# THIS
# FABULOUS
# CENTURY

# THIS FABULOUS CENTURY

PETER LUCK

NEW
HOLLAND

To Penny, Anna and Anthony

## PREFACE

I am often asked, 'Why fabulous?' I usually respond that the word 'fabulous' means given to fable, incredible, absurd and even 'unhistorical'. And I guess that pretty well sums up this century—indeed this book—with its mixture of some profundity and some silliness—we battled two World Wars, and the Great Depression but still found time to invent hula hoops and milk bars.

A note of caution: this is far from a definitive history book. It falls into two parts—a decade-by-decade account of a few of the highlights of the century followed by some stories of the people, places and events that have fascinated, shocked and amused us—and even changed our lives.

But fabulous? Well, just look at this wonderful place where I'm standing —call it Ayers Rock or call it Uluru—and marvel at it either because it's the doorway to the Dreaming, or simply because it's the place where a dingo stole a baby. But whatever, I think you'll agree that it is somehow the spiritual navel of the mighty continent that surrounds it—a continent that is dynamic, mystical, modern and magnificent—and, yes, fabulous.

# Contents...

# INTRODUCTION

*This Fabulous Century* is like a family album—reflecting the people and events that have meant something to the collective Australian family over the twentieth century. Within the television series of the same name, the Edwards family of Newcastle appear as a charming, continuous motif typifying the lives of ordinary Australians throughout this fabulous century.

Millions of Australians watching the television series have been captivated by the unpretentious chronicles of Ken Edwards, his wife Josephine ('Joey'), their two sons Michael and Howard and their wives and kids.

Ken Edwards, who migrated as a five-year-old child to Australia with his English parents, became an engineer like his father in the steel city, and also worked as a photographer. In the early 1930s, Ken bought a movie camera and, as well as recording his industrial surroundings, began a remarkable record of his own life and family, meticulously enshrined in film, photographs and diaries.

The Edwards family epitomises the innocent bystanders to the great ebbs and flows of Australia's history in the twentieth century, from the hard years of the War to the halcyon days.

Over the years, Ken filmed the city of Newcastle almost with a reverence, as though it were Paris or New York—sure it was smoky and grimy but it had some impressive buildings, libraries and art galleries and above all, it was honest and hard working. Indeed, Ken's expertise became so great he was given the ultimate honour of filming the Queen's visit to the city in 1954. But mostly in his films Ken chronicles the balmy days, the kids leading a Huckleberry Finn-like existence in the backyard and on the beach. However, Ken's diaries also reflect moments of pain and heartbreak. At times the Edwards were very poor. During the war years Ken wrote in his diary:

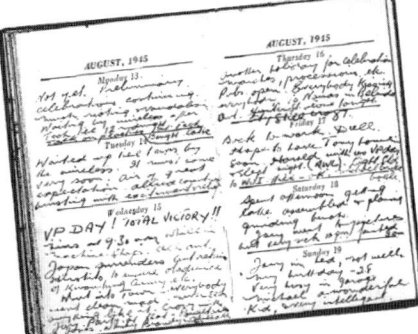

> Joey cried herself to sleep last night. We really don't have anything. I think I'll have to hock the camera.

And yet, set against the minutiae of daily life in the suburbs of Newcastle, are observations of the profound events of the century...

> August 1945 Wednesday 15—VP DAY! TOTAL VICTORY!! News at 9.30 am while still in machine shop. All out. Japan surrenders but retains Hirohito to ensure obedience to Kwantung Army etc., ...
> Friday 17 Back to Work. Dull ... Michael broke bottle.

When son Howard grew up he became a cameraman like his dad. He still works as a television producer and has made it his role to pick up the baton and move into the new millennium as the custodian of his family's precious time capsule of history—a personal archive, in its own way as important as the major film collections of the world. My thanks to Michael and Howard Edwards and their families for sharing their experiences of this fabulous century with us.

DIEU ET MON DROIT

Menu.

BANQUET.
TO CELEBRATE THE
FEDERAL
CONVENTION

SYDNEY TOWN HALL

Sep. 7th 1897.

# As time goes by...

## GROWTH OF A NATION

It seems fitting that the oldest surviving film in Australia, shot just before the turn of the century, includes the Melbourne Cup—maybe the only event in the world which, to this day, stops an entire nation in its tracks.

As *The Bulletin* of the day observed, 'It is something beautifully appropriate that the first Australian picture should be a horse race. Of course it had to be that or a football match.' It was perhaps not so beautifully appropriate that the film was shot by a visiting Frenchman, but that's a long story.

Australia became a pioneer of the world's film industry in a most intriguing way. Just before the turn of the century a Sydney photographer by the name of Barnett was returning from a trip to England. In the Taj Mahal Hotel in Bombay he met a despondent French cameraman who had been told by his employers, the Lumière brothers (who invented motion picture projection), that his shots of life in the East had been ruined by heat and humidity. Barnett suggested to the Frenchman, Maurice Sestier, that he could find work with Falk's photographic studios in Australia.

The idea obviously appealed to him. Sestier caught the next boat for New South Wales.

Australians had seen some film before. At the Melbourne Opera House in August 1896, just a matter of months after the cinematograph had taken Europe by storm, Harry Rickards presented the 'Premier prestidigitateur and illusionist in the world—in his conflux of apparent miracles—the greatest wonder of the nineteenth century.' They don't write spruiks like that any more, except in commercial television.

Left: Queen Victoria enhanced the menu for the 1897 Federal Convention banquet.

Scenes from the 1896 Melbourne Cup—among the oldest surviving film in Australia, shot by Frenchman Maurice Sestier, an employee of the Lumière Company, the inventors of motion picture projection. Sestier was filming in India when his negatives were ruined and he was persuaded by an Australian entrepreneur to come here and produce our first films.

Rickards told the public that for the first time in the Southern Hemisphere a certain Carl Hertz would demonstrate the 'photoelectric sensation of the day'. Australians sat spellbound as scenes of London flickered in front of them: Westminster Bridge, a scene from *Trilby* and the Kempton Park races.

But Sestier, who arrived in Sydney in the following month, would present a spectacle to amaze Australians even more: themselves. The Frenchman, in partnership with Barnett, began filming scenes of Sydney on 60-foot spools of film. The Lumière brothers in Paris were apparently quite happy with the arrangement because they supplied the film stock. But Sestier quickly ran into trouble. Not being a technician, he knew nothing of processing and developing and his first results were a failure. However, an Australian photographer designed some special equipment, and soon Sestier's films were part of the vaudeville program at the Princess Theatre in Melbourne.

Within a few short weeks, however, Australians were already beginning to tire of scenic views and street scenes. Then in November 1896, Sestier produced his sensation—a film of the nags. It caused such excitement that journalists practically fell over their new-fangled typewriters to describe it.

As *The Argus* noted, 'By the Lumière principle a series of views were taken which will carry to London, Paris and St Petersburg an actual presentment not only of the Cup meeting but the most wonderful Cup race ever run over this classic course.' No doubt the presentment of the Melbourne Cup would have gone over in St Petersburg like lead in the saddle, but the point was there. Film was a way of showing Australia to the world—proof that we really were down here on the bottom of the world. According to the advertisements of the day, 'Exhibitions of the wonderful tableaux of the Melbourne Cup were received with thunders of applause and unbounded enthusiasm.' Sestier, though, would share little of the kudos in the industry he helped to pioneer in this country. After some unsuccessful screenings this forlorn advertisement appeared in a Melbourne newspaper:

Cinematographe Lumière. For sale, the original one brought over by Mons. Sestier with all fittings—complete for immediate exhibition. Sixty-three magnificent pictures.

Whatever happened to the foreigner who shot our oldest film is something of a mystery but by the time his camera was sold, Australian films were well on their way. And the men who made our movie history came from the most surprising places.

In the audience of Carl Hertz's first Australian picture show was someone who in his wildest dreams didn't realise that he would become the creator of the first major film presentation, not only in Australia, but in the world. Joseph Perry was, after all, a member of the Salvation Army, not a movie mogul. But around the turn of the century 'the Sallies' were a pretty dynamic bunch. Their leader was Herbert Booth, son of the founder of the Army. He sent Perry to a picture show to investigate the potential of the medium as an aid to evangelism. There was no doubt there were exciting possibilities.

It is difficult to realise now that film was not simply a quaint novelty that amused the Edwardians like some gigantic home movie. Film then, like television today, meant money and a tremendous amount of technological experimentation and development. Even before the turn of the century, the Australian cinema audience was in the millions and the business was subject to the predatory maraudings of celluloid sharks. Studios, cinemas and production houses came and went in rapid succession.

Among this frenetic activity the Salvation Army seemed an unlikely contender. But the Army preached 'Blood and Fire', and ultimately it would hurl itself into the film business with such energy that it would produce the most ambitious work of all—a film production that has often mistakenly been called the world's first feature—but was, in fact, the world's first major audiovisual spectacular.

On the very eve of the twentieth century, the Salvation Army's Limelight Department completed *Soldiers of the Cross*, a truly amazing presentation of film, slides, music, and oratory, which must have been at least equal to the elaborate stage presentations of the future such as *Hair, Jesus Christ Superstar* or *Phantom of the Opera*.

*Soldiers of the Cross* was not strictly a feature film. Although it comprised thousands of feet of re-enactments of the trials of early Christian martyrs, it was interrupted by coloured-glass slides during the reel changes, and some fiery evangelism by Commandant Booth himself.

When the illustrated address was first presented at the Melbourne Town Hall on 13 September 1900, it was billed in a rather low-key manner: 'Town Hall this evening, 7.45 o'clock, Wonderful Limelight Lecture entitled "Soldiers of the Cross".'

Nevertheless, despite the soft sell and atrocious weather, 4000 people attended the premiere. The title was taken from a line in a hymn called 'Am I a Soldier of the Cross?' It was a ferocious epic that might even have turned Cecil B. De Mille white. Martyrs were crucified, beheaded, hacked to pieces, thrown into pits of burning lime, burned at the stake and fed to wild animals. During the filming, demure Salvation Army wives had been transformed into lightly clad maidens of Roman times, and to simulate their ordeal in the Colosseum, they were photographed outside the lions' cage at Fitzgerald's circus in Melbourne. The whole effect was apparently so life-like that women among the audience on the first night screamed and fainted.

The show was such an extraordinary success that within a short time the Salvation Army was encouraged to step up the publicity:

Of Interest to All Creeds
Everyone Captivated from Start to Finish
A Colossal Success
Never Before Witnessed in This or Any Other Country

The Salvation Army's magazine *War Cry* thought that *Soldiers of the Cross* was a 'knockout', a word that the paper's reporter heard used on the steps of the Collingwood Town Hall. 'Thanks for the word, whoever you were,' he wrote. 'Possibly "knockout" is slang but it is rapidly becoming good English, and we like to be a bit ahead of the times. The lecture was a veritable "knockout".'

The Army's elaborate new program included critiques from *The Age* and *The Argus* which were impressed by the 'savage but soul-stirring realism' of the production. They apparently did not notice that the Roman soldiers' cardboard spears bent a little as they prodded hapless Christians into settings which were actually draped across the tennis court netting at the rear of the Murrumbeena Girls' Home at 1219 Dandenong Road. Joseph Perry once told the film buff Eric Reade that in one 'take' the hindquarters of a fake lion fell over and the front portion tried to pull the offending legs upright.

Perry, who had talked the Army into buying a Lumière cinematograph for the filming had been running the Limelight Department for nearly five years when *Soldiers of the Cross* was completed. His first studies had been modest, to say the least: *Wood Chopping at the Metropole* and *Richard Earning His Breakfast*.

*Soldiers of the Cross* was the world's first major audiovisual extravaganza. Produced by the Salvation Army's Limelight Division, it was premiered to Melbourne audiences on 13 September 1900. To construct its 'savage but soul-stirring realism', it featured lightly clad Army wives as Ancient Roman maidens as well as caged lions from a local circus.

But he became more ambitious and was soon taking thousands of feet of film dealing with the social work of the Army. Members of his family also worked on his films and some can even recall playing parts, as children, in their father's epic. Tragically, none of his great work survives. Not long after *Soldiers of the Cross* was shown, Herbert Booth resigned from the Army in a disagreement over policy. There was some suggestion that the problems of the early martyrs had been tackled with perhaps a little too much relish and that this was not the sort of screen violence that the Army should be peddling to the masses. But, whatever the reasons, Booth purchased the film outright for £300, one half of the estimated cost of production. He later exhibited the film in America, but it has long since disappeared. Fortunately the superb glass slides somehow survived and are now a treasured possession of the National Film and Sound Archive, now called *ScreenSound* Australia.

In 1901, the same year that Joseph Perry's great work was lost to history, he was appointed as one of the official photographers to cover Australia's Federation celebrations. The film industry in the colonies was now well under way, but Australia as a nation was not even born.

## THE 1900s

The first day of the twentieth century, January 1901, was a day the whole world had been waiting for with a mixture of confidence and apprehension. In Australia it was a day of tremendous excitement. For us it meant Federation, the time when Australia at last became 'fair dinkum' about being a nation. The first day of the century would see the swearing-in of the first Australian Government. The separate Australian colonies were about to weld themselves together as states of a Commonwealth. It was in fact a truly significant achievement because, with so many rivalries and jealousies between the various cities and their politicians, there had been bitter arguments for many years. At times it had seemed that Federation might never occur at all.

Sir John Robertson, for example, was five times Premier of New South Wales and plainly disliked Victoria. 'We cannot stand that progressive colony,' he said. 'They are rather too insolent.' He commonly referred to his southern neighbour as 'the cabbage garden ... those bloody fellows across the Murray who produce just the same as we do, and all they can send us is bloody cabbages'. God knows what he would have thought of 'Plugger' Lockett and the Sydney Swans.

Freedom of trade of course had a lot to do with the urge to unify the nation, and defence was also a sobering consideration. Rudyard Kipling observed, 'If you want to hurry up Federation, you ought to make a syndicate to hire a few German cruisers to bombard Sydney, Melbourne and Brisbane for 20 minutes. There'd be a Federated Australia within 24 hours.'

Whatever the reasons, on the eve of the twentieth century, most of the differences had been resolved—well, almost. The Federal Parliament was in Melbourne, but the first Prime Minister, New South Welshman, Edmund Barton, would be sworn in at the Federation ceremony in Sydney.

It rained on the night before Federation and there were fierce storms. George Cockerill, a writer for the Melbourne *Age*, sent this report by telegraph:

> The Australian Commonwealth was inaugurated in Sydney today. The old century went out amidst rain and storm; the new one made its advent amidst overhanging clouds and portending thunder. Disunity and parochialism made a tearful exit. Federated Australia was nevertheless ushered into being on a day that was full of sunshine and inspiration of life and hope and the spirit of buoyant youth.

Sydney was decorated like a wedding cake for the proudest day in Australia's history. From the early hours of the morning, groups began to gather in the streets, and soon there were half a million people watching almost five kilometres of procession as it wound its way to the Federation site in Centennial park.

Even the reporter from *The Age* was impressed by Sydney's extravagance:

> There was so much of interest and beauty along that triumphant pageant that human eyesight lamentably lost its range. Look down George Street! The Collins Street of Sydney is bedecked in its gayest apparel as it may never be bedecked again.

At the head of proceedings was Lord Hopetoun, Australia's first Governor-General, who had arrived in the colonies only a fortnight earlier. A young chap with a somewhat daffy demeanour, Hopetoun made a colossal vice-regal blunder by trying to appoint the wrong man as our first Prime Minister. Hopetoun's first choice was Sir William Lyne, Premier of New South Wales and an arch opponent of the whole idea of Federation. Needless to say, Lyne couldn't find the necessary numbers to form a government and the job fell to Edmund Barton. Barton was a brilliant, suave and witty man, but apparently he had such a penchant for the grog he was nicknamed 'Tosspot Toby', and Hopetoun would never be a very popular figure, especially when the taxpayers found he had remarkably extravagant tastes.

But on the great day everyone was determined that nothing would spoil their moment of celebration. More than 150 000 people gathered at Centennial Park, and as the boom of the one o'clock gun died away, the Governor-General approached the magnificent white pavilion. There was so much feathered headdress around the official area that it was almost comic—a veritable gaggle of Gilbert and Sullivan officialdom.

Yet everyone knew this was serious business. Queen Victoria's proclamation was read, Hopetoun took the Oath of Allegiance, a 21-gun salute was fired and 10 000 children sang the 'Federation Anthem'. The Commonwealth of Australia was born.

According to reporters, the beautiful grounds of Centennial Park would always be remembered as the scene of the historic occasion. But how wrong they were. Few people today could say where the Australian nation was officially born. Indeed, the pavilion where the ceremony took place is no longer there. It was made mainly of plaster of Paris and was only a temporary structure anyway. The elaborate Victorian filigreed decorations were stripped away, and the wooden framework and a small brass plaque now stand tucked away in a corner of a quiet suburban park at Cabarita—over 14 kilometres from the original site of 1901. For most of the century, the seminal spot in Centennial Park was marked by an insignificant stone monolith, but in 1988 it was replaced with a much grander monument.

But Australians have never been ones for great political monuments. Federation was, after all, more an idea, more a symbol than a tangible event. And the average Australian in 1901 had more practical concerns.

Simply staying alive was one. At the turn of the century, bubonic plague was still a major problem in the Rocks area of Sydney (that area of the city around the southern pylon of the Harbour Bridge). Conditions in some parts

Edmund Barton, the first Prime Minister of the newly Federated Australia, in 1901. Nicknamed 'Tosspot Toby' because he liked a beer or two, he was a dazzling student and a brilliant sportsman who was called to the Bar at just 22. But his rise to the post of Prime Minister was almost thwarted by a vice-regal blunder.

Top left: Lord Hopetoun, Australia's first Governor-General. He made a colossal gaffe in choosing Sir William Lyne, an anti-Federationist, as the first Prime Minister. Top right: Henry Parkes, 'the Father of Federation'. Unfortunately he died five years before the event occurred. He is buried at Faulconbridge in the Blue Mountains. Bottom: Federation Day, Centennial Park, Sydney, 1 January 1901.

of the inner city were as grim as those depicted in a drawing by Hogarth or a novel by Dickens.

What was life like for the average Australian then? For a start, our population was only a little over three and a half million whites. (In those days we didn't even bother counting Aboriginal peoples.) And those whites were 95 per cent British, and proud of it. We were xenophobic, still trying to rid ourselves of the 'problem' of the Chinese who had flocked here during the 1800s gold rushes, and the black Kanakas who had been brought here as virtual slaves to work the sugar plantations of Queensland.

To make sure that we would remain 'pure' for the rest of the new century, in our first year of nationhood we introduced an Immigration Restriction Bill, a polite way of saying a 'White Australia Policy'. It was a racial filter that we would keep in force for more than half a century. During debate on the Bill, John Christian Watson, who was destined in 1904 to become the first Labor leader in the world to head a national government, delivered this classic utterance: 'The question is whether we would desire that our sisters and brothers should be married into any of these races to which we object.'

In 1901, Queen Victoria was still on the throne, and words like 'world war', 'aeroplane' and 'radio' still had to be coined. Mr Bell's telephone, however, was spreading like wildfire. There were 10 000 in Sydney alone.

The maximum wage for a skilled male worker was 60 shillings a week, whereas female workers were lucky if they could earn five bob. The 48-hour week was standard. It all compared rather unfavourably with Lord Hopetoun's take-home pay of the best part of one million dollars in today's money. However, Hopetoun spent huge sums entertaining royalty for which he was never compensated and he left the country a bitter man.

It was a myth then, as now, that Australia is a 'classless society'. At the turn of the century, the working class aspired to be middle class, and the middle to be upper. A white-collar worker might have earned about £300 a year, and he was extremely mindful of his position in the community. He was the unchallenged head of the household. His wife knew her place. The people at the office called him 'Sir' and his children might have called him 'Pater'.

In 1901, our Mr Middle Class paid only £7/10/– annually in taxes. In New South Wales, it was a flat rate of sixpence in the pound on incomes of more than £200. In Victoria, the rate was only four pence in the pound on incomes up to £1000. There was no federal income tax for another 15 years.

The average Australian male wore clothing which, like his house, was totally unsuited to the environment. The Queen Anne-style villa was all the rage, although within a few years one might have considered a change to 'Federation' style. Traditional terrace houses with their iron lace were already considered 'old-fashioned'. Those that managed to survive would experience a spectacular revival more than half a century later. But then, at the beginning of the twentieth century, architectural emphasis was on elaborate decoration in wood, with soaring towers, turrets and tiled minarets, completely at odds with the landscape and the climate. One of the reasons such elaborate and high-maintenance houses were in vogue was that labour was cheap after the economic depression of the 1890s.

Seventy-five years on, little had changed. Australians were building Tyrolean houses with steep roofs to shed the snow—at Surfer's Paradise. The unique Australian phenomenon—a panorama of red roofs sweeping from the hills to the sea—had also begun before the turn of the century. The Wunderlich tile company was boasting before the First World War that it had 'painted the town red' with the 75 million terracotta tiles which it imported between 1892 and 1914.

What else can one say about the male citizen of Australia in 1901? Certainly he wasn't the easy-going bushman which mythology had led us, and the world, to believe epitomised the average Australian. Between a third and a half of all Australians lived in the cities, and Australia was progressively becoming one of the most urban nations on Earth. Nevertheless, some of the mythology did appear to hold true. We did 'like a drop'. At the turn of the century, the genteel state of Victoria had 50 breweries, and Sydney alone boasted 21.

Our passion for grog was eclipsed only by our love affair with sport. We took great pride in adhering to the lofty ideals of amateur contests such as the Olympic Games—indeed, Australia is one of only three countries which has attended all Olympic Games of the modern era beginning in 1896.

In 1900, the nation's collective bosom (and it was a large bosom in those days when the ideal measurement for a woman was said to be 40–28–40 inches) swelled with pride when Fred Lane won Australia's first gold medals for the 200 metres freestyle and 200 metres 'obstacle race' at the second Olympic Games in Paris. Fred had also entered for the 100 metres and probably would have won except that the organisation of those Games was

Top: Banjo Paterson, one of Australia's 'bush bards' who made famous such legends as 'Breaker' Morant and *The Man from Snowy River*. Bottom: A fine example of Australian Federation architecture, established during the first decade of the century.

somewhat lax—when Fred made it down to the banks of the Seine he found that the race was already over. In 1902, Lane became the first swimmer in the world to break the minute barrier for the 100 yards, using the favoured style of the day, 'the Trudgeon Kick'.

Melbourne's love affair with that remarkable game called Australian Rules was in full flower at the turn of the century. Even before the first decade of the century was over, 50 000 of Melbourne's population of only half a million turned out for the Grand Final.

We also took a healthy delight in a good, juicy scandal, or better still, a murder. A few days into 1901, a 'half-caste Aborigine' named Jimmy Governor was hanged at Darlinghurst gaol in Sydney. Behind him lay a horrifying saga of death and mayhem, which appeared to have been triggered by the problems of a 'mixed marriage'.

Jimmy, who many years later would be celebrated in book and film as Jimmy Blacksmith, married the white daughter of a local miner. He was hardly black himself. With his shock of red hair he was known in Gilgandra district as a good cricketer, fencing contractor and station hand. But one day Governor's pretty white wife overheard the wife of one of Jimmy's bosses discussing a coming cricket match and the words, 'If you pick those blacks for the team, I won't cook any cakes for the picnic.'

This racial slur led to a rampage in which Jimmy Governor killed nine people, including old men, women and babies. Governor, his brother, and a friend were pursued over a good part of New South Wales. The killer's most relentless hunter was Herbert Byers, lover of a murdered schoolteacher, Helena Kertz. Governor was eventually riddled with bullets, but he survived to be hanged and to become the subject of hatred, awe and gossip for much of the first decade of the century.

In all, the turn of the century was an exciting if difficult time for the 'average' Australian. Some of the menfolk were overseas involving themselves in the oriental skulduggery which surrounded the Boxer Rebellion. 'Banjo' Paterson was with other Australians in South Africa chasing Boers and creating legends about such dubious heroes as Lieutenant Harry 'Breaker' Morant—the Australian soldier who was executed by firing squad for murdering South African prisoners. Books, plays and movies have been created around the Morant legend so that the truth of the story has become more and more hazy. Suffice to say that Morant, a poet and drinker, did admit to killing Boer prisoners but said he was only obeying orders and was defiant to the end as he faced the firing squad—'Shoot straight, you bastards.' Morant's friend, another poet named Will Ogilvie wrote that he was 'A chivalrous, wild and reckless lad, a knight born out of his time.' Meanwhile, in Sydney, actress and generally 'naughty' lady Pansy Montague, alias 'La Milo', was scandalising decent and not-so-decent folk with her picture-postcard poses in the nude or at least in a bodystocking. And remember S.E. Gregory? Oh well, people probably won't remember Dennis Lillee, Shane Warne or Mark Taylor in a 100 years either.

If 1901 was a momentous year for Australia, then perhaps it is worth noting what else was happening in the world during those 12 months of the new century. For Britain no doubt the most significant single event had been the death of Queen Victoria. For the United States it was the assassination of President McKinley. He was succeeded by President Roosevelt, who concerned himself with such matters as America's brand new protectorate of Cuba, and the treaty for building a massive engineering project called the Panama Canal. It was in essence a quiet year internationally. Samuel Butler published *Erehwon Revisited*, Kipling presented the world with *Kim*. Toulouse Lautrec died, and Walt Disney was born. Rachmaninoff produced his *Piano Concerto Number Two* and ragtime jazz surfaced in the United States. The hormone adrenalin was isolated, Marconi transmitted radio messages from Cornwall to Newfoundland, J.P. Morgan organised his US Steel corporation, oil drilling began in Persia, Britain launched its first submarine and recognised boxing as a legal sport.

Against this international background, Australia faced the first 10 years of the new century with optimism. Before it was over, the inhabitants of the world's newest nation would see technological changes beyond belief.

Even by 1900 Australians were aware that the motor car had some potential in a country where the 'tyranny of distance' was to become a catch phrase. The first all-Australian car, the Thompson Steam Phaeton, is in fact just as old as the twentieth century. In late 1900, the Phaeton's designer, Mr Herbert Thompson of Armadale, Victoria, drove the vehicle from Bathurst to Melbourne at an average speed of 8.7 miles per hour (14 kilometres per hour). At that rate the journey did much the same for motoring as Burke and Wills had done for the concept of interstate travel. But, after centuries staring at the backsides of horses, it was a novel change.

The year 1901 also saw the first Australian petrol-driven car built by Colonel H. Tarrant. The intrepid colonel went on to prove that the horseless carriage was quite a feasible instrument in which to travel from go to whoa. However, for the majority of citizens the solution to urban transport problems was the tram and it would continue to be for most of the century. The good people of Melbourne have clung on to them until the present day and they may well have the last laugh. While other states have progressively ripped up the tracks in the name of progress, Melbourne's city fathers have nodded wisely and maybe suggested a new coat of paint. Today Melbourne still boasts one of the most efficient tramway systems in the world and other states are bringing back the concept of light rail.

Initially trams were horse-drawn affairs. Sydney was first off the rank, introducing trams to the streets as early as 1861. Unfortunately, in the haste to demonstrate the new wonder, the tracks were laid upside down, which made the streets so bumpy that the line was soon closed.

By 1885, Victoria had unveiled its version of the latest in urban transport, the legendary Melbourne cable tram. It was the beginning of 80 years of rivalry between the two capital cities over which had the better system. In many ways the Melbourne cable tramway symbolised Australia's newfound faith in technology. The massive steam powerhouse which drove the endless miles of underground cables was like some sacred monument to engineering. It was a splendid system, even though only a few years after its introduction it was regarded as obsolete. Actually it would be 1924 before Melbourne reluctantly began tearing up the cableways that had been such a source of civic pride.

If the first decade of the century was marked by great technological change, then it also saw considerable social advances. In 1902, women (dammit, sir) were given the vote, and workers' compensation was introduced making Australia a world leader in social legislation. The shutters were also going up in other areas. Daylight bathing—a symbolic breaking down of the remnants of Victorianism—was pioneered at Manly.

However, in some areas perhaps we tried to change too much too soon. An Australian committee reported in 1902 that it was in favour of adopting decimal currency, but the Mother Country was unwilling to change, and it would be over half a century before our official 'D-day', 14 February 1966. When the new Commonwealth came into being, an entirely new force of public servants had to be recruited and, almost immediately, a search for a suitable site for a capital began. The site had to be well and truly in 'no-man's land', preferably on the border of New South Wales and Victoria, because interstate rivalries were still smouldering. At one stage the New South Wales Premier threatened to withdraw from the newly federated states altogether, and this led to Deakin's classic instruction to his secretary, 'Tell him to go to hell—three pages.' The 'Battle of the Sites' lasted until 1908 and the foundation peg for a new capital would be driven into the earth of the Molonglo Valley five years later.

The year 1904 also saw the ascendancy of that pioneering 'Labour' Government led by John Christian Watson. Actually, Watson was born in Chile and raised in New Zealand and the government was a short-lived minority one—but what the hell, you've got to start somewhere. At the time the government was formed, Labor still had only 24 members in the House of Representatives, but it joined with the opposition to carry an amendment to a controversial bill. Prime Minister Deakin saw this as a vote of no-confidence and resigned. After such a messy start there would be hard times ahead for Labor and it was destined not to govern very long in the ensuing half century. As for that long-running argument whether it should be spelt 'Labor' or 'Labour', that's very complicated. Suffice to say that both spellings have been used throughout the century depending on which movement and which party is involved, but the Australian Labor Party should officially be spelt without the 'u'.

In keeping with the prevailing more egalitarian mood of the times and the collective power of the common man, the Commonwealth Arbitration Court was set up. It was the culmination of decades of struggle, including bitter battles between capital and labour forces that had even ended in bloodshed and death as police and troops had descended on fledgling trade unions created by groups such as the shearers and waterside workers. Out of this had arisen the Federal Parliamentary Labour Party, formed in 1901. One of the new Federal Government's decisions not long afterwards gave some indication of the economic climate of the age. In an award for shop assistants in Sydney the court granted boys under 15 a starting wage of five shillings a week which rose to seven and sixpence after 15.

The captains of commerce, however, were doing quite nicely, and some were well on the way to becoming institutions which would last throughout the century. A firm named William Arnott's Steam Biscuit Company was

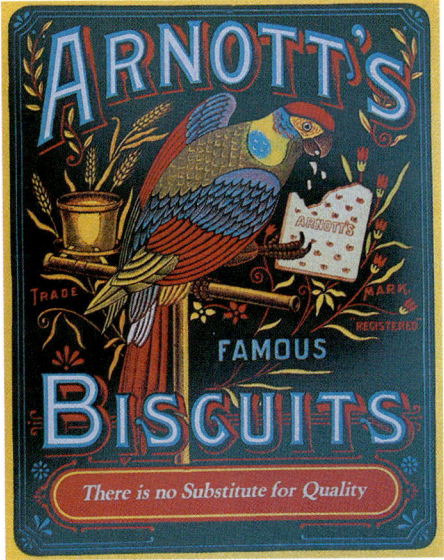

Top left: The famous parrot
motif of the Arnott's biscuit
company, makers of the
best-selling SAO biscuits.
Top right: Artist Norman
Lindsay, whose work wowsers
found to be lewd and
obscene. Bottom: A classic
Norman Lindsay fantasy,
one of his paintings on display
in the red room of
his home at Springwood
in the Blue Mountains.

founded in that year. Soon afterwards they adopted a parrot motif which became almost as familiar to Australians as a boomerang. Arthur Arnott, one of five sons of the founder of the company, was a member of the Salvation Army. One day he christened a biscuit with the initials of the Salvation Army Officer—SAO—and the rest is history. Towards the end of the century, this biscuit still outsold all of its rivals—525 million SAOs a year!

What Australians had to spread on their SAOs around the turn of the century is a mystery because it would be another 20 years before Vegemite was invented. In 1923, an enterprising Melbourne merchant named Fred Walker got himself a contract with Carlton and United Breweries to provide them with yeast. Just a week after the contract was formalised, he appointed a chemist named C.P. Callister to develop a yeast extract as a by-product.

A couple of months later, Walker launched a competition to name his new food product. On a trip to the Dandenongs later in 1923, he mentioned some of the competitors' suggestions to his only daughter, Sheila. She favoured 'Vegemite', which put the clincher on it. Five years later, however, the English beef extract Marmite was selling more than Vegemite, so Fred Walker changed the name of his product and registered 'Parwill'. He used the slogan, 'If Marmite, Parwill.' Needless to say, the public groaned. The change was unsuccessful and in the 1930s, Vegemite was reinstated. The Fred Walker Company became the Kraft Walker Cheese Company in 1926 and has been linked with the American Kraft Company since then.

Two years after the Arnott company was established, another amazing success story began. The Kiwi boot polish company was a dynamic, thrusting concern which relied heavily on ingenious advertising. In fact, one of the oldest film commercials in the world was made by Kiwi in London, and shows a good-humoured digger enlightening two street urchins as to the qualities of the product.

As the new century unfolded and the Victorian influence dissipated, Australians had an extraordinary amount of difficulty in trying to work out their standards of decency and decorum. Norman Lindsay's *Pollice Verso* (Latin for 'thumbs down') caused a national outcry when it was purchased by the Melbourne Art Gallery for £150. The drawing of female nudity in a religious setting aroused the ire of the wowsers to a pitch where they would feel obliged to hound Lindsay for half a century afterwards. Another of Lindsay's drawings, *The Crucified Venus*, caused even greater controversy when it was exhibited in Sydney. Julian Ashton, founder of the famous art school and gallery, refused to remove it from public gaze and eventually there was an absurd compromise. The picture was hung face to the wall. Lindsay, who was still working in his 90th year, outlived his most determined critics, but was somewhat bitter about them until the end.

Meanwhile let's return to that sobering thought that, at the turn of the century, at the dawn of the modern era, bathing in daylight hours was prohibited in Australia. The strong, healthy bodies of a brash young pioneering country were apparently not suitable for public gaze. Wowserism still permeated our soul.

That was until 1902, when in the Sydney suburb of Manly a newspaper editor named William Gocher decided to challenge public morality head-on. In December of that year, clad only in neck–to–knee bathers, Gocher plunged into the sea at high noon. He did it again on two more occasions, each time announcing his intentions in his newspaper.

On the first day a crowd gathered and oohed and aahed but police on the scene took no action. Eventually though, the constabulary decided it could no longer tolerate this flagrant challenge to the law and public decency. The police swooped and hauled Gocher off to court. Nearly 80 years later his daughter, Mrs Marie Mahony, recalled:

> He asked to be taken to the High Court to see Inspector Fosby and the Inspector said, 'Mr Gocher, I've been reading with delight ... you've won the day.' He said, 'All day surfing from now on as long as the women are properly clothed. They must have neck-to-knee costume and the bosom must not be shown.' So of course Dad couldn't get home quick enough and we all went down with him and we were thrown into the water. We all had our costumes and had a lovely swim.

As for that bit about 'the bosom was not to be shown'; well, we'd get around that but it would take us 75 years. In a nice twist of history, nude bathing would be first introduced at Camp Cove where Governor Phillip first set foot in Sydney Harbour five days before declaring Australia 'open' on 26 January 1788. By the 1980s, even on Australia's most popular family beaches such as Bondi, girls appeared topless and the bottoms of their swimsuits were so diminutive that the wags dubbed them 'dental floss'.

Top: At the turn of the century, Australians weren't allowed to swim during daylight hours, as this 1901 picture of Sydney's Bondi Beach shows. Bottom: Fortunately, this prohibition was challenged in 1902 by Manly Beach local William Gocher so that within the year daylight bathing was legalised, much to the delight of these swimmers at Coogee.

The Period 1900-1910 is probably the most forgotten decade of Australian history. With the whole of the first part of the century about to be eclipsed by the 'war to end all wars', those balmy days seem to have almost been lost to time. Yet in those first 10 years, there was a tremendous amount of development in all areas of antipodean life.

Australians had been besotted with sport ever since troopers kicked convicts around the decks of the first fleet. But now Australia was sending stout-hearted men back to the Old Country to wrest a variety of trophies from the British. During 1901, Australian bowlers destroyed the Englishmen in Melbourne, with M.A. Noble taking seven wickets for 17 runs. In 1905 Australia and New Zealand sent a combined team to contest the Davis Cup, and two years later Norman Brookes, 'the Fox', became the first non-British player to win Wimbledon. Then with his New Zealand partner he took the Davis Cup. The following year saw the remarkable Burns–Johnson World Championship bout in Sydney, which was billed as 'the fight of the century' and the first in which a black man became official champion of the world.

Nevertheless, Edwardian life was apparently not without its tensions. The magazine *The Lone Hand* was about half a century before its time when it reported in 1907 that 'what the drink habit is among men in Australia, the headache powder is among women'. Despite the fact that it has been called 'the lucky country', it seems that Australia has always had a massive headache. By the 1920s, the Aspro company—with extraordinary advertising campaigns engineered by a remarkable character, George Davies—was using the slogan, 'Twenty Aspros a day keep a man's pain away.'

The amount of medical and dental quackery in the country would lead to a Royal Commission in 1908, and some of the bogus 'professors' were forced out of business.

As the first decade drew to a close, transport had made some astounding leaps, jerks and bounds. In December 1909, George Taylor made the first free flight in Australia in a glider.

Some Australians had been mucking around with the heavier-than-air machine for many years and, indeed, few people these days realise that Lawrence Hargrave, the man whose portrait appeared on Australia's first $20 notes, exerted a profound influence on the history of international aviation. Ten years before the Wright brothers flew their first powered aeroplane, Hargrave took to the air suspended beneath four box kites. The aerodynamic

Top: Making aviation history—the first real Australian flight of 110 yards was made by George Taylor in a glider at Narrabeen Heads, Sydney, in December 1909. Bottom: Even the Wright brothers used information gained from Australian aeronautical inventor Lawrence Hargrave and his box kites, shown here at Stanwell Park, Sydney, during the 1890s.

knowledge gained from this and other experiments contributed greatly to the development of aviation theory, and the Wright brothers were among the many people who corresponded with Hargrave about his work. A monument on a spectacular headland at Stanwell Park on the New South Wales coast commemorates Hargrave and his experiments, without which the Wright *Flyer* might never have got off the ground. Sadly, Hargrave himself never achieved powered flight, possibly because of the weakness of his propeller designs.

Soon after the turn of the century a number of other Australians were anxious to test their wings. In the same year that Taylor made his glider flight at Narrabeen Heads in New South Wales, Mr L.A. Adamson, headmaster of Wesley College in Melbourne, had been greatly excited by the news of Bleriot's history-making first flight across the English Channel. He sent a young man named Colin De Fries to Europe to purchase a Wright biplane and a Bleriot monoplane. On his return, De Fries did manage to get airborne in that year. But the fact that he could not demonstrate his ability to control and steer his aircraft—for some strange reason considered important to the future of aviation—robbed him of being the first Australian to fly.

By a strange quirk of fate, the first man officially to make a controlled flight in a powered aircraft in Australia was the American escape artist and magician, Harry Houdini. On a tour here in 1910, he brought along his French biplane specifically to attempt the first real flight in this country. After waiting several days for the right conditions, Houdini duly made his ascent at Digger's Rest in Victoria on 18 March, but at the time no-one realised that, just a day before, a young man in Adelaide named Fred Custance had flown an imported aircraft for three miles. Custance didn't seek any publicity, so the honour and glory went to the American magician.

It wasn't long before Australians were keen to get airborne totally under their own steam, and just four months after Custance and Houdini, a young farmer named John Duigan from the Mia Mia district of Victoria became the first man to pilot an Australian-built aircraft. Duigan had designed and built the plane himself, although he'd never seen an aircraft. It was based on pictures of the Wright brothers' aircraft that Duigan had seen in a magazine, and it was lovingly assembled in a barn. On 16 July 1910, Duigan and his home-made plane flew into history books, with stays made from piano wire and fittings fashioned from the steel bands off wool bales.

Top left and right: The first official, controlled flight using a powered machine in Australia was made by the American escape artist, Harry Houdini, at Digger's Rest, Victoria, on 18 March 1910. Bottom: The first Australian to get his licence to fly was the dare-devil dentist from Sydney, William Hart, in 1911. He received a court fine for scaring cows to death.

The first Australian pilot's licence went to a Sydney dentist, William Hart, an adventurous character who bought himself a Bristol Box Kite in 1911. Hart became the pioneer of inter-suburban flying and confounded the local sceptics when he made the epic flight from Sydney to Penrith, a journey of about 40 miles. He took passengers for joy flights at 10 guineas a time and thrilled Sydneysiders by once keeping up with a train travelling at a mile a minute. Hart was fined £10 for scaring some cows to death and he complained that at those prices the future of flying was bleak. Hart, like many other early Australian aviators, was almost killed in a crash.

At the beginning of the 1910s, Australia was already a considerably different country from what it had been in those heady days of January 1901. Science and technology were clearly going to change our society completely. Despite the huge size of the continent, and despite the fact that we were told that we rode on the sheep's back, we huddled in cities on the coastline and prepared for the industrial onslaught.

There were now 360 000 trade unionists in the country. Towards the end of that first decade, miners at Port Kembla went on strike over an issue which would foreshadow the anti-uranium protests of today. Miners considered that the use of electricity in the mines was dangerous. No protesters gathered with chants of 'Keep electricity out of the ground', but here was an early example of what the future was to bring.

## THE 1910s

The next decade of Australian life was dominated by one great and hideous event—the First World War, the 'war to end all wars'—even though it didn't.

Not that Australia was bereft of development in the last few years before the conflict began. An American named Walter Burley Griffin won a prize for his concept of a magnificent new capital city but, as we shall discover, he was destined like another great Danish architect Jørn Utzon to run foul of Australian bureaucracy. Australia also had its first 'skyscraper', a building nearly 52 metres high, Culwulla Chambers in Sydney. The Australian Inland Mission was founded, the Murrumbidgee Irrigation Scheme began, and we even had our first advertising agency.

By now we also had our first true film star, Lottie Lyell, who was described by the producer, Raymond Longford, as 'a little lady, an elocutionist, and strictly religious'. In the days long before Linda Lovelace alliteration was all the go, Lottie Lyell, who was soon to be followed by another great star, Louise Lovely, made a great impact in *The Romance of Margaret Catchpole* and appeared in dozens of films before her death in the prime of her career.

Ultimately Raymond Longford would be remembered for his classic film *The Sentimental Bloke*, but in the years just before the war he made *Australia Calls* which, in its story of a Japanese attack on Sydney Harbour, reflected the popular obsession with 'the yellow peril'. In his film, the visiting American fleet doubled as the Japanese Naval force, and the rest of the action was done with models. However crude it might have been, Longford's film was prophetic. The only problem was he predicted the wrong war. In the First World War, the Japanese were not the enemy, but 30 years later, during the Second World War, Sydney Harbour did indeed come under attack from Japanese submarines.

In 1910, around the same time that William Hart, the adventurous dentist, was earning Australia's first pilot licence, a Melbourne man named Harry George Hawker was flying as test pilot for the legendary T.O.M. Sopwith in England. Hawker, whose legacy became the Hawker Siddeley and Hawker de Havilland companies, was Australia's first professional airman.

In 1914, Hawker was back in Australia to demonstrate a new aircraft. He had an appointment with the Governor-General who then resided at Government House in Melbourne. The story goes that Hawker was late for the appointment, but whatever the truth, when the time arrived, the tranquil atmosphere of the Government House grounds was shattered by the noise of the aeroplane's engine. Moments later the vice-regal couple who were engaging in a spot of tennis were greeted by a Sopwith biplane taxiing through the gardens. Mr H.A.G. Hawker had arrived for lunch.

Flying into Government House became all the rage that year. Another who all but charmed the bloomers off the Melbourne ladies was the Frenchman Guillaux who flew the first air mail from Sydney to Melbourne. Guillaux, who pranged his aircraft spectacularly at the old Ascot racecourse in Sydney, was killed in Europe soon afterwards. Hawker, too, was destined to be involved in many remarkable aviation achievements, and was once awarded £5000 and a medal from the King after an unsuccessful attempt to fly the Atlantic. But, like most of our early aviators, he was fated to end his life in a crash.

Top: One way to achieve fame in the early 1900s was to land an aircraft on the front lawns of national buildings. Here Frenchman Maurice Guillaux is departing after he had dropped into Federal Government House, Melbourne, in 1914. Bottom: Anzacs departing for First World War campaigns like Gallipoli. During the 1915 invasion of this Turkish peninsula, 10 000 Australian and New Zealand soldiers were killed.

The development of aviation during the conflict that erupted in Europe would be remarkable. Once it was found that the aeroplane was useful for killing people other than pilots, its future was assured.

The war did not burst on Australians overnight. The rumblings had been going on for months. But the actual announcements, however, came with surprising suddenness. On the eve of the outbreak, the issues that affected the average Australian male were the Irish crisis, the coming football finals and electioneering. For example, Andrew Fisher, the coal miner who became Prime Minister, was destined to suffer similar vicissitudes to those of Gough Whitlam 60 years later. Against a background of press and opposition cries of 'socialisation', Fisher struggled through three terms as Prime Minister between 1908 and 1915.

With such controversial items in its platform as a decision to form a Commonwealth bank and to introduce anti-monopoly legislation, Labor's position was always precarious. At the general elections of 1913, Labor very narrowly lost its majority in the House of Representatives, but increased its control in the Senate. The Liberals (a title borrowed from the British Liberal Party), in ironic contrast to the events of 1975, had their mandate frustrated by the Senate, and consequently the ministry fell.

During the election campaign in 1914, there was no mention of the imminence of war until the end of July. On the last day of that month, both Fisher and opposition leader Cook broke the expected tension. Fisher made his famous 'last man and last shilling' speech. This was not an original phrase, but it was one that had tremendous effect on the electorate. The next night, Joseph Cook made a similar promise, 'If there is to be a war, you and I shall be in it. We must be in it. If the Old Country is at war, so are we.'

Britain declared war on 4 August 1914, and the British Foreign Secretary made another memorable utterance, 'The lamps are going out all over Europe. We shall not see them lit again in our lifetime.' Over the next four years, Australia would send its sons overseas—sons who were often used as not much more than cannon fodder. Almost 60 000 Australians were killed in action, and nearly 70 per cent of our troops would be killed or wounded—the highest casualty rate of the Empire. In comparison, British casualties were 15 per cent less.

And yet, for every man who went to war, a dozen Australians stayed home. Many of them were women and children, but many of them were men, too.

Life did go on, sometimes with a zest. In 1914, two vaudeville performers, Nat Phillips and Roy Rene formed a partnership which was to become the most successful in the history of the Australian theatre, 'Stiffy and Mo'.

In the same year two brothers, George and Jim Coles, started a store with a motto 'Nothing over a shilling'. It was the beginning of a business which would revolutionise retail trading in Australia. During the war George, Jim and their other brothers, Arthur and Dave, served with the AIF. Jim and Dave were both killed in France, but when the war was over George and Arthur opened another store with the slogan 'Nothing over two and sixpence' and this would be their policy until the following world war.

There was no doubt that Australia enjoyed a blessed standard of living, even in those days. Our diggers were called 'six-bob-a-day tourists' because they were the highest paid soldiers of the war. But the jibes seemed hollow when the 'tourists' were thrown almost as a sacrifice at the cliffs of Anzac Cove, Gallipoli.

In 1915, this little-known Turkish peninsula became a byword for one of the most tragic and inept campaigns of the First World War. No other single event would do more to mould the national psyche. The campaign was not only tragic in its overall concept, but the folly was compounded by the fact that the first wave of Australians was mistakenly landed one mile from its true objective, in an area previously regarded as an impossible place for a night landing. Because the Anzacs were being slaughtered by the Turks, their commanders suggested withdrawing, but the British General Hamilton on board the battleship *Queen Elizabeth* ordered them to hold on.

After eight months of hopeless fighting, trying to wrest the enemy from its topographical bastion, the Anzacs were finally withdrawn. They had lost 10 000 men. The withdrawal itself was a miracle of organisation using some ingenious tricks such as the 'drip rifle'—a gun set up to be triggered by a string tied to a bucket of water which slowly rose as the water dripped out. This fooled the enemy into thinking the Australian troops were still in their trenches. They had, in fact, vacated the peninsula during the night without loss of life.

The Australians' heroism at Gallipoli was such that nine of them were awarded the Victoria Cross. But the enduring hero was a man who was never awarded a medal—Simpson, the stretcher bearer who ran the gamut of Shrapnel Gully with his donkey named Duffy.

Top: Prime Minister Billy Hughes had the nickname 'the Little Digger'. One reason could be that he wanted to see more Australians in uniforms—he tried twice through national referendums to impose conscription, both of which returned negative results. Bottom: Anzacs fighting in the trenches at Gallipoli.

Not all Australians were enamoured of the war and the press reports of deeds of derring-do, however. In 1916, a good many of the Irish community saw the conflict as a 'sordid trade war'. Their leader, Archbishop Daniel Mannix, fought vehemently against conscription. They made a martyr of Les Darcy, the young boxing champion who had skipped the country. There were purges of the local German communities, which admittedly had been rather nationalistic and insular since arriving in the colonies nearly a century before. The Germans were victims of a general hysteria about spies: some German-Australians were incarcerated, place names were changed, and South Australia banned the teaching of German and closed Lutheran churches.

However, these witch-hunts were tinged with irony. After the war was over, for example, the city fathers of Adelaide, as in all Australian cities, decided to build an impressive memorial in North Terrace to commemorate those who'd died fighting 'the dreaded Hun'. Who should be commissioned to carve this elaborate sculpture but my grandfather, Julius Henschke who was, of course, of German descent.

Many of the passions and fears of the time were understandable. On the Western Front alone, 38 000 Australians had been killed. The general mood of the press, which had been strident and tub-thumping at the beginning of the war, grew more sober. The heavy casualty lists appeared each day, surrounded by a black border.

The first Anzac Day was held in 1916 on the anniversary of the Gallipoli landing. By order of Prime Minister Billy Hughes, a dispatch by the British war correspondent Ellis Ashmead Bartlett was read out to school children all over the country. This was the stuff that made loyal Australian hearts skip a beat: '... not waiting for orders, or for the boats to reach the beach, the Australians sprang into the sea and, forming a sort of rough line, rushed at the enemy's trenches. Their magazines were not charged, so they just went in with cold steel.'

By the end of the war, 329 000 Australians had served overseas; 59 330 were killed and 152 710 wounded. Sixty-six Australians received the Victoria Cross.

The cost in cold hard cash had exceeded £370 million. Yet, even then Australia could count herself fortunate. In Europe the daily war expenditure had been £164 million. Eight million people had been killed, 21 million wounded, and seven and a half million were missing.

When Billy Hughes returned from the Versailles Peace Treaty Conference in 1919 he said that he had no real idea of how much the Commonwealth might expect in compensation. Our claim for reparation was £464 million. Of this, Hughes thought we might get £50 million—if we were lucky. In fact, only £5.5 million had been received by 1931, and after that no more payments were made by Germany.

During that conference, Hughes was involved in some celebrated exchanges with the American President, Woodrow Wilson. Hughes insisted on what amounted to a 999-year lease over New Guinea. Wilson was shocked by the Australian Prime Minister's stubbornness in wanting to secure New Guinea and administer it under Australian law (a blatantly white Australian law at that). The following exchange was reported:

> *Woodrow Wilson*: Mr Prime Minister of Australia, do I understand your attitude alright? If I do, it is this: that the opinion of the whole of the civilised world is set to nought.
>
> *Hughes* (adjusting his hearing aid): Very well put, Mr President. You guessed it. That is just so.

This sort of terrier-like activity endeared 'the Little Digger' to many Australians. Australia at the end of the war was much changed from what it had been just five years earlier. It had gone into the Big Stoush as the 'little boy' among the nations and had come out with a bit of a swagger. The returned soldiers formed an elite group in the community and reinforced their position each Anzac Day. They devoted a great deal of their energy to helping their comrades and families. No-one questioned the fairness of the returned soldiers getting preferential treatment in areas such as housing, but whether or not it led to social harmony and industrial efficiency is another argument.

The men who came home from the war found that the cost of living had risen by 60 per cent, and that a bloke couldn't buy a drink in a pub after six o'clock. Still, Australians were better off than the Americans, who were about to go through that extraordinary period known as Prohibition.

In 1919, with the hostilities over, Billy Hughes offered to pay £10 000 to anyone who completed the first flight from England to Australia. Two Adelaide brothers, Ross and Keith Smith took up the challenge. In horrific conditions—at times they nearly froze to death—they completed the journey in a Vickers Vimy biplane. The trip took 28 days, and that time stood as a record for the next 10 years.

The record was finally broken by little Bert Hinkler, the young man from Bundaberg, Queensland, who had been crazy about flying since he was a child. He had built a glider as a teenager and by 1912 he was mechanic for the visiting American flyer Wizard Stone.

Hinkler, who was eventually killed in a crash in the Appenine Mountains in Italy in 1933, was a shy, introverted man who was devoted to his mother. His elaborate and maudlin funeral, stage-managed by none other than Benito Mussolini, would no doubt have caused the flyer acute embarrassment.

When Hinkler took off from Croydon Aerodrome near London in February 1928 in his tiny Avro Avian biplane there was little fanfare. And yet he was about to make the longest solo flight in history—England to Australia—in little over a fortnight. When Bert flew into Bundaberg to see his Mum, the Hinkler backyard seemed to be almost the centre of the universe for this Queensland country town. The entire populace was ecstatic, as indeed was the whole of Australia. All around the nation people cheered him and wrote songs and poetry about him, a favourite being, 'Hinkle, Hinkle little star, 16 days and here you are.'

After being lionised by the Australian nation and the world, Hinkler tried to keep some of his flights, including a remarkable sortie across the southern Atlantic in a midget plane, secret. He shunned publicity and glory and became known as 'the Lone Eagle'. But there was no doubt that for most of Australia little Bert Hinkler, the boy from Bundaberg, was the public hero for the 1920s.

Another of our aviation visionaries wasn't a pilot at all but a pioneering doctor named the Reverend John Flynn, or 'Flynn of the Inland'. Flynn was a schoolteacher in Victoria who was ordained into the Presbyterian Church in 1911. But it was an incident in 1918, the last year of the First World War, which led him to create his famous flying doctor service, now known as the Royal Flying Doctor Service of Australia. A stockman in the Kimberleys named Jimmy Darcy was thrown from a horse and seriously injured. His friends found him lying unconscious, put him in a buggy and drove him an agonising 47 miles to the tiny settlement of Hall's Creek.

Although there was no doctor there the local postmaster had a smattering

Top: Billy Hughes presents his £10 000 prize to Ross and Keith Smith, who in 1919 were the first to fly from England to Australia. The registration letters on their aircraft were G.E.A.O.U—'Gawd 'elp all of us!' Bottom: The Smith brothers' flight created a 28-day time record, unbroken for nearly 10 years, until shy soloist Bert Hinkler completed the journey in a little over a fortnight during 1928.

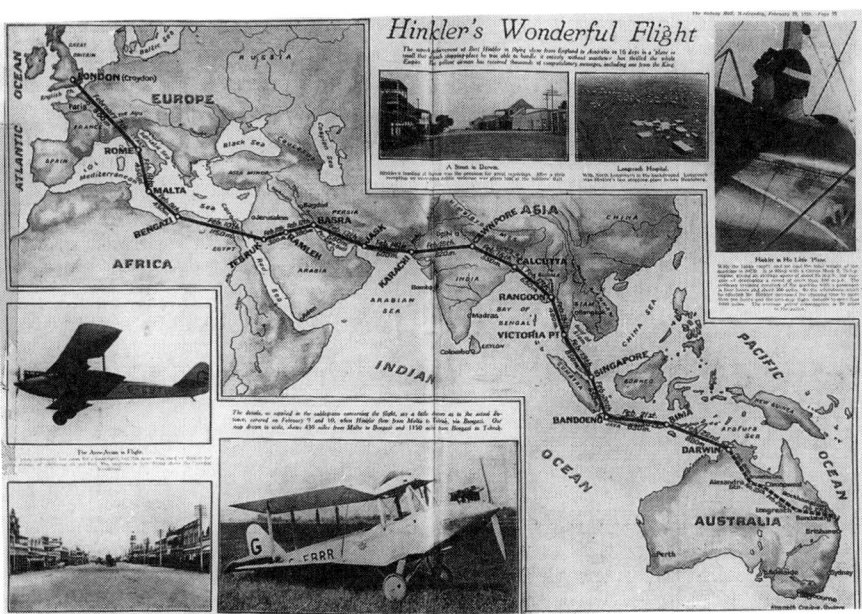

Top: Bert Hinkler's route from England to Australia. A native of Bundaberg, Queensland, he was a national hero of the 1920s. Bottom: Hinkler's Avro Avian plane, housed at the Queensland Museum.

of medical knowledge. He telegraphed Wyndham and Derby, both hundreds of miles away, only to find the doctors at both centres were on holidays. He then telegraphed his former first aid lecturer in Perth, more than a 1000 miles away.

The lecturer, Dr Holland, diagnosed a ruptured bladder and told his friend that he must operate. The patient was strapped to a kitchen table in the Post Office while Dr Holland gave instructions by morse code. The operation took seven hours but then complications set in. Dr Holland himself then set out for Hall's Creek—a journey that took two weeks, Holland travelling by boat, car, horse and finally on foot. When he arrived he found that Darcy had died the previous day.

Haunted by this incident, Flynn struggled over a period of 30 years against tremendous odds to create and nurture the bush's most revered organisation. When government funds were withdrawn during the Depression, Flynn toured the major cities raising money which saved the Service from extinction. When 'Flynn of the Inland' died in 1951, the nation as a whole mourned and newspapers around the world published eulogies. Today the Service's 13 bases and operations cover a third of the Australian continent— more than two million square miles.

## THE 1920s

The popular image of the 1920s is of the Charleston, flappers, crazes—'the Roaring Twenties'. It was a time of gay abandon and sheer joy, before we plunged into the gloom of the Depression at the end of the decade. To a large degree this mood did prevail in Australia. We did try most of the crazes, most of the fashions, most of the drinks and most of the dances. But the 1920s was also a time of intense political and social change.

To most Australians, 'the Bolshies' were little more than a 'bloody nuisance'. But there were real class struggles being fought. Police used bayonets to break up watersiders' demonstrations in Fremantle, and the Broken Hill mines had been closed for more than a year.

Politics was still a rough and ready business. Hugh Mahon, the member for Kalgoorlie, got stuck into the British for their policy on Ireland. That was acceptable, but when he referred to this 'bloody and accursed empire', Billy Hughes organised a move to get him thrown out of the House. (Somehow people had now forgotten what Hughes himself had said about Britain in a fiery debate about the Boer War: 'This is the most iniquitous war ever waged by any race, and I hope that England may be defeated.')

Within a short time some fancy political footwork backfired on Hughes, and he would not taste the Prime Ministership again. In an attempt to placate big business, Hughes appointed the well-heeled Stanley Melbourne Bruce as his Treasurer.

Before long, Bruce himself was Prime Minister and, even though he claimed he hadn't the faintest idea how he got there, he managed to lead Australia through most of the 1920s. In many ways Bruce's aristocratic and stylish image suited the times. We regarded ourselves as considerably more sophisticated than the eager colonial hicks who queued up for places on the troop ships 10 years earlier. When the Prince of Wales visited Australia in 1920, *The Bulletin* urged that the Prince should be seeing 'the Australia that is friendly and hospitable but will lick no man's boots'.

Stanley Melbourne Bruce was our first businessman Prime Minister. And perhaps more by accident than design he ruled over Australia during an unprecedented boom period. By 1928 an increasingly materialistic Australia had 500 000 cars, 300 000 radios and 400 000 telephones. The population increased by 20 per cent, due in part to the influx of 300 000 migrants.

After the stagnation of the war, the country was being pioneered once again. P.J. McGinness and Hudson Fysh, the two young men who had tracked by car the route for the 1919 flight from London to Sydney, formed the Queensland and Northern Territory Aerial Services Ltd, or Qantas for short. Enterprises in the country were both large and small. The Golden Gate, which opened in Sydney in 1921, became the best-known soda fountain in Sydney, while on a slightly larger scale, the boffins finally got serious and decided to call for tenders for a bridge across Sydney Harbour. Even convict architect Francis Greenway had plans for a bridge as far back as 1815, but wealthy ferry owners did their darndest to see that one never came to fruition. And by the start of the twentieth century a bridge was still just a dream. Plans were drawn up by Dr Bradfield as early as 1911 but the project was again delayed by the First World War.

In 1921, a group called the Old Melburnians were treated to a demonstration of the phenomenon of radio at one of their smoke socials. They were advised that it was 'quite unnecessary for any of the windows to be open' for

Top: In the 1920s, Australia fast became a nation of car lovers. In 1924, America had nearly 13.5 million. We were fifth in the world with 100 000 cars, which quintupled by the end of the decade. . Bottom: Spot the spats—Stanley Melbourne Bruce led the nation during the boom period of the 1920s but became the only Australian Prime Minister to lose his seat in Parliament in an election.

the radio waves to get through. I still don't know why you don't need to open the windows.

Prime Minister Bruce allowed much of the frenzied commercial activity to develop unchecked. His motto could well have been 'Life was meant to be easy'; but then, like Malcolm Fraser, who took quite the opposite view so much later, he could be extremely autocratic when the mood struck. His common ploy was to blame the Bolsheviks for all industrial ills. This was a successful tactic taken up by a number of conservative Prime Ministers.

By 1924, Australia was building 20 000 new factories a year. Woolworths went into business. Qantas declared its first profit in the same year that Cobb and Co. ran its last coach in Queensland. Horse-drawn trams were finally phased out, and work began on the Harbour Bridge and the new 'temporary' Parliament House in Canberra. Oil was struck at Lakes Entrance in Victoria, and although nearly 300 000 gallons of petroleum were produced in the next 35 years, it was largely of a poor quality. This discovery was, nevertheless, of great significance in the development of Australia's oil reserves.

Australia was now fifth in the world for the number of motor vehicles according to the National Automobile Chamber of Commerce in New York. Of the world total of nearly 16 million cars, America had 13.5 million and Australia, bless her little heart, had more than 100 000.

By the mid 1920s, Bruce was taking the 'big stick' to the unions, a tactic that would eventually bring about his undoing. He made an abortive attempt to have the ringleaders of the seamen's strike deported.

In 1925, Australia faced a far more insidious problem than some left-wing talk from the Bolsheviks. Over 20 million hectares of Queensland and New South Wales were covered with prickly pear, a vegetable plague, which had multiplied from a single potted plant. The story of how the land was saved from the scourge is one of the great scientific sagas of the twentieth century. Elsewhere in the world, a man named Adolph Hitler unveiled a book called *Mein Kampf*. A chap named Clarence Birdseye succeeded in freezing cooked food and storing it, and Chiang Kai-shek became leader of the Chinese Nationalist Party. On a more parochial level, a Sydney real estate agent named Jack Lang became Premier of New South Wales. Lang was destined to become one of the stormiest and most fascinating political figures in our history, his career culminating in a dramatic dismissal which would not be paralleled until the Whitlam era.

In the same election that saw Jack Lang become Premier, a young man of 31 named Herbert Vere Evatt won the seat of Balmain. Evatt was quick to make his presence felt in Lang's Government, playing a vital role in the framing of legislation introducing widows' pensions. Like Lang, Evatt was also fated to have a spectacular, dramatic and, at times, tragic political career. In Australia, he was eventually pilloried for his politics, but on an international level he rose to the highest position attainable: President of the United Nations.

After his early stint in state politics, Evatt became at 36 the youngest man appointed to the High Court. He left the legal profession to enter politics when the country was at war in 1940, and after the war he helped to set up the United Nations. At home his political career from 1949 onwards was thwarted by the smear that he was pro-communist. In those McCarthyist days, the 'Red' tag was enough to keep him out of office as Prime Minister. He remained Leader of the Opposition for a decade and his own party, the Australian Labor Party, split in two largely because of the strongly anti-communist and Catholic elements within its ranks.

By the late 1920s, however, Australia was still under the benevolent dictatorship of S.M. Bruce. Although there was a general strike in Britain and the Hitler and fascist youth movements were on the rise, Australia was making the most of its 10 years of peace since the First World War. We were happily separated from the gathering turmoil in Europe. The fact that Trotsky had been expelled from Moscow meant little, but the visit by famous Russian ballerina Pavlova excited press and public alike. A young Adelaide man named Helpman changed his name slightly, adding another 'n' for distinction, and joined her company. The year 1926 was a great one for the arts. Others who came were singers Dame Clara Butt, Chaliapin and Toti Dal Monte.

And if Pavlova inspired Robert Helpmann to great heights, she did the same for a Perth hotel chef named Bert Sachse. Why the ballerina's lissom figure prompted Bert to create a highly calorific concoction of eggwhites, sugar and cream is a mystery, but 'the Pav' became one of Australia's favourite ethnic desserts; along with Peach Melba, created by the great Escoffier, and the lamington, a chocolate and coconut-covered cube of sponge cake named after Baron Lamington, Governor of Queensland from 1895 to 1901.

The disappointment of not being able to compete in the 1919 London to Sydney flight caused Kingsford Smith, in the late 1920s, to make the most audacious flight of all—across the Pacific. We now had our own Lindbergh. In fact, there were few international trends we could not match. We even had our own little crime 'czars' like Squizzy Taylor, who culminated his career by getting shot under mysterious circumstances in Melbourne.

Nellie Melba had ruled the international stage for decades, and in 1927 she sang at the opening of the brand new Parliament House in Canberra, while none other than the Duke of York turned a golden key in the door. The inimitable newspaper *Smith's Weekly* sent its boxing writer to cover the affair:

> During a devotional interlude I noticed the Duke cast several nervous apprehensive glances towards the political gallery. Possibly he had just remembered his ancestor George the Third's illuminating outburst, 'Politics is the trade of scoundrels.' Orisons over, the Duke and Duchess vanished into the bowels of the building and the gallant Four Hundred charged the doorway.

As the 1920s drew to a close, Australians could look back on a decade that hadn't been so frivolous after all. The CSIRO had been established, and the Australian Iron and Steel Company was formed to provide the vast sums for the projected Port Kembla steel works.

Australians had made international names for themselves even in the arts, although Frances Alda, prima donna at the Metropolitan Opera House for 20 years, was not too confident about the future. Asked whether she thought grand opera would show a profit in Australia she replied (to the delight of everyone, still with an Australian accent), 'Stick your money on a horse, son.'

In the late 1920s it wasn't only grand opera which was having its financial difficulties. Unemployment, which was a problem of frightening magnitude, rose from 7 per cent in 1926 to 11 per cent in 1928.

As the economic climate worsened, we seemed to look more and more to our heroes for inspiration. Perhaps we took heart from the smiling faces of Smithy and Ulm when they conquered the Pacific, and little Bert Hinkler who flew solo from Britain to Australia. Cyclist Hubert Opperman was voted the most popular sportsman in Europe. Don Bradman played his first Test Match. The name Phar Lap was on everyone's lips. The engineering wonder of the age, the Sydney Harbour Bridge, was under way.

But the reality was that most of us were now battling for a living. The Wall Street crash in America signified the start of the Depression and, although not

Top: During hard times, Australia needed its heroes. Opera singer Dame Nellie Melba was vain, haughty and lived like a queen, but she remains possibly our greatest international star. Here she is waiting to sing for the opening fo the first Parliament House in Canberra in 1927.
Bottom: Beloved Melbourne Cup winner Phar Lap and his strapper, Tommy Woodcock.

hit as hard as some countries, Australia nevertheless suffered severely. Her economy relied heavily on overseas loans and the sale of primary products. Share prices plummeted and, as the value of our money dwindled, businesses closed, farms were abandoned and people who could not pay the rent were forced out of their homes.

Prime Minister Bruce, more and more incongruous in his Savile Row suits and spats, not only lost an election, but suffered the humiliation of being the only Australian Prime Minister to ever lose his seat in Parliament as well. James Scullin, who became Prime Minister after Billy Hughes had led the revolt which toppled Bruce, lost important support soon after winning the election. He refused to intervene in the New South Wales coal strike in 1929. When the New South Wales Government sent troops into the Rothbury mine and killed and injured strikers, many unionists never forgave him for ignoring the call for federal intervention.

It was a dramatic time in Australia. In Sydney thousands of people protested against the killing of the young Rothbury miner, Norman Brown:

Norman Brown's body lies a mould'ring in the grave,
But we'll go marching on.

Labor also failed to gain control of the Senate during the elections, and in March and May of 1930 the Senators threw out money Bills which Scullin considered vital. Scullin also became embroiled in combat with his Labor colleague in Sydney, Jack Lang. Lang tried to protect the people of his state from the effects of the Depression at the expense and in defiance of Canberra, and, more dangerously, Britain. It made him a hero of the people but it killed him politically.

And so the 1930s began with unemployment worse than Germany's, and 125 000 out of work in Sydney alone. The decade would end with another world war.


## THE 1930s

The 1930s was not a happy decade for many Australians, although perhaps because of this, it is a period rich in folklore. Even the crimes of the 1930s have an unsurpassed mystique. The 'pyjama girl' and 'shark arm' murder cases still arouse more curiosity than any of the thousands of murders which have taken place in the half century since. Bradman, Lindrum, Phar Lap and Jack Crawford were just some of the sporting giants of the 1930s. The decade also saw the rise of perhaps the greatest of our political giants, Curtin, Chifley and Menzies.

This whole period was marked by bitter internal dissension in the Labor Party over the handling of the Depression by Scullin. Ben Chifley was one of Scullin's supporters and, because of this he lost the backing of many people in the Labor movement. Perhaps, more importantly, he made a life-long enemy of Jack Lang. In the elections of 1931, during the massive swing away from Labor, Chifley lost his seat. At the same time Lang and his supporters launched a plan to oust Chifley from his own union. The move was successful and Chifley faced 1932 without a seat in Parliament, without membership, and without a job. He spent the next 10 years out of Parliament, but not out of politics, and, after a long battle, he did in turn have Lang expelled from the party in 1936.

After the outbreak of the Second World War, Menzies offered Chifley the job as Director of Labour Supply. Chifley lasted in the job for less than a year. He resigned to contest the seat of Macquarie and within a year his close friend John Curtin appointed him to the post of Federal Treasurer, a portfolio he retained even after he eventually became Prime Minister.

But back in the 1930s, Chifley, Curtin and Menzies were still in the political wilderness. The Prime Minister for most of the decade was in fact a most unlikely character, Joe Lyons. Apart from the fact that he was one of those peculiar political animals who changed horses in mid-stream, Lyons seems an uninteresting character. Or was he? When he put himself outside the government and the Parliamentary Labor Party in March 1931 he was protesting against their handling of the economic crisis and he fully expected that his political career was finished. Yet, within a year he was the country's leader, and he remained so until 1939. The secret of Lyons' success has puzzled many analysts.

Certainly, with the rest of federal politics in disarray in the early 1930s, 'Honest Joe' came through the middle in a fashion not dissimilar to the rise of United States President Jimmy Carter. The Nationalist Party Leader, John Latham, who had gunned down such figures as Billy Hughes, stood aside to let Lyons lead. There had been a hasty move to bury the Nationalist Party and to create the United Australia Party and once again, a Labor 'defector' filled the opposition party leadership and gave it renewed stability. Latham, in turn, had the satisfaction, along with Menzies and Casey, of manipulating the less urbane and seemingly malleable Lyons. But just how much Joe Lyons was a pawn of the party is open to speculation. History has painted Joe and his famous wife Enid as a couple of simple, home-spun, fundamentally decent Christian folks—a little at a loss in the hurly-burly of federal politics. But the idea that a couple could accidentally stumble into the top positions in the country seems absurd. Besides, they had 11 kids—they certainly knew how to organise a chook raffle.

If the leadership of the 1930s was somewhat grey, then life was not altogether dull. We took up most of the Depression crazes: barnstorming, marathon ballroom dancing and mini-golf. There were other rages such as art deco, airships, skiing, 'Odeon'-style cinemas, cocktails, and modern bungalows.

Another important change to the way Australians saw themselves occurred during the 1930s. The newsreels began—Cinesound and Movietone—and they really were the television of their era. They were surprisingly large-scale, dynamic and topical for such a small country, and we flocked to see them. There was a surge of activity in the film business. It was the beginning of the so-called 'golden age' of Australian film, and a not-so-golden start for a strapping young bloke named Errol Flynn, whose first role was in a documentary feature called *In the Wake of the Bounty*. Flynn got £10 a week for his part and had no idea then that he would go on to become one of the biggest stars in Hollywood. In that same year in 'Tinsel Town', Shirley Temple was making her first film, and Johnny Weissmuller made his first appearance in a Tarzan movie.

But while Errol Flynn made a tenner a week, many were getting next to nothing. By 1933, a quarter of the workforce was still unemployed. It was the era of 'bagmen' and 'jumping the rattler', when men caught Murray cod, possums and rabbits to earn a meagre living. They transported themselves in boats called 'Murrumbidgee whalers', and jumped the trains, sometimes slowing them down to a comfortable jumping-on speed by greasing the tracks.

There was no building boom throughout the decade, and immigration virtually ceased. In fact, more people left Australia between 1930 and 1932

Top: Protesters during the Depression years gathered outside Parliament House demanding jobs. Australia's unemployment rate at the beginning of the 1930s was worse than that of Germany. Bottom: A Depression family. New South Wales Premier Jack Lang lost his job fighting to protect such people by refusing to pay state debts.

than entered it. Rural areas were hit just as hard as the cities. In the early 1930s, a country bank manager wrote:

> Merriwagga is a dust storm fenced in, surrounded by mirages, dying sheep and our clients. The principle industries are dust storms and uninhabited farms.

However, in the depths of the Depression, Australia built its proudest monument—that grand old pile of nuts and bolts called the Sydney Harbour Bridge. There was a tremendous amount of fuss at the opening when the political extremist de Groot cut the ribbon with a sabre and stole Premier Jack Lang's thunder. For Lang it was a desperate time all round. At his right elbow on that sunny afternoon in March 1932 was the Governor of New South Wales, Sir Philip Game, who, two months' later, called the Premier to his study at Government House and dismissed him.

For many, the dismissal was an outrage against democracy, but even Lang's sacking hardly aroused the kind of passions which surfaced during the infamous 'Bodyline' cricket tour. Cricket became warfare and the sporting crisis reached diplomatic level. As England kept the Ashes, our only comfort was that Jack Crawford won the Wimbledon singles tennis. But we soon had other preoccupations which would help take from our minds the wounds left by 'Bodyline'. The bizarre 'pyjama girl', whose body was kept in formalin for 10 years until she was identified, was the subject of ghoulish speculation and rumour until the mid 1940s, as were the shady principals of the 'shark arm' case. The case began with an incredible coincidence. A shark in Coogee aquarium disgorged the remains of another shark, which in turn contained a human arm. On the arm was a tattoo, which started police on one of the most frustrating and still unresolved murder cases in our history.

Such newspaper stories as the pyjama girl and shark arm cases, the mysterious loss of Kingsford Smith's airliner *Southern Cloud*, and the race riots in Kalgoorlie, momentarily distracted Australians from the problems of the day. Halfway through the decade there were still 400 000 unemployed. Australia's recovery from the Depression was slow, and full employment did not return until the outbreak of the Second World War in 1939.

However, the extreme severity of the Depression was thankfully not compounded by a collapse of the banks as had occurred in America (and indeed in Australia in the 1890s). As a response to the bank smash just before

While the 1930s might have been clouded by the Depression years, there were more than enough highlights to fill the news headlines. In 1932, the Sydney Harbour Bridge was opened. Jack Lang was ready to do the honours, but he was pipped at the post by right-wing radical Francis de Groot. Meanwhile, Donald Bradman was on his way to becoming one of the greatest cricketers the world has ever seen.

the turn of the century, Australian banks had strengthened themselves with a series of amalgamations, which reduced their total number to nine. Nevertheless, there were many penny-pinching schemes which caused hostility and heartbreak. The New South Wales *Married Women (Teachers and Lecturers) Act* provided for the dismissal of married women teachers unless they could prove hardship. The official justification was that 'the married woman's sphere is the management of the home rather than breadwinning. It is the woman's lot to marry and share the home with the breadwinner'.

Now looking after our interests overseas was Stanley Melbourne Bruce, who after a brief comeback in federal politics, had accepted the job as resident minister in London, a job which he handled with distinction and *savoir faire*. He proved to be a hard bargainer at the Empire conference in Ottawa. At one stage, when Neville Chamberlain (then Britain's Chancellor of the Exchequer) was being unco-operative about meat quotas, Bruce retorted, 'I saved the bloody Empire on Monday. It's your turn to save it now.' This conference did in fact go some way to 'saving the Empire', and established a trade pattern that was to last for 30 years. Chamberlain and Bruce were actually friendly foes. When war seemed inevitable, Chamberlain offered Bruce the chair of the BBC, but Bruce declined.

The situation in Europe was ominous. Hitler amassed 99 per cent of the vote in the 1936 elections. The Spanish Civil War had begun and King Edward abdicated to marry Mrs Wallis Simpson. The world seemed to be falling apart.

And, while the war clouds gathered, some of those who were destined to play major roles for Australia were going through the most traumatic periods of their lives. One was Thomas Blamey, who went on to become Australia's best-known soldier and our first Field Marshal. After a highly successful career in the First World War, Blamey was, in the late 1930s, the Victorian Police Commissioner, but he was involved in some scandals that nearly ruined his career. Soon after he took the post, Blamey's police badge, number 80, somehow came to light following a raid on an 'upper crust' Melbourne brothel. Blamey claimed he had lost the badge some time before the raid, but a public scandal ensued. Nevertheless, Blamey survived the crisis and went on to reorganise the police force. In 1936, however, the chief of the CIB was shot in a gunfight when two men tried to hold him up as he waited in a car with two women friends to meet an informer. Blamey told the press that the superintendent had been shot accidentally while loading his revolver. But the true story came out, and in the storm that followed, Blamey was censured and forced to resign. His official career seemed finished, and for a while he was a broadcaster on Radio 3UZ.

In his talks on the radio, Blamey warned of the growing dangers from Germany and Japan, and in 1939 he was made Controller-General of the recruiting secretariat. A year later he was appointed General Officer commanding the Sixth Division. Blamey was a man with many enemies, and many friends. When he died in 1951, 20 000 people passed through the Shrine of Remembrance.

With the war yet to begin, people still made their plans for the future. Who could have guessed that the world would be at war for half the following decade?

Laurence Hartnett, a little Englishman who had come to Australia to solve some of the problems of the merger between General Motors and the Adelaide-born Holden Motor Body Works, dreamed of an 'all Australian' car. A man named Bill Walkley was fighting to establish the Australian Motorists Petrol Company, which eventually became Ampol. Even without the war, the odds seemed against them from the start. The Sydney Stock Exchange advised its members not to buy shares, and the major oil companies did their best to squash the new company. By 1937, the company welcomed the tanker *Garonne*, carrying its first supplies from the American Richfield Corporation. But the 'big boys' cut their prices to try to force Ampol out of business. Ampol lost more than £18 000 in its first six months, and employees had to hawk shares door-to-door to raise another £100 000 in capital.

The year 1938 was also the 150th anniversary of the founding of New South Wales. Charles Chauvel, watching the procession to celebrate the event, was instantly inspired to make his epic film *Forty Thousand Horsemen*. It was based on the exploits of his uncle, an eminent soldier, during the Palestinian campaign in the First World War, and it put 'Chips' Rafferty and Peter Finch on the road to international fame.

The Lyons Government, which had lasted for almost the whole decade, had been sound but unspectacular. When the Labor Party, led by John Curtin, began to look formidably strong in the late 1930s the conservatives started to carve one another up politically. He who came out on top was Robert Gordon Menzies.

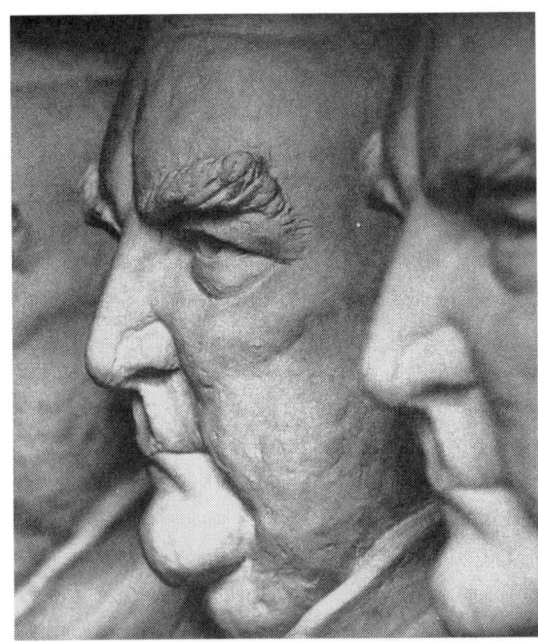

Left: The year 1939 gave Robert Gordon Menzies his first reign. One of his duties as the new Prime Minister was to announce Germany's invasion of Poland, and that Australia was once again at war. Bottom: Another outstanding politician on the rise at the time was Labor's John Curtin, who late in 1941 became Prime Minister for the remainder of the Second World War. Here he is exhorting a Sydney lunchtime crowd to buy War Loan Bonds.

Menzies had already earned his famous nickname of 'Pig Iron Bob' after he had introduced severe punitive measures to break a union ban on the loading of scrap iron for Japan. Menzies was growing impatient with the apparently feeble leadership of Lyons and in 1938 launched a thinly veiled attack on his leader by saying that 'Democracies could not maintain their place in the world unless they provided leadership as inspiring as that of the dictator countries.' It was a prophetic statement.

The speech by Menzies caused a Cabinet re-shuffle which did not suit the ambitious Victorian. For a start, Richard Casey was promoted to Treasurer, and it transpired that Lyons had chosen him as his successor. Within a matter of months, Menzies resigned. His excuse was that the government had failed to carry out its 1937 election promise to create a national comprehensive insurance scheme. Menzies said this was a betrayal of the electors. But, whatever his reasons, neither Menzies nor any other non-Labor leader revived the idea of the scheme.

As fate would have it, Lyons died while the internecine struggles continued, and there was immediately a brutal battle for the leadership. There were desperate plans to revive Stanley Melbourne Bruce as Prime Minister, but he set down a series of impossible conditions for his leadership. The Country Party leader, Earle Page, tried to thwart Menzies and publicly denounced him, but Menzies shrugged off the attacks and formed a new government.

As Robert Menzies posed for his first ministry photograph in 1939, with Casey on his right and Billy Hughes on his left, and with his United Australia Party colleagues and a few renegade Country Party men to back him up, the future looked shaky. Yet even then, it seemed war was not inevitable. The coalition government under Lyons believed, like the British coalition government under Chamberlain, that the aggressors could be appeased. In fact, just a few months earlier, Lyons had rebuked visiting English writer H.G. Wells for describing Hitler as a 'certifiable lunatic' and Mussolini as a 'criminal Caesar'.

On 1 September 1939, Menzies was booked to hold a meeting in the Victoria Hall at Colac, the venue where Andrew Fisher, on the eve of the First World War, had pledged that Australia would defend the Mother Country to 'her last man and her last shilling'. Menzies was dining before the meeting when he was told on the telephone that Hitler had invaded Poland.

He went to the meeting, told the audience of the invasion, and returned to Melbourne to confer with his ministers. At 9.15 p.m. on 3 September, Menzies said in a broadcast to the Australian people:

> It is my melancholy duty to inform you officially that in consequence of the persistence by Germany in her invasion of Poland, Great Britain has declared war on her and that, as a result, Australia is now also at war. No harder task can fall to the lot of a democratic leader than to make such an announcement.

## THE 1940s

More than twice as many Australians enlisted for the Second World War as did for the First, and yet only half as many were killed. While there had been 66 Victoria Crosses awarded in the First World War, only 20 were awarded in the Second World War. It was a different war. No longer was there a sense of derring-do or adventure. It was more business-like, more mechanised and more scientific. There were no bloody years of trench fighting, and medicine had improved. Nobody dreamed that the conflict would end in a futuristic nightmare—the atomic holocaust of Hiroshima and Nagasaki.

At the outbreak, the mood was calm and purposeful, not as excited and enthusiastic as it had been in 1914. Service throughout the war was primarily voluntary—not complicated by the divisive conscription battles of the First World War.

Yet, as in the First World War, Australia turned to a Labor Government for leadership. The Menzies Government's tenuous hold on power led to a revival of calls for a 'national government'. Although many, including Evatt, agreed with the idea, Curtin refused. While Menzies was beset with the problem of dealing with the unions, the Labor movement was strengthened by the return to the fold of the Lang Labor Party.

In 1941, Menzies went overseas and returned to find that his leadership of his own party had been completely undermined. Fadden took over, but two independent members, one of whom described Menzies' fall as a 'lynching', took revenge on his behalf. They combined to defeat the Fadden Government and their action placed Labor in office for the remainder of the war.

In 1941 the new Prime Minister, John Curtin, made a direct declaration of war against Japan without consulting the British Cabinet. It was the first time in Australia's history that the nation had declared war on its own. Curtin also introduced a new era of Australian foreign policy in December of that year when he said:

> Without any inhibitions of any kind I make it quite clear that Australia looks to America—free of any pangs as to our traditional links of kinship with the United Kingdom.

For Australia this was perhaps the major difference between the Second World War and the conflicts that had gone before. For the first time in our history there was a possibility of a direct threat to *our* shores. Within months war would actually come home to Australia, and it shocked the nation.

In the meantime, Australian soldiers underwent a splendid baptism of fire at Bardia, capturing 40 000 Italians for the loss of only 130 of their own men. But we were not so fortunate in Crete. Trapped on the Greek peninsula by the German occupation armies, Australian losses were high. Yet, as with all warfare, the fortunes vacillated. Glorious pages of Australian history were written at Tobruk. At one stage the Australians found they had taken another 27 000 prisoners for the loss of just 49 men. But the untried Ninth Division was routed by Rommel in Tripoli in a retreat which was cynically called 'the Benghazi Handicap'.

In the early days of the war the Australian battleship *Sydney* sank the Italian *Bartolomeo Colleoni* in the first cruiser battle of the war. But in 1941 it met the German raider *Kormoran*, a heavily armed ship disguised as a Dutch freighter. *Kormoran* was on its way to lay mines in the Shark Bay area outside Fremantle, and surprised the *Sydney* as it was returning to port. The ships had closed to about 900 metres before *Sydney* asked for a secret sign of identity. The *Kormoran's* reply was immediate. German flags went up, Dutch flags went down and it opened fire. A full salvo hit *Sydney* amidships. Both ships were crippled in the fire that followed and, as the Germans abandoned ship, they caught sight of the *Sydney* about 16 kilometres away with its hull ablaze. The only trace of it ever found was a life float and lifebelts, and as a result of this lack of details, its demise remains one of the great Naval mysteries.

In 1942 the war came right to Australia's shores. Japanese midget submarines raided Sydney Harbour and Japanese planes raided Darwin—

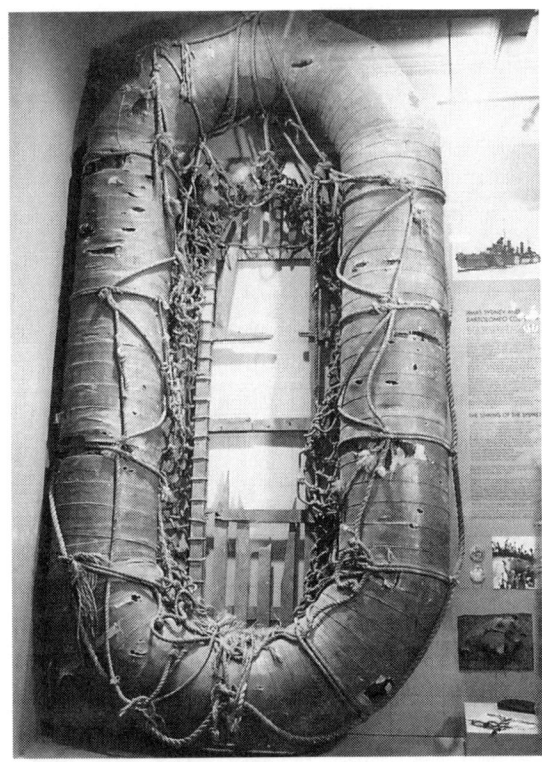

Left: A Carley life float, all that remains of HMAS *Sydney*—sunk in 1941 when caught in a surprise battle with the *Kormoran*, a disguised German ship, near Fremantle, Western Australia. Bottom: The *Sydney's* mysterious end came only shortly after her sinking of the Italian light cruiser *Bartolomeo Colleoni*, seen below.

dropping twice as many bombs on our northern capital as were dropped on Pearl Harbor. They were bleak times. To our near north, Singapore fell, a loss described by Churchill as 'the worst disaster and the largest capitulation in British history'. On 16 February, Major General H. Gordon Bennett, leader of Australia's Eighth Division, escaped from Singapore believing he should return to his country to help in its defence. His reasons, however, were not accepted in Australia and he did not receive an overseas command for the rest of the war. In 1945, he was finally cleared by a commission which decided that he had considered himself a prisoner of war, and that it was his duty to escape.

The American role in the war was paramount. When General Douglas MacArthur arrived in Australia after his mauling in the Philippines, the American President sent a telegram to Curtin saying it would be 'very acceptable' if the Australian Government would nominate MacArthur as the Supreme Commander of all Allied Forces in the South West Pacific. The Australian Government agreed. MacArthur found what he later described as 'a sense of dangerous defeatism' among a large segment of the Australian people. Many disagreed with his assessment, while others took it with a grain of salt.

To get to Australia from the Philippines, MacArthur made an amazing journey through enemy lines and was pursued by Japanese fighter planes even onto Australian soil. On his way south across the continent from Batchelor Field in the Northern Territory, MacArthur's train stopped at the tiny South Australian outpost of Terowie where he said to the press who'd come up to meet him from Adelaide, 'I came out of Bataan and I shall return.' He said it many times again and after running the Pacific war by remote control from the war room in Melbourne, he eventually fulfilled his promise. The Japanese were repelled and MacArthur did return. A brilliant man who liked the sound of his own voice, MacArthur went on to lead a United Nations force in the Korean War but was dismissed when he demanded the use of nuclear weapons against the North Koreans.

Australians were already well aware of the American alliance. By the end of the war nearly a million American troops had passed through Australia, and the influx caused inevitable tensions. The American GI, with roughly twice the spending power of the Australian soldier and a somewhat more dashing uniform, cut a swathe through some of the flowers of Australian womanhood. Eventually, 12 000 girls went to the United States with American servicemen. There's a classic story about a GI who boasted that the Americans had pinched all the girls from the Australians, to which a digger laconically replied, 'You didn't pinch 'em mate, you just helped us sort them out.'

Many Australians really resented the American 'invasion'. They described the Americans as 'over paid, over fed, over sexed and over here'. The liaisons between American servicemen and Australian girls eventually led to 'the Battle of Brisbane'. A group of Australian servicemen picked a quarrel with American military police. In the fight that followed, nine Australians were shot, one of them fatally.

Late in 1942, the Japanese launched a two-pronged attack on Port Moresby down the Kokoda Track and at Milne Bay. For a while it seemed that the Australians would lose Milne Bay, but the invaders were driven back into the sea. On Kokoda the defeat of the Japanese took much longer. The nightmare of the Track—the sheer hellishness of the terrain and the fighting—is known to most Australians. The casualties on both sides were high. In Papua the Japanese eventually lost 13 000 of their 20 000 men.

It is sometimes assumed that when a country is at war all other activity stops in respectful silence. On the contrary, many non-aggressive pursuits flourished during the war years, although not always without problems. The 1943 Archibald Prize for portraiture was marred by a ludicrous scandal which almost destroyed the life of artist William Dobell. An argument taken to the Supreme Court about whether Dobell's painting of fellow artist Joshua Smith was a caricature or a legitimate portrait in the accepted sense was resolved in the artist's favour, although he suffered deeply after the public trial, saying, 'I don't think I can ever forgive them for what they have done to me.'

During the war years the courts also contributed to the humiliation of Max Harris, Sidney Nolan and others involved with an avant-garde literary magazine called *Angry Penguins* after they had sincerely published the works of the poet 'Ern Malley', later revealed to be a hoax. Malley and his free-form poetry had been concocted as a joke by two poets of the traditional school and, to add insult to injury, Max Harris was prosecuted for publishing what were considered indecent extracts from the phoney poet's works.

Lawson Glassop's famous book *We Were the Rats* was also prosecuted for obscenity in 1944. Diggers, it seemed, didn't use four letter words. Around the

Right: *Joshua Smith*, the famous portrait by William Dobell (bottom right) which won the 1943 Archibald Prize. Some unsuccessful exhibitors argued that the painting was a caricature and not a portrait. The ensuing court case became a *cause célèbre* and almost destroyed the lives of Dobell and some of the other artists involved.

same time, Dr Floyd began his record-breaking run of concert programs on the ABC, and the Commission also began broadcasting the legendary 'Kindergarten of the Air'.

In 1944, the year the Liberal Party was formed; Chief Havoc, a Sydney greyhound, broke five track records in one night; 51 people were killed in Victorian bushfires; and the D-day landings were made in Normandy. The Japanese were driven out of New Guinea, 232 Japanese died in a suicidal break-out from a prison camp near Cowra, and the first Aboriginal Army officer was commissioned in Australia.

The year of 1945 was one of the most momentous in the history of the century. It was a kaleidoscope of horror and hope: the Americans entered Manila; British troops reached the Rhine; there was heavy United States bombing of Tokyo; Iwo Jima was captured by North American forces; President Roosevelt died and Truman took over; Mussolini was killed; Hitler suicided; Germany capitulated; the Japanese held out in New Guinea until the end; atom bombs were dropped on Hiroshima and Nagasaki; 35 million people had been killed in the war and 10 million died in concentration camps.

John Curtin, still a hero to many Australians, died just a month before the war ended. Ben Chifley easily won the position as Australia's Prime Minister. The London *Times* said in an editorial, 'Chifley is a true product of the Australian Labor movement. He is solid, hardworking and sincere, and his record suggests that since Curtin's mantle has fallen on him he will wear it worthily.'

On 12 July 1945, Chifley entered the Federal Parliament for the first time as Prime Minister and was greeted by a chorus of cheers from members of all parties. His first job was to announce the surrender of the Japanese, and for this occasion he arranged the first national broadcast from the House of Representatives in Canberra.

Chifley's primary objective as Prime Minister was post-war economic and industrial development. His government set up shipping, aluminium, whaling and atomic energy industries. It started the Snowy Mountains Scheme and took over telecommunications. But it was Chifley's confirmed belief in nationalisation which led to his downfall; first with the airlines and then, more disastrously, with the banks. Menzies, who was then Leader of the Opposition, later recalled:

In my opinion he was the most authentic Labor leader in Australian political history. For him the socialist objective was more than a slogan, it was a principle of action.

Chifley's first attempt to nationalise industry met with mixed success. He did not achieve a true monopoly, but Trans Australia Airlines (TAA), later Australian Airlines and now Qantas Domestic, is still a testament to his success, and his initial sortie into the airline business did no harm to his standing at the next elections. Labor was returned with Chifley firmly in control.

During his second term as Prime Minister, however, Chifley made a decision which militant Labor leaders still regard with distaste. Strikes in the New South Wales coalfields were causing a critical shortage of supply and Chifley, believing a communist plan was at work, sent the Army to work in the mines.

Chifley's most serious tactical error was his attempt to nationalise the banks. Chifley dissented from the findings of a Royal Commission into the banking system and introduced legislation which was passed through parliament in 1945. It gave greater control to the Commonwealth Bank, but the Melbourne City Council mounted a challenge in the High Court, claiming that the legislation was discriminatory. The abortive bank national-isation plans were a nail in the coffin of the old Labor Party, which was about to be cast out of office. Labor would not see power again for 23 years. Ahead lay the agonies of the crippling party 'split' and years in political 'wilderness'. The legacies of Labor in the 1940s are very much with us today. The visionary Snowy Mountains Scheme is one example. Another of Chifley's more symbolic acts in the last months of his Prime Ministership was to welcome the first Holden motor car off the assembly line. Chifley, a constant supporter of Laurence Hartnett, played a considerable part in the birth of the car which became an Australian institution.

The Menzies Government came to power in 1949 with promises of a softer life. Menzies' slogan for the election was 'Tip out the socialists and fill up the bowsers', and he won comfortably.

Whatever the achievements, for most Australians the 1940s was a good decade to leave behind. The first five years had been bloody and sad, the second rather drab and grey.

There's a story, now very much part of our mythology, which comes from the 1940s and which says a fair bit about that decade. An American visitor is sitting down to dinner at an Australian pub and he's given a plate of cold meat and potatoes:

'Do you think,' he asks adventurously, 'that I could have a little salad to go with this?'
'Did you hear that?' the waitress yells back to the kitchen. 'This bastard thinks it's Christmas.'

## THE 1950s

At the beginning of the 1950s, who could have realised that one man would rule us almost until the 1970s. The 1950s and 1960s were the Robert Menzies years. He was in power longer than the combined terms of three-quarters of a century of Labor Governments. Little wonder that they called his reign 'the Ming Dynasty' (from the traditional Scottish pronunciation of his name 'Mingus').

Many Australians look back on the 1950s and 1960s as balmy, troublefree days—a time when a silver-haired father figure in a double-breasted suit gave everyone a Holden, opened the Snowy Mountains Scheme and then went off to watch the cricket at Lord's. Menzies in fact had little to do with any except the last.

The early Menzies years were as politically turbulent as any in our history. When Menzies came to power in 1949 he had already been savagely 'rolled' by his own colleagues years earlier. He knew what political scrapping was about, and his reign began with a tremendous series of battles over the issue of communism. This led to a divided nation and a 'split' which virtually destroyed the Labor Party as an effective opposition. On top of the problems at home, Australia was already fighting in Malaya and was soon to be embroiled in the war in Korea.

The early days of the 1950s were hardly halcyon. Menzies has often been accused of engineering the turmoil to achieve his own political ends. But no politician is quite that clever, and it seems that when Menzies did emerge from the fray as victor, he set about seeking a quieter political road. Some said the secret of his success was that he did nothing at all, and although his achievements do not stand out like beacons, Australia did settle into a long period of stable government.

His legacy is his pioneering work in the development of education and universities. It is also said that Menzies chose his time to be leader nicely, although other countries in the 1950s and 1960s saw the usual turmoil and turnover of political leaders.

There is not much doubt, however, that the period between our involvement in the Korean and Vietnam Wars was a time of contentment and prosperity for millions of Australians. The bogeys of over-population, the energy crisis and the nuclear age were still beyond the horizon.

Australian awareness of a nuclear future had only just begun in 1950. Just a year earlier a lone prospector named John Michael White stumbled across uranium deposits at Rum Jungle. The deposits were proved in 1951 and a jubilant White was paid a reward of £25 000 by the Commonwealth Government.

In those days, nuclear fallout held little fear for Australians. We blithely let the British explode atomic devices all over the country. Yet, by the 1970s, there would be a collective national frenzy against the French who were testing similar bombs on a Pacific atoll 4800 kilometres from our shores.

Looking back, the 1950s seem a somewhat smug period of Australian history. Proud of our lifestyle in 'the greatest little country on Earth' we worried constantly that the 'yellow hordes' might still be casting 'greedy slant eyes' on our vast land. The threat from the north became almost a national obsession as our standard of living increased. Those who preached about the peril of the communist tide drew maps with large descending arrows which showed that communist Chinese and others were going to descend upon us almost by force of gravity. (Some wags said the problem could be solved simply by inverting the map.) To the delight of those who had been predicting an Asian invasion, the situation actually began to get some real tension in the early 1960s during Indonesia's 'confrontation' period under Sukarno. As the Indonesians adopted a menacing stance towards Malaysia and other Anglo-Saxon outposts like Australia, the fear of 'the yellow peril' waxed and then slowly waned again. It would return with the Indonesian invasion of Timor in the mid 1970s and the subsequent turmoil.

Although life in the early 1950s was fairly insular, we soon began to expand our horizons again. Australia sent a Davis Cup team to try to wrest the trophy from the Americans who had held it since before the war. Drysdale and Nolan, the Australian artists, held their first London exhibition.

At the same time, there was an aggressive new school here called The Antipodeans who attacked local abstractionists as 'second-rate imitators of the Europeans'. It was rampant artistic jingoism, and while the big guns of the art world lined up on each side, some painters like Godfrey Miller, Passmore and Fairweather, said it was folly for artists to call themselves anything at all.

In 1950, a young woman named Joan Sutherland, having won a Sydney *Sun* Aria Quest and Mobil Song Quest, would soon be strutting the international stage commanding a fortune as 'La Stupenda'. Other Australian women, however, were still struggling to make a quid. In 1950 the female basic wage was increased from 54 per cent to 75 per cent of the male rate. Today's feminists would no doubt respond 'big deal', but in that year women accepted the adjustment as 'progress'. A large body of Australian women were still a pretty mousy lot who even years later would sullenly oppose the idea of liberation espoused by their self-appointed champion, Germaine Greer. In general, bras remained unburned. Ironically, too, Australian women were slow to adopt a fashion style that eventually we came to believe we had created. In July 1946, the United States began its atomic bomb tests at Bikini Atoll in the Pacific and in that month Louis Reard, a Parisian designer, made world news by introducing the first bikini swimsuit. However, in Australia the summer season of 1949–50 only saw the introduction of the strapless swimsuit, which was quite bold enough, thank you very much.

In 1952, the year Elizabeth became Queen and Australia sent its Second Battalion to Korea, Australians at home began once again to flex their sporting muscles. The 1950s was a watershed for Australian sport, which would culminate in the pride of staging our first Olympic Games in Melbourne. The war had interrupted the careers of some Australian sportspeople, and terminated many more, and in the late 1940s, save for the inexorable progress of cricket and football, sport had been in the doldrums.

Then, with a rush, we found ourselves gathering laurels around the world. Lew Hoad and Ken Rosewall, two 17-year-old tennis players from Sydney, won the Wimbledon doubles. Marjorie Jackson won two gold medals at the Olympics in Helsinki, and the whole nation gave a collective 'tch, tch', when Marj, 'the Lithgow Flash', dropped the baton in the 100 metres relay, then went on to cross the line first just to show that we would have won. Jimmy Carruthers slaughtered Vic Toweel in 139 seconds to win our first official world boxing championship this century.

Top: Lew Hoad and Ken Rosewall were only 17 when they won Wimbledon in 1952. Dubbed 'the tennis twins' they thrilled Australia with their victories against the US in the Davis Cup, then the pinnacle of amateur tennis. Bottom: Marjorie Jackson, 'the Lithgow Flash', won two gold medals in the 1952 Helsinki Olympic Games. She saved for months to buy her running shoes.

That was just 1952. In 1953, Ken Rosewall, at 18, became the youngest Australian singles champion. Russell Mockridge, the great cyclist who was to die in a tragic accident, won the Grand Prix in Paris. In the following year, Peter Thomson won the first of his five British Opens and John Landy, our first four-minute miler, racing against the world's first, Roger Bannister, turned his head in the last few yards to see where his opponent was when Bannister snuck past, and it was all over. It was the beginning of the professional era. Sport started to become big business. Frank Sedgman turned pro with Jack Kramer. There was a strong rear-guard action fought by amateur sporting bodies, but soon ambitious young people in all fields made a bee-line for the big money.

The year 1954 was probably Australia's most momentous political year. Russians Vladimir Petrov and his wife Evdokia defected to Australia in an atmosphere of hysteria. Russia and Australia withdrew their ambassadors, a Royal Commission into espionage was set up, and the scene was set for the Labor Party's exile from government for nearly 20 years.

The Cold War got a little chillier, but life generally was loosening up—less austere than the grey days of the late 1940s. Encouraged by tours by Laurence Olivier and his wife Vivien Leigh, and then the Queen herself, a group of Australians led by Dr H.C. Coombs set up the Elizabethan Theatre Trust. Australian theatre was injected with new life with celebrated plays like Ray Lawler's *The Summer of the Seventeenth Doll*. Australians generally had a sudden new passion for what comedian Barry Humphries many years later would call 'the Yarts'. Sydney even decided to fulfil a grandiose dream and chose a site for an opera house. Three years later, the first Opera House Lottery—£5 a ticket—was introduced and 15 years and some $100 million later, the Queen would open the new Opera House building itself.

One 'cultural' development for which Australians eagerly awaited in the early 1950s was television. In 1950 the Television Advisory Committee sent a group of advisers abroad to study the latest developments. There was considerable argument over many years.

Ben Chifley, for example, had wanted no commercial television whatsoever, and these days there are still a lot of people who wish he had had his way. Others wanted to aim straight away for a colour service, similar to those in other countries. But, by being unadventurous and settling for a black and white, at least we benefited from the technological improvements which had been made at the expense of others. Television was postponed in 1951 because of the economic problems of the time, and the next significant move was the setting up of a Royal Commission in 1953.

The Australian way of life was changing both rapidly and slowly. When Malcolm Muggeridge, the English pundit, came here in the 1950s he noted that Geelong Grammar was 'even more snobbish' than Eton. The 1950s saw a burgeoning of the *nouveau riche*. One of them was a nuggety character with a nose for good dirt named Lang Hancock. In 1952, Hancock, a grazier and part-owner of an asbestos mine, became lost under thick cloud in his light plane while flying with his wife from their West Australian property, and flew into a gorge with rust-coloured walls. He returned later, and took iron ore chip samples. He found that they were of better quality than deposits being processed by the United States and was elated. He claimed that 'the greatest industrial might in the world was built around the Lake Superior deposits, and here is a deposit bigger and better'. Hancock's genius was that he not only discovered the deposits, just as John White had stumbled across uranium at Rum Jungle, but that he was able to hang on to 'a piece of the action'.

Hancock was one of the new breed of Australian millionaires whose fortunes were founded in the 1950s. Australia still had its old rich, who in the 1950s were getting £1 a pound for wool during a boom due largely to shortages caused by the Korean War. But the new social giants were people who found new ways to tap the natural riches of the land.

After flying over promising-looking oil country in the late 1940s, William Walkley took six years to raise the money and equipment to prove his theories. In November 1953, the first oil rose out of a drill site at Rough Range near the southern tip of Exmouth Gulf. It was the 250th well to be dug in Australia, and while several strikes had been made dating back to the 1920s, they ultimately proved to be of limited value. By the time of the first strike, Walkley's company, Ampol, was working with Caltex in a joint venture. As they poured millions into the search for oil, these two companies found just what a difficult and frustrating business it is. The joint venture WAPET spent $35 million before its big strike at Barrow Island.

While some Australians talked in millions of pounds, however, most talked in terms of 10 pounds. The year 1953 saw tremendous conflict over the basic wage. The Commonwealth Arbitration Court decided to abolish the system of quarterly cost-of-living adjustments. The automatic adjustments had been part of the Australian way of life since 1921, and the decision sent a shock wave throughout the trade union movement. The circumstances that led up to the change were not dissimilar to the factors which renewed the arguments in the mid 1970s. The period 1947 to 1953 was one of high inflation and, after a series of extremely rapid price increases, the basic wage had risen in leaps and bounds from £4/18/– to 11 guineas. As it happened, because of a complex series of economic developments, the decision coincided with a drop in inflation. The unions pressed for restoration of the old system, and would continue to do so until nearly a decade later when the Arbitration Board partially reversed its policy. In the 1970s the adjustments came back again and all the old arguments were revived.

In 1955, the Labor movement split and Australia saw a new political force, the Democratic Labor Party, or more commonly the DLP. A group of vehemently anti-communist Labor men, who according to their enemies were controlled by a clandestine Catholic group called 'the Movement', the DLP never took a large share of the vote. But it was always enough, when preferences were distributed to the Liberal party, to keep Menzies in power.

Just how the electoral system works in Australia is a fascinating numbers game. For example, when the DLP was at the peak of its influence in the late 1950s and early 1960s it did not gain even 10 per cent of the vote. But here's how important those votes were. Below is a breakdown of figures for the 1961 election in which the Menzies coalition government won narrowly: ALP 47.99 per cent, Liberals 33.53 per cent, DLP 8.65 per cent, Country Party 8.45 per cent, Communist 0.48 per cent.

The DLP was a staunch advocate of increasing Australia's expenditure on defence. In 1955 Australian forces were committed to the South-East Asia Strategic Reserve.

Since soon after the war our answer to survival in a hostile world had been 'populate or perish', if we didn't fill this country up someone would. So in 1955, our one millionth migrant, Mrs Barbara Porritt, arrived in Australia with her husband Dennis, and was greeted with great ceremony. A shy couple, they retreated quickly from the limelight to live quietly in Canberra where Dennis worked with the CSIRO.

Fifteen years later, the number of migrants had more than doubled. By the 1970s, two and a half million migrants had travelled half way round the world to start a new life. More than 55 per cent of them were of 'British stock',

Top: Migrants arriving in Sydney during the 1950s. By the 1970s, two and a half million migrants had travelled to Australia to start a new life and today four million Australians were born outside the country. Bottom: In 1955, Australia welcomed its one millionth migrant, Barbara Porritt. Her husband, Dennis, worked with the CSIRO and they went to live in Canberra.

compared with 95 per cent in 1901 and the ratio would continue to decline. Despite having a sense of homogeneity, Australia boasts the highest proportion of overseas-born people in the population of the English-speaking world.

In 1956, Australia saw its one millionth road casualty, Sydney got its first parking meter, its first computer and was about to get its first glimpse of Utzon's amazing concept for an opera house. But we really only remember that year for two reasons: the Olympic Games in Melbourne and the coming of television.

The 1956 Olympics were the first held in the Southern Hemisphere, always the favourite sphere of reference for Australian claims to fame. Australian athletes responded by winning 35 medals, to come third behind the giants, the United States and the USSR. Ron Clarke, then Australian junior champion, ran in with the ceremonial torch. *Betty Cuthbert, Shirley Strickland, Dawn Fraser, Murray Rose* and *Lorraine Crapp* all made unforgettable names for themselves at those Games. Australians dominated some of the traditional areas, particularly swimming, and performed admirably in other events. We only narrowly missed a gold medal in the high jump and the men's 100 metres. John Landy, who had injured his foot before the Games, still ran third in the 1500 metres. Rolly Tasker won the points for the gold medal in sailing but had to accept silver after a disqualification. Jock Sturrock won a bronze, and sculler Stuart McKenzie earned a silver. There were also medals in a series of events in which Australia has been completely overwhelmed in more recent Games.

The Games were memorable in many ways. In that same year Russians invaded Hungary and, while a 5000 and 10 000 metres double by Russia's Vladimir Kuts electrified the crowd, a water polo match between Hungary and the USSR literally turned into a blood bath. The Hungarians survived the battle and went on to retain their title.

The opening of television was not so dramatic. TCN 9's first broadcasts were made from a church hall in Sydney. The programs included 'Accent on Strings', 'What's My Line?' and 'The Johnny O'Connor Show'.

Bruce Gyngell, who would go on to be head of the Broadcasting Tribunal, head of Australia's multi-cultural broadcasting service and eventually return to the Nine Network, uttered television's first words as an announcer on 16 September 1956: 'Ladies and gentlemen, good evening and

Top: Danish architect Jørn Utzon won an international prize for a design for a Sydney opera house. His concept was presented to the public in 1956 by New South Wales Premier Joe Cahill (left). Bottom: Melbourne held the Southern Hemisphere's first Olympic Games in 1956. Ron Clarke, Australian junior running champion, lit the torch to begin 'the Friendly Games'. More than 100 000 were in the stadium to see the Duke of Edinburgh perform the opening ceremony.

welcome to television.' For the first few months it didn't matter much what was on. Some Australians were so fascinated they were simply happy to watch the test pattern. But, as time wore on, the programmers were already well aware of the importance of ratings. As Gyngell recalls:

Oh, we had highly educational programs. We started with 'Jet Jackson', 'Rin Tin Tin', 'Jungle Jim'. We had 'Disneyland'. It started on 28 January 1957 on a Monday night. 'I Love Lucy' and 'Father Knows Best' were an enormous success. Frank Packer said to me when we did the first program line up, 'Who was it that decided to put "Jungle Jim" on at 7.30 on Tuesday night?' I said, 'I did.' And he said, 'It doesn't augur well for your future in this business.' But when the ratings came out it turned out that they were highly successful.

Towards the end of the 1950s, Australian society had changed noticeably. The Olympic Games and television alone had heightened our awareness of the rest of the world, and the population itself was tangibly more cosmopolitan. Change was seen on the most mundane level. Australians who would not have dreamed of anything more exotic than a pork sausage began their first hesitant experiments with 'wog tucker' such as salami. Pizza Hut and KFC fast-food outlets were still in the future but the more adventurous Australian housewife now called a buffet supper a smorgasbord.

The most astonishing bestseller of those times was in fact a story about the life of an Italian migrant in Australia and the peculiar way this country has of embracing foreigners. *They're a Weird Mob* was written in 1956 by John O'Grady and published in 1957 under the pseudonym of Nino Culotta. The manuscript was rejected by Angus and Robertson and eventually published by Ure Smith. By 1964, 500 000 copies had been sold, 350 000 in hard cover. It had little success outside Australia although it was made into a film.

Another stunningly successful creation that dates back to this period is Edna Everage, the vaguely malevolent 'mother-in-law' of all Australians. Devised by comedian Barry Humphries, she evolved into a megastar and was even gonged a Dame by Labor Prime Minister, Gough Whitlam, in a facetious dig at monarchistic honours (she has since just as facetiously returned to plain 'Mrs' in deference to the prospect of Australia becoming a Republic). According to her creator, she has all but disowned him since her international success.

But the smell of success is not always sweet. Throughout the 1950s, the chances were that anything with a frame around it was 'a Namatjira'. Albert Namatjira, an Aboriginal painter from the Alice Springs area, is possibly one of Australia's most famous artists, but his story had an almost classical, tragic progression. After picking up a few bob on a mission station carving mulga wood plaques, Namatjira was 'discovered' and fostered by the white watercolourist Rex Battarbee. Namatjira was soon grossing more than £1000 for an exhibition.

However, the black artist was inevitably caught in the land between two cultures and two laws. The traditional law of sharing one's property with relatives meant that Albert's fortune was distributed among as many as 500 people. And white society made its own demands. Even though, according to Australian law, Namatjira was not a full citizen and was not allowed to vote (or drink), he was expected to pay income tax. In 1951, when he tried to buy a house in Alice Springs, permission was refused by local authorities on the grounds that Aboriginal people were not allowed into town after dark. In a marvellous display of hypocrisy, Namatjira was dressed up in a white suit and flown south in 1954 to meet the new Queen of England. In October 1958, the old painter was sentenced to six months' gaol for supplying liquor to his relatives. After a national outcry the sentence was reduced. He was released after two months and shortly afterwards he died, a broken and bitter man.

On the eve of the 1960s, Australia's first nuclear reactor was opened at Lucas Heights. The last trams ran in Adelaide and Perth. Equal pay was now a reality for men and women performing the same tasks. Our population had reached the 10 million mark. Construction of the Opera House began in Sydney and the Myer Music Bowl opened in Melbourne. But if Melbourne led Sydney as a cultural venue, film star Ava Gardner did not seem impressed. While in the southern capital to make the film *On the Beach* with Gregory Peck and Anthony Perkins, she said, 'I came here to make a film about the end of the world and I certainly came to the right place.'

At the end of the 1950s, a phenomenon swept the world. It came to be represented in Australia by a young man who, while not overly talented, was an ebullient little character embodying much of the new spirit of the 1960s. The phenomenon was rock and roll and our local star was Johnny O'Keefe. Johnny was the idol of the generation of Australians now in middle age and with teenage children of their own, 'the Sixties Generation'.

Top: In 1956, Bruce Gyngell was the first person to appear on the long-awaited television broadcasts in Australia, opening with the lines, 'Ladies and gentlemen, good evening and welcome to television.' Bottom: During the 1950s, Aboriginal artist Albert Namatjira gained international respect, but he was given the opposite treatment in Alice Springs, where he tried to buy a house. Here he is with movie star 'Chips' Rafferty.

Johnny O'Keefe gave his life to rock 'n' roll, and a good many Australians at least gave it the best years of their lives. Johnny lived fast and died young. He was the ground-breaker for a whole new breed of Australians with attitude who would go on to have the international success that Johnny always dreamed of but never achieved—performers like INXS, AC/DC, Midnight Oil, Men At Work, Little River Band, Air Supply, Cold Chisel, Rolf Harris, Olivia Newton-John, Natalie Imbruglia, Silverchair, Savage Garden and a litany of others—and the one who'd have the most success even though she was dismissed as 'the singing budgie' is the multi-talented Kylie Minogue. On the other hand, Australia's most popular performer, John Farnham, has never found international fame nor really looked for it even though he was a Pom in the first place.

## THE 1960s

The 1960s began with a 'credit squeeze' which almost cost Menzies his position as Prime Minister. He survived the following election by just one seat—the only really tough moment in his long ride at the top. It was also the closest Arthur Augustus Calwell would ever come to being Prime Minister. From then on, the battered old campaigner—'Cocky' to friend and foe—would cling on to leadership of his party, warding off challenges from abler, younger men who just might have had a chance of toppling Menzies.

On the other side of the world there had been many changes. The Russians had sent an unmanned spacecraft to the moon; John F. Kennedy was President of the United States and Fidel Castro was the President of Cuba; and Nikita Kruschev, Harold Macmillan, General Dwight D. Eisenhower and General Charles de Gaulle, who held summit talks in 1960, were soon gone. But in Australia, the political status quo was preserved and life in 'the lucky country' went on largely cocooned from terrors of the world at large.

Our universal obsession with sport continued unabated. In these pre-swimming pool days the tennis court was still the badge of someone having made it to the upper middle class. 'Muscles' and 'Rocket', two nicknames that only Australians could give to their human sporting heroes, dominated professional tennis for the decade.

Rosewall's professional career quickly surpassed that of his 'twin', Lew Hoad. But, blazing along the amateur circuit was a 24-year-old red-haired, freckled-faced Queenslander. In 1962, Rod Laver became the second player in tennis history (the first was Don Budge in 1938) to win the Grand Slam—the four major world tennis titles: Australian, Wimbledon, United States and French—and the only player in history to win it twice, once as an amateur and once as a professional. When Laver turned pro he was given a hiding by both Hoad and Rosewall and he won only two of his first 23 matches in world professional tennis. But he settled down and by the middle of the decade he and Rosewall would be sharing victories with monotonous regularity. Rosewall was ranked number one player in the world during 1961, 1962, 1963 and 1964, but from 1965 Laver got the top berth by a wide margin. However, Rosewall came back again and again and was still winning tournaments against players half his age in the 1970s.

One who failed in his comeback was the boxer Jimmy Carruthers. And, at the start of the 1960s, Heather McKay was squash champion of Australia for the first of 14 times. Wicket-keeper Wally Grout was on his was to a record 187 dismissals in 51 tests. And 1960 will be remembered by all cricket fans for a long time for possibly the most exciting match in the history of the game—the first-ever tied Test, played between the West Indies and Australia in Brisbane.

In 1961 Yuri Gagarin was the first man in space. And there were even more significant scientific developments back on Earth. Contraceptive pills, still opposed by religious leaders even today, began to be widely used and soon controversy was raging throughout the world. Australians, somewhat conservative about sexual matters, would not join in the debate in earnest until later in the decade.

Frank discussion of sex was not really seen in the media until the arrival of more liberated women's magazines at the end of the 1960s. Until then, the most intimate secrets in them had been about knitting patterns and lamington recipes. Sexual matters were considered 'dirty'. Within a few years, the pendulum had swung so far the other way a woman's magazine in Australia would be considered unsaleable without a generous helping of advice on virginity, menopause, hysterectomy and every other conceivable female concern. The new media genre became known as the 'How to Knit an Orgasm' school of journalism.

But if sex was somehow 'unclean', politics got smutty indeed. At the start of the 1960s Gough Whitlam and Arthur Calwell set out on an unprece-

'Get off the beach. You look obscene.'

The bikini was created in 1946 by the French designer, Louis Reard and named after the atom bomb tests at Bikini Atoll in the Pacific. However, it would take a couple of decades before the fashion was accepted in a then more conservative Australia. In the 1960s, council by-laws stipulated that women must wear at least three inches of fabric (about 7.5 centimetres) at the hip or be arrested like this young lady at Bondi.

dented and much criticised campaign to win support from the press, considered traditionally hostile to the Labor movement. They periodically dined with newspaper proprietors in Sydney and Melbourne. To some degree they succeeded in getting the papers to report ALP and trade union activities more sympathetically and even persuaded the conservative *Sydney Morning Herald* to come out in strong support for Labor in the 1961 election. But Sir Frank Packer's right-wing *Daily Telegraph* was dismayed by the development and it ran an extraordinary report of what it described as a wedding on Broadway (the address of the *Herald*). The story, illustrated by a photograph of Mr Calwell visiting the *Herald*, parodied a political 'marriage'. *The Sydney Morning Herald*, and Menzies himself, followed up with a famous '36 faceless men' campaign which made much of the fact that Labor's Federal Executive, not necessarily the elected members of the parliament, controlled Labor's policy. The politically clever adjective 'faceless' implied such sinister doings that Labor's stocks fell again and Menzies won the 1963 elections with a majority of 10 seats.

Sir Frank Packer was almost as much a colossus on the Australian horizon as Menzies, his friend. The only difference between the two was that with Packer, politics was really only a hobby. Another of the pastimes of the newspaper buccaneer was sailing, and in 1962 he made the first of his quixotic tilts at the most elusive prize in sport—the America's Cup. It was one of the few times that he ever lost anything.

Australians were still faster through the water without a boat. In that year, Dawn Fraser became the first woman to break 60 seconds for 100 metres freestyle. By now the Americans had also put Alan Shepard and John Glenn in space. Here at home our long-distance achievements extended to an STD telephone service between Sydney and Canberra. On the other side of the world, television was transmitted by satellite between the United States and Britain. But if our achievements were not always spectacular they were sometimes just as important. In 1962, the world became aware of the horrors of thalidomide and it was an Australian, Dr William McBride, who tracked down and exposed the reasons for the malformations caused by the drug. Later, McBride would be disgraced for falsifying evidence in his quest to alert the scientific community and the public to the alleged dangers of other similar drugs. It was only after years of appeals that he would be able to practise again, leaving Australia in 1999 to work in a hospital in Samoa.

Another scientific find, which has helped to establish Australia as a leader in radio astronomy, was the discovery of quasars by the radio telescope at Parkes in New South Wales in 1962.

In 1962 the seeds were sown for a tragic end to a decade of peace. Australian military involvement in the quagmire of Vietnam began—as it had for the United States—in an almost minuscule way. A team of 30 Army officers joined American advisory forces training the Vietnamese military in South Vietnam. Later this was increased to 100, as well as six Caribou aircraft and RAAF crews. Inevitably the advisers were drawn into counter terrorism. But, even by 1965, only one Australian had been killed. On 29 April 1965, however, Sir Robert Menzies announced to a half-empty House of Representatives that Australia was to send a full battalion of troops. Within a few weeks of arriving, three men were killed and 10 were wounded in a grenade attack on the American base at Bien Hoa. Australia was at war again. Nevertheless, the general attitude of the Australian public to events in South-East Asia would not turn until later in the decade. The election of 1963 was a disastrous one for Labor, and Gough Whitlam began his long run for the leadership of his party and his country.

Compared with the momentous international stories which dominated the newspapers—the Profumo scandal, the great train robbery, the assassination of John Kennedy, the loss of the United States nuclear submarine *Thresher*—our major events such as the beginning of the Ord River Project seemed like small beer.

Yet at home, one story dominated the front pages of our newspapers for not weeks but months on end. It was a weird murder mystery called the Bogle–Chandler case. On the morning of New Year's Day 1963, the semi-nude bodies of Dr Gilbert Bogle, a brilliant CSIRO scientist, and Mrs Margaret Chandler, a 29-year-old mother of two, were found on a bush track in Lane Cove National Park. They were last seen alive at a New Year's Eve party. Nearly 40 years later, the cause of their death is still officially unknown. Police, scientists and criminologists all over the world have studied the case. Scores of theories, some sound, some bizarre, have been put forward but in the words of former Police Commissioner Norman Allan the case is 'the mystery of the century'.

Perhaps the biggest political issue of the mid 1960s was defence. Spurred on by the clamourings of the right-wing DLP who pointed to the worsening situation in South-East Asia, in 1964 Menzies introduced Australia's most important peacetime program for the armed forces. Selective national service, the compulsory military training of Australian 18 year olds, was introduced in in such a swift and definite manner that there was no chance for a repeat of the great political conscription battle of 1916 and 1917. Besides, as yet there was no war, only a vague feeling of menace to the north.

Although there soon would be a growing groundswell of anti-conscription feeling, Australians in 1964 were more concerned with another war between Dawn Fraser and swimming officials. At the Olympic Games in Tokyo that year, Dawn won the gold medal for the 100 metres freestyle for her third successive Olympics. But her 'antics' in Tokyo, namely the souveniring of an Olympic flag from the Emperor's Palace Hotel, led to her suspension from competitive swimming for 10 years.

Donald Campbell was trying to be the fastest man on Earth. He eventually set world land and water speed records in Australia. This caused considerable excitement. But some other English visitors that year sped the country up even more. The English pop group The Beatles were confronted by the biggest crowds they had seen anywhere in the world—300 000 in Adelaide alone, half the city's population. As if the British had not foisted enough on us that year, they sent scientists here to launch military rockets, including the *Blue Streak*. A good many of the tests ended in disaster. Some critics mocked the experiments but when China exploded an atomic bomb that year some people at least acknowledged that perhaps we should know what a nuclear warhead was.

In 1964, Donald Horne, one of a long line of distinguished editors of *The Bulletin*, wrote a book and gave the nation a new phrase. Almost every Australian has at some time used the words 'the lucky country', even if they haven't read the book. The year 1964 also saw another significant contribution to Australian journalism with the birth of a national newspaper *The Australian*. Sceptics predicted that a newspaper covering one of the world's largest and most sparsely populated countries had Buckley's chance of survival, but the newspaper was still well and truly around for the millennium.

By far the most significant development for Australia in 1965 was that decision to send the first full combat battalion to Vietnam. The announcement took many Australians by surprise. Even men in Menzies' own party and certainly the opposition were unaware of the impending announcement.

The Beatles toured Australia in 1964 and were greeted by the biggest crowds they'd seen anywhere in the world. There were 300 000 in Adelaide alone—half the city's population. They were virtually unknown when signed up by promoters Ken Brodziak and Kym Bonython much earlier for a small fee, but honoured their agreement.

Top: Englishman Donald Campbell used the long, flat salt plains in Australia in 1964 to break land speed records, getting up to 403 miles per hour (650 kilometres per hour) in his *Bluebird*. Bottom: HMAS *Melbourne* on arrival in Sydney Harbour in 1964 after its collision with another Navy ship *Voyager*. Eighty-two sailors were killed.

Calwell and Whitlam had left Canberra a few hours earlier to help to campaign for the forthcoming New South Wales elections. During the day, Calwell had asked Menzies if there were any major statements 'in the wind', and Menzies had replied that it was possible but that he could not say for sure. On the very afternoon of the announcement, Senator John Gorton was asked a question without notice as to whether or not the government was planning to send a battalion to Vietnam and his reply was, 'I know nothing about the matter which the honourable gentleman has raised.'

When the announcement was made, Labor was in some disarray as to its approach to the problem of Vietnam. Labor policy was ambiguous to say the least, although the opposition party did attack the Treasurer Harold Holt on his return from America two days later for trading Australian lives for United States capital. Holt announced that he had successfully dissuaded the American Government from placing severe restrictions on American investment in Australia.

The slogan 'Diggers for Dollars' quickly gained currency but the government rode the storm easily. By the time Labor had resolved its line on Vietnam, Australia was already up to its neck in the mire. Ahead lay a bitter struggle at home and abroad—a struggle which contributed some catchphrases to our vocabulary: 'Make Love Not War', 'All The Way With LBJ', 'Save Our Sons' and 'Hearts and Minds'.

The 1960s was a frustrating decade for Gough Whitlam. When Herbert Vere 'Doc' Evatt retired as leader of the Labor Party, Whitlam only narrowly beat the popular Eddie Ward for the position as deputy to Arthur Calwell. He stayed there but he would have to watch Arthur Calwell lose three elections before having a chance to lose one himself.

In 1966 it seemed that Labor might have had a chance for victory. The indefatigable Menzies had left the stage, the first Prime Minister to retire in office, and given the nod to his chosen one, Harold Holt. Holt was less forceful, had less charisma and there was a strong issue on which to fight an election. But there were problems for the ALP, too. The 1966 election was definitely 'the Vietnam election' but Labor was forced to adopt a difficult stance. With Australians already committed to a war that many supported, any criticism of involvement or the conduct of the war was easily dismissed as the arguments of 'ratbags and commies'. Arthur Calwell said the war was 'unwinnable', and although he would be proved right, his statement wasn't really that helpful as far as the public was concerned. Besides, Australians having been fortunate enough to be on the winning side in most of its wars, did not expect defeat—especially when aligned with the United States against a small, underdeveloped country.

Whatever the arguments, the Liberals won 'the Vietnam election' comfortably. However, the war and particularly the conscription arguments increased in intensity. Australians suddenly found themselves grappling with unfamiliar emotional and intellectual arguments which had not intruded into daily life and the press for 50 years.

The year 1967 saw the bizarre but very Australian death of Harold Holt. Where else in the world could a Prime Minister drown in the surf with not a security guard in sight? Before his untimely end at Portsea, Victoria, Holt had been beset with problems which arose over the issues of VIP aircraft for politicians and the complex aftermath of the collision between the Navy ships *Voyager* and *Melbourne*, which killed 82 men.

It was an unusual time in Australian politics because some of the main critics of the government came from among the Liberal ranks. John Gorton, yet to be Prime Minister himself, at one stage tabled papers embarrassing to the government. A group of Liberals and Independents, led by Edward St John QC, attacked their leaders on the handling of the *Voyager* affair.

No doubt because of the seriousness of the issues involved, and their intensely human consequences, political debate took on a fervour that had not been seen for many years. Humanitarian issues were paramount. Conscription was one, and there was also a revival of the capital punishment issue fired by the hanging of Ronald Ryan at Pentridge Prison in Melbourne. Added to this, great moral argument raged over the dismissal by the RSL of two of its members for opposing Australian involvement in Vietnam.

The 1960s was a decade of ferment but also an era of considerable progress for Australia's minority groups. Harry Chan became the first elected President of the Northern Territory Legislative Council, a distant reminder that at the turn of the century the Chinese population of Darwin outnumbered Europeans seven to one. In that same year of 1967, the Legislative Council passed legislation removing much of the discrimination against Aboriginal people.

Yet the change was not quick enough for some. Charles Perkins led a freedom ride through New South Wales in an attempt to end Aboriginal segregation. A year later, Perkins and Margaret Valadian became Australia's first Aboriginal university graduates. While white Australia was marvelling at the introduction of sinfully modern trends such as mini-skirts and pantihose, Aboriginal people were far more concerned with the results of the two Commonwealth referendums. Traditionally referendums are almost never resolved in the affirmative, and while a proposal to end the nexus between numbers in both Houses of Parliament was defeated as expected, the proposal to end constitutional discrimination against Aboriginal people was approved. Australia proudly patted itself on the back. Within three years, the nation would see its first Aboriginal Member of Parliament, Senator Neville Bonner. In the middle of this fervent period of social change, and perhaps even because of it, the birth occurred of the television program 'This Day Tonight', which in turn would significantly affect the development of the medium during the next decade. Out of it evolved numerous television programs such as 'A Current Affair', 'Willesee at Seven', 'Sixty Minutes' and 'Today Tonight'. The current affairs programs arrived at a time of some turmoil, at least by Australian standards. Holt's death had almost a domino effect on the Liberals, creating a succession of leaders during the following few years.

The electorate, already highly charged because of the war and the instability of the political situation, received an extra shot of adrenalin with a modern version of a gold rush. Australia saw, in the late 1960s, a series of dramatic mining discoveries. Conzinc Rio Tinto announced its first nickel find in 1967. By 1968 the Broken Hill Proprietary Company Limited sent the stock exchanges wild with the news that Esso BHP would be able to supply two-thirds of Australia's total oil needs. The Western Mining Corporation announced fresh nickel discoveries at Kambalda.

However, the most amazing share market flurry of the late 1960s centred around a company with the romantic sounding name of Poseidon. Late in 1969, the directors of the small and almost unknown mineral company excitedly announced a nickel and copper find. During the previous week, rumours alone had almost doubled the price of its shares. When asked by the directors of the Adelaide Stock Exchange for an explanation of the rise, the Poseidon directors replied that the find had yet to be assayed. Nevertheless, the Exchange went wild. A couple of hours after lunch on the same day shares leapt from $1.90 to $6.70. A week later they were $30. One reason for this reaction was that this find, unlike the great nickel discoveries a few years earlier, had been made by a small adventurous company. Nickel was much in demand, and the time was ripe for a rags-to-riches story in the grand Hollywood manner.

At the company's annual general meeting on the eve of the 1970s it was confirmed that the nickel strike at Mount Windarra could be as large as the Western Mining holding at Kambalda. In February 1970 the price of Poseidon shares in London was nearly $300. There were now runs on similar companies such as Tasminex, which merely looked promising. When it was finally announced that Tasminex had no substantial nickel at its Mount Venn site, the shares plummeted drastically until the stock exchanges suspended all dealings pending an inquiry.

Towards the end of the financial year, when money began to tighten up, the trading companies began to sell out, partly to realise their paper profits before the end of the financial year and partly because of a nagging sense that something was amiss. Once the signs of the first crack appeared the general trader began to follow the professionals, and the rush to get out started. Although there was another encouraging report from Poseidon, the market failed to respond. Small companies such as Minsec, which had quickly found that they were theoretically among the biggest mineral producers in the world, saw millions wiped off the value of their shares. Many small investors lost their life savings and in June 1970 a Senate Select Committee was set up to investigate the crash. It was soon realised that some of the principals in the drama had a classic conflict of interests. Short selling, a device whereby the client sells shares he or she does not have in hope of covering the sale by buying at the lower price, was banned.

The end of the 1960s also saw some frenzied activity in Canberra. The most obvious successor to Harold Holt was William McMahon, Deputy Leader of the Liberal Party and experienced in the ways of Treasury. But, as had happened with Billy Hughes 50 years earlier, the Country Party, in particular its leader John 'Black Jack' McEwen, would have nothing to do with McMahon. If 'Little Billy' got up, said 'Black Jack', the Libs could kiss the coalition goodbye.

The remaining candidates included Leslie Bury, who had been twice sacked by Menzies, Paul Hasluck and Billy Mackie Snedden. However,

Top: The team for 'This Day Tonight', the first nightly current affairs program, included from left: Stuart Littlemore, Peter Manning, Terry McMahon, Bill Peach, Peter Luck, Mike Carlton and Tom Molomby. Bottom: 'Jolly John' Gorton, a Prime Minister with the larrikin touch, reigned in the late 1960s, but not for long. During a party vote of no-confidence, Gorton voted against himself and stepped down.

a group of behind-the-scenes power brokers, including Malcolm Fraser, lobbied for another candidate from the almost unheard-of background of the Senate. He was a Victorian orchardist and ex-fighter pilot whose face had a craggy and yet endearing quality caused to some degree by plastic surgery after a fighter crash during the war.

Gorton—'Jolly John' to the press gallery—had been around since the 1940s, had frequently clashed with Menzies and had remained on the backbench for nine years before his promotion to the junior portfolio of Navy. His rough-and-ready 'decent sort of a cove' image impressed the electorate, but his rough-and-ready government soon caused him problems. For a start, he was an iconoclast and an activist, opposed to a 'committee-style' of government. Not surprisingly, the committees did not like it. He made enemies in the public service but if anything this only endeared him to the public. But by far the greatest public intrigue surrounded Gorton's private behaviour.

A visit by Gorton to the American Embassy on the night of the American announcement to halt the bombing in Vietnam became the most contro-versial story of the year. According to the ascetic Edward St John, the evening had turned into a party during which Gorton had preferred to spend his time talking to a young woman journalist while there were matters of great national and international import at hand. Gorton survived the controversy and St John didn't (he lost his Liberal Party endorsement). Nevertheless, the Prime Minister's days were numbered.

The Liberals suffered a set-back in the ensuing election and discontent with the leadership was evident as soon as the voting was over. Gorton remained Prime Minister for more than a year, but his ultimate undoing was brought about by one of the men who had helped put him into office in the first place. Newspaper journalist Alan Ramsay had written a story stating that the Army Chief of Staff, in a meeting with Gorton, accused Malcolm Fraser, the Minister of Defence, of disloyalty to the Army and to the Army Minister, Andrew Peacock.

Gorton released a statement indicating that the details of the conversation were untrue. Ramsay replied with a statement that Gorton had been given an opportunity to repudiate the story before its publication, but had not done so. Fraser then resigned from the ministry (accusing the Prime Minister of releasing news of his resignation before an agreed time and also accusing him of significant disloyalty). Then Gorton attacked Fraser in Parliament and vigorously denied the contents of the story, whereupon Ramsay, in an unprecedented incident, called out from the press gallery, 'You liar.' Soon after this incident Gorton's leadership was again put to the vote, and this time it was a tie between Gorton and McMahon. Gorton, in a puzzling move, cast his own vote against himself and stepped down.

So within a few short years after the abdication of Menzies, the Liberals were in disarray. The kindest observation one could make about McMahon was that he did not have the image of a leader and against Whitlam on the ascendancy he looked progressively shaky. Either way, he would lead the Liberals to their first defeat in 23 years.

And so the 1960s drew to a close. During the decade the government, backed by strong mandates from the people, had felt confident in steadily escalating its involvement in Vietnam. By 1968 more than 8000 combat soldiers, 40 per cent of them conscripts, had been committed to the war.

Some young men unfortunately died in the jungles of Vietnam. For others it was days of wine and roses. In 1967 John Newcombe won Wimbledon. The following year, the first 'open' Wimbledon, was an all-Australian final with Laver beating Roche. The year 1968 saw the 200th Test match between England and Australia. The match was drawn but over the years Australia is ahead in games won. As always, it was a decade of triumph and tragedy, sometimes—as with our first heart transplant—a touch of both. The patient died soon after the operation. There were more *Blue Streak* failures, and a Viscount airliner crashed near Port Hedland killing 26 people, one of scores of fatal plane crashes in a nation that generally believes it doesn't have any. HMAS *Melbourne* was involved in an incredible 'history repeats' collision in which another destroyer was cut in two. A Sydney to Melbourne express train, the *Southern Aurora*, collided with a goods train at Violet Town.

Morally we seemed just as confused as ever. Norman Lindsay died in his 90th year, while authorities in Victoria were still banning posters by the 'Victorian' artist Aubrey Beardsley. The record *Hair* was banned in Melbourne and everywhere there was controversy over the nude scenes in the musical.

With the 1970s just around the corner, two men named Armstrong and Aldrin walked on the moon. Back on the ground, Bob Hawke walked tall as president of the ACTU. What he lacked in size and class he made up for in driving ambition.

# THE 1970s

For many it's hard to look back on the 1970s with a great sense of nostalgia, although even now the remarkable political events of November 1975 have a strong fascination. There has been no bigger political story this century. Only the dismissal of New South Wales Premier Jack Lang in the 1930s really equals the Whitlam dismissal in dramatic intensity and long-term import for the Westminster system of government. After his extraordinarily political demise, Gough Whitlam urged his supporters to 'maintain the rage'. They didn't, but the events of those fraught days are still argued about and still have an impact on how politics is conducted in this country.

The other event of great magnitude in the 1970s was the destruction of Darwin by cyclone on Christmas Eve 1974. With the loss of 62 lives, 1000 people seriously injured and 45 000 rendered homeless it was a disaster only eclipsed by the Japanese air raids on Darwin during World War II, which resulted in the greatest single loss of life in Australia on any day during its history.

The decade began, however, with a collective sigh of relief as Australia announced that it was extricating itself from the unpopular war in Vietnam. The war had cost the lives of 415 Australians and 2344 were wounded. It had been the most controversial war in our history, fought for three major reasons—anti-communism, our geographical position and our traditional reliance on powerful allies.

But as the war dragged on and our television sets carried lingering and disturbing images of peasants in coolie hats fighting an inexorable struggle against the massive technology of Uncle Sam and—as a once beautiful country was systematically defoliated with carpet bombing, Napalm and Agent Orange—the war became increasingly distasteful.

On 8 May 1970 the anti-war protest culminated in a moratorium rally of 70 000 people led by Federal MP Jim Cairns. The sight of such a massive public outpouring in the conservative capital of Melbourne was sobering for many Australians.

For many years after the war ended, Australia dealt with its aftermath. Refugees, or 'the boat people', arrived in Australia by the thousands. These war escapees caused some resentment among comfortable and secure white Australians, but many accepted that, having waged bloody war in someone else's land, we must share the consequences.

After centuries of fear of 'the yellow peril', Australia moved inexorably closer in its relationship with its neighbouring region, no matter how much it considered itself a European bastion in the south seas. The bamboo curtain began to come down when an ALP delegation led by Gough Whitlam visited the People's Republic of China in 1971. By the end of the decade the Australian electorate saw footage of Malcolm Fraser strolling along the Great Wall happily snapping tourist shots with his Japanese camera.

Perhaps the most significant social change in Australia has been among this country's original inhabitants, the Aboriginal peoples. When most of Australia proudly welcomed the Queen of England here in 1970 to celebrate the country's '200th birthday', Sydney's Aboriginal community threw funeral wreaths into the water at Captain Cook's landing place at Kurnell.

The arrival of the twentieth century—a fabulous century for white progress and achievement—had meant little for Australia's black community. Shortly before the turn of the previous century, the Aboriginal inhabitants of one state, Tasmania, had been wiped out altogether. And even in this century, Aboriginal people have been shot, enslaved and humiliated.

Official policy towards the Aboriginal race in Australia has ranged from the Christian-ministering of 'savages' around the turn of the century; to a policy of separate development or apartheid in the 1920s and 1930s; to a half-hearted attempt of assimilation in the 1940s and 1950s; to situations during the 1960s and 1970s where Aboriginal people were finally given some rights to determine their own future.

Some of them, like Neville Bonner of Queensland, chose the white way. Paradoxically, he had managed to become the first Aboriginal Parliamentarian in the state that is generally considered to be the most retarded in its racial attitude. Because he had chosen the 'white' way to power and influence—even to the point of standing for the Liberal Party on the conservative side of the Australian political spectrum—Bonner had to suffer the inevitable criticism that he was an 'Uncle Tom'. But it would be a mistake to think that Aboriginal people are any keener about their own politicians than whites are about theirs, and Bonner was at least as successful in Parliament as some of his Queensland colleagues.

But no story is more symbolic of the Aboriginal struggle in Australia than that of the Gurindjis and their battle for land rights at Wattie Creek, about 800 kilometres south of Darwin. It began in 1966 when a group of Aboriginal stockmen walked off Wave Hill station owned by the British beef

Top: In the wake of the Vietnam War in the 1970s, Australia saw the first of 'the boat people' —pathetic groups of refugees prepared to risk their lives in these craft for a fresh start over the horizon. Bottom: Vincent Lingiari, spokesman for the Gurindjis, whose seven-year battle for land rights at Wattie Creek in the Northern Territory ended successfully in 1973.

barons, the Vesteys. The Aboriginal workers were being paid less than a quarter of the minimum wage of the whites, and sometimes instead they got only rations. The Gurindjis said they were sick of it, they wanted their own place. One day they simply took a bale of wire and fenced off some of the Vestey land. The Gurindjis' leader, Vincent Lingiari, was soon confronted by Mr Morris, the station manager. In 1973, Lingiari told me:

> We all got the wire for the fence and carry them on the shoulder—everybody bring it up here, and we start that morning, cutting up poles, and so we put it up. Straighten her up, right around, finish it. And Mr Morris came along and he said, 'Hey, you steal another man's country.' Oh yeah, that's alright. And I said, 'No, well, what was before the Vestey born and I born?' It was black feller country.

Vincent's statement crystallised the whole story of the Gurindjis' struggle for land rights. A small band of Aboriginal people was prepared to fight one of the most powerful business concerns in the world.

The Vesteys, a collection of English barons and earls, had acquired their original 36 000 square miles (58 000 square kilometres) of the Northern Territory during the First World War. In 1970 they leased Wave Hill from the government for only 55 cents a square mile (2.66 square kilometres), and at that price the Gurindjis could probably have afforded their few acres. But for them the land was beyond value. They maintained that Seal Gorge above Wattie Creek was sacred. They said it was the burial place for some of the thousands of natives reportedly shot by early land holders in the district.

According to local whites, Wattie Creek was no more sacred than a mission Sunday school. 'Next thing,' they said, 'the Abos will claim Pitt Street in Sydney.' But there was no doubt that there was a principle involved that was very hard to argue with. But the Gurindjis found that the Vesteys were not necessarily their main opponents. The company maintained a low profile throughout the affair and, in fact, their approach eventually embarrassed the government. When asked about the land, they would say it wasn't theirs, it belonged to the government. The government on the other hand said land rights claims were out of the question because Vesteys had the lease until the year 2004. But in 1971, Bob Hawke was claiming that the government had known for three years that Vesteys had been willing to surrender the land.

Whatever the truth, the then Minister for Aboriginal Affairs, Mr Wentworth, promised to try to obtain about 21 square kilometres of land at Wattie Creek. Cabinet replied by offering about four square kilometres at Drover's Common near the Wave Hill welfare settlement. The Gurindjis rejected the offer and, considering the welfare people needed jackhammers to plant trees on their settlement, this reaction was not surprising.

In order to pursue its point anyway, the government decided that this would be the new home for the Gurindjis, and they spent $500 000 on building a township there. The town came to be known as 'Dangled Carrot'. Ironically, the Gurindjis helped to build the town as paid labourers, but when applications came in from families to live there, there was only one from a Gurindji. Lord Vestey went over to Vincent Lingiari to ask why:

> He said, 'Why don't you come in a decent house?' 'Where?' 'Down at the settlement and the new town.' 'Oh, no. I don't like going in there,' I said. 'I stay right here where I pick the place.' 'Right-o.' So he move off.

Later in the 1970s, anyone who doubted the determination of the Gurindjis to hold out for their land must have been starting to think twice. Admittedly a benevolent welfare service made life easier and the Gurindjis had support from people 'down south', including some communists and the waterside workers who at one stage raised $10 000 for their cause.

The turning point for the tribe was the 1972 Federal election. On the previous Australia Day, William McMahon had rejected the idea of land rights, and it was clear that if the ALP wasn't going to do something about the situation, no-one else would. Sure enough, after the election the new minister, Gordon Bryant, and a big mob from down south came into the Gurindjis' camp. Captain Major was the one who spoke with Vincent:

> He claim he shall be the minister. He come here, tell everybody he was the boss now. 'You OK out here?' [I] said to him, 'Yes.' He said, 'Alright, you can have this country, and you can put cattle on it and build a new village.'

So, after seven years, the Gurindjis finally had the official blessing of the government of Australia. But there was to be a succession of ministers and, indeed, the whole Labor tribe would soon vanish. Yet the Gurindjis held out.

It has been a remarkable stand summed up in the words of a remarkable song by Ted Egan:

Poor Bugger Blackfella, Gurindji,
Long time work, no wages we,
Work for good Old Lord Vestey,
Little bit, flour, sugar and tea.
From Lord Vestey to the Gurindji.
Poor Bugger Blackfella, this country,
Government law, him talk along we,
Can't givit land long blackfella, see,
Only spoilim Gurindji,
Poor Bugger Me, Gurindji.
Poor Bugger Blackfella, Gurindji,
Suppose we buy im back country,
What you reckon proper fee?
Might be flour, sugar and tea,
From the Gurindji to the Lord Vestey,
Oh Poor Bugger Me.

More importantly Wattie Creek was a symbol of hope for all Aboriginal peoples. Their stand was followed by a series of land rights resolutions. In 1976, the Aboriginal Land Rights Act of the Northern Territory gave Aboriginal people freehold title to form a reserve land. In 1978, Aurukun and Mornington Island Reserves were abolished. The Pitjantjatjara were granted land rights and in 1984, Maralinga land was returned to its traditional owners. The Mutijulu were granted freehold to the symbolic Ayers Rock in 1985.

If the 1970s produced an era of socio-political reform, alas, it was also described as 'the era that style forgot'. With our typical penchant for adopting almost anything American, Australians eagerly embraced the flower-power, hallucinatory drug and rock 'n' roll revolution with hardly any understanding of what it all meant. The worst part of it was that it required a pretty crook wardrobe of brightly coloured flared trousers, feather boas, headbands, Afro hair styles, ridiculously high platform-soled shoes and body shirts with impossibly wide collars that draped across the shoulders like dead seagulls.

In fact, the Woodstock-driven cultural movement was partly a backlash to the imbroglio of Vietnam and in Australia inner-city suburbs soon adopted the trappings of San Francisco's Haight–Ashbury district and all its trendy political causes. The painted Kombivan with its 'Save the Whale', 'Keep Uranium in the Ground' and 'Hug a Tree' stickers became a sort of urban badge of honour—all the better if they were driven wearing a camouflage suit. By the 1980s, yuppie residents of recently gentrified suburbs were into everything from rebirthing to flotation therapy and it seemed that herbal jogging and underwater Caesareans were not far away.

The first day of the 1970s had begun with Bob Hawke succeeding Albert Monk as leader of the Labor movement. By the early 1980s, at the same time that Malcolm Fraser obtained a double dissolution of Parliament, Hawke would replace Bill Hayden as leader of the Labor Party, a coup which led to a famous question from the then ABC journalist, Richard Carleton, 'Have you got blood on your hands?' Hawke's response was indignant but unconvincing. Later some would see it as ironic that he should undergo a similar fate.

Whatever one thought about the opportunistic Hawke, however, he had a certain charisma, as did South Australia's avant-garde Labor Premier, Don Dunstan—remembered by many simply for the fact that he wore pink hotpants into Parliament, but revered more profoundly by others for genuine social changes that he introduced on behalf of working-class people, women, Aboriginal people and other politically deprived groups.

'Civil liberties' was a buzz phrase and, despite some resistance, in 1971 the wearing of seat belts was made compulsory in Victoria and later in New South Wales and Australia generally. While we were strapping ourselves in, others were strapping things on—Sydney's first sex shop opened that year.

There was no doubt that during the 1970s Australians as a whole were becoming politically more aware and internationally more socially responsible. Among the obvious manifestations were the demonstrations against the arrival of the South African Springbok football teams, which showed to the world that Australia was aware of the plight of the majority of South Africans living under the discriminatory rule of Apartheid. Protesters made their stand at some peril to themselves in a series of violent clashes with police. The Queensland Government perceived the unrest to be so dangerous that it declared a state of emergency for the Springboks' visit.

Another pioneering social phenomenon was 'the green ban', a term applied by Jack Mundey of the Builders' Labourers Federation to describe trade union bans on what many considered were socially irresponsible and unsympathetic developments. Certainly, it was Mundey and his followers who saved Sydney's Rocks district—one of the most historic areas in the country because it is just a few hundred metres from where Captain Phillip landed the First Fleet. Without Mundey's intervention, the nation's most significant precinct of historic buildings would have been obliterated. In one of those niceties of history, Mr Mundey in the 1990s became President of the Historic Houses Trust of New South Wales.

Politically, apart from the turbulent events surrounding the Whitlam dismissal in the middle of the decade, the 1970s produced a peculiar mix of adventurism and conservatism. While Don Dunstan reigned in the south, in the north it was the era of Joh Bjelke-Petersen. From the late 1960s, Joh would stride the local political scene like a colossus for two decades, but he came unstuck when, in a sudden attack of delusions of grandeur, he tried to make a run for Prime Minister.

Meanwhile, the Libs continued their in-fighting in the wake of Holt's drowning with a succession of leaders including John Gorton, who voted himself out of office, William McMahon, who got voted out of office, and Billy Snedden, who died on the job.

In the heady early days of Labor's first government in a couple of decades, Gough Whitlam ran the country with a two-man cabinet which he said was the 'best government the nation ever had but was too big by half'. Those seminal days for Labor also offered hints to some of the disasters in the wind. Attorney-General Lionel Murphy and a posse of Commonwealth Police raided Australia's security organisation headquarters, ASIO, to demand information on Croatian terrorists—and to immensely embarrass himself and his government into the bargain.

At the same time the government purchased American artist Jackson Pollock's huge abstract painting *Blue Poles*—wrongly reported to have been painted in a drunken frenzy. The painting cost more than a million dollars, regarded as profligate by the philistines of the day, but now that its value has risen to more than $40 million, it seems with the benefit of hindsight to have been a 'steal'.

The winds of change were refreshing for many. Early in 1974 Gough Whitlam announced that 'God Save the Queen' would be superseded as

Top: Kingaroy peanut farmer Joh Bjelke-Petersen was a long-running conservative Premier of Queensland during the 1970s—an era that was a mix of adventurism and conservatism. Bottom: After Harold Holt's death in 1967, the Liberal Party's leaders in the 1970s included two Billys: Snedden (centre) and McMahon (right), seen here with Phillip Lynch.

Australia's National Anthem after an opinion poll narrowly chose 'Advance Australia Fair' over a couple of other contenders including 'Song of Australia' and 'Waltzing Matilda'.

Around the same time, however, the seeds were sown for the destruction of the government. Firstly, in a move too clever by three-quarters, Prime Minister Whitlam announced the appointment of a much-hated old rival, DLP Senator, Vincent Gair, as Ambassador to Ireland—this could allow the replacement of Gair with a Labor Senator in the forthcoming half Senate election.

In a counter move, the Queensland Premier Bjelke-Petersen issued writs for the return of five instead of six Senators and the scene was set for a dramatic denouement. Just two months later, Gough Whitlam appointed an old colleague, Sir John Kerr, as Governor-General not having the faintest idea how prescient this move would be.

The year ended with the cyclone that devastated Darwin and drew the Prime Minister back home from an overseas trip. Meanwhile, Australia's cultural life continued after a fashion with the birth of 'Countdown', a rock 'n' roll program hosted by the cowboy-hatted Ian 'Molly' Meldrum.

The 1970s period was marred by a peculiar run of misfortune with bridges. Beginning with the collapse of the West Gate Bridge and the death of 35 bridge workers in Melbourne, what followed was a bizarre chain of disasters, including the collapse of the Tasman Bridge over the Derwent when it was struck by a ship, and the awful tragedy of Granville when 83 people were killed and many injured after a packed commuter train from Mt Victoria in the Blue Mountains left the rails and crashed into a concrete overpass in suburban Sydney.

The appearance of a Labor Government on the scene had also fired once again notions of independence and republicanism. In 1975, archaic knighthoods gave way to the Order of Australia and visits by lesser royals such as Princess Anne and Captain Mark Phillips were treated with amiable amusement, particularly when Mark Phillips, who was dubbed 'the Fog' by the wags of the press, rolled over one of the English cars he'd come here to promote.

The Australian Government to its later shame all but welcomed Indonesia's invasion of East Timor in the mid 1970s with open arms. The execution of five Australian newsmen at Balibo during the capture of the town by pro-Indonesian forces remained to haunt those politicians involved. By the end of the century Timor was once again in flames.

To be fair to the pollies, though, the Australian public cared even less about the events on their doorstep at that time and were more preoccupied with parish pump matters. It seemed that everywhere change was afoot. Capital punishment was abolished in Victoria, and 'irretrievable break-down' after 12 months' separation became the sole grounds for divorce. Australia's first legal nude bathing beach was established at Maslin's in South Australia; while in Sydney nude bathing was introduced at Camp Cove, and it wouldn't be long before selected beaches in Sydney would drop their gear altogether. Camp Cove, incidentally, was where Captain Phillip landed in Sydney Harbour five days before raising the flag at Sydney Cove on 26 January 1788, only he was wearing stockings.

In spite of relentless commercial pressure on the community, we finally bit the bullet and banned cigarette and tobacco advertising on radio and television—a move 20 years' overdue. Asbestos, the dangers of which medicos had also known about since the 1920s, became another preoccupation and there was an underlying swell of nervousness in the community about uranium and bomb testing here and in our Pacific neighbourhood.

The year of 1976 ended on a sinister note when an arsonist destroyed half the Navy's fleet of Grumman tracker aircraft, and two days before Christmas, the first of seven young women victims in Adelaide's Truro murders disappeared. This South Australian crime remains an enigma.

Artist Brett Whiteley's *Self-Portrait in the Studio* won the Archibald Prize, an unorthodox change to the normal outcome of the competition. The prevailing small 'l' liberal political mood—which saw the birth of a party called the Australian Democrats, under the aegis of a former Liberal Party MP, Don Chipp—was a source of encouragement for the cultural community. The Democrats, with their vaguely left of centre, environ-mentally green and slightly herbal view of life appealed to the sensitive side of the yuppier electorates and, not surprisingly, also held great appeal for women politicians, a number of whom were frustrated by the macho club of the traditionally ossified parties. Foremost among them have been Janine Haines, Cheryl Kernot, Meg Lees and Natasha Stott-Despoja. However, Janine shot herself in the electoral foot when she tried to make the transition from the Upper to Lower House and found herself without a seat at all.

Among those contributing to the rising success of the Australian Democrats was former leader Cheryl Kernot, who would later 'jump ship' to join the Labor Party in the 1990s. Here she's demonstrating that the power of the sisterhood in Parliament transcends party boundaries—her mate in the photograph is none other than Liberal, Bronwyn Bishop.

Cheryl Kernot also led her party well but shattered her colleagues when she suddenly announced that she was jumping ship to join the Labor Party—a move that her colleagues saw as a betrayal of all the principles of a party whose sole self-appointed role had been 'to keep the bastards honest'.

Meanwhile, the radio serial 'Blue Hills' ended its run of more than 30 years—the last gasp of a radio medium that still called itself 'the wireless'. The film industry was having one of its many false dawns with good movies like Bruce Beresford's *Don's Party*, Donald Crombie's *Caddie*, Henry Safran's *Storm Boy* and great films like Fred Schepisi's *The Devil's Playground*.

The decade drew to an end on a somewhat ominous note. Crime scenarios, worthy of the worst American movies that were flooding into the country were becoming increasingly familiar. In 1976 it was 'the great bookie robbery' when bandits stole 1.4 million dollars from the Victorian Racing Club.

In 1977, an escaped convict, gaoled for the Faraday School kidnapping five years earlier, kidnapped nine more school children and their teacher at Woreen in Victoria. He was arrested after a high-speed chase, and the drama and the bravery of some of those involved was later encapsulated in a feature film of its own.

In February 1978, a bomb exploded outside the Hilton Hotel, the scene of a meeting of Commonwealth Heads of Government, and three people including a policeman were killed. The episode would be followed by a murky and protracted series of proceedings which cast suspicion not only on those alleged to have committed the crime but on the justice system itself. The fact that the principals were involved with a mysterious Indian sect, the Ananda Marga, and were accused of murdering the leader of the Nazi-style National Front, added to the intrigue which still surrounds the case.

The death of Donald McKay had thrust the menace of drugs clearly into the public psyche and from now on Australians would have to get used to the periodic spectacle of its citizens being arrested in tough Asian countries for smuggling illegal substances. Among the high-profile figures involved in these proceedings was Sydney Rugby League footballer, Paul Hayward, arrested in Thailand for attempted heroin smuggling. Mostly Australians had little sympathy for its citizens apprehended overseas; however, when some of them were unceremoniously hanged for their crimes, shock waves reverberated throughout the community.

# THE 1980s

The 1980s was the era of 'Greed is Good', a robust period which saw the rise of the 'entrepreneur', particularly in Australia's financially wild west. Indeed, Western Australia saw such a flurry of dodgy activity that eventually a Royal Commission was set up to examine what had become known as 'WA Inc.' It was a period that saw the meteoric rises of careers and spectacular falls of men like Laurie Connell, Alan Bond and former Premier Brian Burke.

But, at least, said their critics, these men stayed to 'face the music' and even gaol for any financial misdemeanours. The entrepreneur who has Australians most hostile *en masse* is Christopher Skase, a former financial journalist who became a media baron almost overnight then fled into exile in a Mediterranean resort after his empire crashed, leaving hundreds of angry shareholders skint.

In just a few years, Skase had metamorphosed himself into a sort of antipodean Randolph Hearst with all the grotesque trappings of Citizen Kane. He and his wife, Pixie, luxuriated in the lavish resorts that he developed with money still being sought after. Life for the Skases was an endless party, decadently decorated with elaborate kitsch, most of which was allegedly smuggled overseas as the empire began to crumble. Revved up by the aggrieved investors, the Australian Government has spent the best part of a decade trying to wrest Skase from his Majorcan manor, but the wily entrepreneur has eluded the authorities by repeatedly parading a life-threatening illness.

Perhaps the one that fascinated us most, however, was the mining magnate, Lang Hancock. For all his millions, Hancock would probably have aroused little interest but for the fact that in his dotage he married his Filipino housekeeper, Rose, a worldly-wise woman who has managed to keep a considerable part of the Hancock fortune despite legal forays by her *bête noir*, Hancock's daughter Gina. Andy Warhol claimed that everyone had 15 minutes of fame, but in her case it's been 'Hancock's Half-Hour' as she's beguiled the press with her histrionics and gutsy courtroom appearances.

As a country that started its life in chains, Australia has always been pretty good at nefarious pursuits and the 1980s were full of them. Merchant banker Frank Nugan was found dead in his car in Lithgow, the culmination of a mysterious financial scenario.

A couple of months later convicted bank robber Darcy Dugan was released after spending more than 30 of his 59 years in prison. He was rearrested and charged then with the armed hold up of a service station. Nothing if not consistent, old Darce.

In 1981, alleged crime boss Robert Trimbole fled Australia alerting Australians to the really dark side of crime and links with the Mafia, drugs and death. Much of the activity centred on the Riverina town of Griffith, which in the late 1970s had seen the disappearance of handsome young anti-drug campaigner, Donald McKay, presumed murdered. Trimbole would be arrested in Ireland three years later.

A few days after Trimbole's defection, Jack 'Putty Nose' Nicholls, due to give evidence in the Costigan Royal Commission, was found shot dead in his car at Wangaratta. The Costigan Commission into the Painters and Dockers' Union named some prominent citizens but the Commission was terminated and inconclusive. A few days later, a Royal Commission into drug trafficking, headed by Justice Stewart, was established and any Australians who were in any doubt were now well aware that Sydney and Melbourne were up there along with the crime capitals of the world.

The early 1980s also saw some new crimes that were generally regarded as 'un-Australian'. A bomb exploded in the Woolworths store near the Town Hall in Sydney, the third bombing of the chain in a million-dollar extortion attempt.

And even our most respected institutions, the Parliament and the Courts, were not immune. Justice David Opas of the Family Court was shot dead on the doorstep of his Woollahra home. A few days later, New South Wales politician Peter Baldwin was beaten up by an intruder in his Marrickville home following attempts to clean up Sydney's Labor Party branches. In 1984, Justice Ray Watson of the Family Court in Sydney narrowly escaped death but his wife was killed when an explosion devastated their Greenwich home.

But the case which fascinated Australians like none other this century began on a holiday weekend in August 1980 at the spiritual heart of the continent, Ayers Rock (Uluru). Baby Azaria Chamberlain disappeared from a campsite there and the words of her distraught mother, Lindy, both chilled and mystified the nation: 'A dingo's got my baby.' What followed during the next decade is the most bizarre and convoluted saga in the history of Australian courts.

The Australian public was quickly polarised as to who killed the baby—a dingo or Lindy herself. Rumour, innuendo and half-truth spread like a brush fire and Lindy aroused little sympathy with her seemingly cold demeanour during her public appearances.

On 20 February 1981, the Alice Springs coroner Denis Barritt found that a dingo did kill Azaria Chamberlain, but this was only the start of the Chamberlain's legal vicissitudes. New evidence and new experts emerged to blind one another with forensic science, and the Chamberlains were destined to face three Coronial Inquests, two Appeals, a Royal Commission and a Court of Criminal Appeal hearing. During that time, Lindy would spend part of a life sentence in gaol before being pardoned in 1987.

The case would continue to enthral Australians throughout the 1980s and even the 1990s while many of the major events of those decades have been forgotten. Ronald Reagan was President of the United States, which was fighting Iran; Maggie Thatcher was Prime Minister of Britain and was fighting the Falklands; and John Lennon was fighting no-one but was assassinated anyway.

Another who would meet a violent end for no apparent reason was Dr Victor Chang, who in 1984 carried out Australia's first truly successful heart transplant. Australia was already on its way to becoming a world leader of in-vitro fertilisation, a program headed by Professor Carl Wood, which kicked off the decade with the birth of Candice Elizabeth Reed, the world's third test-tube baby.

In the joyous big-spending days before his financial ruin and disgrace, Alan Bond became a national hero when his sailing boat, *Australia II*, with a winged-keel designed by Ben Lexcen, took the America's Cup from the United States for the first time in the 'the Auld Mug's' 132-year history. At home, a 61-year-old potato farmer named Cliff Young also became a national hero after winning the first gruelling Sydney to Melbourne Westfield marathon.

Criminal acts abounded on the international scene when Soviet fighters shot down Korean jumbo flight KAL 007, killing all 269 people on board, including an Australian family. The world's worst industrial accident occurred at Bophal in India when chemicals leaked from the Union Carbide insecticide factory, killing at least 2000 people.

In the mid 1980s, Australia's crime spree continued when several people including a 14-year-old girl were killed in a shoot-out between bikie gangs, the Bandidos and the Comancheros, at the Viking Tavern, Milperra Sydney, on Father's Day. Thirty received sentences from five years to life.

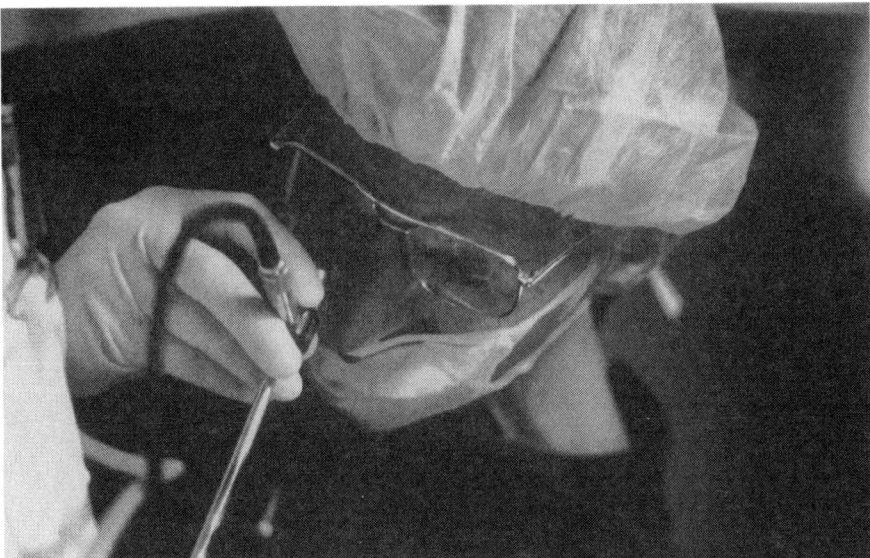

Top: Professor Carl Wood, head of the world-leading team in in-vitro fertilisation during the 1980s. Bottom: *Australia II*, winner of the elusive America's Cup in 1983, at the Maritime Museum in Sydney. Its novel winged-keel design by Ben Lexcen created a psychological advantage for the Bond syndicate, sending the Americans off to decide whether or not it was legal.

Top: Greg Chappell, one of the famous cricketing brothers and a superb batsman— the one who blotted his copybook somewhat when he instigated the infamous underarm bowling incident against New Zealand in 1981. Bottom: Bowling legend Dennis Lillee, who set a new world record with 310 Test wickets and went on to take 355.

It would be unfair, though, to create the impression that Australia was in the grip of anarchy and our streets were bathed in blood like Chicago of the 1920s. In fact, the general crime rates have increased very slowly and sometimes been reversed in the latter part of the twentieth century, and Australia has enjoyed a remarkably peaceful and pleasant existence during the last quarter century—but the same can't be said for politics where the warfare continued.

At the beginning of the 1980s, Andrew Peacock, 'the Colt from Kooyong', the well-heeled and elegant young liberal considered by many of his peers to be 'born to rule', began his run in politics.

In 1981, Peacock resigned from Federal Cabinet accusing Prime Minister Fraser of gross disloyalty but 'as sure as night followed day', he'd be back. And back. And back. Peacock's political adventures would take him to within a whisker of the Prime Ministership, and his high profile enabled him a liaison with an American actress, Shirley Maclaine, and an ambassadorship to Washington.

Meanwhile, Trevor Chappell, at the behest of his brother Greg, caused a bit of hysteria on both sides of the Tasman when he bowled the last ball underarm in a World Series cricket match against New Zealand, to prevent the Kiwis scoring the six runs they needed for a draw. It was regarded as extremely poor form, behaviour not even worthy of a school yard, but elsewhere on the sporting field, there were some triumphs too. Bowler Dennis Lillee set a new world record with his 310th test wicket. Part Aboriginal brothers, Glen, Mark and Gary Ella starred together in Australia's Rugby Union Test team, and Jan Stephenson won the Women's World Golf Championship.

Pat O'Shane became permanent head of the New South Wales Department of Aboriginal Affairs, the first woman to head a government department in Australia. It was an appointment hailed by the progressives. More than a decade later, she would once again feature strongly in the Australian consciousness as she and the nation grieved and fretted over the fate of her tiny relative Tjandamurra O'Shane, horribly disfigured in a random act of cruelty. The little boy suffered terrible burns when a man came into his school yard, poured fuel over him and lit it.

The 1980s saw a number of significant advances for women, whose political fortunes had started out so promisingly a century earlier. Not only had Australian women been the second only to New Zealanders in being allowed to vote, they'd been granted the right to own property and to attend university since the 1870s, and allowed to practice as doctors since the 1880s. By the 1980s, having achieved equal pay 15 years earlier, they began training alongside men in the Army and were ordained as Anglican Deacons. In 1985, Australia saw its first woman Ombudsman, Mary Beasley of South Australia, although there was still no such thing as an 'Ombudswoman'. In 1986 came the first woman Speaker of the House of Representatives, Joan Child, the first woman appointed to the High Court, Mary Gaudron, and the first woman leader of a Parliamentary Party, Janine Haines, Democrat. But there was better to come. In the 1980s, women were allowed membership of the MCC. That was something they'd been holding their breath for.

There were, however, other sinister spectres on the horizon. In November 1982, the first case of AIDS was diagnosed in Sydney. For most Australians it seemed remote and meaningless. It would be a while before we even knew what it stood for—Acquired Immune Deficiency Syndrome. The Australian in the street identified much more strongly with another initiative—random breath testing.

By now Australia's population was more than 15 million and yet another demon that would continue to haunt us was unemployment which by then already exceeded half a million. Australians became more peripatetic in the search for work and New South Wales dubbed those Victorians coming north to seek jobs as 'Mexicans'. On the other hand, there were plenty going south too, with Queensland cane toads reaching Coffs Harbour in New South Wales.

The year 1983, one of Australia's most volatile political years, began against a background of flames. In January, four fire-fighters were killed in Victoria and the Ash Wednesday fires two weeks later would take 72 lives and destroy 2000 houses. Meanwhile, Brian Burke became Premier in Western Australia and Bob Hawke, having rolled ALP Leader Bill Hayden, won the 5 March election for Labor. Malcolm Fraser, a man who'd stood by to accede the throne when a democratically elected government was dismissed by the Queen's representative, a man who'd ridden through numerous bloody political crises, now sat beaten with his lower lip quivering and a tear in his eye. Tough game, politics.

As the Hawke Ministry was sworn in, Andrew Peacock was elected Liberal party leader, Prince Charles and Princess Diana with their new baby Prince

William visited Australia and God was in his heaven, but not for long. Within a month after holding a triumphant economic summit, Hawke ran into his first crisis when the Soviet Embassy First Secretary, Valeriy Ivanov, was expelled for alleged spying, and the Canberra lobbyist and former ALP Federal Secretary, David Coombe, was declared *persona non grata* by the Federal Government for his association with Ivanov.

It was a generally fraught time for Labor. 'Four Corners' reporter, Chris Masters, the producer of a number of exposés on political shenanigans made a program called *The Big League*, which led to New South Wales Premier, Neville Wran, stepping aside while a Royal Commission investigated allegations that he attempted to influence the magistracy. Wran was exonerated and resumed his post as Premier. However, the repercussions of the program were profound. Chief Magistrate Murray Farquhar was charged with perverting the course of justice and later sentenced to four years' gaol.

In 1984, Justice Lionel Murphy was named in Parliament as the judge referred to in the so-called '*Age* tapes', and later that year, the Director of Public Prosecutions, Ian Temby, decided that Murphy should be charged with having attempted to pervert the course of justice. It was a complicated matter centring around an acquaintance of Murphy's named Morgan Ryan—'My little mate.' At the same time, the Australian Jockey Club 'warned off' Bill and Robbie Waterhouse following the substitution of a dud race horse named Bold Personality for a better one named Fine Cotton.

Lionel Murphy was found guilty in 1985 then granted a new trial. He died of cancer in the following year, just a month after a special inquiry into his conduct had been dropped. The justice system was under attack from all quarters, when Ananda Marga members, Ross Dunn, Timothy Anderson and Paul Alister were pardoned and released from gaol after serving seven years of a 16 year sentence in relation to the Hilton bombing.

The hills were alive with the sound of takeovers: Coles took over Myers to become Coles Myer, and John Howard took over from Andrew Peacock, not to become Howard Peacock, but Andrew's former wife Susan was destined to become a type of serial bride—Susan Rossiter Peacock Sangster Renouf at the time of writing. Geoffrey Edelsten took over the Sydney Swans and the Aboriginal people took over Ayers Rock (Uluru) and Maralinga, site of atomic bomb testing during the British 'dreamtime' of the 1950s.

Not that Australians could be accused of simply mucking around with frivolous pastimes; on a more profound level we were keeping up the good work with the booze, averaging 115 litres of beer, 22 litres of wine and a litre of spirits per head per year.

And we knew how to spend a quid. It's said that Aussies will gamble on two flies crawling up a wall or even the sunrise, and our national game— indeed, the only illegal one officially sanctioned on that holy of holies, Anzac Day—is two-up. We built our most famous building, the Opera House, using money raised by a lottery. By the 1960s we were spending one and a half billion dollars a year on gambling and by the 1990s it was $10 billion—$500 a head for every man, woman and child in the country. Assuming there's not much gambling going on in our kindergartens, the figure is probably closer to $1000 a head.

Sadly, though, it was crime that continued to dominate the headlines of the 1980s—the horrific Anita Cobby rape and murder by five men. A car bomb exploded outside of the Russell Street Police Headquarters in Melbourne, killing a policewoman, and a man was sentenced to life imprisonment for conspiring to murder the anti-drugs campaigner Donald McKay. Robert Trimbole, however, escaped the long arm of the law but died in Spain.

Five people were shot dead in the Hoddle Street Massacre, and a few months later another lunatic shot nine people dead and wounded five more in a Melbourne office building before plunging 11 storeys to his death.

Fortunately, though, all this death and destruction was transcended by happier events: Pat Cash won Wimbledon, Greg Norman won the British Open, Wayne Gardner became the first Australian to win the World 500cc Motor Cycle Championship, and Jeff Fenech won the WBC Super Bantam Weight boxing championship and became the first Australian to have held two boxing World Titles.

Above all, the 1980s are remembered for the wonderful celebration of the Bicentenary of European settlement. Sailing ships re-enacted the voyage of the First Fleet and there were numerous sporting, cultural and political events culminating in the magnificent spectacle of Australia Day on Sydney Harbour in 1988. Aboriginal groups were not happy about the celebrations and no-one expected them to be, but two and a half million Australians—the biggest ever crowd to attend a single Australian event—showed that despite our trials and tribulations, we really had something to celebrate.

Around two and a half million people—half the population of Sydney—turned out to celebrate the Bicentenary, 200 years of European settlement, on 26 January, 1988. Tall ships which had re-enacted the arrival of the First Fleet—those 11 ships that brought the first convicts to Australia—were greeted with ecstatic enthusiasm, although Aboriginal groups were understandably not impressed.

# THE 1990s

It seems somehow appropriate that Australia found itself on the eve of the twenty-first century under the stewardship of Prime Minister John Howard. After hovering in the upper ranks for so many years, 'Little John', often deemed unlikely to succeed to the top job, seemed simply to have eventually worn through. Certainly, he proved to be the most persistent, if somewhat plodding, politician in the Parliament—and, in a way, he is a sort of metaphor for the way Australia itself stumbled through the twentieth century.

Considering that, during those hundred years we took part in half a dozen wars, a Great Depression and other economic downturns, numerous natural disasters and various other catastrophes, we somehow got through in one piece. Maybe not with huge distinction, but at least we could lie pretty straight in bed knowing that we hadn't had a war or an uprising on our own soil, and that we had accepted migrant people from over a hundred countries.

The population of Australia was now 17 million and nearly two million of them were aged over 65. Grey power will only increase as medical technology improves. Four million Australians were born overseas, and by the 1990s, the best part of two million had a university degree or higher qualifications. Not that qualifications helped much to get a job. There were still around a million unemployed and the largest occupation group in the country was of clerks who make up 15 per cent of the employed population of seven million.

Yet, on the whole, we were pretty well-heeled at the beginning of the 1990s. Australia's 1.6 million private dwellings that were being purchased were being bought with mortgage repayments of $1000 or more a month. Nearly 12 per cent of these dwellings had three or more motor vehicles in their garages or carports.

For the Queen at least, 1992 was *annus horribilis*, which roughly translated is 'a pain in the arse'. Not surprisingly, Paul Keating, who'd wrested the Prime Ministership from Bob Hawke in much the same way that Hawke had ousted Hayden before him, tried to convince us to break away from the Mother Country. In typical Keating fashion, the boy from Bankstown scandalised Australian conservatives when he lightly touched the Queen on the back to guide her through a crowd. From their reaction, one might have thought he'd stuck his hand up her dress. Meanwhile, Laurie and Noeline Donaher showed the Poms in a television series called 'Sylvania Waters' what life down under was really like and despite the vista it wasn't always a pretty sight.

The Liberal Party, perpetually trying to choose between John Howard and Andrew Peacock as leader, had a brief flirtation with a new one named John Hewson who, for the electorate, put up the preposterous idea of a GST. A 'goods and services tax', or 'consumption tax', call it what you will, was given a huge thumbs down by voters, particularly when Hewson embarrassed himself publicly by not knowing which parts of a birthday cake were subject to which tax. To get into office for his first term, John Howard of course promised that no such thing would be introduced in the future.

And while Hewson was saying let them eat something or other, the year saw the passing of the eye surgeon and humanitarian, Fred Hollows, along with one of Australia's all-time greats, Sir Edward 'Weary' Dunlop, who'd been a Christ-like figure to Australians held prisoner by the Japanese in Second World War.

The year 1995 was the 50th anniversary of the end of that war, and with more than a million Japanese visitors to our country every year, we were given to some reflection—in particular, a shared guilt relating to the innocent victims of Hiroshima and Nagasaki, as well as our own shattered souls who returned from places like Changi.

Throughout the 1990s, we became even more crazy about sport than we had been. There was Kieren Perkins' against-all-odds second gold medal victory in the 1500 metre freestyle final at the Atlanta Olympics. Fittingly, also at those games Dawn Fraser was saluted as one of the all-time sporting greats, along with the likes of Mark Spitz and Muhammad Ali. To the bemusement of the Rugby League, which was in all sorts of strife after a power play between two proprietors, Australian Rules football, once considered safely exiled to states that didn't matter, spread its tentacles into New South Wales and became a huge success. It was a success largely due to the efforts of such master players as 'Plugger' Lockett. Michael Doohan won his fifth 500cc Motor Cycle World Championship, Greg Norman had another heartbreaking collapse in the final round of the US Masters, and Karrie Webb became the first woman golfer to win over a million dollars.

As we made our run towards the new millennium, international and national events had a momentum both inexorable and a little scary. Perhaps because of that we turned our attention away from the big picture to the

Right: In 1992, Federal Treasurer Paul Keating wrested the throne from Bob Hawke to become Prime Minister. A pro-Republican leader, Keating saw Australia's future as being closely linked with our Asian neighbours. Bottom: Captain Cookiyaki—in the 1990s, Australia is host to more than one million Japanese visitors a year. Japanese photographers take time out while waiting to film the tourists who flock to Captain Cook's Cottage, reconstructed in Melbourne.

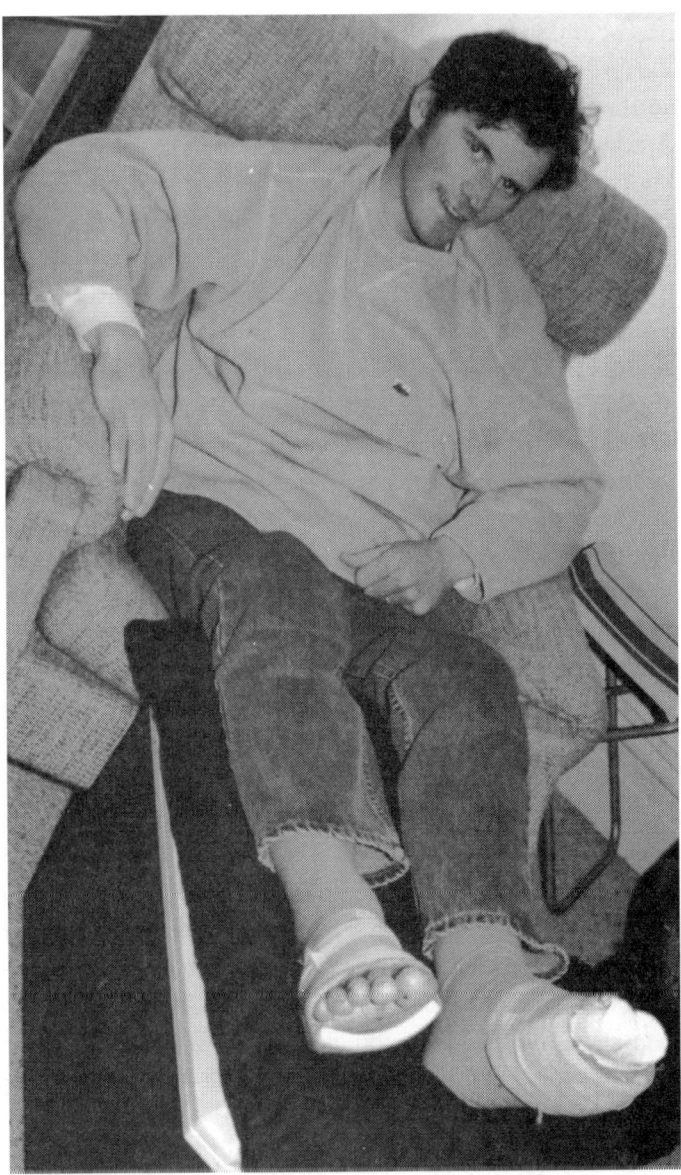

Stuart Diver, sole survivor of the Thredbo disaster of 30 July 1997 when two ski lodges were destroyed in a midnight landslide. A majority of the Australian population sat glued to their television sets watching the rescue attempt and, when Diver was brought to the surface after 65 hours, a collective cheer rang through the nation.

compulsion of individual human drama such as 'Would Kate Fischer get Jamie Packer, son of Australia's richest man, to the altar?' 'No way,' said the cynics, and they were right. Swimsuit model Jodie Meares stole his heart.

However, in 1997, the event which mesmerised us all was the rescue of young skier, Stuart Diver, trapped in a horrifying landslide at one of Australia's winter playgrounds, Thredbo. The fact that a few million Australians visit this tiny village each year made the disaster seem even closer, and when television pictures of the rescue were beamed, live, into our living rooms, the whole nation was transfixed. From Perth to Sydney and from Darwin to Hobart, a collective cheer went up as, after 65 hours in below zero conditions, Stuart was brought out alive. Eighteen others, including his wife, lying beside him, perished when they were buried alive.

The decade was distinguished by the usual political chicanery and in-fighting, and for a nervous moment we saw the rise of Queensland politician Pauline Hanson, founder of the One Nation Party. Claiming her right to free speech, the one-time fish and chip shop owner criticised what she saw as preferential treatment of Aboriginal people and migrants, the former because they were taking our money, the latter because they were taking our jobs.

Traditionally, the likes of Pauline Hanson and other political fringe dwellers such as the member for Kalgoorlie, Graham Campbell, have had little influence on Realpolitik. However, such has been the evolution of the electorate over this century that support almost became polarised into equal groups for each of the two major parties, Labor and Liberal. This led to the phenomenon whereby smaller breakaway parties such as the Democrats and a number of independent candidates such as Hanson, Brian Harradine and Mal Colston found themselves, to much of the electorate's dismay, wielding enormous amounts of influence over social and business policy.

To add piquancy to the proceedings federally, Brian Harradine and Mal Colston, two Senators who for some years controlled the entire destiny of the nation, were like characters out of Dickens—Harradine, a thin, morally upright Catholic from the Apple Isle; and Colston, an overweight, frequent flyer from Queensland, who ratted on his party, Labor, when he failed to get a nomination as Deputy Leader of the Senate.

The decade was dominated by the bogey of economic rationalism and extraordinary technological development such as Marshall McLuhan's famous prophesy of 'the Global Village' came true. Australia, as it has always tended to do, embraced the mobile phone, the Internet and cable television with even greater alacrity than the rest of the world. Paradoxically, it has also fretted more than the rest of the world about the perils involved, such as the millennium bug, which in 1999 had latter-day Luddites leaving for mobile ashrams stocked with food, water and copies of Nostradamus.

Above all, Australians still love their bread and circuses, and the circus this time was indeed maximus—the Olympic Games, allocated to Sydney for the year 2000 by only one vote over Beijing. Although, maybe not. The Olympic President, Juan Antonio Samaranch, actually awarded the games to a place called 'Siddenay'. New South Wales Premier, John Fahey, achieved a new personal best for the high jump at the announcement. However, subsequent revelations about the behind-the-scenes machinations required to win the bid did not make proud reading. The Games, held under the mock banner of amateurism, involve billions of dollars. Some of these behind-the-scenes manoeuvres were deemed to be unethical and there were some spectacular falls in the last furlong in the race towards opening day, 15 September 2000.

In the meantime, Prime Minister Howard with his usual dogged determination eventually forced through his dream of a GST, to come into effect after the year 2000, but his tax package was only a shadow of its former self after it had been severely mauled by the Democrats and two of those independents in the Senate mentioned earlier, Harradine and Colston.

Nevertheless, having hypnotised the electorate with his hip-pocket preoccupation, Howard had managed to distract the punters completely from more profound issues such as reconciliation with the first owners of Australia, the Aboriginal people, and the small matter of whether Australia wanted to become a Republic. Fortunately for him, the Republicans' conference managed to show exactly the sort of division that Republics are meant to eschew.

To Howard's credit, or to his Menzian good fortune, the country found itself at the end of the century with an economy appearing to be in good shape. In short, Australia arrived at the doorstep of the twenty-first century looking different but in many ways the same as it had at the beginning of the twentieth—a bigger more mature and more diverse country and yet still strangely British, still preoccupied with the comings and goings of the British royal family, still somewhat insecure about its place in the antipodes with Asia looking over its shoulder, but still proud of its achievements and, more than anything else, very optimistic about the future.

# Heroes...

## OUR GREAT FOLK HEROES

Traditionally heroism is about war—slouch hats and fixed bayonets—acts of conspicuous bravery—the Spirit of Anzac.

And yet, who really remembers our military heroes? Of the scores of soldiers awarded the Victoria Cross in the First World War, only the name of Albert Jacka is still well known, and, strangely, more recent VCs are even harder to recall. Some Australians remember the late Frank Partridge who became famous as a contestant on Bob Dyer's 'Pick-a-Box' show on television. Very few Australians remember the names of the four men awarded the VC in Vietnam—'Dasher' Wheatley perhaps; but Badcoe, Payne and Simpson? Such is the price of military heroism.

In fact, our truly unforgettable heroes come from a variety of unsoldierly vocations—particularly sport, and never from politics. Perhaps John Curtin came close to being a political hero, but in general Australians accord the honour to a remarkably select group of people—and animals.

So, too, do our heroes have heroes of their own. When I asked runner Cathy Freeman who her heroes were, she didn't have to go far from home: 'Oh, it would have to actually be my mother, definitely, but also my stepfather Bruce Barber. He was the one who told me when I was 10 years old that I could go to the Olympics one day. He was the one who had the vision.'

The ABC character Aunty Jack, a.k.a. Grahame Bond, also didn't have to travel far for a hero. On his way to being a successful young architect, news that he suddenly wanted to play the fool as a moustachioed woman in a velvet dress and a boxing glove might have been greeted with some dismay

Left: Sir Don Bradman was nearly twice as good as any other batsman.

by the average doting parent, but Grahame's father said simply, 'No, son, you'll be successful, whatever you do.'

Rock group Midnight Oil's charismatic lead singer cum evangelistic environmentalist, Peter Garrett, is somewhat more expansive about the notion of heroism. For him life is full of heroes—those volunteer bushfire fighters, lifesavers, meals-on-wheels workers; indeed, a host of thankless souls who help others. More specifically, he lionises Dr H.C. 'Nugget' Coombes, former governor of the Reserve Bank, a man who served and was a confidante of governments on both sides of the political spectrum. He was, Garrett notes, a person who could have safely stayed in a cocoon of power and privilege but chose to spend a good deal of his time working with underprivileged Aboriginal people in the bush.

One who spent a good part of his life doing just that and without a background of power and privilege was a doctor many modern Australians nominate as their hero for all seasons, the late Fred Hollows. Hollows was a driven man and could be irascible but he had a passion to save the sight of the world from outback Australia to the war-ravaged jungles of Vietnam.

And, of course, there's the man nominated more than any other Australian as both saviour and hero, Dr Edward 'Weary' Dunlop, who worked tirelessly to save the lives and spirits of prisoners in disgusting hell holes like Changi. According to blokes who were there with him like Tom Uren, a former boxer who later became a champion of the working class as a Labor politician, Weary often put his life on the line for others and, to prevent his mates from being brutalised by their cruel captors, would often be brutalised himself.

Clive James:

My idea of the Australian hero is not necessarily a victor but someone who behaved well under impossible conditions—our prisoners of war in World War II—the day-to-day endless string of moral decisions made when you are staring destruction in the face—that's the kind of heroism that interests me the most.

Prime Minister John Howard nominates Sir John Monash, the Jewish general who led Australia's military force in the First World War and went on to a distinguished peacetime career as a public servant. Howard's other great hero is that one from sporting's Mt Olympus, 'the Don'. Which raises an interesting point—why is it that our super heroes tend to have come from the 1930s?

Is it because that's when we might have needed them the most; needed people whose life stories were so extraordinary that they stretched beyond the mundane concerns of life during the Depression?

In the 1930s Sydneysiders used to say that they were three 'ours' ahead of Melbourne: 'Our 'arbour, Our Bridge and Our Bradman.' Don was a national demigod because he swung a cricket bat better than anyone on Earth. Nellie Melba simply sang like an angel, and Kingsford Smith conquered the heaven that was left—the first man to fly the Pacific. But surely, only in Australia could our greatest national hero have been a racehorse? Certainly it had something to do with his mysterious demise at the height of a young and brilliant career. And, certainly, the legend of Phar Lap remains intact because only he, of all the heroes, did not have feet of clay. There are no scandals, no chinks in his wonderful armour. All too human behaviour surrounded him but the legend of Phar Lap is unassailable.

## PHAR LAP

Dawn in America on Tuesday, 5 April 1932; a grey light floating through Australian eucalypts growing on a Californian ranch. In the stables, devoted strapper Tommy Woodcock was sleeping, as he often did, beside his pet horse 'Bobby', a giant red gelding known to the rest of the world as Phar Lap.

Soon after midday, Phar Lap was dead. The horse collapsed in the arms of young Tommy who, later at the age of 75, still talked about it with tears in his eyes:

I woke up about a quarter to five and when I went to hand up the sugar to him I felt he was hot. The vet came down and said he might have a slight touch of colic and his temperature was starting to rise. It was over a hundred. I led him around and I thought he was going to die. I thought—you know, I didn't know what to do. I just led him in the box and he gave one squeal and he haemorrhaged and just dropped dead.

The news was relayed from America by wireless and newspapers to the millions of people who had followed the spectacular, three-year career of 'the Mighty Conqueror'. Many claimed Phar Lap had been 'nobbled by the Yanks—like Les Darcy', the Australian boxing champ who had died in Memphis back in 1917. It was the beginning of a legend.

Phar Lap—Siamese for lightning—has enjoyed the reputation of being one of Australia's national heroes for 70 years, which isn't bad for a horse, especially one that was not even an Australian. Like so many Melbourne Cup champions, Phar Lap was bred in New Zealand. There was little in the stud book to show that he would be perhaps the greatest horse of all. Nothing about this ugly, ungainly colt suggested that he would go on to win 37 out of his 51 starts and rank favourite in 41 out of 42 consecutive races.

Harry Telford, a trainer from Sydney, didn't have the money to buy him, but persuaded a wealthy racing enthusiast, David J. Davis, to put up the auction bid—a paltry 160 guineas. At the price, Phar Lap must have been the biggest bargain in turf history. Yet when the horse reached Australia, Davis thought so little of him that he agreed to lease him to Telford for three years.

Phar Lap was unplaced in most of his early races and it seemed the playful two-year-old would never find form. The horse was a clown, playing tricks with his track rider Woodcock, pulling the jockey's hair with his teeth and ripping stableboys' shirts. He ran track work at half pace with his feet hardly off the ground, and he was always tripping himself. Nevertheless, he had an awesome fascination for world champion jockey, Scobie Breasley, who even though he'd ridden against him three-quarters of a century earlier could still recall being impressed by the way the horse walked with such huge strides.

Then, after a drought came a flood. In September 1929, Phar Lap won his first race and soon he was off on a series of winning runs that made him the favourite for that year's Melbourne Cup. The November classic, which had started with a prize of a few hundred pounds in 1861, was now worth £9000 to the winner. Phar Lap carried only 7 stone 6 pounds (about 47 kilograms), but he was headstrong and the horse and jockey fought each other from the start. Finally, the jockey gave up trying to hold him and let him have his head. Phar Lap tired in the straight and finished the race a close third.

After a summer spell, 'the Red Terror', as they called him, went on another winning rampage, at times winning by 50 lengths. He was favourite four months before the 1930 Melbourne Cup, even though he was to carry 9 stone 12 pounds (about 62.5 kilograms), a massive 15 pounds (about 7 kilograms) over weight-for-age. His win was, in fact, so certain that turf rivals tried to kill him. Two men in a car, with a rifle wrapped up in newspaper, fired at the horse. But Tommy Woodcock, riding the white pony that always travelled with the champion, shielded Phar Lap against a fence and no-one was harmed. From then on, Phar Lap's movements were kept secret. He won the 1930 Melbourne Cup at 11 to 8 on, making him the first 'odds on' favourite in the history of the event.

Phar Lap earned £12 429 at the Melbourne carnival, winning five major races in 14 days. His proud jockey, Jim Pike, in the now famous red, white and black silks, told the cameraman: 'They can breed 'em with wings on and get Kingsford Smith to ride 'em, and I doubt whether they'll beat him then.'

Telford's lease expired at the end of 1930 and Davis agreed to sell him a share of Phar Lap for £4000. From then on the two men worked in a partnership marked by many differences of opinion. By 1931, Phar Lap had grown to a gigantic 17.1 hands, standing 6 feet 10 inches (208 centimetres) from the ground to the top of his head. That year, the Victoria Racing Club decided the only way to curb him was to introduce special handicapping. He was to carry an incredible 10 stone 10 pounds (about 68 kilograms) in the Melbourne Cup, and Telford was strongly against him starting. His partner overruled him and Phar Lap came in eighth.

This was to be his last race in Australia. His owners wanted him to take on the world, and in January 1932 Phar Lap was hoisted aboard a steamship on his way to Tijuana in Mexico. The target was the Agua Caliente ('hot water') Handicap, then the richest horse race in the world. Phar Lap romped home first, with the race commentator at Tijuana calling:

> ... a great debut for the Australian beauty Phar Lap, one of the handsomest horses seen on an American track—a little temperamental but what star isn't? In one race he's proved himself, and how the fans love it.

The triumphant Australians returned to their base camp, a training ranch outside San Francisco. Sixteen days later, Phar Lap was dead. To this day there has not been a satisfactory explanation of the fatal illness. The initial explanation was that the horse's death had been caused by 'intestinal tymphany' blamed on highly fermentable green pasture. However, Scobie Breasley supports 'the Les Darcy scenario', arguing that there were sinister forces at work who didn't want to lose their money and kudos to a nag from down under.

And the mystery only deepened as, after two autopsies, bits and pieces of the famous horse spread around the world—his skeleton to his homeland of

In 1931, Phar Lap was a giant red gelding, 17.1 hands high. He came third in his first Melbourne Cup race in 1929. The next year, he won it, even though he carried nine stone 12 pounds —15 pounds over weight-for-age. The frequency of his subsequent victories meant that, for the 1931 race, he was weighted with a massive 10 stone 10 pounds. Needless to say, he didn't win. It was his last race in Australia.

THE "RED TERROR" LIVES AGAIN

Which is The Live Horse? The Horse On The Phar Lap Right is the famous bones and hide. On the left is the well-known American

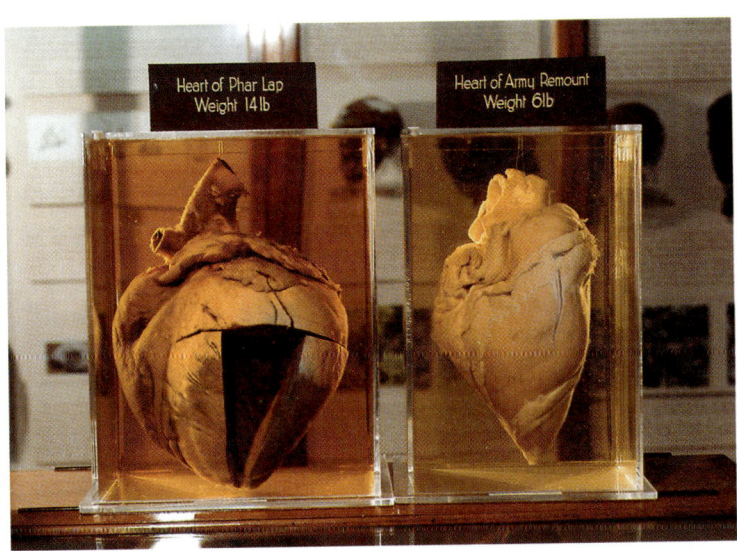

Heart of Phar Lap
Weight 14lb

Heart of Army Remount
Weight 6lb

Phar Lap died suddenly—some say suspiciously—near San Francisco on 5 April 1932. His skeleton was sent to New Zealand, where he was born, and his hide was sent to Melbourne. That's Phar Lap after taxidermy, above right. It is displayed at the Museum of Victoria and has been seen by millions of Australians. His heart is kept in Canberra.

New Zealand, his hide to Melbourne, where he was painstakingly recreated for display in the Museum of Victoria and, of course, his mighty heart, which would go on display in the old Institute of Anatomy in Canberra and would be seen by literally millions of Australians.

But, much later, doubts began to arise about the heart's authenticity, particularly when Mrs Mary McCann, the daughter of Bill Nielsen, who did the original autopsy, made this startling revelation:

> One day I told my father I was going down to Canberra and while I was there I was going to have a look at Phar Lap's heart and he said, 'That will be clever because it's not Phar Lap's heart.' It was the heart of a draughthorse.

Dr Nielsen carried the secret of the heart to his grave but it now seems unlikely that the organ is genuine for a variety of complicated technical and historical reasons. During a horse autopsy, the major organs are usually cut to ribbons, yet rarely seen documentation shows that the famous heart arrived in Australia intact—and this was after not one but two autopsies. The small, neat triangular incision in the heart, which has been seen by so many Australians, was in fact made by a vet after the heart had arrived in Australia. So the plot thickens.

In the long run, though, it doesn't really matter whether Phar Lap's heart is genuine or not. During the three-quarters of a century since his death, the object well and truly became an Australian icon. It's sort of our sporting Shroud of Turin and, like the Shroud, it's deteriorating so much so that these days television crews can only videotape it under very low light conditions. All in all, a rather poignant end for a racehorse that once literally shone in the Aussie sunlight.

## NELLIE MELBA

In 1861, the year the first Melbourne Cup was run, a girl was born at Richmond, Melbourne, and christened Helen Porter Mitchell. Later, in a manner peculiar to Australian stars of the opera, she would change her name to Melba, in honour of her home city. Others who underwent similar patriotic name changes were Florence Austral, Elsa Stralia and June Bronhill, but none made such an impact on the musical world as Nellie Melba.

Madame Melba became the singing sensation of the century and dominated international music for nearly 40 years. Perhaps more importantly, she was the first Australian to be well known as an Australian outside her own country. By the end of the First World War, Melba had been made a Dame of the British Empire for her contributions to music and for her charity concerts and fund drives in Australia, which raised more than £60 000 for the war effort.

Gounod coached her in the role of Juliet for his *Romeo and Juliet*. Puccini acclaimed her as his ideal Mimi for *La Bohème*, and it is said he created the role of Madame Butterfly especially for Melba, although she never publicly sang it.

Melba's early life was not a happy one. She had a wealthy father whom she adored, although she began an unhappy marriage which took her to a sugar plantation in Queensland. The role of wife of the manager of a mill in the steamy tropics did not suit her, and soon after the birth of her son she left Queensland and her husband behind. She was turning her back on marriage. In 1886, she took her young son, George, to London. She had collected a clutch of letters of introduction but they seemed to lead nowhere. However, one letter was from the wife of the Austro-Hungarian consul in Melbourne to Madame Mathilde Marchesi in Paris, then the world's most renowned singing teacher. After Melba had sung just one line it was said that Marchesi announced: 'I have found a star.'

Melba's first operatic performance took Brussels by storm. She was called to the royal box after her first performance in *Rigoletto*. Soon afterwards she was singing at London's Convent Garden. The British critics, however, chose to ignore the newcomer, and the young star, already seeing herself as a prima donna, swore never to return. A personal invitation from the Princess of Wales soon changed her mind.

Now there were invitations to sing for Queen Victoria at Windsor, and for Czar Alexander III in Russia. Melba conquered all, even the notoriously critical audience at La Scala Opera House in Milan. After she had sung the famous 'mad scene' from *Lucia di Lammermoor*, the frenzied applause lasted 10 minutes. Melba quickly rose to an exalted position among European high society. She entertained royalty at her sumptuous mansion in London, which she had decorated after the style of the palace at Versailles.

A stately, headstrong woman, Melba was always intolerant of imperfection. She preferred the company of men and political debate to the 'idle chat of

Right: The great chef Escoffier created the Peach Melba desert at her suggestion. Bottom: When Nellie Melba returned to Australia in 1902, she was given a triumphant 'royal' tour and adulation from the public, which lasted through to her 'Farewell' tours in 1929.

Helen Porter Mitchell, later known as Dame Nellie Melba (after her home town), was born in Melbourne in 1861. Taking her son with her, she left behind married life on a Queensland sugar cane farm and headed for Europe, to take up leading roles in some of the world's best opera houses. She returned to Australia an international star. Melba died in Sydney on 23 February 1931.

women'. Once, in Germany, after the Kaiser had criticised her singing, she told him she would never dream of criticising his government. The Kaiser turned on his heel and walked away.

At 30, Melba fell in love with the suave, wealthy Duke of Orleans. They were constant companions for many years, and the resulting scandal almost ruined her career. Marriage was impossible for the Catholic prince with a commoner who was already married. The scandal spread to Australia where Melba's husband, Queensland sugar producer Charles Armstrong, began divorce proceedings. Finally, British diplomatic influence was brought to bear and the whole affair died down.

There were to be many more liaisons and friendships, including that with the legendary tenor, Enrico Caruso. Like Melba, 'the Great Caruso' enjoyed playing practical jokes and one night, while he sang the aria 'Thy Tiny Hand is Frozen' during *La Bohème*, he pressed a hot sausage into her hand. Furious, Melba flung it across the stage into the wings.

But Melba was herself a practical joker. Early one April Fool's Day, she ordered a bathtub to be delivered every quarter of an hour to the composer Bemberg. By midday he was begging her to stop. To add insult to injury, he had to pay for the baths and organise their removal.

Aloof and imperious, Melba made enemies, and there were many prepared to invent scandalous stories about her style of life. She ignored most, but she always denied reports that she once advised British singer Dame Clara Butt, while touring Australia, to 'Sing 'em muck. That's all they understand.'

Dame Clara's autobiography was recalled to the printers so that the pages referring to this incident could be removed. When Australia's most famous daughter returned to Melbourne in 1902, it was a triumphant 'royal tour'. Tens of thousands of people lined the streets, and at Lilydale, outside Melbourne, where she later bought Coombe Cottage, Melba was welcomed by a special edition of the local newspaper printed in gold ink on blue paper. By 1926 Melba had started her famous 'farewell' tours. Yet the legend that led to the phrase 'more farewells than Melba' was unjustified according to Melba's piano accompanist, Lindley Evans, who told me:

The whole point about a farewell was that she was leaving this city to go somewhere else, but people took up this word 'farewell' as if she was saying: 'This is my final concert. I'm never going to sing again,' which is stupid.

Melba came home for the last time in November 1930. After falling ill on the ship, she was taken to St Vincent's hospital in Sydney where she died on 23 February 1931. She was 69 years old.

For a woman who brought whole cities to a standstill there is little to perpetuate her memory. Her recordings, made on primitive apparatus, give no real indication of how great her voice must have been. As a memorial there is the Melba Auditorium in Melbourne and, at her suggestion, the great Escoffier created the Peach Melba dessert for her. But perhaps her most lasting monument will be the suburb of Melba in Canberra. With its rows of brick veneer houses, it is a far cry from her sumptuous home at Great Cumberland Place in London. But there is no doubt that the naming of part of our national capital was an honour which Melba, an intense patriot, would have taken deeply to heart.

## DONALD BRADMAN

In the 1930s it was said that Bradman made more records than a gramophone company, and that wasn't far wrong. In a career that spanned more than 20 years, Don Bradman scored an incredible 271 centuries.

He captained Australia for 12 years, and had a personal Test match average of 99.94 runs. Just one more six over the fence, or even if he hadn't played his last match at all, he would have brought up the amazing average of a century for every Test innings he played. In the words of another of our sporting heroes, Greg Norman:

> When you sit down and you read the stats and you think that his average is almost double the average of most modern-day Test cricketers, and when you think no helmets, you know, different equipment, the ball, the pitches were different, the variations that there were in those days just like golf courses, you've got to sit back and go 'wow'—like Babe Ruth in the United States with baseball—those guys are the real icons of their respective sports

Bradman's batting record was indeed almost twice as good as anyone else's in history. When you look at the graph of the average scores of the world's batsmen over their lifetimes they all finish up at what's called the 'natural brick wall', an average of about 60 runs: Sobers, 57; Hammond, 58; Pollock, 60; Lara, 60;

and Jimmy Adams, 62. And even more amazingly, while other legendary batsmen like Sobers, Hammond and Border actually totalled more runs than Bradman in their lifetimes, the Don only played half as many innings as they did. Bradman scored 6996 runs in his Tests; Sobers scored 8032 in 160 innings—exactly twice as many as Bradman's 80.

Donald George Bradman, born in Cootamundra on 27 August 1908, was to be labelled the Phar Lap of cricket. The now hackneyed metaphor 'a run-getting machine' was invented for him. At one stage the English press seriously suggested the rules of cricket be changed to put a limit on Bradman's runs. A smart entrepreneur even persuaded Bradman to make a gramophone record. Thousands of fans heard the Don playing the piano on one side and teaching cricket on the other.

The young batsman was the idol of Australians from the day in 1927 when he scored a century in his first Sheffield Shield match. He was just 19 years old. Then, in 1930, he piled up a world record 452 not out in 415 minutes against Queensland. Off to England with the Australian team that year, Bradman became a national hero, amassing a score of 334 in one day (including 105 before lunch) in the third Test at Leeds. His boots, still preserved behind glass at Lord's, commemorate that epic innings.

Bradman's tour aggregate for that year was 2960 runs from 36 innings—more than many batsmen make in a lifetime—and it was his massive scores against the English Eleven that led the British bowlers to invent 'Bodyline', perhaps the most infamous weapon in the history of cricket. Bodyline, or 'Leg Theory', a style of bowling attack that intimidated and even injured batsmen, was used to demoralise the Australians in the 1932–33 Test series. While Bradman did adapt to the bowling, he was able to notch up only one century against the Bodyline attack. The fast bowler Harold Larwood, who spearheaded the English attack and who later migrated to Australia, said: 'They said I was a killer with the ball without taking into account that Bradman with the bat was the greatest killer of all.'

Just why Bradman was unique is still a mystery, although there are some clues. As a boy in the New South Wales country town of Bowral, he spent hours in the backyard of his home hitting a golf ball with a cricket stump against the brick base of the tank stand. Who knows whether this practice made Bradman see the ball just that much bigger than other cricketers?

**Daily At Dawn**

## The Natal Mercury

**Saturday July 12, 1930**

# BRADMAN VERSUS ENGLAND

PUBLISHED BY THE CENTRAL NEWS AGENCY, LIMITED.

Sir Donald Bradman, born in Cootamundra, New South Wales, in 1908, stayed at the crease as long as some entire teams. His career Test average is 99.94 runs per innings— and at the end of the century, it still remains almost twice that of any other player.

Bottom: The Don practised strokes using a cricket stump and golf ball. Some believe it was this simple trick that helped him see the cricket ball that much bigger than anyone else.

Bradman's contemporaries tend to speak about him not so much with affection, but with awe. Bill O'Reilly, the incomparable test bowler, gives some idea of the Bradman determination:

> This man, Don Bradman, was born to be king as far as the game of cricket was concerned. He fell into it like a duck falls into water, and God help anybody who tried to take it from him.

As stirring as Bradman was on the pitch, he was always careful to preserve his privacy. Another Australian test cricketer, Jack Fingleton, said of Bradman:

> He didn't seek the friendship of other chaps. He was quite happy to be on his own. He was such an intent businessman. He was tied up in all manner of things so that I don't think he had time to think about mateship, and that, to most of us, meant a lot.

And Bradman, still in his 20s, told an English interviewer:

> I think one of the main reasons why I am able to carry on so long is the fact that I don't drink and I don't smoke. I really don't do anything to get myself out of condition. Consequently, I haven't got to train to get myself into condition to play a match.

Bradman, who led Australia's Test teams from the 1930s through to the late 1940s, was consistently the best batsman in the world. According to a later Test captain, Bobby Simpson:

> Bradman saw the ball a lot quicker and he was able to transfer that thought to movement. He could make a success of any sport or business he took up— he had so much natural intelligence.

The 1948 tour of England, when Australia won the Ashes undefeated, is remembered as the Don's farewell. In one of the great anti-climaxes of the game, he went for a 'duck' in his last innings.

Bradman was knighted in 1949. After his retirement from cricket, he was a stockbroker and company director in Adelaide and served as a selector for

Top: Bradman in full flight. The Don played such havoc with traditional bowling like this that in the 1932–33 Test, the English side employed the intimidatory attack called 'Bodyline' to try to curtail Bradman's huge scores. Bottom: Bradman was a skilled user of media, including radio.

the Australian Cricket Board. Having been feted, analysed and criticised all his life, he has shunned public appearances. Years ago he broke his silence to criticise the new World Series Cricket and more recently he gave his imprimatur to Sachin Tendulkar as a batsman of his own calibre. He's also the living centrepiece for an Australian cricketing shrine, The Bradman Museum, at Bowral. There's no question, however, that he's become possibly the most revered Australian hero. In the words of one of his devotees, John Howard:

> He also represented to a lot of people in his and later generations a sense of 'Australianness' many of us would like to see in ourselves. He was essentially a boy from the bush but he gave a lot of hope and inspiration to people during a difficult time. He was Australia's first great celebrity and unquestionably our greatest at a time when there were fewer celebrities around and we weren't as celebrity conscious. And the other simple fact is that we have only one truly national sport and that is cricket. For a nation of 18-odd million people we are remarkably divided and eclectic in our football tastes. Cricket is the one game that brings all Australians together, not all of them, but Australians in different parts of Australia together, quite uniquely.

The reason for Bradman's success is simple. He was uncannily good. But that still does not explain the slightly unreal aura that surrounds his name. It was a time of economic depression, a time of depression in body and spirit, a time when just some of the worries could be forgotten under the glorious arch of a red ball sailing into the crowds. Perhaps his kind of heroism was needed in the 1930s when they literally sang his praises.

## CHARLES KINGSFORD SMITH

On 3 December 1906, the newly formed Bondi Lifesaving Association gave its first demonstration of rescue using the line and reel. Just 11 days later, two young boys who had been swept out to sea were rescued by the novel method. One of them, who had almost drowned, gave his name as Charlie Smith.

This near tragedy would in fact afflict 'Smithy' with a phobia throughout his short life. Yet his 'aquaphobia' as he called it, and the terrifying panic attacks it induced, would not prevent him from making the greatest flight in history across the Pacific Ocean. That boy on Bondi Beach would, of course, go on to become Sir Charles Kingsford Smith, described in his time as 'the Columbus of the skies'.

After his first flirtation with death as a child, there would be many more near misses for Smithy even before he was 20. As a teenager he served at Gallipoli and, as a pilot in the Royal Flying Corps, he had three toes shot off.

Immediately the war ended, Smithy suffered one of his greatest disappointments. He was refused permission to enter the £10 000 competition to fly from England to Australia. The Australian Prime Minister of the time, Billy Hughes, told the young flyer that he lacked the experience and the backing. To rub salt in the wound, the competition was won by two other young adventurers also called Smith—Ross and Keith—from Adelaide.

Smithy continued his life of adventure and, for a while, was barnstorming for the silent movies in Hollywood. At one stage he almost lost his life in a trick which called for him to hang upside-down from the undercarriage of a plane. He underestimated the strength of the slipstream and only managed to climb back into the cockpit with the utmost difficulty.

But, in 1928, Smithy was planning a feat more serious and more daring— in fact, the most audacious flight of all time. Lindbergh had just flown the Atlantic, but Smithy and his mate Charles Ulm wanted to be the first to fly across the Pacific from America to Australia. For £3000 they bought a Fokker Tri-motor monoplane, an enormous aircraft for its day. The plane had to be specially rebuilt for the flight. Smithy and Ulm recruited two Americans, Harry Lyon, a navigator, and Jim Warner, an experienced radio operator.

Smithy was at the controls on 31 May 1928 when the *Southern Cross* left San Francisco: ahead of the enthusiastic crew were 8000 nautical miles of flying. Conditions on board the Fokker were almost unbearable. The vibration rattled their teeth. The constant thunder of the engines made it impossible to speak, and all communication was by handwritten note.

Smithy and Ulm flew up front in the semi-open cockpit exposed to wind, rain and biting cold. After 27 hours, they arrived in Honolulu to be greeted by a battery of questions and welcoming speeches. They heard nothing of it—all four were temporarily deafened from the roar of the engines. By this time, the whole world was beginning to hear about their progress. They flew through heavy storms to Fiji, then onto Brisbane. Smithy had achieved his dream in just 83 hours. In Sydney, 300 000 people turned out to watch them land. They had tamed the Pacific with their epoch-making flight.

Top: Aviator Charles Kingsford Smith in the cockpit of the 'Old Bus', a Fokker Tri-motor he called the *Southern Cross*. With his friend Charles Ulm, navigator Harry Lyon and radio operator Jim Warner, Smithy piloted this plane on the first flight across the Pacific Ocean, from San Francisco to Brisbane in 1928. Bottom: Smithy's view of the cockpit.

Top: Smithy speaks to Australia after breaking another aviation record. Next to him in the stylish fur is his fiancée Mary, who was destined to become his widow even though he always told her 'Poppa's going to die in bed with his socks on.' Bottom: Such was Smithy's fame on both sides of the Pacific that he was accorded a ticker tape parade in New York.

In the words of another flyer named Smith—Dick Smith, the electronics millionaire who himself has flown around the world solo in a helicopter and who has maintained a scholarly interest in the life of Smithy:

> We don't realise that, in the early days, going in an old Fokker Tri-motor which was quite unreliable really and knowing that if any one of the three engines had failed that you were down in the water [and] basically you were dead; there's no doubt about it that flying in very bad weather conditions at night—because they had to fly day and night because the plane was so slow it only did about 140 kilometres per hour—and that meant that the journey took a tremendously long time. The aircraft would typically stay in the air for 26 to 27 hours and there was no autopilot, so quite an extraordinary achievement.
>
> But, Kingsford Smith was unique … he was known throughout the world, he was given a ticker tape parade in New York when he eventually arrived in New York after completing the circumnavigation of the world, so he was a hero right around the world.

But the adulation that was accorded to Smithy and Ulm was soon to change to animosity. He would even be cursed in the streets. The troubles started within a year of the trans-Pacific flight. This time Kingsford Smith and Ulm were heading for England on yet another attempt to break a long-distance flying record, and also to buy aircraft for a new airline venture. They were farewelled by huge crowds. However, in the far north-west of Australia, they landed on a mud flat. They said later there had been a violent sandstorm and they had lost radio contact.

Smithy was missing and Australia's first big air search was launched. The lost crew were found after 13 days on the mud flat they called 'Coffee Royal', after their coffee and brandy rations. But two of Smithy's friends, who went searching for him in a little plane called the *Kookaburra*, were forced down and suffered horrible deaths from thirst and starvation. A Sydney newspaper suggested that Smith and Ulm had staged the whole air drama, and when they returned to Sydney, 'Coffee Royal' was the dirtiest tag in Australia.

Eventually the affair became such a *cause célèbre* that the Prime Minister called for a public inquiry. During the hearing Smith and Ulm found their business acumen mildly criticised, but nothing was proved that cast doubt on their motives. Smithy's reputation was gradually restored, but he was plagued by rumour and gossip for the rest of his life. Dick Smith believes he was unfairly maligned:

> He got lost in very bad weather and did the most amazing landing ... I've been to the area where he landed at Coffee Royal. He got the *Southern Cross* down in one piece and he and his three other crew members lived there for 10 days off what they called snails—they were little sort of shell fish and it was quite an extraordinary feat, but certain people claimed that this was all done as a stunt to create publicity. It certainly wasn't but it caused Smithy quite a lot of problems for a while and I think then he was treated as a hero again as he should have been.

To many Australians, Smithy was still the ultimate hero. He made the headlines again after an amazing incident during the trans-Tasman mail run. Part of the propeller on the *Southern Cross* broke off and carried away part of an engine. While Smithy fought to keep the plane aloft, his co-pilot, P.G. Taylor, walked out onto a wing strut, drained oil from the damaged engine into a thermos flask, and transferred it to a second engine which was overheating. The operation, which had to be repeated many times, won Taylor the George Cross for bravery.

These were Smithy's lucky days. With his cheeky grin and his deeds of bravado, he was a much sought-after prize for the Sydney social set. He disappointed them by marrying a Melbourne girl, Mary Powell. They had a son, Charles Arthur, who was born in 1933 and who would also go on to fly the Pacific, solo, in the 1970s.

But Smithy suffered more setbacks. It was a sign of his failing fortunes that the passenger airline company he and Ulm started, Australian National Airways, collapsed after the pride of their fleet *Southern Cloud* disappeared in the Snowy Mountains. The wreckage of the plane was not found until 20 years after Smithy's death.

Smithy ran into more trouble during preliminaries for the 1934 centenary air race, firstly because he proposed using an American plane. The authorities refused to let him name it *Anzac*. They need not have worried; Smithy was forced to withdraw from the race because of technical problems. Then, as if his worries had not been great enough, he was sent abusive letters and even white feathers for being 'too cowardly' to compete.

Top: A demonstration of the dangerous lifesaving action of one of Smithy's co-pilots, P.G. Taylor who, in mid-flight, drained the oil from a defunct engine into a thermos flask to transfer it to another engine that was overheating. Bottom: Smithy stands with the ill-fated *Lady Southern Cross*, the aircraft in which he would disappear over the Bay of Bengal in an attempt to break the record between England and Australia in 1935.

By 1935 Smithy had sold his all but immortal aircraft *Southern Cross* to the government. He was disappointed in the price, which he considered an insult, and now in his 38th year he seemed generally tired and dispirited. Ulm was now dead, killed in a crash. Close to bankruptcy, Smithy decided to make one last record attempt in the plane he had bought for the great air race. In a letter to a friend just two weeks before take off, he confided: 'The pressures are becoming too great.'

On 25 October 1935, with Tommy Pethybridge as co-pilot, he set off in the *Lady Southern Cross* in his last race against time. His aim was to lower the record of 71 hours for the trip between England and Australia. Somewhere between Rangoon and Singapore, the plane disappeared. A huge search was led by Australian pilots, and backed by British bombers and flying boats from Rangoon. Leaflets printed in local dialects were dropped to villagers living along the coast.

By the end of November, the search was called off. Not a trace of the pilots or their plane was found. Nothing, until 18 months later when the port wheel from the *Lady Southern Cross* was washed up on an island in the Bay of Bengal.

Smithy's widow told me how she still vividly remembered the horror when she heard of her husband's death: 'It just didn't seem possible to me that he wouldn't come back. He always did. He used to say to me: "Just don't worry, because Poppa is going to die in bed with his socks on." '

Lady Mary Kingsford Smith was destined to be widowed three times and died in Florida in 1997 aged 86, but shortly before she passed on she told Smithy's biographer, Ian Mackersey, that she 'beseeched him to abandon the flight and come home by sea. But he wanted that England–Australia record so badly he just drove himself to do it.'

Mackersey speculates that Kingsford Smith's demise may well have had something to do with his phobic condition—his ironic dread of flying out of sight of land. Mackersey points to cockpit notes such as 'I want to vomit, will be back in 10 minutes' and, 'Can you carry on for a while … feel a bit sick.' While flying over water, Smithy would, in Mackersey's words:

… become so hopelessly disorientated he would sometimes lose control of the plane. It didn't matter when a co-pilot sat beside him, but on solo flights the attacks threatened disaster. On one occasion he'd been so overwhelmed over the Timor Sea he'd been swept with the urgent desire 'to break out of the cockpit'.

And this:

> During a 1931 Australia–England record attempt in an open-cockpit biplane, he had written: 'Suddenly I had a horrible feeling that I didn't know who I was or what I was doing. I knew that I was flying the plane and that I had to reach land which was out of sight. But who I was, or why I was there, I didn't know ... I was in a peculiar condition of half consciousness. The next moment I was diving at a fairly steep angle for the sea.' Had his last flight ended like that?

In some ways Smithy had all the makings of a tragic hero in the Greek sense. But he had something which endeared him especially to Australians—a touch of 'Sydney or the bush' about him. He could walk with kings and princes and he did, but he could also drink a glass of beer standing on his head. His plane was grandly named *Southern Cross* but to him it was always 'the Old Bus'. It took smart planners and accountants to make a business out of the routes Smithy pioneered. It took science and technology to transform the paddock which Smithy used to approach with a wing and a prayer. But when it came to a name for Sydney's first major international airport, it could only ever have been Kingsford Smith.

## DOUGLAS MAWSON

In November 1912, the bodies of British polar explorer Robert Scott and his companions were found, entombed in snow just 18 kilometres from a food and fuel depot which could have saved their lives. The story of how they died after reaching the South Pole, to find they had just been beaten to first place by the Norwegian, Roald Amundsen, is a classic saga in Antarctic history.

But at the same time, on the ice 1600 kilometres away, the bizarre and tragic story of Dr Douglas Mawson was unfolding. Mawson, then 30, was making a scientific expedition which would end in madness and death. As the only survivor, Mawson, after many weeks, struggled back to base only to see his rescue ship steaming off over the horizon.

Top: Dr Douglas Mawson, later Sir Douglas, the Antarctic explorer, who became world famous after he survived his tragic first expedition during 1911–13. His face appears on the original Australian $100 note. Bottom: Mawson (left), with two team members who perished, a Swiss, Xavier Mertz (centre), and Englishman, Belgrave Ninnis (right).

## DR. MAWSON BACK FROM THE ANTARCTIC

Dr. Mawson.          Dr. Mertz.          Lieutenant Ninnis.

After two years of Antarctic exploration in Adelie Land, Dr. Mawson has reached Port Adelaide. He returned on the Aurora, the ship of the expedition. Lieutenant Ninnis and Dr. Mertz were two members of the party who perished.

Half mad from eating the livers of husky dogs, with his skin falling off, his hair gone, no soles on his feet, and weighing half his normal 95 kilograms, Mawson would have to wait another year for the ship to return to the remote base. But he went back later—providing more scientific knowledge of the Antarctic than any man of his time.

Mawson left on his fateful journey with Xavier Mertz, a Swiss aristocrat and champion skier, and a handsome young Englishman, Lieutenant Belgrave Ninnis of the British Royal Fusiliers. With other teams, they planned to explore the land, over 2400 kilometres of coast and inland. Captain Moreton Moyes, another member of that expedition, told me at the age of 93:

> We had to sit and make our own sledge harness. We were all provided with our needles, you know, and little gloves they called palms, to push the needles in and he stood over us while we made our sledge harness a copy from his. And he would stand there and say, 'Now don't forget,' he said, 'if you go down a crevasse and this harness gives way say to yourselves as you go down it's my blanking own fault, you can't blame anybody else,' he said.

They would be prophetic words:

> Mertz was walking out in front, a kind of guide, and Mawson looked up from his sledge, he had the next sledge, at one time and saw Mertz stop and hold up his hand, which meant that there was a crevasse there. So when Mawson reached that area he saw the lidded crevasse—you generally can see where the edge of it is—and so he jumped on his sledge and the dogs took him across and shortly afterwards he looked up and saw Mertz stop again and pointing backwards. So he turned around and found ... Ninnis and his sledge had disappeared.

They were about 515 kilometres from base. The two survivors stayed at the hole, shocked and sickened, for three hours before taking stock of their situation. The lost sled carried all the dog food, some of their food, and vital equipment. They decided as each dog became weak from hunger, it would have to be killed for food. Within a day of Ninnis's death, the men ate their first meal of dog, unaware of the horrendous consequences.

As the weeks passed, they were surprised to find the dogs' livers fairly appetising. What they did not know was that husky liver contained toxic doses of vitamin A. Indeed, it was only in that year that the term 'vitamin' was coined. The poison had horrifying effects, stripping their skin, swelling their spleens, and causing severe disorientation. But the men did not know why. The dogs were dying out, one of the last being Pavlova, the husky that had been patted on a wharf in London by the great ballerina herself. Pavlova, who had been sent to see Mawson by none other than Nellie Melba, said to him: 'Take it with you, instead of me.' Mawson ate Pavlova's paws in a stew.

Mertz slowly became insane, even biting off one of his fingers. When he died Mawson was left with only the instinct to survive. He planned to travel 5 miles (8 kilometres) a day, often against headwinds of 80 miles per hour (about 130 kilometres per hour). The soles of his feet fell off completely. He fell down a crevasse, hanging from his sled. He was saved by his harness and, after numerous attempts to climb out, somehow made it to the top. He woke from unconsciousness in the snow, unable to remember getting out.

Then a miracle occurred. Mawson stumbled across a cairn of stores which had been left by one of the parties out searching for him. This gave him the strength and encouragement to reach a small depot called Aladdin's Cave, where Mawson made a new pair of wooden shoes with nail spikes for the final treacherous walk down to the main base. The soles of his feet, which had completely come away, were tied back on with lamp wick.

When at last he staggered into the base camp, the men did not recognise him. As they peered at what seemed like a living skull, one of the men cried out: 'My God, which one are you?' Mawson was then greeted with some numbing news. His ship *Aurora*, the one contact with civilisation, had left that very day and could not return for 10 months. In hindsight, Mawson felt it might have been a blessing. He did not feel he would have survived the journey. Yet his days as a scientist and Antarctic explorer were far from over. While he never completely recovered from his ordeal, he managed more scientific work on that trip before returning to Australia.

Mawson joined up for the First World War and later resumed his geological work. He was, in fact, the first man to find uranium in Australia. During the 1920s and 1930s he returned to the Antarctic, and is said to have contributed more to Antarctic research than any man before or since. In his later life, Sir Douglas Mawson became an ardent campaigner against the slaughter of whales, and he would become familiar to millions of Australians 50 years after his adventures as the face on the $100 note.

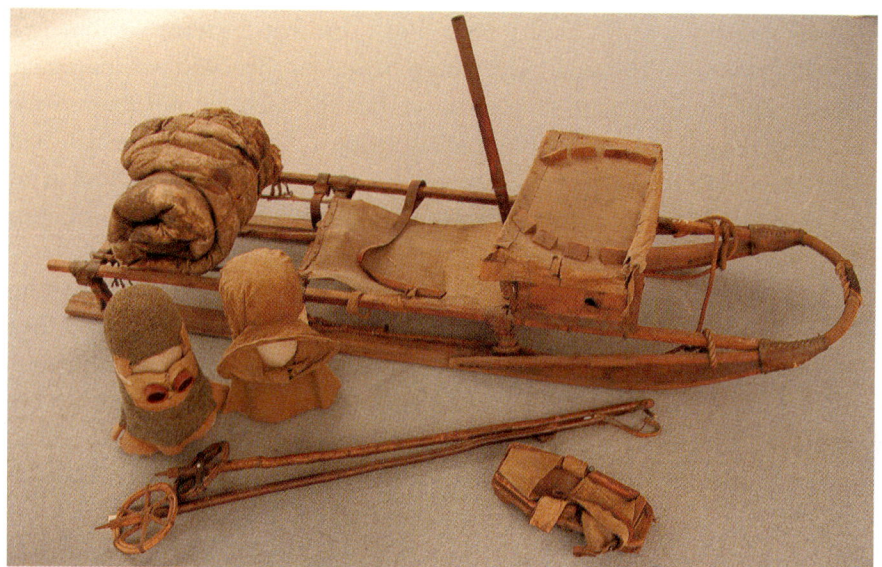

Top: Mawson's sledge, kit and handmade shoes or 'crampons'. Bottom: A crevasse similar to that into which Ninnis disappeared together with his sledge, which carried some of the men's and all of the dogs' food. As the huskies died from hunger, Mawson and Mertz ate them, not knowing that the dogs' livers contained toxic levels of Vitamin A.

Top left: Xavier Mertz with one of the huskies. Eating the dogs sent Mertz insane and he eventually died. Top right: Captain Moreton Moyes—another member of the Mawson team—at the age of 93. Bottom: The vitamin poisoning stripped skin from Mawson's face and feet. He used lamp wicks to reattach his soles to his feet, wrapping them in his shoes, in order to tramp across the snow back to base.

# Humour...

## WHAT MAKES AUSTRALIANS LAUGH?

Is our humour really so special, or are we much the same as anyone else? Here's a joke, and if you laugh, you probably are Australian:

> There's an old swaggie walking along a road about a hundred miles back o' Bourke. It's 110 degrees in the shade and the dust and flies are really crook. As he's trudging along in the heat a ute pulls up and a grazier sticks his head out the window and says: 'Would you like a lift?' The swaggie looks at him for a while and then says with a slow smile: 'No thanks, mate, you can open your own bloody gates.'

It may not be the ultimate Aussie joke but it does say a lot about our humour—ironic, laconic, sardonic and a bit moronic. It has often been said that humour is born out of adversity and Australians have had plenty of that ever since the convicts were flung onto this fatal shore in chains.

For most of its history, the Australian comic tradition has been rooted in the bush. It's a kind of grim comedy that comes from the struggle to survive and eke out a decent living in a vast, tough land. As an old cocky said, 'You can't expect to beat this place ... the best you can ever hope for is a draw.'

If there is something special about Australian humour then it is perhaps the 'Well, I'll be buggered' feeling about it. As Melbourne humorous columnist Keith Dunstan says: 'There's a feeling of hardship and toughness ... funny lines like "the harvest was so crook that the sparrows had to get down on their hands and knees to get at the wheat".'

Left: Actor Barry Humphries as his alter ego, the megastar Edna Everage.

'What else can any Australian do but laugh?' says another renowned wit, Phillip Adams. 'You're drowning in floods one minute and being cooked in bushfires the next.' Author and columnist Max Harris had a theory that Australians have an innate verbal humour that descends from:

> ... a lot of garrulous Irishmen in the nineteenth century. Fortunately, most of them never took to the stage, never became professionals, and never relied on the lavatory innuendo and the 'prawns and beer' syndrome, but basically on their quick verbal wit. That is, if we're busy, we're 'flat out like a lizard drinking'.

Now that's not uproariously funny; it's a metaphoric usage that brings the element of wit into what would otherwise be a pedestrian statement. 'Flat out like a lizard drinking' goes back to the 1890s. This love of metaphor has continued throughout two centuries. Even today, an Aussie when asked about his health might say, 'Well, I feel okay, but I wouldn't get through rego.'

Of course, there wouldn't have been bush humour without being able to tell a good yarn. Not only were there bush heroes to tell stories about, but there were also 'anti-heroes'—characters whose naivety laid bare the most embarrassing aspects of the typical Australian's personality. 'Dad and Dave' is still probably our best-known radio serial and no less than 16 feature films were made about the exploits of these rustic yobbos. Indeed, our only two Academy Award winners for Best Actor, Peter Finch and Geoffrey Rush, as well as a star we claim as our own, Mel Gibson, all played Dave in 'Dad and Dave' productions. There are literally thousands of Dad and Dave gags. A typical offering sees Dave at a smart Melbourne hotel booking a room for his wedding night. 'Would you like the bridal suite?' inquires the female receptionist. 'No thanks, dear. I'll just hang onto her ears.' And they were not so naive, either. While Dave was invariably the butt of the jokes, Dad had wisdom and a wry wit, like the time he won the lottery and an eager reporter asked him what he was going to do with all the money: 'I don't know. I'll just keep farmin' 'til it's all gone.'

But even at the turn of the century Australia was becoming a nation of city slickers. In 1900, about half our population lived in towns and the capital cities, and we were rapidly becoming one of the most urban nations on Earth. Not surprisingly, our humour started moving in the same direction.

Left: 'For Gorsake, stop laughing—this is serious!' —one of Australia's most famous black-and-white cartoons. Drawn by Stan Cross for *Smith's Weekly* in 1933, it tickled the funny bone of an Australia in the grip of the Depression. Bottom: Arthur Hoey Davis as 'Steele Rudd' created the classic *On Our Selection*, home of Dad and Dave.

Around the turn of the century, our black-and-white artists had tired of gags about so-called knowing graziers, stupid farmhands, lazy Aborigines and evil Chinese, and began to explore the comic possibilities of city life. In *Smith's Weekly*, Stan Cross gave us easily our most famous cartoon with the caption: 'For Gorsake stop laughing—this is serious!' It was a joke built on a modern phenomenon, what we used to call 'skyscrapers', but it still used the classic device of Australian humour—laughter in the face of adversity. Below the rigger is certain death, but above him is the scrawny nakedness of his mate, whose pants he's clinging to.

Films, too, now reflected our awareness that we were no longer a nation of 'bushies'. *The Sentimental Bloke*, the classic working-class ballad by C.J. Dennis had sold 100 000 copies before the end of the First World War, and Raymond Longford's marvellous film of the book was just as popular. The Bloke, and his mate, Ginger Mick, who spoke 'wiv ixprissions thick' were the 'ockers' of yesteryear. Certainly the Bloke himself was a little Aussie battler—a boozy, brawling bard, putty in the hands of his girl, Doreen, and embarrassed to the extreme by anything that smacked of culture. 'Put in the boot!' he cries during the duelling scene from Shakespeare's *Romeo and Juliet*, which Doreen has persuaded him to attend.

Like Mo McCackie, George Wallace, Barry Humphries, Paul Hogan and Norman Gunston after him, the Bloke and his language were criticised for being grotesque and embarrassing caricatures. But C.J. Dennis, for one, had a good ear, and he certainly summed us up in his anthem 'The Austral-aise', which he entered anonymously in a competition run by *The Bulletin* in 1915:

Fellers of Australia, blokes and coves and coots,
Shift your—carcasses, move your—boots,
Get a—move on, get some—sense,
Learn the—art of, self de—fence.

Most assumed that there was a 'bloody' for every dash, but in the trenches in the First World War, the poetic 'ixprissions' were somewhat richer. But even if we are slightly crude, it's very delicate and gentle. For instance, if a horse starts off first from a barrier a race commentator is likely to say: 'He's off like a bride's nightie'—it's got a certain amount of innuendo about it, but nonetheless you get a sense of speed.

Top: Dave and his girl, Lil, favourite black-and-white film characters based on Steele Rudd's *Dad and Dave* yarns. Bottom: C.J. Dennis, writer of the ballad verses, *The Sentimental Bloke*, the story of a little Aussie battler, written before the First World War.

Keith Dunstan notes the Australian preoccupation for rhyming slang and the love of the metaphor for the impossible situation. He says:

A line they love to use is: 'It hasn't happened since Christ played full-back for Jerusalem.' Australian humour has become a bit more subtle in the twentieth century, but it also has a nice twist. My favourite joke concerns the digger and, of course, it's a war joke:

There's a wounded digger and he's being carried across No Man's Land by another digger, and there are bullets coming from everywhere. The fellow that's on the other fellow's back says: 'How about turning round and going backwards? You're copping the VC and I'm getting all the bullets.'

According to Dunstan, there's great exaggeration and also a waspish cynicism in our humour, like this famous convict joke:

A convict was out on a property at Parramatta, and his boss told him he wanted him to deliver a letter to the magistrate. The convict knew damn well what was in that letter—he was to get 25 lashes. So he goes all around the district and finally pleads with a nice young fellow to deliver the letter for him to the magistrate. And the magistrate reads the letter, sees the nice young fellow, promptly puts him up on the pole and gives him 25 lashes.

Of course, to the convict, that's an immensely funny joke. There's an earthy contempt for authority in Australian humour. It helps you to hate the magistrate.

Such irreverence for authority continues to be a part of Australian humour. 'Taking the micky' out of someone, to put it politely, is still being used these days to bring down our 'Tall Poppies', those famous—or infamous—people who take themselves too seriously. But perhaps the most droll summary of Australian humour comes from Phillip Adams, whose almost jaundiced views are in themselves part of the Australian comic tradition:

Is not Australia one great big joke? Now, I see the map of Australia looking like a great pair of buttocks spreading across the wrong end of the world— the bum of the world—you've got Perth as a hip and Adelaide as a sphincter, Sydney as a hip. And, of course, all the animals in Australia have great big bums. Have you ever noticed that in the coat of arms you've got this great big fat bummed kangaroo and on the other side this enormously bummed emu? But the whole country is a joke—a great piece of irony surrounded by water. You get dumped here—'Against the Wind' extras, that's how everyone got here to Australia—you're sort of dumped on this forlorn continent. Great humour comes out of misery. The more Draconian the context, the funnier the response. It's no joke that the world's greatest comedians are Jews.


## ROY RENE

Roy Rene, 'Mo', Australia's most famous comic for the best part of the century, had an act with which no other Jewish comedian could compete. His grotesque stage character, a sort of lewd, leering Shylock who slobbered over the sheilas, upset the Jewish press to the point where they recommended that readers avoid his shows. But Mo loved upsetting people, and the more he called them 'mugs' the more they came. He was everybody's favourite mug lair, the eternal prankster and lurk merchant. Dame Sybil Thorndike called him 'the greatest living clown'. Jack Benny watched him again and again to learn the secrets of his timing.

Roy was born Harry van der Sluice in Adelaide in 1892, the son of a Jewish Dutch cigar manufacturer. He began his career as a boy soprano and was 'Boy Roy' as long as he could get away with it. When his voice broke, he took the name of the famous French clown, Rene. Everyone was amused by his talents, except his own family. Sadie Gale, the pretty young vaudeville soubrette Mo married in 1929, says his own family planted stooges in the audience 'to give him the Richard the Third—the bird. They wanted to break his heart. They wanted him out of show business.'

But Mo was unstoppable. By 1914 he had perfected the Roy Rene character with black-and-white stage paint mask and painted moustache, and when he teamed with comedian Nat Phillips, the 'Stiffy and Mo' double became the most successful comedy act on the Australian stage. The partnership had tremendous ups and downs but it lasted a total of 18 years, and by that time Harry van der Sluice was the biggest thing in the business. Stiffy and Mo were experts in innuendo, an art later exploited just as successfully by their admirer Graham Kennedy. In one celebrated Mo routine there's a large blackboard on which Mo writes the letter 'F':

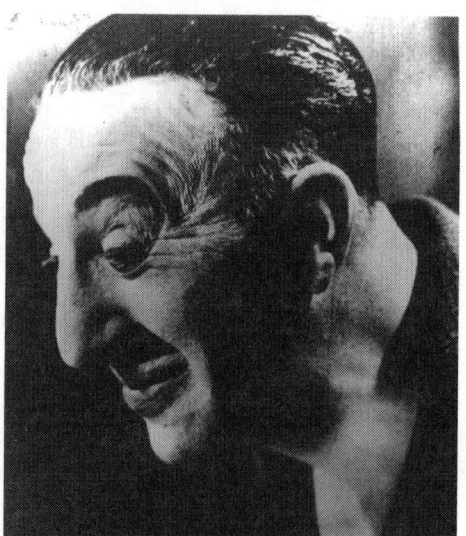

Top left and right: Roy Rene, better known as 'Mo', a grotesque, lewd, leering character who slobbered over the sheilas and called his audiences 'mugs'. During his half-century career, he made famous such lingo as 'coming the raw prawn', 'cop this', 'you beaut', 'strewth', and 'strike me lucky'. Bottom: Out of character, Roy Rene was a reserved, private person. Here he is with his wife, Sadie Gale.

*Mo*: What's that?
*Stiffy*: 'K'.
*Mo*: How come every time I write 'F', you see 'K'?

And Mo laid the mugs in the aisles with the simple ones:

*Woman*: Do you have the time?
*Mo*: Yes, but I don't have anyone to hold my rifle.

Even though Mo looked a bit like a sly Al Jolson, his humour was 100 per cent Australian. Mo invented his own language and to the dismay of 'correctly spoken' citizens, many 'Mo-isms' became popular slang. Mo's 'mots' included expressions such as 'coming the raw prawn', 'cop this', 'you beaut', 'mug lair', 'strewth', 'strike me lucky', 'you little trimmer', 'cheeky possum', 'one of my mob' and 'suck it and see'.

Mo made just one film, *Strike Me Lucky*. It was unsuccessful because the producers failed to come to grips with his distinctive style and because the comedian himself found it hard to work without a live audience. Nevertheless, it has its moments of brilliance and some surprisingly bold lines. 'I know who you are,' says Mo as he stumbles upon Robinson Crusoe and his pet goat. 'Cat Whittington and his dick (splutter, splutter) no, I mean Dick Whittington and his cat.'

For all of his adult life, Mo was troubled by ill health. An unbroken stage career of 30 years took its toll. Yet, against all advice, he took on even more work; this time on radio. The legendary 'McCackie Mansions' show was born and Mo conquered a whole new generation that had never seen him perform in the great old days of vaudeville.

Mo was such a giant on the Australian comedy scene that he probably could have become an international star. He was tempted by overseas offers but declined them, usually with the same words: 'The people here understand me. I work in their language. My stuff is folklore stuff. I don't think I'd go over anywhere else.' And he once told his sister, who came to visit him after 23 years in New York: 'Break it down, love. Look what happened to Les Darcy and Phar Lap when they went to America.' He was content to be the big fish in a little pond, and he was undismayed by the fact that the big overseas stars who appeared on the same stage as him were earning thousands of pounds: his only concern was that he was getting £10 a week more than anyone else on the Tivoli circuit.

He was a man of modest ambitions, but his legacy was enormous. By the time he died in 1954, his unique style had influenced the course of Australian humour. The former Governor of New South Wales, Lord Beauchamp, once wrote to him and said: 'Your art is an important expression of the Australian ethos.' Mo cracked back: 'Gorblimey, I hope that's a compliment.'

## GEORGE WALLACE

Like Mo, the other great star of Australian comedy, George Wallace, ascended from a vaudeville double act, 'Dinks and Onkus'. But, apart from that, Wallace and Mo had little in common. While Mo could be quite blue on stage, he was reserved, even something of a prude, in private life. Wallace, on the other hand, was never smutty in his act but he could be quite risque off stage. And, while Mo made only one unsuccessful film to pass on to posterity, Wallace made five major movies, all of them hilarious. His greatness lay in his movement. With his uncanny timing and sublime sense of motion, he was the closest Australia ever had to Chaplin. Most Australians remember him as the fat bloke with the hat half on and a few grogs under his belt, and even when it seemed he could hardly scratch himself, his feet barely touched the floor as he improvised his eccentric dances. His impressions of 'the great Russian ballet dancer, Palmolive' laid his audiences in the aisles.

In films like *Harmony Row*, *Let George Do It*, and *Gone to the Dogs* he was the classic Aussie battler, but with a nice sense of the absurd. Accused by his boss of sleeping on the job, he responds: 'We weren't sleeping, Mr Austin; we were unconscious.' Being questioned by the inevitable police sergeant:

'Now then, what's your name?'
'Wallace.'
'Wallace ... What initial?'
'S.'
'S for Samuel?'
'Tom.'
'S for Tom? How do you get S for Tom?'
'I don't know. I just don't care, that's what it is.'

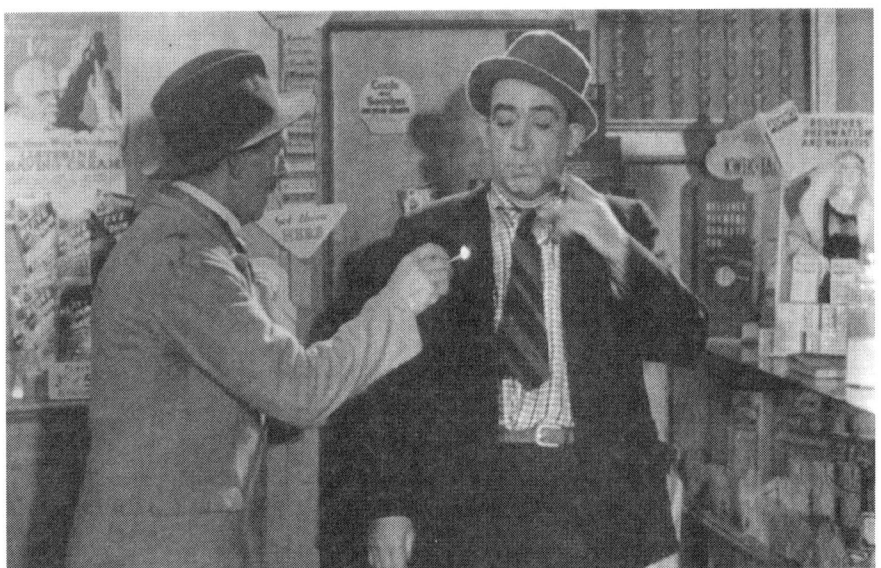

George Wallace was another great master of Australian vaudeville, then film comedy for nearly 40 years, from the 1920s to the 1960s. He could sing, dance, tell a perfectly timed joke and, together with his 'Dinks and Onkus' partner, Dinks Paterson, he performed top gags. Some characters that Wallace 'grew' were 'Sophie the Sort', 'the Drongo from the Congo' and 'Fanny Shovelbottom's Friend'.

And, after one of his thousands of brilliant pratfalls, he picks on a bloke for deliberately pushing him: 'Listen, I've had 78 fights and 78 losses, but me luck's liable to change any minute.'

It was Wallace's endless supply of gags, his musical skill and superb stagecraft that allowed him first to compete with Mo and then eclipse him; but in fact, George Wallace got his start, indirectly, through Stiffy and Mo. Wallace's family had been in show business and George was a would-be comedian. But he had not had much luck and, to support his family, he'd been cane cutting in his home state of Queensland. One night in 1919 he was sitting in the car park of Sydney's Tivoli theatre with another would-be comedian, Dinks Paterson, listening to the audience roaring with laughter at Stiffy and Mo. In Paterson's words: 'George said suddenly, "There's the opportunity for us. Why don't we team up and start a double act too?"'

The 'Dinks and Onkus' partnership got its first laugh in 1919 and ran for the next five years in four Sydney theatres. But Wallace was clearly a huge individual talent, and he evolved out of the partnership to create a whole range of characters: 'Sophie the Sort', 'the Drongo from the Congo' and 'Fanny Shovelbottom's Friend'. They brought him fame and fortune, and he was earning £90 a week in the middle of the Depression.

He had a dazzling array of talents. He wrote a good deal of the scripts for his films as well as a score of radio plays and more than 30 songs. He exhibited watercolour paintings, sculpted, made novelty dolls, played five musical instruments, ran a chicken farm outside Sydney and performed on stage six days a week for more than 40 years.

The best known of his songs was the digger's favourite, 'Brown Slouch Hat', which Wallace wrote at a moment's notice for one of his co-stars, British singer Jenny Howard, who teamed up with him for their happily married sketch called 'The Love Burglar'. The best part of half a century later, Miss Howard still had vivid recollections of their introduction:

I arrived at a producer's office in 1940 to meet Wallace, and I can honestly say I have never seen such an apparition. I think he'd been out the night before and, having never seen anyone keep their pants up under a big fat stomach without braces, I was fascinated. They stayed up all that morning, much to my amazement.

He had a tie spotted with tomato juice and orange. And he had stains and all kinds of things down his suit. Having just arrived from England, and being a little bit British, I was stunned. Then he spoke to me in a very hoarse croaky voice. He said: 'I'm a natural lair.' Well, I thought that must be an Aborigine of some kind, I'd never heard the expression 'natural lair'. We don't have such a thing in England as a lair.

By the time Wallace died in 1960, aged 66, he had carved a career through vaudeville, then radio with the Macquarie Network, and he was one of the first people to appear on television in Australia. All the Onkus stories could never be told in one sitting, and a great many cannot be repeated in polite company, but there's one which shows how the country bumpkin and sometime amateur fighter from Queensland always enjoyed a chat.

A backstage visitor at the Tivoli one night reminded Wallace that he had once been time-keeper when Wallace took on a blacksmith in the boxing ring at Walkerston, near Mackay. That was all the urging Wallace needed to invite the man for a drink. They talked about the old days in Queensland and the visitor commented: 'Well, George, you've come a long way from the cane fields.' Wallace thanked him and added, as an afterthought: 'By the way, what are you doing these days?' His visitor grinned and said: 'Oh, struggling along. They've just made me Prime Minister.' He was Arthur Fadden.

## JACK DAVEY AND BOB DYER

The two big 'D's—Davey and Dyer—were the biggest names in local radio for 20 years. Yet, ironically, neither was an Australian.

The second son of a steamer captain, John Andrew Davey was born in New Zealand. When he breezed ashore in Sydney in 1931 at the age of 20, he had already failed as a signwriter and used car salesman. Somehow he talked Radio 2GB into giving him a job as a singer. In the words of his lifetime friend, aide and biographer, Lew Wright:

They said: 'Oh, yes, you can sing for us, Mr Davey, at three guineas.' So he said, 'OK.' He had to sing three times a week. But even at three guineas, it's an actual factual story, which I have from a person who knew him all his life, that he went into Park Street in the city and he bought three suits, ties, shoes and a motor car, within an hour of getting a job at three guineas a song. But when the end of the week came, he received a cheque for nine guineas. He said: 'Lew, if they're that careless with their money, they could have had me for three. I knew this is where I belonged.'

Three months later, Davey had his own breakfast show, and within two years he added a daytime quiz program, a music and variety show in the evenings, and another job compering Movietone newsreels.

At the same time, a poor white boy from Nashville, Tennessee, was carving out a name in show business the hard way. His name was Bob Dyer and he had come to Australia with a vaudeville group as a banjo-strumming comedian. His star turn was an act called 'the Death of Willie'. This was a send-up of the craze for singing cowboys. Harry Griffiths, 'Young Harry' of the Mo McCackie days, recalls:

> Bob could stamp his foot and sing—the Martins and the Coys they were reckless mountain boys—there was no doubt about it when he told a gag— whack! You know, there was no uncertainty about anything he ever did.
>
> We had a big variety show once; Dick Bentley, Roy Rene—all these people were in the show—and Dyer was on and he did his bit. When he came off the boys were all sitting there in the chairs looking at him, and as he walked toward them through the curtains he said: 'Well, I may not be the funniest comedian in Australia, but I'm the loudest.' And Roy Rene said: 'Yeth, you thed it, pal.'

Dyer liked Australia, stayed, and was soon into radio. In those frenetic early days he relied heavily on the comedy tricks he had learned in vaudeville. It was 'slapstick radio', designed as much for the eye as the ear; and the reason was that the audience was there, packed into the auditorium, to see those radio shows being made.

The Jack Davey style was almost the opposite to Dyer's; Davey's strength was in his verbal wit, and his optimistic, ad-libbed humour was the most familiar sound on radio for nearly 20 years. It is said that, while his quick wit went straight to the point, it rarely hurt anyone. He was a master at extracting humour from other people, turning the joke away from them, and yet somehow scoring points for the result. A typical exchange is recalled by Lew Wright:

Top: Jack Davey, an entertainer and writer of boundless energy, was one of Australia's biggest names in radio for 20 years, particularly during the 1950s. His style of humour was based on quick, verbal ad-libs. Bottom: Davey with contemporary, Bob Dyer, a lifelong friend, who began his comic life as a Tennessee hillbilly in vaudeville.

He said to a boy contestant: 'What is a brazier?' [A brazier is a pot with glowing coals in it which is used for a soldering iron, and making morning and afternoon tea.]

The boy thought for a minute and said: 'Have I got to answer that one, Mr Davey?' And Jack said: 'If you don't, you don't get the pound!' It was 'Snatch and Grab'.

The boy said: 'I'll cop hell when I get home, but it's that thing that holds a woman together.' Jack said: 'Together, or apart?' And away they went again, you see? The audience loved it. But he turned the humour back to people themselves. He had an innate confidence in people themselves.

Davey's mark was entertainment, making people laugh. And his golden voice was money in the bank. At his peak he commanded five million listeners a week, and even if you missed his shows the voice was there in commercials for everything from electric shavers, to aspirin and radio valves. He commanded a healthy income, but his personal extravagances cost more. Big boats like *Sea Mist*, and fast cars like his famous D-type Jaguar, became his trade mark. He gave away huge sums of money to people in need, and some not so desperate. While he was known to buy silk pyjamas for all the patients in a pensioners' home, he might also tip a drink waiter £40 at a time.

For himself he gambled heavily, entertained in lavish style and generally seemed hell-bent on trying to out-do his own playboy image. In the book *The Jack Davey Story*, there are dozens of 'Daveydotes' and this is typical:

He always thought and acted big. Like the time he was going to do a show for the Wool Bureau and he haggled with the Macquarie Network for six months about how much he was worth. He wanted £500 a week and he fought and fought until he got it. When they finally agreed, he charged them £5 a week, but he'd had to establish that he was worth £500 before he'd agree to it.

Davey headed his own radio production unit; writing, producing, directing and starring. At the same time, the American radio king Art Linkletter boasted of making 32 shows a year. Davey had made 680. His personal motto was: 'Bite off more than you can chew, and chew like buggery.'

But if Davey was the gallivanting bachelor, Dyer was the devoted married man. In fact, his life was really a double act with the ubiquitous

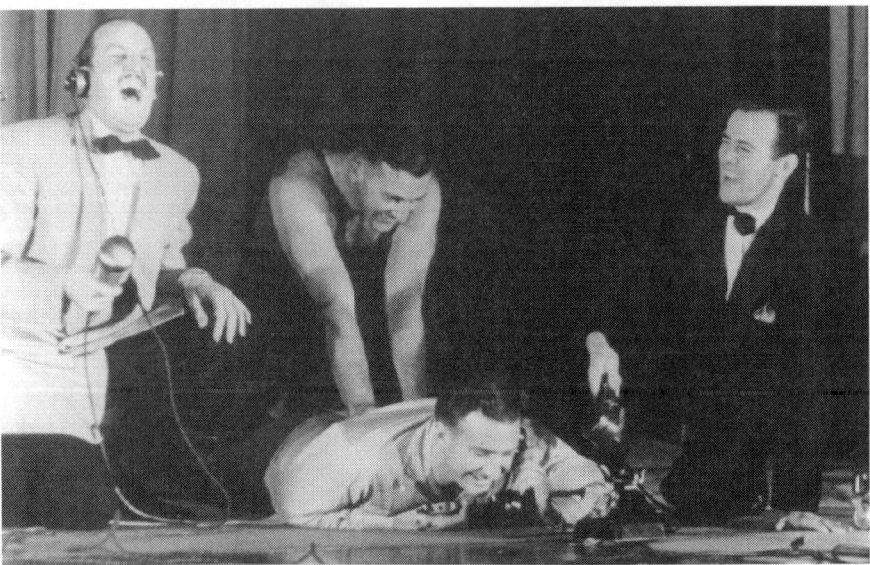

Top left: Such was Jack Davey's frenetic 'work hard, play hard' life that he died at only 49 years of age. Around 150 000 fans gathered for the biggest funeral in Sydney since the death of Billy Hughes. Top right: Unlike Davey, Bob Dyer made the transfer from radio to television successfully. Bottom: A stunt on Bob Dyer's 'Can You Take It?'.

Dolly Mack. By the 1950s, Davey and the Dyers controlled the airwaves, and they revelled in it. They were so unassailable they could indulge themselves in friendly public rivalry; playing practical jokes on each other, putting each other down, even appearing on each other's shows.

However, while Davey was keeping up his playboy image all over town, it was really Bob and Dolly who were having the good time. Davey was now a sick man, and while the Dyers travelled the world chasing sharks and marlin, Davey was in and out of hospital. The combination of 'cigarettes, whisky and wild, wild women' were taking their toll, and Davey was hospitalised nine times in the next seven years.

When he died, more than 150 000 fans packed the streets to watch the cortège pass by; the biggest funeral Sydney had seen since the death of Billy Hughes.

Bob Dyer's career, on the other hand, still had a decade to run. Whereas Davey had failed on television, Bob and Dolly took to the new medium like marlin to water. Dyer understood television. He had the voice, the stagecraft and, above all, an astute business brain. Bob and Dolly owned everything they ever did, and they knew how to sell it. And, unlike Davey, Dyer knew how to pace himself. Having quickly made his mark in television, he decided to change his style almost immediately:

> I ceased being an entertainer after the first year of television. I found that being an entertainer was too much, too much of a demand. It ate up too many people and put too many people in their graves and insane asylums, so I started being myself and became what I would call an entrepreneur. I'm not an entrepreneur, I'm a showman. And being a showman is being myself; engineering things and deciding situations such as a quiz show, which I used to look down my nose at. Quiz shows in vaudeville? I wouldn't be in it. I thought anybody can ask questions and give money for correct answers, but there's more to it than meets the eye.

Dyer was an entrepreneur, an electronic circus ringmaster, and now and again he discovered a star who would help carry him through yet another year of his many years at the top of the tree. One was Barry Jones, destined to become Australia's Minister for Science and President of the Australian Labor Party, whose bumptious mastery of the quizzes kept millions of Australians spellbound. Here's a typical exchange:

*Dyer*: Who was the first British Governor-General of India?

*Jones*: Now, there are two ...

*Dyer*: His name?

*Jones*: Now, it could be either Canning or Mountbatten, because Canning was Governor-General of India in 1858 and Mountbatten was Governor-General of India in 1948. Now it could be either of these two.

*Dyer*: One of those two, ah?

*Jones*: Mmmm.

*Dyer*: Ah, the first ...

*Jones*: You mean with the actual title of Governor-General of India? The former Governors-General were called Governor-General of Bengal, and earlier of course, the first Governor-General of Bengal was Warren Hastings. But he was only Governor-General of Bengal. He was in effect (laughter) Governor-General of India. He only held the title of Governor-General of Bengal ...

*Dyer*: Customers, I find myself in a dilemma.

While Dyer might have been the loudest stage comedian, on television he knew how to hang back. He played straight man to the waspish Barry Jones, who left the show with more than £58 000 in cash and 'Pick-a-Box' prizes and left his hosts that much wiser and richer.

Dyer's work in the 'Pick-a-Box' and 'BP Super' shows earned him an OBE in the Queen's honours, and in 1971 the television industry honoured him with its highest award, a gold Logie.

## NORMAN, HOGES, EDNA AND BEYOND

Australians love to laugh at themselves. For decades now, Australian audiences have queued up to be knocked down, to have their own failings and pretensions thrown back at them—even down to the colour of the water in their toilets, which in this country is invariably royal blue.

At the top of this tradition is Barry Humphries, perhaps the cleverest comic of all. Humphries is both uproariously funny, and at the same time acerbic, a viperish wit whose characters punish the audience as much as they amuse and entertain it. Humphries' most successful character, 'Dame Edna', is a combination of everyone's mother and mother-in-law. She envelops her audience, confides in it and scolds it—a mixture of mum and malevolence:

*Question*: Is there anything of your mother in Edna?'
*Answer*: Well, that depends what you mean. (pause) I suppose there is something of my mother in Edna. (longer pause) I used to think there was a lot of my mother in Edna. (wicked pause) That was until I met your mother.

Edna, who was made a 'Dame' by the Australian Prime Minister Gough Whitlam during his cameo appearance in the movie *The Adventures of Barry McKenzie*, but has now slyly renounced the Damehood in deference to the coming of the Republic, is Humphries' most durable and most successful character. Some have come and gone, but among the other notables is 'Bazza' himself, who was actually created for a comic strip in the English satirical magazine *Private Eye*; Sandy Stone, the suburban returned soldier now appearing as a ghost; and Sir Les Paterson, former Labor Minister for 'the Yarts' and Australia's roving cultural attaché.

The Arts community, and particularly its penchant to dip into government subsidies, is a favourite target for Humphries. When one, for example, went to dinner with one of his trendier creations, Neil Singleton, and asked directions to the bathroom, the reply was, 'Second past the Whiteley on the left.'

Dame Edna, the matriarch for all Australians, is really a little over 40 years old. Humphries tells how she was born:

Well, Edna began not as a monologue, but a very real character with whom I feel very little personal affinity at all, except that from time to time I find traces of Edna's make-up on my collar in the mornings.

But Edna started as one half of a dialogue, a two-handed sketch that was written in 1956 at the time of the Olympic Games in Melbourne. At that time, I was working in a repertory company in Melbourne. The director was Ray Lawler, who, in his spare time, was hatching *The Summer of the Seventeenth Doll*, which was presented later that year. Ray suggested that for the Melbourne Theatre Company's presentation of the Christmas pantomime, or review, Noel Ferrier and I do a sketch together in which Noel interviewed me disguised as an Australian housewife.

Left: Edna Everage, before
she became a megastar.
Made a 'Dame' by Prime
Minister Gough Whitlam,
she has since become a
Republican and returned to
plain 'Mrs'. Edna is one of
Barry Humphries' most famous
and enduring characters.
An Australian matriarch,
she is a mixture of mum
and malevolence. Below:
Humphries in an interview
with the author.

The reason they decided that I would be good as an Australian housewife was because we'd been on tour with *Twelfth Night* early in that year and, between country towns, each member of the cast tended to improvise, sing songs, recite, just to while away the boring hours on the bus. One of the things I did rather well was a falsetto, and my falsetto could frequently be heard from the back seat of the bus imitating the lady mayoress of the next country town we were going to. She would invariably make a speech over the lamingtons, thanking everyone for 'doing' Shakespeare so wonderfully and bringing culture to their country town.

Ray said: 'You know, you ought to do that character on stage.' And I said: 'I could do the voice from the wings and one of the girls could act it, you know.' He said: 'Oh no, you ought to do it yourself. We'll dress you up as a housewife.'

Dame Edna may be a figure of fun, but she does not tolerate fools gladly. However, as long as Humphries creates characters who continue to give offence, his success is assured. His audiences love to be insulted by him, and his style is now so assured that no-one would dare step into his stiletto-heeled shoes to challenge his position as the doyenne of our comedians.

But there have been other Australian 'anti-hero' comic stars who have made fortunes from our capacity to laugh at ourselves. Paul Hogan, 'Hoges', achieved wealth and success on television by reviving the stock cliché of the brash battler—the ocker working-class hero with a modicum of guile and wit. In a real life rags-to-riches scenario, Hogan was once a rigger on the Sydney Harbour Bridge and was literally discovered through a 'New Faces' talent quest. He went from there to becoming a larrikin commentator on Mike Willesee's current affairs television show, then on to a successful comedy television career of his own, and eventually into movies where he still holds the claim for the most successful Aussie flick ever, *Crocodile Dundee*.

Just like Barry Humphries' creations of Barry McKenzie, Les Patterson and Lance Boyle, and Ross Higgins' character in 'Kingswood Country', Hogan was the apotheosis of the ocker that many middle-class and newly sophisticated Australians found somewhat embarrassing, and he compounded their fears by becoming in the 1980s Australia's major international selling tool for tourism worldwide. In his highly successful television commercials spruiking the joys of down under, Hogan had to commit a few little cultural travesties

Top: Back where he began. Comedian Paul Hogan was a rigger on the Sydney Harbour Bridge when he took part in a talent quest that triggered his meteoric rise to television and movie stardom. Bottom: During the 1970s, Paul's character, Hoges, typified the ocker working-class hero who had a modicum of wit—and guile.

such as chucking a 'shrimp' on the barbie. No Australian had ever called a prawn a shrimp, but it seemed a small trade-off when the tourism dollars started to pour in. The Americans had to perform similar translations for Paul's character Mick Dundee; but in general, the irreverent gusto of the movies remained undisturbed and indeed was the major reason for their success in a stultified market place.

Humour today means television; a monster that chews up a year's worth of material in a single night. One of the medium's most original and successful talents is actor Garry McDonald, who created a unique comic character in Norman Gunston, and who had further success with the television show 'Mother and Son'. Gunston, the little Aussie Bleeder, revived an era of humour that had lain dormant since the 1920s, 'the theatre of embarrassment'. He's been described as a symbol for the inspired amateurism of Australia as a whole: a naive walking disaster who doesn't even know it.

His deliberately awkward interviews had us aching with laughter—not just at Gunston, but at the international stars who had little clue about how to read him. Among those totally bewildered were Mick Jagger and Burt Reynolds. Sally Struthers, on the other hand, was totally 'corpsed' and laughed so much even Norman was thrown. At a press conference for the superband, Kiss, Norman was there as part of the gallery. Answering another interviewer's question, Gene Simmons mentioned something about when the band 'hit the road' as part of being on tour. Gunston stood up to address his question to Gene, 'Ah, did you hurt yourselves?' After some awkward silence from the band members, he embellished, 'When you hit the road, did you hurt yourselves?' As usual the conference disintegrated.

Comedy has many casualties but an act, having passed first base, can be remarkably durable. Mo dominated stage and radio for decades, Barry Humphries has entertained a couple of generations, and so too has Daryl Somers with 'Hey Hey It's Saturday'. It started as a Saturday morning kids' show but it was so full of naughty double entendres for the parents that it moved to prime time. During three decades, Daryl and his collection of desperadoes have commandeered Saturday nights with a live mix of riposte, repartee and rank jokes from a team including Ozzie Ostrich, Dicky Knee, John Blackman and Red Symons, the hiss-boo vaudevillian villain who judges the 'Red Faces' segment, which lets anyone have a go at television.

Garry McDonald, creator of the little Aussie Bleeder, Norman Gunston, reflects on the success of another Australian comedy icon, Mo McCackie. Not strictly a comedian but a brilliant comedy actor, Garry has played Mo on stage and lived with his alter ego, Norman, for three decades.

Australians seem to have a soft spot for amateurs—Paul Hogan is the best example but more recently 'The Footy Show' has shown that any mug can get a laugh, particularly if he wears a dress. 'The Footy Show' caters for the Falstaffian end of the market, even down to the fart jokes, and at the other end of the spectrum we've been treated to the incredibly sharp and witty Andrew Denton and the totally off-the-wall Doug Mulray.

Their forebears, who laid the groundwork from both these extremes of the market, were comedy pioneers like Gordon Chater, Ronnie Frazer, Noeline Brown, Carole Rae and Barry Creyton—the former Phillip Street Revue team who gave us the classic 'Mavis Bramston Show'. As with all old comedy, its slapstick now seems rather tame and its political satire rather lame, but in the context of its era, the 1960s, it was outrageous, shockingly funny stuff. Among the many performers who cut their teeth at Phillip Street was Reg Livermore, who for 10 years was almost as big a name as Barry Humphries on the comedy stage.

It's not surprising then that, given all these ingredients, Australian television was used as the springboard for a plethora of skit-based comedy shows during the 1980s and 1990s such as 'The Big Gig', 'D-Generation', 'The Comedy Company', 'Full Frontal' and 'Fast Forward', to name a few. Symptomatic of the changing nature of comedy was the fact that by far the most popular character spawned by 'The Comedy Company' was Mark Mitchell's Con the Fruiterer. It's said that an ethnic group has fitted comfortably into its larger community when it has no trouble laughing at itself and certainly this has been one of the most distinctive highlights in the evolution of Australia's modern comedy.

'Wog humour' has been one of the great comic success stories. In much the same manner that Barry Humphries decided to hold a somewhat cracked mirror up to Australian society in the mid 1950s, by the time the 1980s came around Australia's Greek community was ready for some of the same treatment at the hands of two of their own in Mary Coustas and Nick Giannopoulos. Initially, Nick had tried to become an actor by a more traditional route, auditioning for *Romeo and Juliet*:

> But I was told by a director that I didn't look right and I said to the director, 'Did you know Romeo was Italian?' And he said, 'Oh yes, that's right ... I think you're right, but we ... still ... our Romeo's got to be blond-haired and blue-eyed.' I said, 'No, that's Hamlet.' (laugh) So it was tough.

Top left: Hung Le, comedian and one of the boat people who can remember when 'the war came into our living room'. Top right: 'The Comedy Company' cast send up '60 Minutes'. Bottom: 'The D-Generation' spawned stars such as Marg Downey, Rob Sitch, Michael Veitch and Magda Szubanski.

Then he hit upon the idea of something closer to home:

> 'Yeah, that's exactly right—I was the Barry Humphries of the late 1980s ... Barry Humphries used to do Dame Edna to the Dame Ednas; well, I was doing the Spiros, the Petroulas, the cleaning lady and the cab drivers ... to those people I was putting up a mirror and showing them what their lives were like in this country—that whole way that we live within two cultures.
>
> And that's when the show really started to take off. That's when it became very satisfying for me because all of a sudden I had people who looked like my parents in the audience laughing at this material ... *Wogs Out of Work* ran for three and a half years and about 650 000 people came to see it, which was incredible ... and that was only two families!

The theatrical shows in turn spawned the highly successful television show 'Acropolis Now', but if the wogs had had their turn it was also time for the ascension of the women comics. If Dame Edna is the epitome of the 1950s housewife, then typical Australian females from later decades were expertly exemplified by Magda Szubanski (Chenille the depilatory artiste), Jean Kittson (Candida), Maryanne Fahey (Kylie Mole), Marg Downey, Rachel Berger, Wendy Harmer, Elizabeth Gorr (Elle McFeast) and Jane Turner.

Yet we have not forgotten that it is the people themselves who create our most current and often most everlasting humour. 'Where do they come from?' is the question most asked about jokes, after all. And the answer is from the pubs or more accurately, the people. It can be spoken, or even written on walls in the tradition that dates back to the cavemen. We have had some wonderful graffiti—perhaps the most famous example, possibly apocryphal, occurring outside a Melbourne Church. The local reverend had written on his noticeboard: 'What would you do if Christ came to Hawthorn?' And someone wrote underneath: 'Put him at centre forward and shift Peter Hudson to the wing.'

Keith Dunstan argues, in fact, that we have always been better at written rather than spoken humour, which may or may not be true. Certainly, the great Aussie tradition of humour of words has been continued in more recent times by the 'minimalists'—men who are not exactly comedians but say very funny things such as John Clarke, Rampaging Roy Slaven and H.G. Nelson (John Doyle and Greg Pickhaver), and Andrew Denton.

In the long run it is, of course, impossible to make generalisations about humour, even this one. Not even a familiar ambience will allow a joke to travel through one era and out the other and yet there is something about certain thoughts and situations that seem to make all Aussies laugh.

Tell you what. Why don't I tell you another joke and if you laugh, well, you probably are an Aussie. Stop me if you've heard it …

This one is about a natty little gent who rolls into a country bar in Queensland and orders a gin and tonic. The locals in the corner of the pub delegate one of their number to go to check out the blow-in.

'G'day mate,' says the local introducing himself. 'So, what brings you up these parts?'

'Well actually,' says the city slicker, 'I'm a taxidermist.'

'Oh, yeah?' says the local suspiciously. 'And what have you been doin' around here?'

'Well, I've had a simply wonderful week. On Friday I managed to stuff a very large red kangaroo, and on Wednesday I found a wonderful specimen of the hairy nosed wombat which I've also stuffed. And tomorrow I plan to stuff one of your marvellous emus.'

'Oh … well … I'd best be getting back to me mates,' says the local.

When he returns the group, they are keen to know. 'What's his story then?'

'Well,' says the delegated one. 'He reckons he's a taxi driver … but I reckon he's a drover like the rest of us.'

That, of course, takes us back to the beginning and the bush. But what of the humour of the future? Well, perhaps that's embodied in a new breed of comedians such as Hung Le, who arrived here as one of the Vietnamese 'boat people'. He said: 'People say that Vietnam brought the war into people's living rooms—yeah, you're telling me, and we didn't even have a television.'

In fact, Hung Le's family lived right opposite those gates of the Presidential Palace that the world saw being smashed through by tanks during the fall of Saigon. Life for Vietnamese refugees has not been all beer and skittles and perhaps this is why during the 1990s we are seeing a new genre of humour that's both funny and poignant, with just a tinge of bitterness. Hung Le: 'How do you know when a Vietnamese guy has robbed your house? Your dog's gone and your homework's done.'

# War...

## AUSTRALIANS AT WAR

Before Australia's baptism of fire at Gallipoli in 1915, we didn't beat around the bush when it came to ideas of bravery.

'How'd you like to win a VC?' said the recruiting posters, as though we were going to an armed version of the Olympic Games.

Indeed, if it weren't for the terrible cost in human lives, an outside observer could almost be excused for thinking that Australians actually like going off to war. Every generation since Federation has had its own war to fight and die in—we were even at war before the loose collection of colonies was unified as a nation in 1901. Not surprisingly, the exploits of Australians at war have formed a major part of our international reputation.

In all, Australian forces have been involved in a dozen conflicts ... Taranaki, New Zealand ('Maori Wars'), Sudan, Boer War, Boxer Rebellion, China, two world wars, Malaya, Korea, Indonesian confrontation, Vietnam, the Gulf War and Timor. Australia has several hundred peacekeeping personnel stationed around the world, including Israel, Lebanon, Syria, Sinai, Bouganville, East Timor, former Yugoslavia, former Macedonia, Kuwait, Mozambique, Cambodia, the United Nations headquarters, and Seoul.

## COUNTING THE COST

It has been said that Australia really came of age through war; that although we became a nation in 1901, we did not gain international status until we signed up for 'the Big One' in 1914. That may be true, but at what cost?

Left: Australian servicemen have been involved in a dozen wars.

Only one in three men
who went to the First World
War returned unharmed.
Just two decades later,
Australian women again
watched their menfolk depart
for far off battlefields.

At the Australian War Memorial in Canberra, the roll of honour lists 102 389 names of Australian men and women who died in our many wars, from the Sudan in 1885 to 1972 when we left Vietnam. That's a pretty high price to pay for taking our place among nations.

The loss of life during the First World War was staggering. Of the 330 000 who embarked for overseas service, more than 200 000 were killed or wounded; a casualty rate of 66 per cent compared with 51 per cent for the British Isles.

Why the diggers suffered disproportionately is still a matter of conjecture. It could be wrongly concluded that they were simply not very good soldiers—and certainly the young nation of Australia, only officially 14 years old, was inexperienced in the ways of war—but then there's also a lingering bitterness that the Colonial forces were used somewhat as cannon fodder in a series of disastrous campaigns like Gallipoli.

It seems, too, that Australia, which even called itself 'the little boy among the nations', was anxious to prove its worth in the international club. Certainly, the diggers impressed the Allies with their bravery, their cockiness and their independent egalitarian spirit. The British General, Sir Ian Hamilton, said this of the Anzacs:

> It was the physical appearance of the Dominion soldiers—Colonials as they were then called—that captivated everybody who came to Anzac Cove, and there is hardly any account of the campaign which does not refer to it with admiration and even a kind of awe.

And from the passionate pen of Scottish writer, Sir Compton Mackenzie:

> ... their tallness and majestic simplicity of line, their rose-brown flesh burnt by the sun and purged of all grossness by the ordeal through which they were passing, all these united to create something as near to absolute beauty as I shall hope ever to see in this world ...

In August 1914, Australia responded to the news that the Empire was at war with a spontaneous outburst of patriotism. Today, we tend to forget that the original 'diggers' made up an entirely volunteer army. Around Australia, converted passenger liners were packed to the gunwales with cocky young

In 1915, Australian and New Zealand soldiers—Anzacs—landed on the little-known Turkish peninsula of Gallipoli. Ten thousand died there during the eight months before their withdrawal. The events of Gallipoli, however, didn't stop the Australian soldiers from wanting to fight overseas during the First World War. In all, 330 000 left Australia. More than 200 000 were killed or wounded.

"The Australian and New Zealand troops have indeed proved themselves worthy sons of the Empire."
GEORGE R.I.

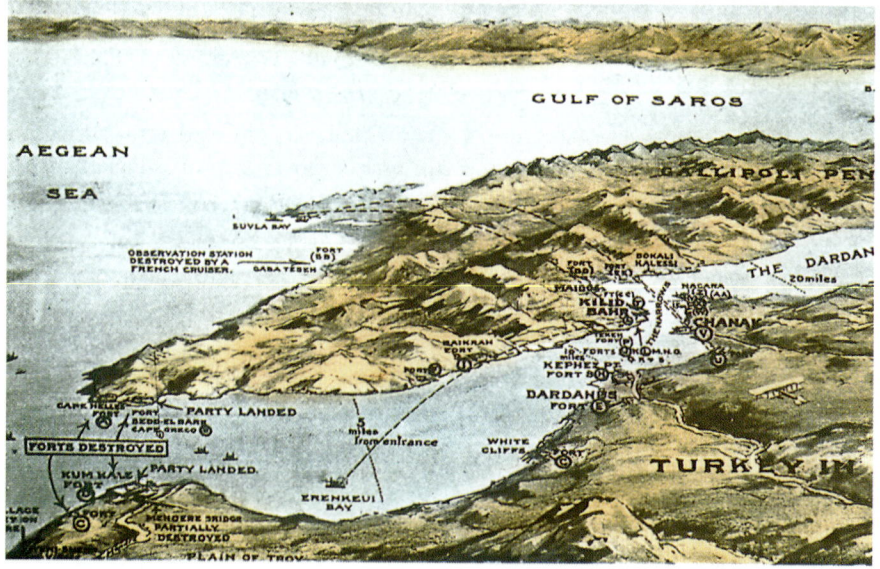

soldiers ready to steam across the equator. For weeks those ships were their parade ground, horse stables and barracks.

Patsy Adam–Smith, author of *The Anzacs*:

> You stood on the sidelines and you cheered and you called out: 'You're going to your baptism of fire.' They didn't know until then that a baptism of fire took off an arm and a leg, and sent a man mad.
>
> You see, Gallipoli didn't really stop them. The casualty lists—well, they expected it and it showed what Australia could do. But France was different. Those hideous casualty lists—and by this time the men were writing back and telling them what war was like.

Paradoxically, as the machinery of war has become infinitely more destructive, with a single warhead capable of inflicting as much damage as an entire battalion of men armed with rifles, the casualty lists of our fighting men have actually decreased. Twice as many Australians went to the Second World War as the First but the casualties were relatively fewer. The war in Vietnam lasted as long as the two world wars combined, with only a fraction of the total casualties. By the time we got to the conflict in Kuwait in the 1990s, despite the awesome barrage of missiles and potential possibilities for total devastation, the Australian force suffered no casualties at all.

## CONSCRIPTION

By 1916, most of the young men who wanted to fight, and who were old enough, were already overseas. After the horrifying death toll at the Somme in France, Great Britain was demanding that we supply even more men for the war. In England, Australia's new Prime Minister, Billy Hughes, agreed to send more troops. But the only way to swell the Army's ranks was to introduce conscription. Back home, Billy Hughes faced two hurdles. The trade unions and his Labor Party were implacably opposed to conscription. Hughes decided to take the issue direct to the people in the form of a referendum. With the Establishment press behind him, he was absolutely confident of victory.

'The Little Digger' launched his 'Vote Yes' campaign, fighting his opponents in typical style. Hughes branded them 'scabs' and 'blacklegs'. He

"I'LL HAVE YOU!"

In response to Great Britain's plea to its Empire for fresh troops to fight the First World War, Billy Hughes agreed to send reinforcements. In 1916 and 1917 he tried to introduce conscription to get the numbers. He failed to do so.

ordered soldiers to break up anti-conscription meetings, often sparking violent street fights. This heady period of Australian politics culminated in the celebrated 'Warwick eggs' incident in the town of Warwick in Queensland, where the Prime Minister was campaigning for the 'Yes' vote. From Melbourne *Argus* writer, Lloyd (later Sir Lloyd) Dumas:

> The moment the Prime Minister stepped from his carriage, he was surrounded by a mob. They commenced hooting and groaning and hurling vile epithets at him. An egg thrown from the crowd just missed him. A second one, better aimed, broke upon the Prime Minister's hat and knocked it off.
>
> Fists were flying everywhere, and the Prime Minister was in the thick of it striving to get at the man who had assaulted him. Mr Hughes was hustled and jostled by men twice his size ... but the Prime Minister was daunted by nothing.
>
> He demanded assistance from the police in apprehending the man. Although Mr Hughes demanded in his capacity as Attorney-General of the Commonwealth that they should take action against his assailant, Senior-Sergeant Kenny declined to do so, declaring that he recognised the laws of Queensland and would act under no other.

This particular incident led Hughes to form Australia's Commonwealth Police Force. For half a century, until a shot was fired at opposition leader Arthur Calwell lacerating his chin during another conscription row, 'the Warwick eggs' event represented the summit of political violence in Australia.

Through two referendums, Hughes fought tooth and nail to convince the people to vote 'Yes'. But he met his match in the fiery Irish Catholic Archbishop of Melbourne, Dr Daniel Mannix. The anti-British Dr Mannix addressed public meetings attended by hundreds of thousands of people throughout the country. He attacked Hughes at every opportunity, arguing that the European conflict was in reality a 'sordid trade war', and that Australia should not conscript its sons for 'cannon fodder'.

Hughes had the entire Establishment press on his side, and used propaganda material including cartoons depicting Belgian women with their breasts cut off by 'the filthy Hun'. He also invoked the Defence Act to suppress the huge flow of anti-conscription pamphlets, magazines and newspapers.

Billy Hughes' two conscription referendums, in 1916 and again 1917, were both knocked back by the Australian public. Two major anti-conscription agents were the Irish Catholic Archbishop of Melbourne,    Dr Daniel Mannix (top); and the melodramatic poster titled 'The Blood Vote' (bottom), released at the time of the first referendum.

Pro-conscription propaganda posters during the First World War increasingly played on fear and guilt—powerful emotions. Billy Hughes, with the Establishment press on his side, even used propaganda material depicting Belgian women whose breasts had been cut off by 'the filthy Hun'.

One of the most effective weapons for the 'No' voters turned out to be a melodramatic poem. This ballad persuaded most women, and many men, to vote 'No'. It was called 'The Blood Vote':

Why is your face so white, Mother?
Why do you choke for breath?
O, I have dreamt in the night, my son,
That I doomed a man to death …
They gave me the ballot paper,
The grim death-warrant of doom.
And I smugly sentenced the man to death
In that dreadful little room …

Perhaps the poem tipped the balance. On 28 October 1916, Billy Hughes' conscription proposal was defeated by a narrow margin. Undeterred, he mounted a second referendum in 1917. He lost yet again, this time by a more substantial majority.

Twenty-five years later, John Curtin, the young anti-conscriptionist who had authorised publication of 'The Blood Vote' in 1916, became the Labor Prime Minister of Australia. By a strange irony he would in fact be the man who would eventually introduce conscription to Australia.

In the Pacific campaigns of the Second World War, Australian forces looked pitifully small alongside the massive United States armies led by General Douglas MacArthur. As the war came closer to home, to New Guinea and then to Darwin, John Curtin began to believe that our purely volunteer army was no longer adequate. Curtin spoke to the nation:

Clearly and specifically every human being in this country is now, whether he or she likes it, at the service of the government to work in the defence of Australia. For no longer shall this government appeal, it shall order and direct.

Curtin's message was that Australian men were to be conscripted for military service. Australian law allows for the compulsory enlistment of men into the Army only in the event of a direct threat to Australia. Curtin interpreted this to include the Pacific war zone. With the Japanese closing in, Australians this time accepted conscription without quarrel.

Top: Prime Minister John Curtin (seated, right), seen here with American Pacific campaign leader General Douglas MacArthur, was the one who eventually introduced compulsory conscription to the Australians during the Second World War—an irony because he, in fact, was the young anti-conscriptionist who gave the approval to publish 'The Blood Vote' in 1916. Bottom: The next time Australians were dragooned was in 1964, under the instrument of Menzies' national service. Soon after, Australian conscripts were being sent to the Vietnam War, a war against which thousands of people protested.

In 1964, when Sir Robert Menzies re-introduced a form of conscription, he brought in new legislation and renamed it 'national service'. There was some criticism from the Labor party and the trade unions, but to most Australians it seemed that 'a dose of Army discipline' would not hurt our young men. Within a few months the Australian Army, conscripts included, had joined the Americans in Vietnam.

But not every young Australian was prepared to accept that fate. Simon Townsend was the most prominent of a small band of people who decided to take their opposition to conscription before the courts. As a conscientious objector, Townsend refused to obey his call-up orders. He found himself a prisoner in solitary confinement living on bread and water in an Army prison.

It took three years, one court-martial and five civil court cases before a Sydney magistrate in June 1968 finally decided that the Simon Townsend's objections to military service were indeed conscientious.

Townsend told me that among the 'tea chest' of letters he received was a selection of venomous correspondence:

> In a small bundle there were 22 hate letters. They were quite extraordinary: white feathers, a silver bullet with my name scratched on it. Really vile letters that made me realise that people, who'd never met me, hated me so much they would have preferred to see me dead.

It was November 1972 before conscription and Australia's involvement in Vietnam was finally halted by the incoming Labor Government. But it was too late to save the lives of young men like 21-year-old Private Errol Noack. In 1966 he was one of the unlucky winners of a national lottery when his birth date was drawn out of a barrel and he was conscripted into the Army and sent to Vietnam. Just 10 days later, a sniper's bullet ripped through his stomach as he was washing in a creek. Private Noack became the first of 187 National Servicemen to die. Ironically, we had managed to win the First World War without conscription, then lose Vietnam with it.

Australian diggers have always volunteered to fight against nations that they believed to be a threat to freedom, but Australians have shown that for more than 50 years they will not easily accept the concept of compulsory enlistment. Future governments will surely think twice before introducing conscription again.

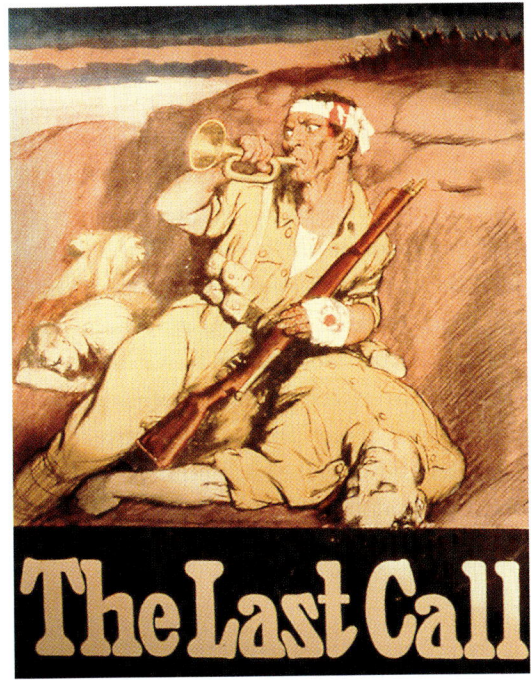

**The Last Call**

Left: *The Last Call*, one of Norman Lindsay's propaganda posters. Bottom left: Englishman John Simpson Kirkpatrick (standing, right) joined the Australian forces in Perth and was sent to Gallipoli. He used donkeys to take wounded Anzacs through the treacherous Shrapnel Gully. Within a month he had rescued hundreds of men, until he was shot. Simpson was not awarded the Victoria Cross for his brave and selfless acts; however, he was commended. It is his image that appears on the Anzac medal (bottom right).

## THE DIGGERS

Exactly how the Aussie digger came by his legendary name is a little obscure. Of course 'digger' dates back to the gold diggings and the Battle of Eureka Stockade, but how it came to be the universal word synonymous with the Australian foot soldier is not recorded—for a start it doesn't apply to personnel in the Navy and the Air Force. Most likely it seems that the diggers saw themselves as simply the 'shit kickers', infantry who dug the trenches of the First World War, and often their own graves; tough fighting men who, throughout their history, died for causes that were never quite their own. Almost invariably they fought other countries' battles and on other peoples' soils. Whatever its precise origins, the word digger, and its diminutive 'dig' is synonymous with mate. Prime Minister Billy Hughes was immensely proud of his nickname 'the Little Digger', but no doubt Rupert Murdoch is not so enamoured with his sobriquet 'the Dirty Digger'.

Interestingly, Australia's most enduring hero of the First World War was not an Australian. He didn't receive a Victoria Cross, and he didn't even carry a gun. By today's military standards, he might even have been court-martialled for desertion. John Simpson Kirkpatrick was a young British adventurer, sailing the world on a steamship. When war was declared, he went ashore in Western Australia and joined the Australian forces to fight overseas. At training camp, Simpson, as he called himself, proved a bit of a larrikin. He played jokes on the other men, and made friends with the camp dogs. He loved animals and even carried a possum on board the troop ship.

Simpson was assigned to the Third Australian Field Ambulance. When he stepped ashore at Gallipoli on 25 April 1915, he was the second man off his boat. The first and third were killed beside him. That initial confrontation with death in the Dardanelles had an immediate effect on the young man: he disappeared and was reported missing.

By the next day, Simpson had been found. He was walking through Turkish sniper fire leading a donkey that carried wounded men from the frontline carnage back to the medical team on Anzac Beach. He had not even bothered to join his unit. In just 25 days, 'the bloke with the donkey' became a legend.

Simpson had found his first donkey 'Duffy' on the beach. They defied death to run their one-man ambulance service, working all day and half the night. The wounded who couldn't walk were straddled across Duffy's back, while Simpson helped other diggers to limp to safety.

Another stretcher bearer at Gallipoli, Mr N.W. Faulkner of Melbourne, remembered him:

> He was a law unto himself. He just did it on his own. He got killed eventually. He was an absolute target for the snipers. It was bad enough when you had to get yourself under cover, but you can't put a donkey under cover very well.

By 19 May Simpson had rescued hundreds of men and acquired a second donkey. That day, he stopped for breakfast before starting his trek through 'Shrapnel Gully'. Breakfast wasn't ready, so Simpson said: 'Never mind, get me a good dinner when I come back.' He was returning through the gully with the two donkeys and two wounded men when he was shot through the heart by a Turkish sniper. Simpson was only 22 years old. The next day, Colonel John Monash wrote from Anzac Beach to the Australia–New Zealand headquarters:

> I desire to bring under special notice the case of Private Simpson. Private Simpson and his little beast earned the admiration of everyone. Simpson knew no fear and moved unconcernedly amid shrapnel and rifle fire, steadily carrying out his self-imposed task.
>
> Enquiry solicited that he had belonged to none of the units of this brigade. He had become separated from his own unit, and had carried on his own perilous work on his own initiative.

There were 66 Victoria Crosses awarded for service in the First World War, but nothing for Simpson. Why? Well, there are a number of reasons. One was that stretcher bearers in the First World War were not generally recommended for the VC for rescuing wounded because in doing so they were only carrying out their normal duties. Interestingly, though, the first VC awarded in Gallipoli was to a British stretcher bearer, Lance Corporal W.R. Parker.

It seems more likely that Simpson was a victim of bureaucracy—his citations did not go through the strict protocols and procedures as laid down in Recommendations for Awards, and it also seems that the fact that Gallipoli was a humiliating loss and not a glorious victory didn't help matters politically. Yet, his story of heroism has lived longer than any other. Today, Anzacs march with the image of the man and his donkey on their medals. To them, Simpson is Gallipoli.

Simpson's war was described as 'the Great War', 'the war to end all wars' but, less than a generation later, the courage of thousands of Australians was tested once more, sometimes on the same battlefields. More than 750 000 Australians enlisted for the Second World War and only 20 received the Victoria Cross. Of these, just 10 lived to tell the tale.

Sydney newsreel cameras filmed one of the heroes, Lieutenant Roden Cutler, 25 years old, when he arrived home on crutches after the 1941 campaign against the Vichy-French forces in Syria. The young officer had, on a number of occasions, distinguished himself by 'remarkable acts of gallantry', and saved the lives of the men serving under him. His VC citation reads:

This gallant artillery officer inspired the infantry to press on and his name became a byword amongst the forward troops with which he worked. At Merdjayoun on 19 June an infantry attack was checked after suffering heavy casualties from an enemy counter-attack with tanks. Enemy machine-gun fire swept the ground, but Lieutenant Cutler pressed a continuation of the attack. With another artillery officer and a small party he pushed ahead of the infantry and established an outpost in a house. The telephone line was cut. He mended this line under machine-gun fire and returned to the house. The enemy then attacked this house with infantry and tanks, killing Bren gunners and mortally wounding other officers. Lieutenant Cutler and another manned an anti-tank rifle and a Bren gun and fought back driving the enemy infantry away ...

Lieutenant Cutler then personally supervised the evacuation of wounded members of his party. Undaunted he pressed for a further advance ... With a small party of volunteers he pressed on until finally, with one other, he succeeded in establishing an out-post right in the town which was occupied by the Foreign Legion ... The enemy attacked and he was cut off ... He was forced to go to ground but after dark succeeded in making his way through enemy lines ... On the night of 23–24 June he was in charge of a 25-pounder sent forward to silence an enemy anti-tank gun and post, which held up our attack. This he did ...

Left: Sixty-six Victoria Crosses were awarded to Australians in the First World War, but only a handful were awarded for service in the Vietnam War. Bottom: One VC went to Keith Payne, who helped to save dozens of lives.

Later at Damour on 6 July, when our forward infantry were pinned to the ground by hostile machine-gun fire, Lieutenant Cutler, regardless of all danger, went to bring a line to his outpost when he was seriously wounded and 26 hours elapsed before it was possible to rescue him. His wounds at the time had become septic, necessitating amputation of his leg.

Sir Roden Cutler survived to become an Australian Ambassador to Washington, and later the 32nd Governor of New South Wales; indeed, the longest-serving state Governor in Australian history. He was always somewhat bemused by the whole idea of the VC, observing wryly that the citation didn't even mention the three machine gun nests that he'd single-handedly put out of action. He described his moments of personal heroism thus:

I was damn frightened, if you want to know. I think everyone is. If there is a dangerous situation and you can see some way you might rescue the people with you, then you act pretty quickly. You don't have time to sit and think. But, by jove, when it's getting pretty close to you, you're very frightened; and it's overcoming fear that really matters.

At the end of the twentieth century, Sir Roden is one of only three surviving men awarded a VC.

Perhaps because war has become increasingly technological, the notion of deeds of valour has diminished. While there were 66 Australian VCs in the First World War, when it came to Korea and Vietnam there were only a few —and yet who could argue the soldiers were not as brave?

Warrant Officer Keith Payne was in command of a Mobile Strike Force Battalion monitoring supply routes near the Laos border in May 1969. After the withdrawal of American heavy artillery, his battalion became isolated and surrounded on three sides by North Vietnamese troops.

Short on firepower, the Australians were pinned down. But on the third day, they made a desperate move. In the ensuing fire fight, the company was splintered, with some men left trapped and many of them wounded. Keith Payne modestly plays down his heroic efforts to return single-handed and rescue many of his comrades.

Keith was awarded the VC for his actions, which helped to save dozens of lives. Those grateful survivors are scattered to the four corners of the world, but when they have been reunited, it's clear those bonds will never be broken.

Yet if there was joy in reunion, it was at the end of a long and bitter road. The Vietnam veterans had returned from an unpopular war to a country divided over its own involvement. It would be two hurtful decades before Keith Payne and his fellow veterans finally received the welcome home they deserved.

## WAR IN OUR OWN BACKYARD

It was morning-tea time on 19 February 1942 when Australians at home had their first real taste of war. Darwin's telegraphist, Archibald Halls, was telling his counterpart in Adelaide: 'Wait a sec, there's another air raid alarm. I'll see you shortly ...' He never did. Halls was one of 10 people killed in the post office when the Japanese bombed Darwin, just three months after Pearl Harbor.

The Darwin attack was Australia's first experience of war on the home front and, like the Americans at Pearl Harbor, we didn't exactly distinguish ourselves with our preparedness. Despite a warning received at 9.30 a.m., the alarm wasn't sounded for another 28 minutes. By then Japanese bombs were ripping apart the large naval and merchant fleet anchored in Darwin Harbour. Two hours later, the bombers returned to attack the airfield. It was all over by lunchtime.

The toll was 238 dead, 320 wounded, eight ships sunk and 23 aircraft destroyed. And, after the raid—panic. By mid-afternoon, the main road out of town was crowded with cars, trucks, horses, bicycles, people on foot, and even a sanitary cart, as Darwin's population fled inland. Local wags dubbed the whole affair the 'Adelaide River Stakes', but to the authorities it was a matter of serious concern, which would lead ultimately to a Royal Commission. Many of those who did not flee, including service personnel and police, took to looting. An air-raid officer in Darwin at the time, Mr Ray Fosky, described the confusion:

> We were delegated to go and collect some rations, and we ran up against the police. They were more or less helping themselves. We couldn't challenge them. They had authority over us because everyone assumed it was martial

Japanese fighter bombers raided Darwin on the morning of 19 February 1942. On this single day, Darwin was hit with twice as many bombs as were dropped on Pearl Harbour, killing 238—the greatest single loss of life on any day in Australia's history.

Top: Sydney Harbour was raided by Japanese midget submarines on the terrifying night of 31 May 1942. The subs, transported by larger 'mother' submarines, snuck into Sydney Harbour and aimed torpedoes at the US warship *Chicago*. One mother ship surfaced at Bondi Beach and fired shells at Bellevue Hill and Rose Bay. Bottom: The Naval dormitory ferry the *Kuttabul* was sunk during the raid, killing 19 men sleeping aboard.

law, although it was never made very clear at the time. It wasn't until three or four days after that before things settled down.

Prime Minister John Curtin announced the Japanese raid on Darwin with the words: 'The government has told you the truth. Face it like Australians.' In fact, what we were told was often far from the truth.

Wartime censorship suppressed the horrifying casualty figures, and the panic which followed. Detailed newspaper reports of the raid were banned by the Federal Government and the full story of the Darwin raid would not be known until many years later.

A Royal Commission later investigated reaction to the raid. It discovered that groups of airmen were found up to 110 kilometres away, while one was 640 kilometres away and another covered 4500 kilometres to Melbourne in 13 days.

The official inquiry found that some Darwinites behaved shamefully during Australia's first encounter with the enemy on its own shores, but some sympathy must be extended to those who lived in a completely isolated outpost with poor defences, which was hit in a single day with twice as many bombs as were dropped on Pearl Harbor—a violent act which totally traumatised the United States and, indeed, dragged it into the war.

In fact, Darwin was bombed 58 more times and, during that period, the city of Sydney had its own visit from the Japanese Imperial Forces.

On Sunday night, 31 May 1942, three months after the first Darwin raid, the calm of Sydney Harbour was shattered by the sound of warfare. Searchlights swept the waters seeking a target. Shells whistled overhead and the crack of machine-gun fire was mixed with the muffled explosion of depth charges. Patrol boats criss-crossed the harbour trying to locate the enemy and co-ordinate a defence.

It was dawn before most people realised what had happened. During the night, three Japanese midget submarines had sneaked into the harbour. One became entangled in the submarine boom just inside the Heads and the crew blew it, and themselves, up. Another submarine was destroyed by depth charges. The third fired two torpedoes at the US cruiser, *Chicago*, moored near Garden Island Naval base. The torpedoes missed, but one blew up beneath the ferryboat, *Kuttabul*, converted to a dormitory for Naval ratings. Nineteen young men asleep on board were killed.

It was soon established that the 80-foot (25-metre)-long midget submarines were launched from a convoy of 'mother' submarines. Now there were embarrassing questions for the defence chiefs to answer: How did these larger ships cruise so close to our coastline, undetected and unchallenged? How adequate was the harbour's submarine boom if two of the three invaders could get through? While these questions were still being pondered, one of the mother submarines surfaced off Bondi Beach and calmly shelled the suburbs of Bellevue Hill and Rose Bay. Property values plummeted, but the only injury was to an engineer who'd fled Germany to escape Nazi persecution—his leg was broken as an unexploded shell landed on his bed.

After the war, Australian journalist Richard Hughes interviewed Ito Susumo, a Japanese pilot who flew over Sydney the night before the midget submarine raid. *The Melbourne Herald* published his report on 2 April 1949:

> ... a pack of six long-range 3330 ton Japanese submarines surfaced 35 miles north-east of North Head (at the entrance to Sydney Harbour). Three submarines carried a midget two-man submarine each. The other three carried a tiny scouting plane. Ito and his observer took off from their submarine at 3 a.m., just before moonrise ... 'I flew in over North Head and descended to 600 feet to fly up the harbour while my observer sketched the position of the boom and its entrance', Ito told me. He came down and flew over Farm Cove, skimmed towards the bridge, climbed again and circled over Cockatoo Island Naval base.
>
> Trying to get his bearings, he sought Mascot aerodrome. Mascot apparently mistook him for a friendly plane and turned on the landing lights.
>
> He flew back towards Farm Cove, observed a ship on the north side of the harbour and flew out towards the sea. He had been over Sydney for about 10 minutes ...

The midget submarine that blew up the *Kuttabul* was never found, but wrecked parts from the other two submarines were later assembled as one complete vessel. The 'submarine' was installed at the War Memorial in Canberra: the last relic of Sydney's night to remember. Two hours after the attack on Sydney another Japanese submarine fired 34 shells at Newcastle but damage was slight. However, during this period submarines sank dozens of ships along Australia's eastern seaboard.

## PRISONERS OF WAR

In the Second World War, thousands of soldiers saw only a fleeting glimpse of tanks and machine-gun fire. Their war became a battle of personal survival of another kind. They were the prisoners of war, who spent years 'behind the wire', often subjected to torture, starvation and disease.

There were many tales of utter horror. The last members of the Australian Army Nursing Service to leave Singapore embarked on the *Vyner Brooke*, which was bombed by aircraft and sank. Twelve sisters were lost at sea and 22 who surrendered to the Japanese were ordered to walk into the sea. They were machine-gunned, and all but one of them were killed. Thirty-two surviving nurses from the *Vyner Brooke* became prisoners of war in the Netherlands East Indies, where they suffered terribly. Eight more died before the war ended.

And yet, while the Second World War was responsible for 20 million violent deaths, some of its participants experienced miraculous luck. Melbourne taxi driver, Gerald Carroll, was one.

He went to the war on a whim. After a broken love affair he decided, on the spur of the moment, to leave his taxi and keys at his depot, told the boss to look after his cab until he got back, and enlisted. After three months in Crete, Private Carroll was taken prisoner and eventually sent to Stalag Luft 3, site of the famous 'wooden horse' escape. He was determined not to waste the time he knew he had to spend in the prison camp, so he set up a laundry service for well-off British officers too lazy to do their own washing. With no money on hand, Carroll operated on credit. He explained the method:

> The officers made out a slip of paper like a bank cheque and I gave it to the postal authorities. Through the German authorities, the letter would go to the Red Cross in Switzerland and then to the Commonwealth Bank in Australia House in London. They processed it through the officers' bank accounts.

After the war, Gerald Carroll went to London. 'I just fronted the teller and introduced myself. The bank account was there, and the figures were satisfactory.' When he returned to Australia, five years after he'd left, Gerald Carroll walked back into his old taxi depot, picked up his keys and went back to work.

Not many POW stories had such a happy ending. However, if the Japanese had it their way, we'd have believed their cruel camps were run like luxury hotels. In late 1942 or 1943, the Japanese made a propaganda film titled *Calling Australia*. It showed Australian POWs eating hearty meals and drinking beer, sunning themselves beside swimming pools and playing golf on the island of Batavia, site of one of the harshest POW camps in the war. No-one knows exactly why the film was made, or how a copy came to end up in Australia after the war. But the most curious question is: Why did Australian soldiers cooperate with the Japanese to apparently misrepresent their treatment? As yet, there is no official answer. With Australian voices used throughout the film, the script reads in part:

> Necessary commodities are supplied to us, not plentiful, but rationed enough to keep everybody going on a normal scale. Nevertheless, the boys need the extras such as cigarette lighters, a pack of cards or a bottle of beer.

And in another scene, two officers are playing golf:

> *First Officer:* Perfect! How do you do it?
> *Second Officer:* Constant practice still keeps me fit, sir.

Warrant Officer Adrian Knowles of Melbourne acted as an interpreter between the Japanese soldiers and the other Australian prisoners on Batavia. Mr Knowles said of a scene in *Calling Australia*, which shows Australians apparently relaxing at a mountain holiday resort:

> To get the people to go, the Japs said they were having a holiday camp for officers and they called for volunteers. On the face of it, it looked reasonable and some of the officers went. A meal was set forward, and before they could eat it, it was taken away. They would have become suspicious of course, but they'd committed themselves. What could they do? I imagine a lot of what they did and said was to reassure people back in Australia.

The film, which incorporates a background of 'Waltzing Matilda' and other familiar Australian sounds and voices, goes on to show officers sunning themselves in deck-chairs at the 'cool mountain sanatorium'. 'You are not

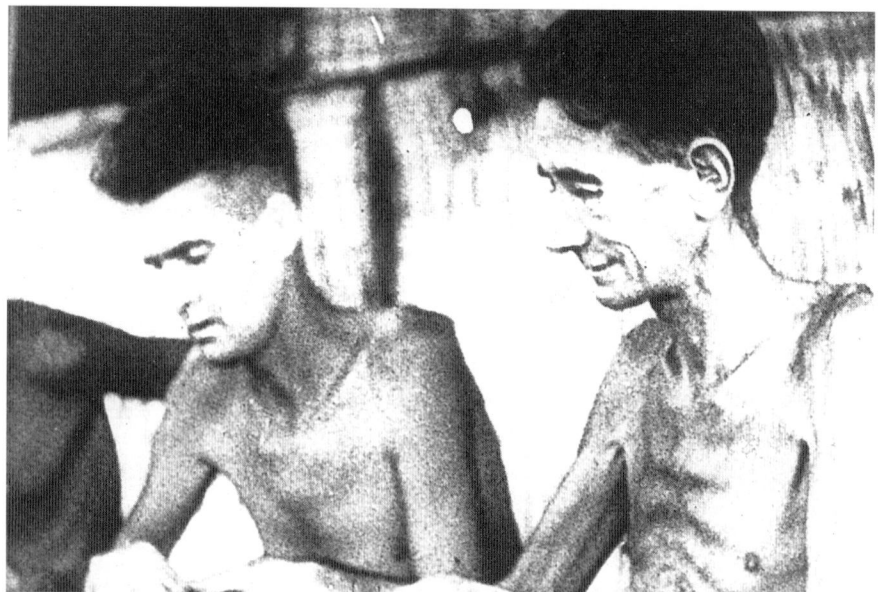

Top: Australians liberated from POW camps after the Japanese surrender in 1945. Bottom: A scene from the Japanese propaganda film, *Calling Australia*, in which Australian POWs spoke of their benevolent, even luxurious treatment, in a war camp in Batavia. It was a misrepresentation of life in the camp, and the reason for the film's existence is a mystery.

looking at a bungalow in Rose Bay,' the Australian voice says, 'though it is very much like it ... a real home for officers. This privilege, as stated in international law, is given only to officers who have pledged their word of honour.'

Overall the film is frightening in it persuasiveness. But for the fact that its Australian cast all have shaved heads, one might be excused for thinking that life in prison camps on Batavia was indeed 'all beer and skittles'.

But we know it wasn't, so how this film was made remains a mystery. However, there are even greater imponderables: Why was the film made at all? What purpose was gained in showing Japanese captors as noble and kindly souls? Was it made for audiences in Australia or Nippon? Only the Japanese who conceived and made the film know the answers.

The true story of the POWs in Asia is often too horrifying to recount. The raw statistics alone are terrible enough. In fact, one third of all Australians who died in World War II did so as prisoners of the Japanese. One third of all Australians who became prisoners of the Japanese died in captivity, while of the 7000 Australians held in Germany or Italy, only 242 died. And even then we considered ourselves lucky. The survival rate of the Australians was in some cases four times greater than that of other nationalities, partly because of the extraordinary tradition of Aussie mateship. The rule in the prison camps was that, 'No-one was ever alone. No-one ever died alone.' And how did anyone manage to stay alive at all? In the words of Tas Knight, a former member of the 2/40th, 'We had faith, you see, I was always convinced I was going home.'

## SHOOTING WITH CAMERAS

Australians at home watched the bloody battles of the Second World War through the eyes of newsreel cameramen. Much of our understanding of war was framed by the action films we saw in the picture theatres. They were shot by men like Damien Parer, one of the greatest war cameramen of modern times, who went bravely to the front lines carrying film instead of bullets. Parer's famous documentary film, *Kokoda Front Line*, won Australia's first Academy Award. Tragically, however, Parer never lived to see his 'Oscar'.

Damien Parer was born in 1912 in Melbourne, and grew up on the barren landscape of King Island off the Tasmanian coast. His father was a Spaniard, an artistic man who ran the local store and hotel to support his large family. His mother was an Australian of strong Irish 'gold-digging' stock, and deeply religious. This volatile mixture produced a man of extraordinary character.

By 1941, Parer was with the Australians at Tobruk as an official war cameraman for the Australian Government. In Libya, Greece and Syria he built a reputation for his films and the risks he was prepared to take.

War correspondent Maslyn Williams was Parer's friend and colleague. They covered most of their war assignments together:

> He browned me off, I can tell you. You'd say: 'Well, Damien, we're going—you know such-and-such has happened today and we've talked to the Intelligence Officer and the General and so forth.' And he'd say: 'Well, the best place to shoot this is there.' I'd say: 'But Christ, you'll get your head shot off if you do that.' And he'd say: 'No, where else would you go?' Just as simple as that. 'I've got to get the shots. I've got to be there.'

While *Kokoda Front Line* won Australia's first Oscar, the cameraman was never really happy with the final film. Within weeks he was back in New Guinea with his camera and the Australian soldiers he admired so much.

Parer prayed often, sometimes loudly, under fire. Yet the man's intense religiosity blended easily with his coarse Army 'language', and the soldier's 'vices' he loved so much. It is said of Parer that he never drank liquor before the war, and then, he never learned how. He poured himself anything from the bar and drank it in double time, which didn't help his gambling around the 'Slippery Sam' tables.

In New Guinea, Parer covered the slow retreat down the Kokoda Trail. Like the soldiers, he had to throw away his personal belongings to lighten the load. He even threw away one of his cameras but he held on to the precious film that won the 1943 prize.

As much as Parer loved filming the war, he hated the more mundane propaganda assignments back in Australia that were also part of his official work. His handsome, tanned face and his encouraging speeches in the newsreels were familiar to most Australians, so when he decided to join the Americans there was wide criticism.

Maslyn Williams agreed with Parer that he should have been allowed to keep his talents for the battlefield. Williams said:

Left: Damien Parer, a great war photographer, who revered the Australian digger. His recording of the Japanese retreat along the Kokoda Trail, called *Kokoda Front Line*, won Australia's first Oscar in 1943. Parer was shot dead while recording American soldiers in action in the Pacific during 1944. Bottom: Scene from Parer's film taken in New Guinea in 1943.

He loved the Australian digger. Quite frankly, I'm a snob and I don't like the Australian digger. But Parer literally loved Australians, those boozy fellows with a can of beer.

He said what great men they were, and it broke his heart to work with the Americans. He did it because the peanuts who were running our organisation would not let him do what he had to do.

The Americans literally had more cameramen than they could use, but they could see Parer was in a class of his own and they offered him complete editorial freedom. He was with the marines when they invaded the island of Guam. He followed the tanks in their advance from the beach, filming the infantry in amazing close-up. Four American cameramen were killed in that bloody combat, but it did nothing to stop Parer.

Often he filmed from ahead of the American lines and, in getting those scenes, he was more exposed than the men he was filming. Parer wanted to be in front of the front line, to have the soldier's face on film, a technique he'd discussed with Maslyn Williams. Williams said:

I wouldn't have a bar of it. He said the best way to film a war was to get between the two combatants and get the reactions from both sides. A nice idea, but …

Just before Parer left to join the Americans in the Pacific, he confided to one of his brothers:

I think that before the war ends I will die if I continue taking photographs the way I am doing. I feel that it's my duty to try to portray the truth and the honesty, the justice and the beauty in the soul of every soldier that dedicates his life to fight and, if necessary, die for his country. I will go on taking photographs the way I know I should, even though I die taking them.

Parer died just two weeks later on 17 September 1944, when the marines landed on the island of Pelelieu. He was racing across open ground when a machine-gun opened fire from a Japanese pillbox about 18 metres away. Bullets ripped through his chest killing him instantly. He was 32 years old, and had been married just six months.

In total, Australians have spent about a quarter of the past century at war, and who knows where in the future? It is impossible to say through the stories of just a few individuals what war has meant to us as a nation, how it has affected the collective psyche. It would be encouraging to think that this young nation would not find itself embroiled in another war. Nevertheless, our attitudes to war have changed. Our feelings are summed up by Sir Roden Cutler, VC:

> Most of us have reacted against war. We don't like it. We think it's senseless, and I think people express this view in many ways, one of which is this changed attitude towards what we were brought up on: deeds of derring-do—you know, 'the thin red line' and all that sort of stuff. That's gone out of fashion long ago, and I think rightly so.

# Sport...

## THE AUSTRALIAN OBSESSION

The English observer, Jonathan Aitken, wrote: 'Sport is the religion of Australia, and Saturday is the day of worship. Gallup Polls indicate that two-fifths of the population play some sport regularly, and that three-quarters of the population watch it.' That might have astounded an Englishman, but most Australians are more likely to be wondering what the remaining quarter have managed to find to do with themselves.

## SWIMMING

As a race, Australians are so besotted with our swimming prowess it's a wonder we haven't started to grow fins. Yet it was an Englishman who introduced us to the art of social swimming, and a Solomon Islander who taught us 'the Australian Crawl'. The history of swimming in this country is in part the story of the amazing Cavill family. Fred Cavill, a former British Navy man, was a self-styled 'professor' of swimming, whose list of distinguished pupils included the future Queen Mary.

In the early 1900s he came to Australia and set up baths at Lavender Bay in Sydney Harbour. On a trip home soon after, he won his fourth medal for bravery —leaping into the sea to rescue a woman passenger who tried to drown herself. Cavill also had the dubious honour of posing as the torso for a statue of King Edward VII before coming back to Australia to continue his remarkable career.

Cavill had nine children, most of whom became Australian or world swimming champions. Two of his sons died in strange circumstances: one was

Left: Cathy Freeman is Australia's athletic heroine of the 1990s.

frozen to death while trying to swim Seattle Harbour, the other was killed by poisonous gas during an underwater demonstration in baths in California. Dick Cavill, another son, was the first man in the world to swim 100 yards in less than a minute, and Sydney St Leonards Cavill invented the butterfly stroke. A grandson, Dick Eve, was the only Australian to win an Olympic gold medal for diving.

Australia's first Olympic gold medals for swimming were won by Freddie Lane in Paris in 1900. Lane was an exponent of a style called 'the Trudgeon Kick', a frog-like stroke which would soon be swept aside by the Australian Crawl. It seems extraordinary now, but the two events that he won were the 200 metres freestyle and, believe it or not, the 200 metres obstacle race. This was an event organised by those who obviously thought swimming was a bit too easy. It consisted of going over and under rowing boats and needless to say it was never held again after those 1900 Olympics. The 200 metres freestyle was included in the 1904 Games but did not surface again until 1968 when Michael Wendon won. Perhaps because of his training in the obstacle race, Freddie went on to become a sprinter.

The Crawl was introduced to Australia by Alick Wickham, a teenage schoolboy from the Solomon Islands. Wickham thrilled Australians with his daring aquatic displays, including '200 foot dives'. He beat all rivals with his Islander's style of crawling across the water. The stroke caused a sensation and was quickly adopted by other swimmers, including Arthur 'Tums' Cavill, who introduced it to the Americans.

At the 1912 Stockholm Olympics, Australia's Fanny Durack became the first woman in the world to win an Olympic gold medal. By 1920, the swimming hero was Frank Beaurepaire, who held every Australian title from 200 metres to a mile. Beaurepaire is better remembered for the tyre company which still bears his name, and for rescuing someone from the jaws of a shark.

In 1924, the great Swedish swimmer, Arne Borg, was brought out to Sydney, at the age of 22, to swim against Australia's new champion. He was Andrew 'Boy' Charlton, only 16 and already a giant, blond lifesaver. He seemed to swim mostly with his arms, which were more powerful than other men's legs. The organisers of the Borg–Charlton clash packed 7000 fans into the old Domain baths. Moss Christie, a 1924 Olympic swimmer, recalled Charlton's victory over the Swede:

Left: Freddie Lane (centre) the first Australian swimmer to win an Olympic gold medal, at the 1900 Paris Games. Bottom: Swimming sensation Andrew 'Boy' Charlton, who won Olympic gold and bronze medals, also in Paris, in 1924. Boy Charlton Pool in Sydney's Domain is named after him.

After the race, Borg put Charlton in a boat and rowed him up and down the baths calling: 'Boy is champion.' Of course, the crowd just cheered and cheered. It was fantastic.

When Charlton got on the Manly ferry to go home, he couldn't get off. All the people were on the wharf at Manly. They crowded around so much, they had to get the police.

At the Paris Olympics that year, Charlton proved his potential by winning a gold and bronze medal from older, more experienced champions like Borg, Johnny 'Tarzan' Weissmuller and Duke Kahanamoku, the Hawaiian who introduced surfboard riding to Australia.

Despite his success, Charlton was often a reluctant racer. He never won an Australian title because, at the time of the championships each year, he was jackarooing up near Gundagai. After the 1932 Olympics in Los Angeles, Charlton 'retired' to live on a sheep property. He died in 1975, aged 68.

It was more than a quarter of a century before Australia saw a new breed of swimming champions, triggered largely, of course, by the incentive of the first Olympic Games in the Southern Hemisphere in Melbourne in 1956. The great Murray Rose for example—good looking, charismatic and always fascinating, particularly when he revealed to a conservative Australian public of the 1950s, whose most exotic culinary experiment was putting a bit of Kraft cheddar on their Vegemite toast, that part of his training regimen involved the partaking of seaweed. Other swimmers who thrilled the nation were the Konrads kids—one of the early examples of multiculturalism at work. John and Ilsa Konrads actually learned to swim at a remote migrant camp near Wagga in New South Wales.

Born in Latvia, the youngsters astonished Australia by both breaking their first world record while only 15 and 13-years-old. They held records between 200 and 1500 metres and we were quick to claim them as our own.

But always one length ahead of the pack was Dawn Fraser; a 'tomboy' of the 1950s who could thrash all the boys at the local pool. When coach Harry Gallagher saw her, he commented that her swimming style was 'rough' and so were her manners. Gallagher took two years to persuade 'the wild kid' to join his squad. Dawn began training early in 1955. In just 20 months she was ready for the Olympics.

Top: Swimmers John and Ilsa Konrads, who broke world records at the ages of 15 and 13 during the 1950s. Bottom: Dawn Fraser, the only swimmer to have won three Olympic gold medals for the same event, the 100 metres freestyle—in consecutive games in Melbourne in 1956, Rome in 1960, and Tokyo in 1964. In trouble for souveniring an Olympic flag from a hotel's grounds while in Japan, she was suspended by Australian officials for 10 years.

The Fraser legend began before a delirious home crowd in Melbourne in 1956. Dawn, then 17, won the 100 metres freestyle in world record time. She won it again in Rome in 1960 and again in Tokyo in 1964. Dawn Fraser is the only swimmer to win three Olympic gold medals for the same event.

But, behind the scenes, trouble was brewing. In Rome, Dawn fought with officials, refusing their dress and swimming instructions. Her subsequent ban from touring (despite a written apology) left her in tears. Then, in Tokyo, she was caught 'souveniring' an Olympic flag from what the press described as 'the Emperor's Palace' but this is what happened in Dawn's words:

> I wasn't with the Australian team when I stole the flag ... and I had permission to leave the village to go and stay at the Imperial Palace Hotel, and of course still today, you know, people say it was the Imperial Palace, they forget the word 'hotel'.
>
> We'd had a few drinks and we were daring and one of the guys said, 'Come on Fraze, we're going to go out and get a souvenir flag.' So we did.
>
> They made a film later on and they had a scene in it where they had the girl running through the palace ... Well, that wasn't so ... No one could get into any palace in the world because of security.

Dawn injured her ankle trying to make good her escape. Hiding her pain, she led the Australian team in the closing ceremony. And in another bizarre twist, the Japanese authorities later presented her with an Olympic flag. Perhaps they'd hoped to save her further embarrassment.

When the team returned to Sydney, Dawn crossed the tarmac in a wheelchair. But there'd be no sympathy for the wounded campaigner. There were many old scores to settle—and the Australian Swimming Union suspended her for 10 years.

> I didn't have an opportunity of going to the Swimming Union and stating my case ... I was just trialled and sort of slaughtered if one can use that word ... my career was finished. My husband and I had talked about it that I was going to try out for the next Olympic Games, and I felt I could have done that.

Even without another Olympics, Dawn would be the greatest swimmer ever. But will we ever know just how great? 'I feel sorry for Australia, because we could have won another gold medal.'

Today, Dawn Fraser is more than just a name to Australians. She's been everything from a publican to a politician and she represents qualities many of us would like to claim: sporting prowess, a healthy disregard for officialdom and, above all, the courage to say what she believes. No swimmer since has generated quite such a public affection. The fact that, for 10 years, she swam faster than any woman, and most men, in the world, is icing on the cake.

Whenever a youngster starts making some impressive times down at the local pool, even today people ask could this be the next Dawn Fraser? Seven years after Tokyo, it seemed as though we'd found her. Shane Gould was very much an unassuming sporting hero, with her shy smile and modest manner. But in the pool she was lethal. At one stage, she had the amazing distinction of being world record holder in every distance from 100 to 1500 metres.

Born just a day after the opening of the Melbourne Olympics, by the age of 15 she was destined for stardom at the 1972 Munich Games. Shane was to compete in a gruelling five individual events and a relay, and stunned the world by winning five medals—three of them gold—in world record time. It was the greatest ever performance by an Australian at a single Olympics—but then it was over. What happened?

I always looked for meaning. I asked, I questioned myself when I was 16: 'What does this all mean? What does it mean to be an Olympic champion, to be an Australian hero, Australian of the Year?' I didn't find any meaning in material things. I'm very satisfied that I've achieved things. I'm very proud that I've represented Australia. I'm very honoured to be Australian of the Year, but I always knew there was something more.

Still a teenager, Shane quit swimming, married, moved to Margaret River in Western Australia, and virtually disappeared from public gaze:

That very extreme intense involvement with swimming and competition and the public life—I needed something to balance it so went to the opposite extreme, and the hippy movement and an alternative lifestyle—the counter culture—was around at the time, so I dropped into that.

More than 20 years later, Shane emerged from that soul searching, lending a hand to a new generation:

The Olympic spirit is not so much the winning, it's the struggle—not the victory but the struggle to get the victory. My Olympic medals really don't matter much to me—the actual physical thing—but what matters to me is what I've learned because of them that's what's important.

Despite her early retirement, Shane's achievements were an inspiration to a new breed of Australian world champions: Tracey Wickham; 'the Mean Machine'; Duncan Armstrong; Susie O'Neill; Ian Thorpe; and of course, Kieren Perkins. Anyone who thinks that Kieren was just a little boy who drank milk is wrong:

I had this great aversion to putting my head in the water, you know, face down, and the coach used to walk along the edge of the pool with a broom and sort of keep pushing my head under as we were going along and they weren't pleasant memories I have to say. And it got to the point where we'd learn with these big foam kick boards and every few weeks you'd progress along and he'd break it in half, so you'd have a little bit less kick board to float with, until it got to the point where I had, like, an inch-square piece of foam. But I wouldn't go near the water if I didn't have that piece of foam in my hand.

Kieren says he was influenced by swimmers such as Tracey Wickham and the feats that she achieved in the 800 metres freestyle, and he was inspired by the three successive Olympic gold medals of Dawn Fraser.

But no-one who hasn't lived the life of a long-distance swimmer can possibly understand how tough a life it can be, and the heart breaks and the disappointments that can come even after you've reached the exalted heights of Olympic gold:

Well, I was, you know, for a number of reasons, myself and my family had gone through hell in the lead up to Atlanta just with the negativity and 'He can't do it.' 'He,' you know, 'he's past it,' and this, that and the rest of it. No matter how much you like to ignore it, it does have an effect. And it may not have an effect on you individually but the people around you—they still read it and they get upset because they love you and they don't like to see people saying nasty things about you and that causes stress and anxiety.

It's true that pretty well everyone had written off the great Kieren Perkins, who'd struggled to get to Atlanta and made it by the skin of his Speedos. All the more triumph for him when he thrilled Australia in that mighty race:

> When I hit the wall I was happy for myself and proud because I'd overcome a lot of setbacks and difficulties going into that race. I think I was happy that I'd vindicated the support the people had for me—they probably got more joy out of that gold medal than I did and that's great.

Thanks, Kieren. I think you're right.

## TENNIS

In 1899, a young Harvard student called Dwight Davis asked his wealthy father for a silver cup as the trophy for a tennis match he was organising between his American friends and some visiting Englishmen. Davis won his first cup in 1900. But by 1907, a combined Australasian team had joined the contest, and that year 'the Davis Cup' made the first of many visits 'down under'. Young Dwight said later that had he known how his idea would grow he would have asked his father for a gold trophy.

Norman Brookes, the first Australian to win Wimbledon, helped to win the 1907 Davis Cup, and captained five more winning sides. He was called 'the Fox' because of his uncanny anticipation. Brookes successfully played forehand and backhand strokes on the same side of his racquet, using what the British called 'the colonial grip'.

Brookes was a sombre, poker-faced fellow who played even on scorching hot days dressed in long trousers and heavy woollen cap, dabbing away with his flat-topped racquet, which he continued to use long after they were out of fashion. Legend has it that he sipped champagne between particularly gruelling sets to keep up his strength. Brookes' international acclaim started a frenzy of tennis playing at home. Australian 'liberated' women in full Edwardian costume came out in the mid-summer heat, to play one of the few games they were allowed to play against men. The tennis court became as familiar as Ayers Rock, and often the surface wasn't much better.

But Australia's dominance of the tennis world early in the century did not continue. Dozens of other countries became just as passionate about the

Top: Mixed doubles and dog. Tennis is still one of the few games where women play with and against the men. Bottom: Poker-faced Norman Brookes, legendary champagne drinker between sets, was the first Australian to win Wimbledon in 1907 and he helped Australia and New Zealand combined to win the Davis Cup.

sport, and just as skilled. It wasn't until the 1930s that Australia produced another enduring international great, 'Gentleman' Jack Crawford, a beautiful stylist on and off the court. In 1933, shorts were all the rage at Wimbledon. But Gentleman Jack wasn't the favourite of Queen Mary for nothing. Aged a mere 25, he announced he would have none of the new-fangled fashion, and in long 'creams' he stepped on to the court to win the title before the Queen.

Crawford was the great champion of his time, but it was Harry Hopman, another player of the 1930s, who would influence Australian tennis perhaps more than anyone else. During the next 20 years, the canny tennis genius coached 14 Davis Cup teams; discovering, urging and orchestrating talents like 'the terrific twins' of the 1950s, Lew Hoad and Ken Rosewall.

Hoad and Rosewall first played each other when they were 10 years old in an exhibition match in Sydney. An old newsreel film of the match shows Rosewall wearing the little 'security' cap that was his trademark for many years. The score in that first clash was Rosewall d. Hoad 6–0, 6–0.

'The twins' as the press called them later, were nothing alike. Hoad was built like a locomotive. Rosewall was tiny but, in one of those nice Australian ironies, it was Ken who was always called 'Muscles'.

Hoad and Rosewall won a Wimbledon doubles final by the time they were 17, and they were clearly Australia's hope to win back the Davis Cup. On the eve of the 1953 challenge, the two juniors beat the Americans Vic Seixas and Tony Trabert in the New South Wales championships.

But the Cup challenge matches would not be so easy. After three rubbers, Australia was down 2–1. On a treacherous, rain-sodden court at windy Kooyong, Lew Hoad, the kid from Glebe, played the match of his life to equal the score. It was a heart-stopping affair. Hoad, playing for the first time with spikes, fell over often, broke strings on his racquet, and generally had the crowd on the edge of their seats. He eventually beat Trabert in five sets. Rain stopped further play and Rosewall had a sleepless night waiting to play Seixas. He won brilliantly the next day. It was a victory even the laconic Rosewall will never forget:

When the match was finished, after four days, to see all those cushions being thrown into the centre of Kooyong stadium was really something.

And then the inevitable. The Americans were turning professional and if Hoad and Rosewall could beat the best of the Yanks, then they must be worth money too. Within weeks the lucrative cash offers were flowing in; yet they both declined.

Lew went into the Army and the newspapers and newsreels followed the all-Australian boy in khaki. The cameras were out again in 1956 for Ken Rosewall's marriage to Wilma McIver. With his new responsibilities, Rosewall decided to turn 'pro'. Hoad joined the professional ranks too and played in epic series like the 100-match tournament against Pancho Gonzales before trouble with his back forced him out of the professional game. Ken, however, looked as though he would go on forever. Hoad said of Rosewall:

I used to think it was an ego thing with Ken—to prove that he could beat all the up-and-coming guys. But I think that he just basically loves tennis.

In reply, Rosewall told me:

Well, I think everybody has got to have some kind of ego. It helps you keep pushing yourself along.

Both Hoad and Rosewall were a credit to tennis. In the 1950s they were criticised for letting the amateur side down, but they bore the 'name calling' with dignity. They had their futures to consider and it paid off.

By the end of the century, Rosewall was still a hero to younger players and a god for any man over 60 and still playing. Lew carved himself out a very comfortable living with a picturesque tennis ranch in Spain but he contracted Leukaemia and died of a heart attack in 1994. He was only 59.

In 1961, another Australian sporting legend was discovered when Mr Bill Kurtzman, president of the tennis club at a small Riverina town called Barellan in New South Wales, told some talent scouts for Sydney coach Vic Edwards about a promising nine-year-old part-Aboriginal girl who seemed something of a prodigy. The little girl, named Evonne Goolagong, started her tennis training by seeing how many times she could hit a ball against a brick wall.

With parents who were not too well off, Evonne had to borrow her racquets, but after she had become the most improved player in the club,

Mr Kurtzman gave her her own. Edwards was delighted with his find. In his words:

> All I could see with the girl was the keenness and the movement and the rhythm. Stroking is quite easy to build if you have all that and she seemed to have that. Also there was another reason. Evonne was part-Aboriginal, and I had in my early days been in the back country, and I always felt that if you could find somebody like this in that race, with their natural movement and so on, you could develop. I think that had quite a bit to do with it.

In a move which brought him some criticism over the years, Edwards virtually adopted the little girl from the country and soon she was making headlines. The press was amazingly prophetic, predicting even when she was 12 that she seemed set for a Wimbledon victory in 1970. Another glimpse into the future came when Evonne could barely see over the net. She met and had her photograph taken with the great Australian tennis champion Margaret Smith (later Court).

In 1971, Evonne met Margaret in the most prestigious tennis event in the world, the Wimbledon singles final. Goolagong defeated Court 6–4, 6–1. She'd be runner up in 1972, 1975 and 1976 and win it again in 1980. She also won the Australian Open three times, the French Open, the Italian Open and the US Indoors. She married Roger Cawley and went to live on Hilton Head in South Carolina to run their private club called LTFG (Looks Terrible Feels Great), but over the years she's spent much of her time travelling between the United States and Australia, where she now lives in Queensland.

There's no question that Evonne, with her easy charm was probably the most popular of the Australian tennis players, particularly with the English press who in those pre-politically correct times described her rather embarrassingly as, 'the chocolate drop darling'. But there is also no question that Margaret Court was the greatest player we ever produced. The second woman in the world and the first Australian to achieve the Grand Slam (French, Australian, Wimbledon and the US Open). She won the singles, doubles and mixed doubles of every major championship in the world, including three Wimbledon, seven US Opens and 11 Australian Opens—the latter seven times in succession.

Top: Margaret Smith (later Court) meets 13-year-old Evonne Goolagong (later Cawley). Court's record was extraordinary even by world standards. Bottom: Later, Evonne herself would claim Wimbledon victory, first against Margaret in 1971 and again in 1980 against Chris Evert-Lloyd.

In many ways she was the antithesis of Evonne, who'd come from the outskirts of a tiny country town. Margaret moved in the right Perth circles. She married the son of the Western Australian Premier, Sir Charles Court, a bastion of conservative politics and white middle-class Australia. She always gave much of the credit for her success to her faith—a devout Christian she experienced charismatic renewal during a visit to Perth by evangelists of the Pentecostal Church—a factor which did not go unnoticed by her opponents as she calmly worked on what seemed to be a level above everyone else.

As far as the Aussie men were concerned, after Hoad and Rosewall there was Sedgman and McGregor and Newcombe and Roche who thrilled Australians in those years when the Davis Cup, like the Ashes in cricket, was really only a contest between a super power like the United States or Britain and our little country with something to prove. All were great players, particularly Newcombe, who won three Wimbledon singles championships and six doubles with Tony Roche. He also won the US singles twice and the doubles three times and the Australian singles twice and the doubles five times, but after this exciting period in the 1960s and 1970s, Aussie tennis experienced something of a drought, alleviated by Pat Cash's single Wimbledon win in 1987 and the continuous success of the doubles champions, 'the Woodies', Todd Woodbridge and Mark Woodforde.

It would take the arrival of Pat Rafter in the 1990s to restore Australian tennis to its former glory. Rafter's two dogged wins in the US Open, and his thrilling 'It ain't over till the fat lady sings' performances in the Davis Cup, have inspired a new generation of players in a game that has become infinitely tougher and now involves well over 100 countries.

You can cop an argument in any pub in Australia about who's been the greatest Australian player this century. For example, Roy Emerson won more tennis titles—including 12 Grand Slam singles matches and 16 Grand Slam doubles matches—than any previous player. He was ranked the world's No. 1 as far back as the mid 1960s.

But despite the greatness of others, from Brookes to Rafter, most of the experts seem to agree that the best ever was a tiny, red-headed bloke from Queensland named Rod Laver, 'the Rockhampton Rocket'. If he wasn't the greatest, he was certainly the first player to win a million dollars on the circuit, and the only player ever to win the Grand Slam twice, first in 1962 as an amateur, and then seven years later as a pro.

Right: The legendary left-hander, Rod Laver, who is the only player ever to win the Grand Slam twice, as an amateur and a professional.
Bottom: Tennis champion of the 1990s, Pat Rafter, who won the US Open in 1998 and 1999.

Laver was brought up on a cattle property west of Rockhampton which had a clay court. When he just 11, a coach named Hollis saw him play and took him to Brisbane. Laver was talented but so frail that Hollis taught him to carry a squash ball all the time and squeeze it, to the point where his left wrist eventually became noticeably bigger than the right.

It was that famous left arm which did all the damage—like the branch of a tree, dipped in molten metal. Apart from that, little Rod Laver never looked like a great athlete at any stage in his career. Off the court he could be just another Sunday slogger with zinc cream and hat. But he was uncannily fast, had extraordinary anticipation and a stunning range of top-spin shots upon which the modern game is based. After a very erratic start to his career he became the king of tennis in some vintage years. For his second Grand Slam he beat Ken Rosewall for the French title, John Newcombe for Wimbledon and Tony Roche for the US. Rod retired to the United States in 1976 with only fabulous wealth and success to remind him of his time at the top. In the late 1990s, he suffered a stroke during a television interview but recovered well enough to be seen only months later swinging a tennis racquet.

## BOXING

Boxing is one of the more bizarre sports still with us, a mixture of ballet and battery, blood and big money. The idea of 'a good stoush' has always appealed to Australians, but it wasn't until 1908 that we had our first real taste of the boxing big time. The Canadian heavyweight champion of the world, Tommy Burns, was challenged for the title in Sydney by the American Jack Johnson. Burns refused the fight on the grounds that Johnson was 'a Negro', but an offer of £6000, win or lose, helped Burns to overcome his racial objections and he was soon in training at Rushcutters Bay in Sydney.

Sydney promoter, Hugh D. McIntosh, who had turned a Chinese market garden into an outdoor stadium, sold 30 000 tickets, and hundreds who had paid 10 shillings or £1 for seats were turned away. McIntosh billed it as 'the fight of the century' and, considering the century had barely begun, this seemed like a safe prediction. But in truth it was a farce. Johnson stood six inches over the champion and was almost two stone heavier. He knew he was to get only £1500, so it must have given him some satisfaction to humiliate the champion.

Jack London, the novelist, who was in Sydney to cover the fight for an American newspaper, described it as 'an Armenian massacre':

> The fight, if it can be called a fight, was like unto that between a colossus and a toy automaton, and had all the seeming of a playful Ethiopian at loggerheads with a small and futile white man.

Eventually police had to stop the fight. Before Jack London left Australia he called on the white race to provide a champion to 'wipe the smile off Johnson's face'. But Australians wanted better than that, they wanted a home-grown champion. And soon they had one.

Les Darcy has often been described as the greatest fighter Australia produced. Gene Tunney called him the greatest middleweight of all time. But he was more than a boxer. He was this country's first real martyr of the twentieth century. Darcy was born in East Maitland, New South Wales, in 1895, the second of 11 children. His parents were poor and he helped support the family by working as a blacksmith.

By 1914 his spare-time boxing career had developed so quickly that his first fight in Sydney was the biggest event since the Burns–Johnson fight. He fought Fritz Holland, one of America's most skilled boxers, and when he lost after a controversial points decision, Darcy's followers tried to burn the stadium down.

Darcy went on to beat all comers but he had one tragic flaw in his timing: the time he chose to be champion. Just when he was ready to take on the world, it was falling apart. Australia was at war and some of his critics were asking what a strapping young man like Les Darcy was doing fighting at home for money when many young men were laying down their lives for practically nothing at Gallipoli and the Somme.

From then on the Darcy story has been clouded with emotion and mystery. He became a hero to many, particularly the Roman Catholic community, while others branded him a shirker and a coward. It must be remembered that the whole nation was split on the issue of conscription, and two referendums would barely resolve the argument. Darcy was on the verge of greatness and some thought he should be allowed to 'have a crack at a real title'. By this time he had beaten anyone they could send to Sydney but he knew the real champions were overseas.

According to Darcy's defenders, he had 'tried to do the right thing by his country'. He had tried to enlist, but his mother had refused on the grounds that he was still a minor. Whatever the truth, in the midst of bitter argument about Darcy's motives, he made a rash decision. On the eve of his 21st birthday, and in defiance of the War Precautions Act, which forbade people from leaving the country, he stowed away on a ship for America. The press, particularly the British press, were incensed. Their headlines screamed 'Darcy Bolts', but there were many Australians who cheered him on.

One who would defend Les Darcy at every opportunity was his younger brother Joe, who maintained that Les had become a political football:

> Others were getting passports to go overseas at the time—vaudeville acts, but the government refused Les repeatedly. He offered to go for six months and deposit £1000 here. He would return in six months and enlist. But this was refused.
>
> He became a political football, more or less … they offered him a captain's commission to go straight in as a captain in a recruiting campaign to go around the country as 'Les Darcy in uniform' and in this way get the youth to enlist. Now, he didn't want this, he didn't want to feel he was being in any way used just as 'bullet bait', as he said, for the war.

At first, Darcy was greeted enthusiastically by the Americans, and headlines predicted spectacular bouts with huge purses. But soon the doubts crept in. Where were the promised fights? Months passed, until Darcy was even forced to join a vaudeville troupe to make money. There is little doubt strings were pulled to prevent him fighting. The Australian Government could not afford to let him become a hero.

Then at last, in late 1917, it seemed that a fight had been arranged. Darcy went into training in the American deep south. There was excited speculation in the press. But Les Darcy never made it to the ring. Just days before the fight, he was taken to hospital in Memphis, Tennessee, where he died aged only 21.

The rumours of foul play and poisoning still persist, but the death certificate stated 'septicaemia' (and pneumonia), thought to have been caused by infected teeth loosened in an earlier bout. Darcy's cortège resembled a state funeral by the time it reached San Francisco. In Australia, 100 000 people viewed his embalmed body.

Top left: Les Darcy, boxing's legendary martyr. His career thwarted by the First World War, he stowed away on a ship to America in 1917. After failing to get a championship fight he became ill and died, aged only 21. Top right: Three-times boxing world champion, Jeff Fenech. Bottom: Bantamweight World Title winner of 1952, Jimmy Carruthers.

In many ways, Darcy's dilemma parallels that of Cassius Clay so much later: whether to choose his own destiny, or run with the mob to fight a distant war. Like Clay, Darcy decided to be his own man and, like Clay, he was left with an unofficial title. After Darcy's tragic death, it was nearly half a century before Australia had a boxer who could claim to be the undisputed champion of the world.

Like thousands of kids in the 1930s, Jimmy Carruthers, 'the Paddington Paperweight', started boxing in the Police Boys' Clubs. By 1946, he was New South Wales amateur bantamweight champion, and two years later he won the Australian title. Jimmy was going right to the top, but he would go right down again, too.

In the amazing World Title knockout of 1952, South Africa's Vic Toweel responded to the Australian's 147 blows with just one punch, and it missed. In a great Australian understatement, Carruthers said: 'I visited him in hospital later and tried to mag with him, but he was a bit browned off with me.'

Carruthers went on to defend his title, including an exotic bout fought barefoot in heavy rain in Thailand. Then he retired and put his money into a pub. It was a financial flop, and 10 years after his big fight, Carruthers tried to make a comeback. He put in some creditable performances, but never regained any of his former championships.

Jimmy Carruthers was a tough character and he bounced back again, this time to share his 'secret of success'. Natural foods had served him well in the good days and for many years before his death in the 1990s, Jimmy Carruthers' vegetable juice and health sandwich counter opposite Hyde Park was a landmark in Sydney.

The second Australian to win a boxing World Title, Lionel Rose, came from a vastly different background—the wrong side of the tracks—and how he dragged himself to the top from 'an atmosphere of booze and beltings' in the tin shacks at the end of Jackson's Track in the Gippsland bush of Victoria is inspirational. Lionel was the son of a tent fighter and the family of nine lived in absolute poverty—Rose recalls being hungry enough to eat a rabbit raw. At age 15, drinkers of the Warragul Hotel in Victoria chipped in a few dollars to send him away to further the one thing he'd showed promise at—boxing. In Melbourne he came under the spell of trainer, Jack Rennie and his wife, who in the manner of Professor Higgins and Eliza Doolittle, coached him in boxing, elocution, English and maths.

When he finally got a chance at the World Title against Japan's 'Fighting Harada', he had to accept a pittance in prize money and entered the ring a four-to-one underdog. The whole of Australia rejoiced when he won and then defended his World Title three times. For a while he organised his life and financial affairs well, but ran into many problems and his life since the triumphs of Tokyo in 1964 has been tinged with some tragedy.

So, too, with Johnny Famechon, our third boxer to win a world championship. Famechon lost only five of his 67 fights and successfully defended his World Title twice. After retirement, Famechon was severely injured when he was knocked down by a car but has bravely struggled to rebuild his body and his life and is still an inspiration to young fighters who remember the days when he was called 'a complete artist of the ring'.

Boxing, of course, is not everyone's cup of tea, even in sports-mad Australia. But few Australians fail to respond to that phrase 'I love youse all' made famous by Jeff Fenech, 'the Marrickville Mauler', who won three boxing World Titles. Fenech was a scrapper from the streets of working-class Marrickville in Sydney and became world champion within six months of turning professional. He defended his title three times, retired, played a few games for a second grade Parramatta Rugby League side, tried a comeback and retired again. As shrewd outside the ring as he was in it, Jeff now lives a comfortable life as a fight promoter.

## CYCLING

In 1928, more than one and a half million readers of a French magazine voted a young Australian cyclist, Hubert Opperman, 24, as the most popular sportsman in Europe. They loved his endurance, his loyalty and his eternal smile, although Australians at home joked that he had to smile because he didn't know what the French were saying.

On endless back tracks around Australia, 'Oppy' trained for the 1000-mile (about 1600 kilometres) cycling championships he won in Europe. His greatest victory was the Paris–Brest–Paris marathon in 1931. Oppy kept himself awake on the 726 mile (1168 kilometre) non-stop race by slapping his face and singing. In sight of the finishing line, he pedalled past the field leaders and won by a length.

Top: Adoring crowd for Hubert Opperman, cycling champion. His greatest victory was the 1931 Paris-Brest-Paris marathon, of 726 miles (1168 kilometres). Left: 'Oppy' became Australian Minister for Immigration, but 40 years earlier, when he was 24, he was voted the most popular sportsman in Europe by French magazine readers.

The name Opperman is synonymous with Malvern Star, a bike Oppy found in a one-man Melbourne cycle shop. The young man behind Malvern Star was Bruce Small. They soon formed a partnership and became lifelong friends.

But that was only one of Bruce Small's business coups. Even in retirement, Sir Bruce Small was making millions, buying land on the south coast of Queensland to build Australia's richest playground, the Gold Coast. If Small and Opperman had anything in common it was energy. Sir Bruce told me:

> Once from Perth to Sydney, I found [Opperman] so exhausted I told him to have four hours' rest. Then I tricked him. I put the coffee on and timed him for 10 minutes, then woke him. He thought he'd lost four hours, and he rode away as if he was just starting fresh in a sprint race.

Opperman's self-discipline served him well when he retired from competitive cycling. In 1949, he entered federal politics and served as a Cabinet Minister. Sir Hubert Opperman was later appointed Australian High Commissioner to Malta, where he served until his retirement in 1972.

Another of Australia's most brilliant cyclists, Russell Mockridge, proved that bike racers and runners should share the same training techniques. It did not really matter whether your feet were on the ground or pedals, as long as they kept on turning. Mockridge rode Australian bike circuits in the 1950s, in the days when thousands of spectators turned out to watch cycling championships in Australia. Before a big race, Mockridge used to go down to the beach at Portsea, near Melbourne, where he joined athletic coach Percy Cerutty's merciless sandhill sprints. Cerutty's spartan sandhill runs helped Mockridge win a gold medal at the 1952 Helsinki Olympics.

Soon after, Mockridge was killed in a collision with a bus during a bike race.

Interestingly, in recent years, Australian cycling has seen more biff and blood than boxing. There have been triumphs with names like Gary Neiwand (silver medallist, Barcelona) and Dean Woods (gold medallist at the 1984 Olympics and gold and silver medallist at the 1986 Commonwealth Games). Sadly, however, the impression left of Australian cycling in recent years is of bitter, internecine warfare between women cyclists such as our first Olympic woman gold medallist, Kathy Watt, and Lucy Tyler-Sharman.

As to what the disputes are about, no-one in the wider community seems to know or care—maybe one's faster than the other.

## RUNNING

Not long before he died, Mockridge ran up Percy Cerutty's so-called 'killer sand dune' and established a time that would never be beaten by the world's finest athletes. It was on this tortuous, almost vertical track in the Portsea dunes that Cerutty developed his intense physical and psychological conditioning of athletes like John Landy and Herb Elliott.

Cerutty's sandhills helped to cut more than 12 seconds off Landy's time for a mile (about 1.6 kilometres). Landy broke the four-minute mile 46 days after England's Roger Bannister in 1954.

Australians also remember John Landy for another incident, which reveals his personality as much as it demonstrates his track performance. Before a crowd of 22 000 at Melbourne's Olympic Park in 1956, Landy was running behind team mate Ron Clarke, when Clarke fell and was spiked by Landy's shoe. Already further down the track, Landy turned back. When Clarke convinced him to keep running, Landy was 60 yards (about 55 metres) behind the field. He started off again and, in one of the most spectacular feats in athletic history, he ran to the lead and won the Australian Mile Championship. Clarke got up and ran in fifth.

At Rome in 1960, it was Herb Elliott's turn to put Cerutty's sandhill training into practice. As Elliott started to run in the 1500 metres event, the eccentric old coach, then in his 60s, jumped the barrier and ran on to the arena, waving a yellow cloth to spur Elliott forward. The Italian police had to remove the coach forcibly.

Elliott won the gold medal 18 metres ahead of his nearest contender. His time of 3 minutes 35.6 seconds remained the world record for seven years. Elliott later described his victory:

> I planned in the race to go from the half-mile mark. I remember getting there and some mad bloody Frenchman had got out in front, and he set almost a world record pace for 800 metres.
>
> I recall thinking, 'I'm buggered.' I then had the split-second decision: Will I stick to my plan or take the rest of the race as it comes? I stuck to my plan.

It was probably one of the most courageous decisions I have made in my life. It wasn't easy.

I remember the fear once I actually hit the front. If some guy passed me I was gone. I can remember very well the absolute relief when I got to the finishing line. There is a photograph of me like an animal ready to pounce, all aggressive and mean and attacking. Probably that is just the big sigh I was letting out at the end.

In the next two weeks, Elliott broke the four-minute mile three times. Then, only a month after the Olympics, he announced his retirement from competitive running and moved with his wife and child to England to study science at Cambridge. In recent years his profile has been high again in Australia as an ambassador for the Sydney Olympics 2000.

Like running itself, it's hard to know when to start and stop. In general, though, perhaps because Australia is such a bloody big place we tend to be better over longer rather than shorter distances. Not since Jimmy Carlton was briefly the fastest sprinter in the world in the 1930s have we stood much chance in the premiere event of all, the 100 metres—indeed, no white man stands much of a chance these days.

When it comes to distances there's a litany of great names such as Elliott, Landy, Clarke, Robert de Castella and Steve Moneghetti—but the bottom line is that apart from Edwin Flack, only two other Australian men have won track gold medals.

Our women athletes have fared a little better than the men. Six Australian women—Marjorie Jackson, Shirley Strickland, Betty Cuthbert, Maureen Caird, Glynis Nunn and Debbie Flintoff-King—have won 10 individual track gold medals. In more recent years, the young woman who gave us our most hope and our most frustration was Raelene Boyle—'the most controversial track and field athlete in Australian history'.

Among the lows, her disqualification for breaking twice at the Montreal Olympics and her personal decision to withdraw from the Moscow Olympics. Among the highs, three silver medals in three Olympic games and seven gold medals in four Commonwealth games, including the climactic win at Brisbane in 1982. And then, the biggest battle of all, the battle against breast cancer which she's approached in the same gutsy manner as she took on all her adversities in sport.

Top: Herb Elliott, 1500 metres runner who won Olympic gold at the 1960 Games. Bottom left: John Landy goes back to help Ron Clarke who'd fallen during the Australian Mile Championship in 1956. Even with this delay, Landy still managed to win the race. Bottom right: John Landy broke the four-minute mile 46 days after England's Roger Bannister in 1954.

Australia's athletic star of the 1990s, however, once again came leaping out of left field—Catherine Astrid Salome Freeman. The girl with the exotic name also had an exotic background—her mother was from Palm Island off the North Queensland coast. Her sporting career was fostered by her father, an ex-boxer, and later her stepfather, Bruce Barber. As a kid she was such a charming innocent she didn't realise she was being discriminated against— that she would win a race and not even notice that the white kid who came second got a prize while she didn't:

Well, see, this is the thing I didn't realise at the time. I didn't care too much about the prizes I just really ran and I realised I loved running and I enjoyed it and so long as I was always able to run I was fine. I probably didn't get what I deserved in some cases … those prizes and the trophies … but I was a little girl and, you know, let the adults take care of all that stuff. Obviously it hasn't changed the course of my life so whatever happened happened.

Sadly, though, the discrimination continued, when Cathy was to represent her state of Queensland—suddenly there wasn't a track suit for the young black athlete:

Yeah, I'm so blasé … I mean I haven't changed a single bit … but these are things that, you know, my stepfather and my mother realised. I mean, they'd go with the money to pay for this and that and expect what they'd paid for and were obviously more concerned about looking after my pet dog or making sure that I had my friends and, you know, I was like any other child, just more concerned about those sorts of things.

But the incident Cathy is most remembered for is draping herself in the Aboriginal flag after her 1994 Commonwealth Games gold medal win. It was an incident that outraged Australian conservatives, particularly Australia's top Games official, Arthur Tunstall. Cathy, however, has a view of life tempered by the fact that she has a sister with cerebral palsy and that nothing should be taken for granted. It's given her a broad perspective and this is what she has to say about that flag business:

Quite frankly, I don't care if the public remember me or not … I mean it's fantastic that people do remember me, for sure, but I'm more concerned about making sure people close to me bloody remember what [laugh] I am and what I'm really all about. What I did in 1994 certainly stands out in my—and most Australians' minds—and people in the street still say, 'Oh, good on you, Cathy. You keep flying both those flags.'

## SAILING

The America's Cup always seemed such an impossible prize to capture that some Australians wondered if it were even worth our while trying. There were fears that the entire New York Yacht Club might commit collective suicide if the Cup was finally taken from them after 130 years. Indeed, the Yanks had done almost everything short of piracy to keep the old, dilapidated mug, which did not belong to them in the first place.

It was originally called the Hundred Guineas Cup, and its contenders sailed in England off the Isle of Wight. When the US schooner *America* won the Cup in 1851, the crew handed it over to the New York Yacht Club. Its name was changed and the race rules revised unashamedly in America's favour.

It was those rules that stopped Australia's first challenge for the America's Cup in 1887 by Walter Reeks, a Sydney businessman. Reeks was told he would have to sail his yacht to America before he could qualify to race. So Australia's first challenge fizzled out. That left the racing to Canadian and British sailors, including the famous English tea baron, Sir Thomas Lipton. He spent six million pounds in five attempts, but never succeeded in winning the Cup back for England.

Australia, meanwhile, was breeding generations of tough sailors aboard the legendary 18 footers. First built near the turn of the century by Charles Messenger for the Sydney retailer Mark Foy, they carried so many crew they were called 'troop ships'. A favourite trick when the wind dropped was to unload half the crew on the nearest buoy to lighten the boat for the final run home.

At the end of the Second World War, some bright spark had an idea of a yacht race from Sydney to Hobart. At first it seemed a bit ambitious, but the 1050 kilometre ocean classic soon became an institution, eventually attracting even the Americans to the other side of the world. One of the men who owned a Sydney to Hobart yacht was Sir Frank Packer, a Sydney newspaper buccaneer who knew a thing or two about cut-throat competition. He wanted a new boat for harbour racing, but by the time he'd commissioned Alan Payne to design a yacht, he'd changed his mind and decided to 'go the whole hog and have a crack at the America's Cup'.

It was then 70 years since Walter Reeks and his crew had been sent packing, but by 1962 Australia was ready to challenge the invincible Americans again. Public excitement, nudged along considerably by Sir Frank's newspaper, *The Daily Telegraph*, was intense when the 12 metre yacht *Gretel*, named after Lady Packer, was launched. It was shipped off to America and with Jock Sturrock at the helm, promptly lost its first race to America's *Weatherly*. While *Gretel* had finished much closer than the British yacht *Sceptre* had done in the previous challenge, it seemed that we were going to get a nice pat on the head for trying, and be sent home empty-handed. But the second race was to provide one of the most exciting moments in the history of Australian sport. What happened that day would help explain why, 20 years later, Australia would still be plotting, still arguing, still spending millions, in their quest for 'the Cup'. Jock Sturrock tells the story:

> It was the second race where it blew up to 25 knots and *Gretel* sort of came into her own in those conditions. It was a thrilling race. We were eight seconds behind after racing for eight miles, and then our crew did an excellent job. They set their spinnaker faster than what the crew on *Weatherly* did, and just as the spinnaker set, we managed to catch a wave which carried us past. As *Weatherly* behind tried to sort of luff up to do the same thing to us, to take our wind, her spinnaker pole bent and that made it very difficult for her to catch us for the rest of the race.
>
> It was just one wave—and the spinnaker set and the boat just seemed to fit into that particular wave, and away she went. She kept on the wave for maybe 200 or 300 yards which was enough to drop us off about 200 yards ahead of *Weatherly*.

In fact, *Gretel* won no more races, but that single win was enough to give the Australians a taste for victory. Next time it was Australia's *Dame Pattie*, defeated 4–0 by the Americans in 1967. By 1970, Sir Frank took *Gretel II* to Newport for what proved to be one of the most controversial races in the Cup's history.

Top: Media baron Frank Packer's America's Cup contender, *Gretel*, which won the second of the 1962 races. Twenty years later, the Bond syndicate gained the success the others had vainly sought for 132 years. Bottom: Start of the ill-fated 53rd Sydney to Hobart race, Boxing Day 1998. In the huge storms that followed, some race yachts lost crew overboard and six men were drowned in the 80-foot swells and 80-knot winds.

At the start of the second race, the American *Intrepid* cut across in front of *Gretel* and the two boats collided. Consequently, the Australians were left about 90 metres behind at the start. *Gretel* caught up on the last leg, winning by just 67 seconds. Then *Intrepid* lodged a protest claiming that *Gretel* had caused the collision. The New York Yacht Club declared *Intrepid* the winner and *Gretel* lost the race, on a protest over a starting incident which had put it well behind!

A challenge for the America's Cup requires almost unlimited financial backing. As Alan Payne, designer of the *Gretel* challengers, said:

In the two times I tried to win the America's Cup for Sir Frank, he never once asked me what anything would cost. I think that's a wonderful quality in an America's Cup sponsor.

The late Sir Frank, who gave the reason for his crusade as 'alcohol and delusions of grandeur', can take the credit for launching Australia as the toughest modern competitor for the America's Cup. Following his quest, the Southern Cross syndicate also tried and failed, and then along came another man with too much money and not enough sense—a brash and cocky former signwriter who'd become a self-made squillionaire in Western Australia. His name was Bond—Alan Bond—he'd originally come to Australia from England as an orphan and he had lots to prove.

After nearly 10 years of quixotic tilts at sailing's holy windmill, Bond challenged for the Cup in 1983 with a remarkable yacht called *Australia II*. It was designed by an erratic genius named Ben Lexcen, formerly Bob Miller, whose name, like his yachts, had been idiosyncratically invented. For this yacht Lexcen had created a peculiar winged keel which, even if it gave no technical advantage, certainly gave a psychological one.

Nevertheless, the two boats raced neck and neck until all hinged on the last race—no, even more nail biting than that—the last leg of the last race which developed into an incredible 'tacking' duel the likes of which are rarely seen in big boat match racing. In a desperate ploy to gain the advantage American skipper, Dennis Conner, changed tack 47 times and even tried dummy tacking to lure *Australia II*'s skipper, John Bertrand, into a mistake. Tacking duels in yachts like these are mentally and physically wearing, but after an hour of manoeuvrings while the whole of Australia sat on the edge of its chair, John Longley, the port grinder (one of the crew operating winches) crept back and whispered to his mates, 'I think we're going to win the America's Cup'. He was met with total silence—the rest of the crew were holding their breaths and too scared to speak.

When the gun sounded as *Australia II* crossed the line first, cheers erupted all over Australia. Prime Minister, Bob Hawke, celebrating with others in a sea of champagne, declared a public holiday saying that any boss who expected workers to turn up the next day was 'a bum'. The crew and their skipper and particularly their patron, Alan Bond, became national heroes. The victory, along with other sporting triumphs, buoyed the national mood and helped to give Bob Hawke a record popularity rating in the polls. Alas, such are the quirks of history that only a few years later the little orphan boy who made good would be painting self-portraits behind bars in an Aussie gaol. As the Bond Corporation empire collapsed, many Australians realised to their chagrin that it was just as well they'd been thrilled by *Australia II*'s victory—after all, they'd paid for it.

## CRICKET

It is a sight unique to Australia—the vision of a man in shorts, towelling hat and thongs, lugging his Esky of beer and leading his friends or family to the cricket.

We played our first official game of cricket back in 1826, a match between the Military Club and the Australian Club on the Turnpike cow paddock, which later became the Sydney Domain. Those early matches soon became an institution in the new colony. A respectable picket boundary fence was erected and games were played on a semi-regular basis.

The original habitués of 'the Hill' were not so regular. Wagers were placed at every turn, and there are reports of bets laid in livestock, grain, rum and even lumber. Unconventional crowds notwithstanding, the game continued at the Outer Domain, the cradle of Australian cricket, until the 1850s when someone burnt the boundary fence down. It seems that with the colony just two generations old, some people still thought cows more important than cricket. They quickly became the minority.

Just 30 years later, we were making our mark in international cricket, beating the English at their own game and on their home grounds. To rub

Top: In the 1860s the first Australian international touring cricket team—comprised totally of Aboriginal players from Lake Wallace, Victoria. Bottom: Not much of a crowd—in fact the only spectator's got a gun—but what would you expect in Tobruk during the Second World War?

salt into the wound, a death notice was published in the *Sporting Times* periodical of London:

> In Affectionate Memory of English Cricket,
> which died at the Oval, 29 August, 1882.
> Deeply lamented by a large circle of sorrowing
> friends and acquaintances. R.I.P.
> N.B. The body will be cremated and the ashes taken to Australia.

In Sydney the next year, an urn containing the ashes of a burned cricket bail was handed over to a victorious English team. 'The Ashes' now stay permanently in the Members' Pavilion at Lord's and the word has come to mean the ultimate prize in cricket: Victory in England versus Australia Test matches.

Since the Ashes began, no event in the history of cricket has been as controversial as the English plan to use 'Bodyline' bowling to 'get Bradman', the Australian wonder batsman of the 1930s. The principle on which Bodyline worked was simple: outright fear. At the third Test in Adelaide in 1933, the English bowlers Bill Voce and Harold Larwood bombarded the Australian batsmen with short-pitched deliveries down the leg side. The close infield was lined with men in catching positions. Playing the ball meant the risk of being caught; while not playing the ball meant the even greater risk of being hit.

The Australian captain, Bill Woodfull, was struck by a speeding ball near his heart. Then Bert Oldfield landed one on the temple. When the English team offered sympathy, Woodfull made his famous comment:

> There are two teams out there on the oval. One is playing cricket, the other is not. This game is too good to be spoilt. It is time some people got out of it.

As furious telegrams flew between the cricket officials in Australia and London, Bodyline was revolutionising Australian batting. The batsmen were padding their bodies against the onslaught, and traditional footwork was replaced by evasive ducking and swaying. Australia lost the Ashes that year, but bounced back in the next series under Bradman's brilliant leadership. In fact, since Test matches between the two senior cricketing nations began in

Top: The birth of cricket's Holy Grail, 'The Ashes'—this R.I.P. notice, along with a cremated cricket bail in a small urn, set off more than a century of fierce competition between England and Australia.
Bottom: The infamous 'Bodyline' attack. Without protective clothing, wicket-keeper Bert Oldfield was hit on the temple. He was carried off and was unable to continue the innings.

In Affectionate Remembrance

OF

*ENGLISH CRICKET,*

WHICH DIED AT THE OVAL

ON

29th AUGUST, 1882,

Deeply lamented by a large circle of sorrowing friends and acquaintances.

R. I. P.

N.B.—*The body will be cremated and the ashes taken to Australia.*

1877, Australia still retains a comfortable margin of wins over the traditional enemy, the Marylebone Cricket Club, at Lord's.

Much of the animosity between the two nations can be traced to subtle differences in their approaches to the game. Until the rise of Kerry Packer's 'World Series Cricket', there was no real professionalism in the game. Good players emerged from Saturday club competition and gradually worked their way through the state side until they were chosen for Australia.

During the same period, England always had two kinds of cricketers: 'gentlemen' and 'players'. The gentlemen were the amateurs, usually selected from the strong university sides of Oxford and Cambridge. The players were the professionals: talented working-class lads who turned their ability to play the game well into their meal-ticket. The class distinctions were maintained until well after the Second World War. Although playing in the same side, gentlemen and players entered and left the field through separate gates and, although a player might be the finest cricketer in the side, the captain of England was always a gentleman. These relics of aristocratic snobbery incensed the Australians, and helped to fuel the special animosity which has coloured England versus Australia matches.

In 1977, exactly 100 years after the very first Test match played between England and Australia, a special commemorative Test was played in Melbourne between the two modern descendants of those first sides. In a hair-raising finish, which could not have been stage-managed better, Australia won in the dying moments of the game by just 45 runs. The result was an exact repeat of the outcome when the same match had been played a century before—amazing.

The most significant change in cricket in modern times has been the intervention of Kerry Packer, son of Sir Frank and a media mogul in his own right who, like his father, gets what he wants. In this case what he wanted was cricket as fodder for his television stations—something that was cheap and that Australians liked to watch for an awfully long time.

Unable to gain a monopoly in cricket broadcasting, Packer signed up most of the leading international players to World Series Cricket, and for a couple of seasons, the game was split into two major camps in much the same manner as Rupert and Lachlan Murdoch have tried with Rugby League and Super League in more recent times.

To add insult to injury for the traditionalists, Packer was accused of reducing cricket to circus entertainment. However, it was clear that the longest game in the world, which can take five days and still not achieve a result, was not designed for television. Thus, one-day cricket came into the ascendancy—a game that saw the players clad in bright colours and the batsmen slashing at the ball in a most untextbook-like manner, that had the old boys muttering in their gin and tonics. However, the public loved it and Kerry loved it even more—he got gate takings as well as the television revenue.

One-day cricket has changed the game forever. Test matches are still played, but without the same focus and passion from the public as they used to generate. Nevertheless, supreme triumphs are still accorded the same reverence as those of the vintage days and one of these was during the 1999 Test match against England when Mark Taylor equalled Sir Donald Bradman's 334. When the Don scored his record 334 in the third Test of the 1930 Ashes series, he was front page all over the cricketing world. It was an Australian record that would stay intact for 58 years, until almost the end of the century, when the Australian captain equalled the feat but went no farther, as a mark of respect to the great man, declaring his team's innings over.

## FOOTBALL

Australian Rules, according to the experts, evolved from Gaelic football, influenced by the large Irish population in Victoria last century. The game was uniquely Australian, with its own cult following in all states except New South Wales and Queensland. However, in 1982 those south of the Victoria–New South Wales border whom New South Welshmen are fond to call 'Mexicans', decided the time had come. As with the rabbit, the prickly pear and the cane toad, it was time to spread throughout the whole country and the infiltration was begun by sending a team with the rather benign name of the South Melbourne 'Swans' into the heart of Rugby Union and Rugby League territory to see if they could attract a crowd.

Among the initial owners of the Swans were unlikely footyphiles such as media magnate, Mike Willesee, and Geoffrey Edelsten, a rich doctor with a penchant for blondes, Porsches and pink helicopters. Initially, they met with some head-high tackles from rival codes and a distinct ennui from the local populace, but as the Swannies overcame their initial setbacks, girded their well-displayed loins and shrunk their shorts still further, they gathered more and more fans. When they won a few games against the top Melbourne sides and then, heaven forbid, actually ran within a whisker of winning a Premiership, they were home town-heroes. By the mid 1990s, AFL was well and truly entrenched in Sydney.

Like all cults, it has bred 'super heroes' like Sydney star and all time record goal kicker Tony 'Plugger' Lockett, and Melbourne, of course, has a whole pantheon of heroes with Barassi, Bartlett and Whitten up there among the immortals. The name that's lasted above all, however, is that of high-leaping Roy Cazaly. It is said that in wartime Australian infantrymen from Melbourne shouted 'Up there, Cazaly' as they began bayonet charges. During the last 20 years, Michael Brady's song by the same name has become an anthem for the AFL—such is the enduring power of Cazaly's name it still invokes reverence, like Bradman's, more than half a century after he stopped playing.

Barassi, who played for 16 seasons, was in seven successive Grand Finals, coached North Melbourne to its first ever Premiership win and coached four Grand Final Premiership-winning teams, has contributed more to the game than most. He even took an Australian Rules team to Ireland to beat the Irish at Gaelic football. But there is not much Irish influence in Australian Rules today. As he once said:

> You call it Australian Rules. Who are the Australians? Think of all the star names ... Kekovitch, Schimmelbusch, Barassi, Jesaulenko, Ditterich ... Take out all the foreigners, and what are you left with? The donkeys—that's from Sam Kekovitch.

Despite all of this, New South Wales is still the home of football codes that mock AFL as 'aerial ping pong' and 'a bunch of bloody ballerinas'—not that you'd often want to say that to their faces. In fact, rugby was only one code until, in 1907, a player called Alec Burdon broke his arm and had to pay his own medical expenses. That led a team of players to break away and professional Rugby League was born. In those days, footballers like Dally 'the Boot' Messenger were 'brought over' from Union for £150. Today, Rugby Union players are wooed with 'confidential' payments and gifts sometimes totalling hundreds of thousands of dollars.

Top left: The shorts are now shorter and the game of Australian Rules has spread from Victoria like an octopus. Top right: Legendary high marker, Roy Cazaly goes 'up there'. Bottom: A special Melbourne tram service in 1908 which took footy-mad fans to the Essendon v. South Melbourne clash.

Top: Australia's 1909 Kangaroos—our national Rugby League team.
Left: 'The Gladiators'— rival Rugby League captains Norm Provan and Arthur Summons left the field of the 1963 Grand Final almost as mud statues. Their end-of-game embrace became an iconic image enshrined in the Winfield Cup trophy, shown in the foreground.

Among Union's immortals are Ken Catchpole, the Ella Brothers and David Campese, although there are scores of others who became household names; indeed, as a finale for the Rugby Union's Centenary Dinner at the Sydney Town Hall in 1999, 32 living Wallaby captains attended, from Trevor Allan, who led Australia in 1947, through to David Wilson, the then skipper. Over the past 100 years, as with cricket, our traditional enemies have been the Poms. It was to England that the first Wallabies went in 1908—not only to play England and Wales, but to win the gold medal in the 1908 London Olympic Games. We're still the current medal holders in that event. Australia beat England in the 1991 World Cup final but England in turn beat us in the quarter finals of the 1995 World Cup in South Africa. The Centenary Test was won by Australia—so there.

Sadly, Rugby League, which has flourished for much of this century, was almost destroyed in the battle between media proprietors in the mid 1990s. Once again the protagonists were the Murdochs with their global empire and the Packers with their Australian empire.

The Murdochs, who had already commandeered a number of sports to feed their insatiable television networks, made a pre-emptive strike to buy up players for a global Rugby League competition called Super League. The Packer camp, whose winter television schedule is fuelled by Rugby League and which enjoys some of the highest television ratings of the year with an artificially contrived three-match battle between Queensland and New South Wales Teams called State of Origin, did not take the attempted plunder lightly and fought back with its own legal kicks to the groin.

Inevitably, of course, the players became cannon fodder in the battle between the media heavies and there were some poignant casualties. Contracts were broken and unbroken, lawyers made millions, the teams were fragmented and their coherent identities lost to the point where the public began to lose interest in the game itself. The immediate winners were the lawyers, Rugby Union and AFL, which benefited from the hiatus.

But the battle was far from over and with so much at stake the two media empires involved would invariably make the game work again, even if they had to do what they've done in the past and that's get into bed together, however distasteful that might seem. As the new millennium approached and a new era dawned, the horse trading began in earnest. Kerry and Rupert were in their dotage and the public watched entranced as the heirs apparent to the two media empires traded blows: James Packer fighting to stop the Murdochs snatching television rights from the Packers' Channel 9 Network, and young Lachlan Murdoch leading the Super League attack, while the games officials and players have been carried off in stretchers.

Meanwhile, there was yet another footy force on the horizon. After the Second World War, thousands of migrants arriving from Europe introduced Australian cities to soccer, a game previously played mostly in the coalfields of New South Wales. By the mid 1970s, Australia had made respectable attempts at gaining Olympic and World Cup honours.

Soccer in Australia is in a frustrating position. It's the code with by far the biggest following in the world and it has the biggest number of actual participants of any football code in Australia; however, due to a complex set of factors, not the least that it's regarded by many Australians as 'wog ball', it has disproportionately small public and media support. The game's organisers have attempted to redress this problem with aggressive Aussie advertising, even to the point of calling the national team 'the Socceroos', but inevitably it's a case of success breeds success. Australian sporting fans are as fickle as any others, and the moment the Socceroos have looked like winning, their audience support has increased dramatically. The greatest tragedy for the future of the game was the national team's heart-breaking 1998 loss after leading 2–0 against Iran in the critical game that would have seen them go into the World Cup.

With nothing to look forward to, the game has had to rely on the success of Australian players overseas, such as Mark Bosnich, who continues a traditional way paved by players like Craig Johnston, who was transferred to Liverpool in 1981 for $1.3 million, the highest transfer fee of the season. Johnston in turn follows in the footsteps of lesser-known successes like Aboriginal activist, Charles Perkins, who trained with the English team Everton in the 1950s.

## MOTOR SPORT

As soon as cars began travelling as fast as race horses it was pretty clear that they could be used for some sort of sport. It's believed that the first actual motor race was held at the Maribyrnong gymkhana in Victoria in 1903.

But the sight of cars thundering along at 20 miles per hour (about 32 kilometres per hour) was not exactly soul stirring. Before long a host of other events became popular—hill climbs, rallies, intercity record-breaking attempts and one particular event which was to eventually become an Australian mania, the reliability trial.

In 1905, the Dunlop Rubber Company conducted two events to test the reliability of the horseless carriage. Both of them involved routes between Sydney and Melbourne. In those days, reliability was fairly easily defined— a reliable car was the one that finished. The problem with those first rallies was that even though most of the field was eliminated, half a dozen of the vehicles kept going. Even when the course was lengthened considerably, some of the infernal mechanical beasts refused to be cowed. So, by the mutual consent of five surviving drivers, the Dunlop Cup was inscribed with the performance of all the cars that finished. *The Daily Telegraph* in Sydney was moved to comment:

> The keen interest taken in the motor contest is something more than a sporting interest. It is the recognition that in the development of the motor lies the solution of many transit problems of the future, and, among these, the problems of our great dry spaces West and South West. The fascinations of speed are already irresistible once they have been tasted, but what is really wanted for outback conditions is a car that will be modestly capable of 20 miles per hour with engine and tyres warranted to withstand the roughest bush tracks.

Australia is often credited with the invention of motor cycle speedway racing and so far no one seems to have contested the claim. According to legend, a group of young blades from the Maitland district in New South Wales were bored with the prospect of hacking around the rough country roads, so one day they took their machines on to the local trotting track. One thing led to another and, in 1925, J.S. Hoskins organised the first official races at the Maitland Agricultural Show. Within a few years the sport had developed from a national to an international sport, climaxed by the famous test matches between England and Australia at Wembley Stadium.

The 1920s also saw a boom in the sport of motor racing and a thrill-seeking public demanded more and more excitement from the competitors. At one stage a favourite contest was between a motor car and an aeroplane which, in the 1920s, were capable of about the same speed.

Top: Jack Murray, master of the Redex reliability trials, run over 10 000 miles (16 000 kilometres) in the Australian outback between 1953 and 1955. Left: Sir Jack Brabham, three-times Formula One World Champion (in 1959, 1960 and 1966) and the only person to win the World Drivers' and World Manufacturers' Championships in the same year.

It must have been hair-raising stuff, because in the earlier days a racing car wasn't much more than the biggest motor a driver could find, bolted to the strongest chassis.

A favourite machine was the Brooklands Riley and one of these cars, driven by Billy Thompson, won Australia's first grand prix, a 200-mile (about 320 kilometres) handicap event.

The most popular New South Wales track was at Penrith outside Sydney, and it was the site of many accidents. Three spectators in the crowd were killed during a race in 1938. The car, a MacKellar Special, was hardly damaged. Its co-driver, Warren Brown, remembered the crash:

> We had come around the corner and the car went into a slide and it wouldn't come out, just stopped in the slide right up the straight and the crowd was very much thicker there. Everything happened so quickly. We didn't realise what happened until the car pulled up right on the safety fence. By that time a tremendous number of people had been injured and there were people lying all over the place, including us. I've never stopped thinking about it. You would like to forget it but human nature won't let you forget certain incidents in your life, especially a thing like this.

But no matter how many lives it claimed, Australians were hooked on the quest for more speed. In 1964, we played host to the world's most celebrated land-speed record attempt. Englishman Donald Campbell, in his futuristic *Bluebird*, flashed across the salt flats of South Australia's Lake Eyre, setting an incredible new world record of 403 miles an hour (almost 650 kilometres an hour). The enormous cost and danger of Campbell's exercise was justified by the claim that the technical knowledge gained by his challenge would be used in the design of cars for the general public.

But it all seemed a long way from a Sunday afternoon spin with the family. Most Australians were driving compact six-cylinder cars like the Holden and Falcon, and we were more interested in how reliable these cars were than how fast they could go in a straight line.

The Redex Trials, the legendary tests of men and machines over outback roads, were run between 1953 and 1955. Redex itself was a petrol additive, and through the spectacular publicity the trials received, it quickly became the best-known petroleum product in the country. The three round-

Australia car trials organised by the Redex Company brought whole towns out to line the highways as car after car flashed through the dust or limped into the next checkpoint.

The contests were a typically Australian mixture of shocking roads, rugged conditions, cheery improvisation, all mixed together with a generous helping of larrikinism. But what the Redex Trial did test, and in merciless style, was whether an ordinary family saloon could stand up to the punishment of 10 000 terrible miles (about 16 000 kilometres).

The acknowledged master of those early reliability trials was Jack Murray, affectionately known as 'Gelignite Jack' because of his quaint habit of punctuating the outback silence with the odd stick of explosive. Murray won the 1954 Redex Trial, and he was an inexhaustible source of great Redex yarns:

> We came over the top of a hill about 100 miles out of Alice, and there's this Volkswagen sitting in the sand. They had hit a big 'roo, an old bloke about 20 years old. So they said, 'Will you take a picture of it?' They propped the 'roo up and one of them took his coat off. I said, 'Why don't you put it on the 'roo because they're easy to dress up?'
>
> I got the Box Brownie and I'm taking the picture, but the 'roo was only stunned. The 'roo leapt about 20 feet, just missed me and shot off.
>
> I roared out laughing and this fellow said, 'What are you laughing at? That coat's got £200 of mine in it, and me bloody licence!'

Australia has had its fair share of lunatics dashing around the countryside knocking over records and 'roos, but before Jack the best known was Norman 'Wizard' Smith. In the early 1920s, Norman drove his famous Essex racer from Sydney to Melbourne in the record time of 13 hours—an average of 70 kilometres per hour—and then from Melbourne to Adelaide in 13 hours 21 minutes, despite running into a flock of sheep. Interstate record breaking was banned in 1935 because it was too dangerous—not the least to the wildlife. The Wizard then took to high-speed driving in a straight line and he set a number of Australasian records, including one for a mile (147.64 miles per hour) which stood for 10 years. Then, on New Zealand's Ninety Mile Beach, in a car that was eight metres long, weighed 3000 kilograms and was powered by a 24-litre Napier water-cooled engine, Wizard got himself travelling at almost 370 kilometres an hour but because of bad conditions failed to beat the world record set by Malcolm Campbell (Donald Campbell's father).

His last great exploit was in 1939 when he drove around Australia, 16 000 kilometres in 45 days, with no stops for repair. Following in Wizard's tyre tracks came men like Sir Jack Brabham, who started out in dirt track races in the 1940s and went on to become three times Formula One World Champion and the only person to win both World Drivers' and World Manufacturers' Championships in the same year. His successor on the world scene was Alan Jones, son of another famous racing car driver, Stan Jones. Jones won the Formula Grand Prix in 1977.

When it comes to the crunch, however, no racing driver has thrilled Australians as much as a local hero, Peter Brock, 'King of the Mountain' at Australia's most popular motor race, the Bathurst 1000. Brock was doubly exciting for Australia's rev-heads because, while his first 102 wins had been in a dinky Austin A30, his big wins at Bathurst were in brutally powerful Holdens—four wins in Toranas and three in Commodores in just 11 years.

But the motor racing stars of the 1990s raced on two wheels, not four. Australia claims to have invented dirt track motor cycle racing and has a long tradition of international expertise, first at places like Wembley, but more recently on the 500cc Grand Prix circuits. It's a hair-raising profession—one rider had 19 crashes in the 1999 season alone—and the Australian kings of the sport such as Wayne Gardner, Mick Doohan, Troy Corser, Anthony Gobert and others have collectively broken almost every bone in their bodies. The rewards, however, are great, and whereas early Australian car and bike racing heroes were happy to win a cup or two, the new breed are racing each year for tens of millions of dollars.

## OLYMPIC GAMES

It says something about our sporting spirit that Australia is one of only three nations which has competed in every Olympic Games of the modern era, beginning in 1896. The 1956 Olympic Games were the first to be held in the Southern Hemisphere and before crowds as big as AFL grand finals—100 000 or more—local athletes bagged more gold medals than in any other games.

Invitations were sent to 91 countries and 67 finally sent teams after Holland, Spain and Switzerland withdrew to protest against the Russian

Top: 1956 Olympic gold medal winners gathered with the author for a television reunion in 1998. Left: Perhaps Australia's most famous living woman. Dawn Fraser, pictured here with her daughter Dawn Lorraine, was the first swimmer to win the same event in three consecutive Olympic Games and the first female to swim 100 metres freestyle in under one minute.

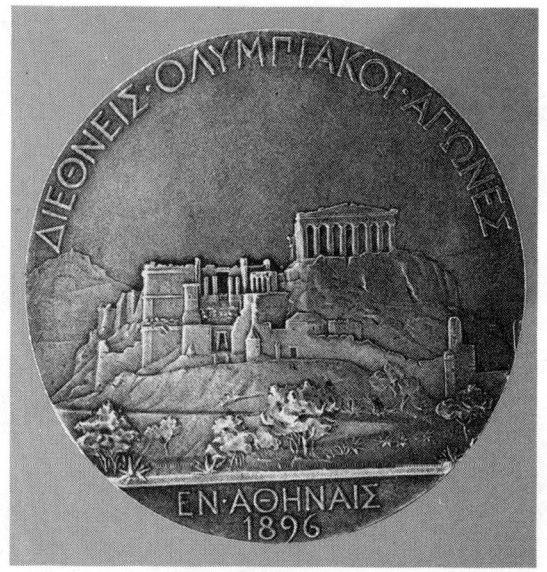

Australia is one of only three countries in the world to have competed in all the modern Olympics which began in 1896 in Athens. Pictured is the face and obverse of one of two medals won by the runner Edwin Flack, the sole Australian competitor at these games.

invasion of Hungary. The Cold War tensions turned the swimming pool to boiling point when teams from these two countries met and there was literally blood on the tiles. More than 200 athletes from communist countries sought political asylum here.

Despite this incident, however, the Games were also known as the 'Friendly Games' and held in great spirit. The young Melbourne athlete, Ron Clarke, who later became one of the greatest distance runners in the world, entered the stadium with the Olympic torch which had been carried, burning, all the way from Greece—its longest distance ever. From Athens a Qantas flight transported it in a special container to Darwin. A Royal Australian Airforce aircraft then flew it to Cairns and from there a relay of 2830 runners carried the flaming symbol, day and night, to arrive at the Olympic stadium at 4.32 p.m. on 22 November.

Typically for Australians, though, not everyone took the Games deadly seriously. Earlier some university students in Sydney had pulled off a stunning hoax by delivering 'the Torch' to Sydney's Lord Mayor, Pat Hills, in front of a crowd of 30 000 rapt citizens—it was actually a jam tin, atop a chair leg with a flame fuelled by three old pairs of Army underpants.

The Australian team won a record number of 13 gold medals in Melbourne: athletics—Betty Cuthbert (100 m and 200 m), Shirley Strickland (80 m hurdles), women's team (4 × 100 m relay); swimming—Dawn Fraser (100 m freestyle), Lorraine Crapp (400 m freestyle), women's team (4 × 100 m relay), Jon Henricks (100 m freestyle), Murray Rose (400 m and 1500 m freestyle), David Thiele (100 m backstroke), men's team (4 × 200 m relay); cycling—Ian Browne and Tony Marchant (200 m tandem).

The USSR won 37 and the United States 32. All in all, Melbourne staged a hugely successful Olympic Games at the princely cost of eight million pounds.

# Leaders ...

## THE DELICATE BALANCE OF POWER

Australia has two kinds of leaders: those elected by the people and those given to us by decree of the Crown. And disputes between the two are nothing new. From the time we first became a nation our chosen leaders and our appointed ones have been involved in skirmishes, and usually it's the politicians who have lost. The names Barton, Lang and Whitlam span this century in Australian politics, and there is a common thread in the stories of these men. Each was the victim of an extraordinary political decision taken on high, each was a leader with a tremendous following, and yet each was thwarted by the supreme authority in this country, the vice-regal representative. Only days before Australia became a nation on 1 January 1901, our first Governor-General, Lord Hopetoun, ignored the obvious and popular choice for Prime Minister and with a vice-regal bungle chose instead a man who could not even muster a handful of men to form a government.

Thirty years later, during the Depression, the Governor of New South Wales, Sir Philip Game, demanded the resignation of the state's dynamic Premier, Jack Lang, and got it. In 1975, the Governor-General removed the Prime Minister, Gough Whitlam, from office while his party still held a majority in the Federal Parliament.

## EDMUND BARTON

In 1900, Edmund Barton was the man most Australians wanted, or at least expected, to be the first Prime Minister of the new Commonwealth of

Left: Gough Whitlam, elected Labor Prime Minister in 1972 and dismissed in 1975.

Australia. Barton, a protégé of Sir Henry Parkes, was the acknowledged leader of the Federation Movement—he was almost symbolic of the new spirit of national unity.

The nation's first Governor-General, Lord Hopetoun, a British aristocrat, arrived in Sydney ill from typhoid just two weeks before Federation. It was his task to choose a Prime Minister who, in turn, would choose a government until the first elections could be held. Hopetoun could in fact appoint whomever he liked, but he had been well briefed in England about the political climate in the colonies, and it was expected that he would make the popular choice. But Hopetoun, after consulting the Chief Justice of New South Wales, Sir Frederick Darley, astonished the country by inviting Sir William Lyne, the Premier of New South Wales, to form Australia's first Federal Government.

It was rather an extraordinary decision considering that Barton had been one of the main forces behind the whole idea of Federation, whereas Lyne had been its arch enemy. Despite this, Lyne accepted the commission but then found himself unable to dragoon the necessary 10 men to govern with him. So, on Christmas Day, Lord Hopetoun went feathered cap in hand, to Barton to invite him to form a government, which he did without any difficulty. To help save face for the Governor-General, and generally diminish the embarrassment all round, the affable Barton included Lyne in his govern-ment. Fortunately, the vice-regal bungle was virtually forgotten until a pesky journalist like myself brought it up again a hundred years later.

Meanwhile, on 1 January 1901, more than 150 000 people had gathered in Centennial Park, and as the sound of the one o'clock gun died away, Barton and Hopetoun entered the white swearing-in pavilion, a magnificent confection of Victorian plaster of Paris, which all but melted in the Aussie sun. The Queen's proclamation was read, a 21-gun salute set the maggies squawking, 10 000 kids sang the 'Federal Anthem' and Australia the nation was officially opened for business.

## JOHN THOMAS LANG

J.T. Lang was 'the Big Feller', loved by the working class, hated by the Establishment and a good deal of the press, and even by his Labor colleagues in Canberra.

He was called 'the people's champion' and he earned the title. He makes the history books for his legislation alone. In the late 1920s his government was the first in the world to introduce widows' pensions. He brought in child endowment, reduced the working week from 48 to 44 hours, and improved workers' compensation.

His government was defeated in 1927 but he came back into power two years later to face the task of governing New South Wales for the most difficult period in its history, the Great Depression.

Lang opposed even his own colleagues in the Federal Labor Party in their philosophy that the economic burden should be shared equally by the community. In 1930 he introduced an anti-eviction law to help unemployed tenants keep their homes. The Act allowed house buyers more time to pay off their mortgages.

By 1931 Lang was embroiled in bitter conflicts with the Federal Labor Government. He was refusing to pay interest on funds New South Wales had borrowed from Britain, claiming his state needed the money more than those 'bowler-hatted bastards' in London. Lang dropped New South Wales domestic interest rates to 3 per cent to help people borrowing money. He continually refused Federal Government demands to cut wages, pensions or social benefits.

The depressed workers all but worshipped their champion. He could be a snarling tub-thumping orator, and they turned out in their thousands to hear him speak at rallies. But the conservatives, and especially the extreme right wing, detested Lang with a vehemence uncharacteristic in Australia.

In 1932 a certain Captain Francis de Groot, a member of an extreme group called the New Guard, stole Lang's thunder at the opening of the Sydney Harbour Bridge by riding up on his horse and slashing the ceremonial ribbon.

But Lang had greater problems to concern him than this embarrassing incident. By now he had completely polarised the electorate. Sections of the press were calling him 'the mad dog'. Finally the Federal Government honoured the New South Wales interest debt to London, intending to make Lang repay it. True to character, he refused.

In the meantime, in the tranquil oasis that is Government House, Sir Philip Game, a small, pert and somewhat nervous man, knew that, as the King's representative, he would soon have to intervene. But in his remote sandstone

Right: NSW Premier Jack
Lang tries to tame his
New South Wales electorate
during the wild days of the
Depression—the cartoon
caption is 'One twist too
much'. Bottom: Lang's
refusal to repay state debts
saw him sacked by the
Governor-General,
Sir Philip Game (right),
in 1932.

castle he was cut off from the goings-on outside, and, according to his daughter, Rosemary, who was then 13, the family employed some extraordinary methods to find out what was happening:

> Well, Mr Lang held a rally in the Domain during the period before the dismissal and my mother wanted to go and hear what he was going to say— dress up incognito—but my father really wouldn't allow her. He didn't think it was very wise, and anyway she wouldn't get past the police all round the house. And so the butler went—Mr Turner—and he came back very upset, and very fussed, and said that Mr Lang had had a crowd of 50 000 there, and he had asked the people: 'Do you want to be governed by the people you've elected to represent you, or do you want to be governed by the Governor?' They shouted back: 'We want to be governed by you!' And poor old Turner was very upset at this and came back and reported it to my father.

Nearly half a century after this tense period in Australian politics, another vice-regal representative, Sir John Kerr, would be severely criticised for taking and making public the advice of the Chief Justice of the High Court and former Liberal lawyer, Sir Garfield Barwick. But in 1932 it seems that Sir Philip Game was not averse to taking a little backroom legal advice. As his daughter recounts:

> Mr Lang said that he couldn't pay the interest due to the British bondholders. Of course, that was a terrible thing to do, because it was a debt that he couldn't honour. So my father thought that he should ask a lawyer about this, and he got my brother to drive him to New South Head Road and told him: 'Drop me at the house of this lawyer and go away and come back for me in about an hour. I don't want the car standing outside.' Because, with the crown on it, the people would know whose it was.

If that clandestine meeting had been made public all those years ago it might have created a sensation. But it wasn't, and while the identity of Game's Double Bay lawyer is a secret of history, it seems fairly clear what his advice must have been.

By May 1932 the Federal Government had introduced new economic measures for the nation. Lang hit back with his own legislation, negating them in New South Wales. Game then made his move, withholding the Royal Assent from the 'illegal' New South Wales Act introduced by Lang, Game demanding an assurance that Lang would not disobey federal law. Lang refused. On 13 May 1932, the Governor called the Premier to his office at Government House and asked for his resignation. To the amazement of Lang's supporters their hero surrendered. Lang said many years later:

> What would I have fought—the entire military forces of Australia? Who would I have fought with—the flesh and blood of the men and women of New South Wales, people of peace, order and goodwill? It's always been my unchangeable principle, something I have never changed, and please God I never will, the Labor Movement doesn't need to disobey laws; the Labor Movement has the power when it will to change the law and change the power peacefully, without bloodshed, without murder, without death.

Lang's days as a political leader were over. But 'the Big Feller' would hover in the political wings for the rest of his long life. At the age of 99, he was still catching the train to work each day and publishing his own newspaper, *The Century*.

## EDWARD GOUGH WHITLAM

Gough Whitlam was impressed by the irony of the date when he was dismissed by the Governor-General, Sir John Kerr, in 1975. It was 11 November, Remembrance Day, the national day of mourning. His speech, made to a stunned nation from the steps of Parliament House, Canberra, is now famous to some, infamous to others:

> Well may we say 'God save the Queen', because nothing will save the Governor-General. The proclamation which you have just heard read by the Governor-General's official secretary was countersigned 'Malcolm Fraser', who will undoubtedly go down in Australian history from Remembrance Day 1975 as 'Kerr's Cur'.

The previous days had been ones of Machiavellian high drama. Just a few hours earlier, Malcolm Fraser had been in one room of Government

Top: *The Australian* cartoonist Bruce Petty's comment on Governor-General Sir John Kerr welcoming Malcolm Fraser as Prime Minister, after the shock dismissal of the Whitlam Government in 1975. The Senate refused to pass tthe Whitlam Government's budget, creating a Double Dissolution of Parliament. Bottom: Gough speaks for posterity: 'Well may we say "God Save the Queen", because nothing will save the Governor-General...'

House—his car parked out of sight around a corner—while the Governor-General, Sir John Kerr, informed the Prime Minister, Mr Whitlam, that his commission had been withdrawn. Minutes later, Fraser was sworn in as caretaker Prime Minister.

It was a remarkable climax to a period of government that had started out so buoyantly. Before the 1972 election, Labor had been in power only 16 of the 72 years since Federation. The Liberals, on the other hand, had been in office for 23 straight years, and the government was starting to fall into a state of decay. The Liberal Party had seen a couple of leaders since the retirement of its founder, Sir Robert Menzies, and the crown had finally fallen on the head of the most unlikely pretender, William McMahon.

It was clearly time for a change, and using just this theme, 'It's Time', in a massive media campaign, Gough Whitlam had little trouble pushing his weak opponent aside.

But the new Labor Government quickly ran into difficulties. Fired with a zealous urge to reform, the changes came too thick and too fast for much of the electorate. The shift in emphasis from the private to the public sector caused considerable heartburn. The government's economic measures exacerbated the effects of a general international recession, and the problems of inflation and unemployment became major preoccupations.

The Whitlam Government suffered further from public scandals which resulted in a series of sackings and resignations. The relationship between the Deputy Prime Minister, Jim Cairns and his assistant, Junie Morosi caused a furore, and the complex and mysterious series of events which became known as the Loans Affair, led eventually to the demise of the government.

By 1975, the Liberal opposition had managed to create such a public controversy about the Labor Government's proposals to borrow huge sums of money from non-traditional sources in the Middle East, that the conservatives felt confident enough to try to bring the government down. Even though Whitlam had a working majority in the House of Representatives, the Liberals had a slender advantage in the Senate. In September 1975, the Senate blocked the Appropriation Bills, effectively cutting off the money supply to all government departments and authorities.

The rest of what happened is dramatic history that most Australians will never forget. As the nation became bogged down in what seemed to many as an almost tedious Constitutional crisis, Kerr made his sudden and sensational move. Still reeling from the shock of his sacking, Whitlam told a stunned nation that such an event had not happened since the days of King George III. But he had to go no further than the days of Jack Lang for proof that Australia is not so much a democracy but a monarchy, where the ultimate arbiter is the Queen's representative.

Whitlam asked his supporters to 'maintain the rage', but despite talk of a coup d'état the conservative status quo of Australian politics was soon restored. Once again, the Labor party gathered its tattered remnants to face the future in its almost traditional role as opposition.

Despite the Liberals' promises, five years after the most significant single event in Australian politics, inflation, unemployment and industrial unrest were still the country's major problems. In the long run, little had changed except the names, and the drastically thinned group of Labor men in Parliament House were living testimony to what happens if you rock the political boat just that little bit too much. Yet, politics often moves in an exquisitely vicious cycle. Such is the fickleness and short memory of the electorate that within the decade, Labor's fortunes would be restored, largely due to the bumptious but charismatic Bob Hawke, and the nation would be treated to the sight on television of the man once called 'Kerr's Cur' evincing just the smallest whimper as he conceded defeat in March 1983.

## HUGHES AND BRUCE

If Barton and Hopetoun, Lang and Game, Kerr and Whitlam were studies in contrasts, then Hughes and Bruce were the Laurel and Hardy of Australian politics—so different, yet so alike.

William Morris Hughes and Stanley Melbourne Bruce were two Prime Ministers who showed just how fragile power can be, and just what strange bedfellows politics can make. As 'Billy and Stanley' they could have been in vaudeville, except that they basically couldn't stand each other. Hughes was a tough, rough diamond. Bruce was the sort who wore them in his tie clip—all class, right down to his spats. They spent years fighting each other; sometimes in the same party, sometimes in rival ones. They got each other into power and out of it again. They made one of the most intriguing double acts in politics.

Hughes said to the Australian people just before he died in 1952:

> Many of you will remember me. Some of you will know me quite well. You should. I have been in public life a very great while. In fact, I've been there over half a century.

In fact, Hughes was a member of Parliament for a total of 58 years. Even at the turn of the century, this wrinkled, gnome-like little man never looked young.

Hughes was born in Wales in 1864 and emigrated to Australia when he was 20. He tried his hand at dozens of different jobs, from boundary riding to umbrella repairing. In Sydney he became involved in the hurly-burly of Labor politics and, as secretary of the wharfies' union, he sat in the New South Wales Parliament.

Hughes used his backroom connections to gain a seat in the first Federal Government in 1901. By 1915 he was Prime Minister, and his carefully cultivated image as 'the little Aussie battler' and patriotic war-time leader served him well. Author Donald Horne, who wrote a biography of Hughes, said:

> Hughes is seen by some people as a symbol of national unity. He was, I think, probably the greatest symbol of national disunity we had. He was either, at best, a true blue koala bear patriot or, at worst, a very devious unprincipled little character.

Hughes was always like that—a bit of both. He'd been a staunch unionist, yet he beat unions into submission and persecuted socialists. Those of the working class who actively opposed him were sometimes jailed, yet he called himself the working man's friend.

Although his party was against it, Hughes wanted to introduce conscription. He broke away from his own men to fight two unsuccessful referendums on the issue. Each time the alliance of Catholic Church and trade unions combined to defeat him. Somehow, Hughes survived the referendum losses, a split in the Labor Party, and endless internal squabbling. Always the campaigner, he used his fierce rhetoric and political cunning to cling to the Prime Minister's job from 1915 to 1923.

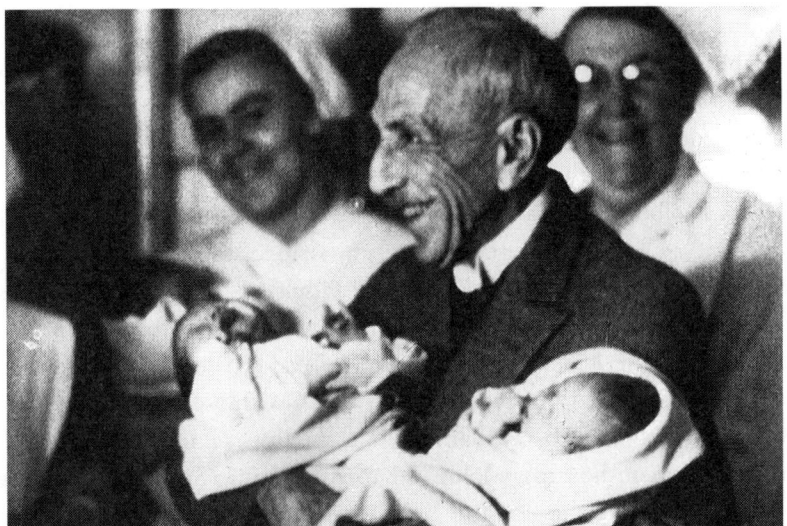

Top: An irascible little ratbag, Prime Minister Billy Hughes, also known as 'the Little Digger', entered politics before the turn of the last century and remained there until his death in 1952. Bottom: Billy Hughes (Prime Minister 1915–23) and Stanley Melbourne Bruce (Prime Minister from 1923–29) were chalk and cheese. They held each other in healthy contempt. This handshake was strictly for the newspaper photographers.

But his days as leader had been numbered. While Labor saw him as a traitor, the Establishment believed he was 'dangerously socialist'. In an attempt to placate big business, Hughes appointed the well-heeled S.M. Bruce as his Treasurer. As a political move, it backfired completely. Within a short time Bruce, in harness with the Country Party's Earle Page, was the nation's new leader.

Stanley Melbourne Bruce was everything 'the Little Digger' was not. Aloof and imperious, he cut a smart figure in pin-striped suits and spats.

While Hughes had literally dragged himself up from the back streets, Bruce lived in stately luxury. His grand home stood on 500 acres (about 200 hectares) of land in Melbourne. Designed by Walter Burley Griffin and built in 1926 for £26 000, it reflected a lifestyle despised by the working class.

Bruce tumbled into Parliament almost by accident. Educated at Cambridge, where he took a 'blue' for rowing, young Stanley quickly made a mark for himself at the London Bar. He served at Gallipoli with the Royal Fusiliers. On his return to Australia to manage the family firm, he represented success, wealth and class—the epitome of the Melbourne Establishment.

Victoria's business community drafted young Bruce to stand for the seat of Flinders, and the campaign was organised for him. He won easily, but Bruce had taken so little interest he maintained he wasn't quite sure whether he had gained entry into the Victorian or Federal Parliament. Five years later he was Prime Minister, aged just 39.

Bruce led, perhaps ruled, Australia for most of the 1920s. In terms of his legislative record he introduced compulsory voting for white Australians, established the Loans Council (to bargain state–federal finances) and specialised in the economy. In 1927, he moved the seat of the Federal Parliament from Melbourne to Canberra. He cut a smart figure in tails at the opening of the new Parliament House, which he presided over with such notables as the Duke of York and Nellie Melba.

Underlying his suave exterior, however, Bruce could be a tough, even savage, Prime Minister. The trade union movement, with its demands for an eight-hour day, its protests and processions, was growing in militancy. Bruce responded with 'the big stick'. He provoked union leaders and in turn blamed 'the Bolsheviks' for industrial unrest, demanding in his propaganda films that 'the Reds' be kept out of 'white Australia'.

On the eve of the Depression, Bruce tried to gain more power over industrial workers, and then virtually set about dismantling the arbitration system. For his old rival, Billy Hughes, who had been a pioneer of the arbitration idea, it was time for a killing. In 1929, on a motion introduced by Hughes, the Bruce Government was brought down by just one vote.

For Bruce, the ensuing election was a personal and political debacle. He could claim the dubious honour of being the only Australian Prime Minister to lose not just an election, but his seat in Parliament as well. Perhaps only a man of Bruce's independent means and superior attitude could have survived such a defeat. He was back at his office in Flinders Lane on the following Monday, for the first time in 10 years. He got back into Parliament in 1931 but, stripped of his old rank, he was happy to accept the post of Australian Commissioner to London. In the tense diplomatic negotiations before the Second World War, he emerged as one of the Empire's most distinguished ambassadors. Bruce's friend and diplomatic colleague, Alfred Stirling, said:

> He worked terribly hard before the war trying to avert the disaster, and then trying to ensure that Italy didn't come in, and above all, that Japan didn't come in. He galvanised the Australian War Cabinet into more aircraft production and he was involved in keeping Turkey and Spain neutral as buffers to prevent Germany breaking through into North Africa. Either of them would have been a terrible disaster and Bruce, almost more than anybody in London, saw the need for keeping Spain and Turkey neutral, and worked very hard at it.

After Billy Hughes had toppled Bruce from the leadership, his own days as leader were also over. In the same year as Bruce took the London job, Hughes suffered a great personal tragedy. His private life had revolved around his daughter, Helen. But in 1931, soon after she turned 21, she died after an operation. Hughes was greatly affected by the loss, but the ingrained fire and ambition of the born politician never died. He held a number of portfolios; he served in the Menzies War Cabinet; he even came within a whisker of getting back the leadership. He was the fighting man's idol, and every Anzac Day his failures and excesses were forgotten under the weight of affectionate nostalgia. When he died in 1952, aged 88, he was still a Parliament member.

His funeral was the biggest in Sydney's history, with 150 000 people lining the streets to see the cortège, and the newsreels tapping a well of almost mawkish sentiment. And Stanley Melbourne Bruce, who would survive the

Little Digger by 15 years, showed that even in his dotage he could look back on his old enemy with a wry affection:

> He had indomitable courage. It was no fun for Billy to annihilate some half-wit on the back benches of Parliament. Billy liked a foeman worthy of his steel. And I may be peculiar, but I'd say there's nothing dirty he hasn't done, or didn't do in his day, but when he died I had a certain regard and affection for him.

## ROBERT GORDON MENZIES

When Sir Robert Menzies left the Canberra stage in 1966, he was more than our longest-serving Prime Minister. For half of the population, he was the only Prime Minister they'd known. When Menzies spoke on television to the nation for the last time as leader, it was in his usual indulgent manner:

> There are very many people who are looking in tonight. I'm told it's almost compulsory, this. It's not an ordinary decision. It's something that doesn't happen very frequently for a man to go out of office under his own steam. I've gone out of office before today under somebody else's steam, but this time— under my own.

Sir Robert Menzies was a father figure to the modern generation of Australians. He was, after all, the man who had led us through the 1950s and 1960s, and somehow it had all turned out pretty well. A large man, with an ego to match, he manipulated others in and out of government, ignored his critics and spun words in wondrous webs of oratory. He was a master of the meandering, often witty, speech that often told us nothing; for example, in this interview after one of his frequent visits to London:

> There are matters to consider, and therefore they won't be considered in a light-hearted way. But I quite agree that the people of Australia are entitled, at the first possible opportunity, to be told what we want to do and how we would like to do it and what proposals we have, if any, for achieving it.

Needless to say, they never were. Australian political writer, Rob Chalmers, says of Menzies:

Top: Her Majesty and her loyal subject, Prime Minister Robert Menzies, who proudly followed the Queen into a state dinner in 1963, during which he quoted the now famous lines: 'I did but see her passing by ...' Bottom: Menzies had held the top post for 17 straight years, before he retired after his farewell speech on Australia Day, 1966.

He knew in the fifties and sixties, what was required to govern. It was to do nothing. That was the Menzies' masterpiece.

He was regarded as a great political leader by the average Australian who then, much as now, wanted his Holden and his television set. In the Menzies era he got it. Menzies knew what he had to deliver, and he delivered it.

He wasn't a man of innovative turn of mind. If you look back at his domestic policies, at the real achievements of the Menzies era, there are only two.

The first is Canberra. It was Menzies who took the bit between his teeth and decided that he was going to force the public service and the service brass out of Melbourne, and build this place as the national capital, instead of 'the old bush capital' as Jack Lang derisively called it.

His other achievement was to realise that the universities were about to be strangled of all funds in the mid 1950s. He set up the Australian Universities Commission, which saved the day.

The Snowy Mountains project was the initiative of the Chifley Labor Government. Certainly, the Menzies government carried it through. It's hard to think of any other concrete achievements.

Robert Gordon Menzies was born in the small country town of Jeparit, in the Victorian shire of Dimboola. He was a chubby, happy little boy, bright and ambitious from the start, learning to read as soon as he could hold a book. His parents could not afford an expensive education for their son, so he sat for and won a scholarship to Melbourne's exclusive Wesley College.

At 17, he won a scholarship to Melbourne University where he edited the university magazine and was president of the Students' Council. His writings at that time reflect his conservatism.

After a shining academic and legal career and a spectacular rise in politics, Menzies was just into his 40s when he began challenging the leadership of the ailing Prime Minister, Joe Lyons, and was accused of disloyalty.

Then in 1939, in the midst of a bitter party struggle, Lyons died. The Country Party leader, Earle Page, fought to keep Menzies out of the Prime Minister's chair, but to no avail. Menzies was sworn in as Prime Minister on 26 April 1939. Page attacked him at every opportunity. Yet it was typical of each man's pragmatism that they could work together in the same Cabinet 10 years later.

After only six months at the helm, Menzies addressed the nation to announce the outbreak of war; and he took on the role of war leader with energy and oratory using these words to inspire:

We can't be beaten except by ourselves. We can't be beaten except by disunity within our ranks, by the occasional ugly acts of treachery within our own ranks.

The following year, the Prime Minister was overseas supporting the diggers. With his home movie camera, double-breasted suit and trilby hat, he made an incongruous figure beside the troops in the hundred-degrees heat of the Middle East. But the real enemy for Robert Menzies was waiting at home.

Menzies was away four months, including eight successive weekends, as a guest of Churchill, staying at Chequers. In Australia, the Queensland 'bush boy', Arthur Fadden, was Acting Prime Minister, and to most of the party he seemed easier to get along with than the imperious Menzies. When Menzies arrived home, colleagues in the United Australia Party turned on him and, in the upheaval that followed, Menzies was forced to resign and Arthur Fadden became Prime Minister. It was a short reign.

In 1941 the Labor Party and its forceful leader, John Curtin, were elected to government. Curtin's charismatic leadership, combined with the total disarray of the opposition, gave Labor another victory in the 1943 elections. Chastened by the defeat, Menzies made his master stroke. At a conference in Albury in November 1944, the Liberal Party of Australia was born, with Menzies as both mother and midwife.

The strain of the war years literally killed Curtin. He died just a month before peace was announced on 15 August 1945. The new Prime Minister, Ben Chifley, inherited the problems of economic reconstruction and was forced to extend wartime austerity measures, such as petrol rationing.

When the Labor leader tried to nationalise the banks, the press and public reacted strongly. By 1949, with the war over four years, people resented not being able to keep their petrol tanks filled, and the general hangovers of austerity. In the elections that year, Menzies' campaign of promises was based on the issues of rationing and the growing international fear of communism. His simple slogan 'Tip out the socialists and fill up the bowsers' worked, sweeping him into office on 10 December 1949 to again become Prime Minister of Australia. When he and his wife, Pattie, moved into the Lodge in

Canberra, no-one could have predicted they would stay for such an incredibly long time. Menzies 'ruled' for a record term of 17 years. So long, in fact, that by the end Australians were calling it 'the Ming Dynasty'.

This second term as Prime Minister saw a marked shift in the Menzies' style. His hectic first 20 years in politics had taught him how to survive, and he determined not to make the same mistakes again. Menzies' emphasis now moved from simply gaining power to making sure he held it. Any danger from inside his own ranks could be solved with an occasional Cabinet reshuffle or an inspired diplomatic appointment. He even learned to live with old enemies, including Earle Page. He needed Page in his 1949 ministry, and Page went in with him.

The new government was quickly blooded in a tremendous struggle over the issue of communism. No Australian leader has realised the electoral potential of 'Red-baiting' more acutely than Menzies. By the 1950s, Australia was embroiled in a local version of America's McCarthyist war against 'the Reds'. Menzies wanted to outlaw the Communist Party and ban its followers from trade union and government positions. But in 1951 the Party went to the High Court of Australia and Menzies' Communist Party Dissolution Bill was voted unconstitutional. But Menzies was undeterred. As Hughes had done with conscription, Menzies flew in the face of even his own colleagues, and put the communist question to the people in the form of a referendum. Australians—traditional 'No' voters—once again preserved the status quo and Menzies' so-called 'Red Bill' was vetoed by a slender majority of 52 000.

Taking a personal interest in the court case against Menzies' Red Bill, and campaigning against the referendum question was the new Labor leader, Dr Herbert Vere Evatt. Evatt's popularity was increasing towards the 1954 elections and, with unemployment high, it was clear Menzies might need another magician's trick to win. He found it just 46 days before the votes were cast. The central character of the drama, and the man who would give his name to the whole affair, was Vladimir Mickailovich Petrov. On Friday, 11 April 1954, Petrov left work at the Russian Embassy in Canberra with a sheaf of papers under his arm. On 13 April, Menzies announced in Parliament:

It is my unpleasant duty to convey to the House (that) Mr Vladimir Petrov voluntarily left his diplomatic employment and made to the Australian government a request for political asylum. The request has been granted.

left: In 1949 Menzies wooed an electorate tired of wartime rationing with the promise of filling the nation's petrol tanks. The voters also registered their disapproval with Ben Chifley's plan to nationalise the banks. Bottom: In a stroke of good fortune, just before election time in 1954, Menzies gained support for his anti-Communist campaign when Russian Embassy staff member Vladimir Petrov, and later his wife Evdokia (centre), defected.

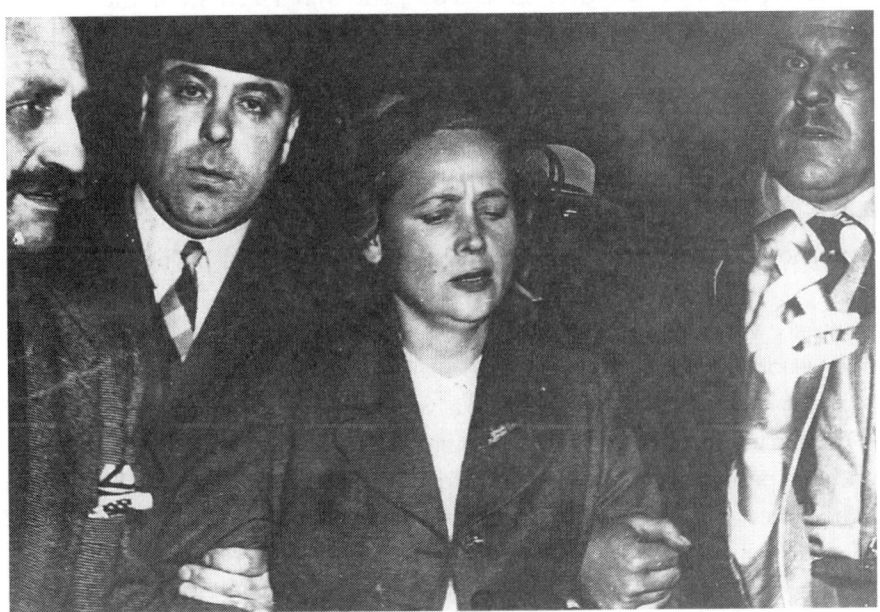

Petrov's 'defection' was ideal election ammunition, but not even the imaginative mind of Robert Menzies could have dreamed up the melodramatic spy scenes that followed. Australians were told how Petrov used his Third Secretary's appointment at the embassy as a cover for espionage activities for the Russian secret service, the MVD (later called the KGB). He turned over documents to the Australian Security Intelligence Organisation (ASIO), although the importance of these was later questioned.

As election day drew nearer, Petrov was seen as a Cold War ally for Australia—a Russian communist who had seen the light, and Menzies was his valiant rescuer. In fact, Petrov, a weak, heavy-drinking man, had been persuaded to defect after a two-and-a-half-year campaign by ASIO.

Evdokia Petrov, Vladimir's wife, also an MVD agent, had been held incommunicado at the Russian Embassy since her husband's defection. On 19 April two Russian couriers escorted Evdokia to a commercial air flight leaving Sydney's international airport. In a demonstration of emotional hysteria, more than a thousand shouting people, mostly migrants from 'Iron Curtain' countries, crowded on to the tarmac trying to pull Mrs Petrov back from the aircraft door.

On board the aircraft the drama continued. An air hostess, briefed by ASIO, approached Mrs Petrov in the ladies' toilet. Mrs Petrov was persuaded to defect and, on stopover in Darwin, she was taken from the helpless Russians by Northern Territory police and returned to Sydney to join her husband who was being carefully hidden.

The carefully stage-managed Royal Commission that followed was a mixture of fact and farce worthy of a B-grade movie. Journalist John Stubbs, who with Gough Whitlam's son Nicholas, later wrote a book on the whole affair called *Nest of Traitors*, tells of an extraordinary incident involving Petrov and another celebrated figure at the hearing, Dr Michael Bialoguski:

> Well, what happened was that Bialoguski, who was the host, was entertaining Petrov at his home. He knew that Petrov drank to excess when given the opportunity. Bialoguski was pretending to be a communist sympathiser and went to a demonstration for clemency for the Rosenbergs, some people caught up in the McCarthy era persecutions in America and, in fact, later executed.
>
> When he returned Petrov had drunk himself unconscious, and he went through his pockets and went to the lavatory and copied them down on the

only paper that was available. By the time he had finished copying the entire contents of his pockets he'd got to the core of the toilet roll, and the core of the toilet roll was in fact produced at the Royal Commission. A translator looked at what these secrets were on the documents and they were some very rude words written by Petrov who was trying to teach himself Australian swear words.

A lot of other documents were just as irrelevant, probably more irrelevant, but that incident did prove that Petrov had been thinking of coming over, jumping the wall, defecting to Australia, for some time.

It also says a couple of other things—that he did like drinking, that he was an unreliable sort of personality, that he was in trouble with people in Russia. He wasn't terribly interested in going back to Russia and was looking for a way out.

What made the Petrov affair so destructive for the Labor Party and such a weapon in the hands of Menzies, however, was that secretaries of Dr Evatt were named in documentary evidence supplied by the Petrovs. Neither they nor any other Australians named in the documents were ever charged, but the mere innuendo was damning enough. Press headlines such as 'Red Agent In Evatt's Office', didn't help matters and Evatt's own political judgement was often questionable. For example, at a time when half of Australia was hysterical about 'Reds under the bed', Evatt told Parliament that his old United Nations 'friend', Russian Foreign Minister Molotov, had assured him that the Petrov documents were forgeries.

Menzies used the Petrov sensation to his advantage to win the 1954 election, and in the months following, the right and left wings of the Labor Party split—largely over the issue of communist influence in the unions.

In 1955, the Catholic right wing helped found a new party, the Democratic Labor Party (DLP). The DLP directed its second preference votes to the Liberals, helping to consolidate Menzies' position for the next decade. The Petrovs, after giving evidence at the Royal Commission set up by Menzies, faded into obscurity. They became official residents of Australia protected by a special 'D' notice, a gentlemen's agreement between the government and the media not to disclose their whereabouts. Petrov died in Los Angeles in 1991. He was 84 and had been treated in hospital under the name of Sven Allyson for several years. 'Doc' Evatt never regained his political composure. He resigned his leadership to become Chief Justice of New South Wales, but died an invalid in 1965. But he's remembered as a great man and on his gravestone is perhaps the most impressive epitaph of any Australian in history: 'President of the United Nations Assembly.'

The 1961 'credit squeeze' election was Menzies closest brush with defeat. Even with the help of the DLP, Menzies scraped back into government by just 32 votes. But for most of the time Menzies ran the country with consummate ease, almost as if it was an enjoyable hobby.

Outside politics, Menzies worshipped cricket and the Queen. He was Australia's most vocal royalist, and in 1963 during a royal visit to Canberra, the Prime Minister made the young Queen of England blush, when he recited sixteenth century poet Thomas Ford's sentimental stanza:

> There is a lady sweet and kind,
> Was never face so pleased my mind;
> I did but see her passing by
> And yet I love her till I die.

When Menzies retired as Prime Minister on Australia Day, 26 January 1966, the country had never been richer or stronger. But sadly, all his legacies to Australia were not so kind. Before he left he had committed Australia to conscription and Vietnam, and there were hard times ahead.

## CURTIN AND CHIFLEY

If the Liberal Party has one true god in Bob Menzies then Labor has two— John Curtin and Ben Chifley. They are still among Australia's most respected Prime Ministers on both sides of the political spectrum—remarkable really, considering both had working-class backgrounds and Australia, on the whole, has not been well disposed towards Labor Governments. Curtin and Chifley served as Prime Ministers for only a few years each, compared with Menzies' two decades in power; and yet, the two Labor leaders appear to have made tremendous impact on the national psyche, perhaps because they ruled Australia during the most difficult and threatening periods of its history.

John Curtin was the political hero of a later Prime Minister, Bob Hawke, who had a well-publicised battle with the bottle and went on the wagon to become the nation's leader. (In fact, Hawke once held a world record—12 seconds for drinking two-and-a-half pints of beer!) Curtin also had to fight alcoholism in his early years. According to his biographer, opposition Labor Leader, Kim Beazley:

> John Curtin was a dedicated man and a great Prime Minister, but he was not thick-skinned, and in many ways was not well equipped personally, to withstand indefinitely the immense pressures involved in leading a country in wartime.

Nevertheless, Curtin was this country's leader during the most difficult four years of its history. It was the time when Australia actually faced invasion, the time when Australia was seemingly left in the lurch by its 'Mother Country' Britain, when it took its own destiny in its hands and sought a new ally in the United States. It was perhaps the birth of modern Australia, but it killed Curtin.

Curtin was born in 1885 in the little country town of Creswick, Victoria, which was also the birthplace of the artist Norman Lindsay. Outwardly, it would be hard to find two more different characters. Lindsay was a libertine but conservative politically. Curtin, the son of a Catholic policeman, was dour, studious and morally upright. He once played cornet and was a torchbearer in a Salvation Army band in Brunswick. He was, however, an advanced political thinker, inspired by Tom Mann, who early this century was one of the world's most notable radicals.

Curtin began his working life as a copy boy on *The Age* and later became a clerk. Even by his early 20s he was a socialist and he became secretary of the Timber Workers Union in 1911. He took a passionate stand during the great conscription debate of 1916 and 1917 and when Western Australia, unlike the rest of the country, voted for conscription in both the referendums, Curtin was asked to be editor of the *Westralian Worker*. Clearly someone was needed to 'educate' that state on the conscription issue.

As a young socialist he made a name for himself as a strident soapbox speaker in the Domain on the banks of the Yarra. Years later he could electrify Parliament with that same oratory.

In 1928, Curtin turned his ambitions from journalism to politics proper. He won the seat of Fremantle in that year, and again in 1929, but lost his seat in the Scullin debacle of 1931.

Right: Two of Australia's most respected Prime Ministers. Labor's John Curtin (left) was Prime Minister during the Second World War. The strain of the job contributed to his early death the month before peace was announced in 1945. His successor, Ben Chifley (right), initiated the Snowy Mountains hydro-electric scheme, a massive project (bottom) where many 'New Australians' found work.

In the following few years, Curtin would be drawn into faction fighting more vicious than that which he eventually encountered from his enemies. Labor was then split into two camps, who, among other things, then couldn't decide if 'u' was in the word labour—Federal Labor, and a group called Labour (non-Communist) led by the fiery Premier of New South Wales, Jack Lang.

During these hard Depression years, Curtin became a heavy drinker and for a while it seemed that his career would be ruined. It was a surprise to the Press when he won leadership of the Federal Labor Party by one vote in 1935. However, with the global situation rapidly worsening, the determined, teacherly looking socialist set about strengthening himself and his party. Just two months before Japan began the Pacific War, John Curtin became Prime Minister.

Within months Curtin was in headlong conflict with Winston Churchill. The British Prime Minister was somewhat cavalier about the threat of the Japanese to Singapore and other areas of the region. Curtin, on the other hand, was deeply disturbed by the Japanese threat and decided to recall a substantial part of the Australian force from the Middle East.

Churchill, who in the time-honoured tradition virtually regarded Australian troops as his own, was outraged by this gesture of colonial defiance. He subsequently blamed Curtin for the loss of Burma.

To rub salt into the wounds of Britain, Curtin sought a direct alliance with the United States and, therefore, General Douglas MacArthur, with his famous statement of 27 December 1941: 'Australia looks to America, free of any pangs as to our traditional links or kinship with the United Kingdom.' It was truly a turning point in our history.

The strain of the war years literally killed Curtin; he died just the month before the war ended. Churchill, in his war memoirs, expressed regret for the tone of his cables to Curtin and paid tribute to his personality. MacArthur said, 'Mr Curtin was one of the greatest of wartime statesmen, and the preservation of Australia from invasion will be his immemorial monument.'

Ben Chifley easily won the position as Australia's Prime Minister. *The Times* of London said in an editorial, 'Chifley is a true product of the Australian Labor movement. He is solid, hardworking and sincere, and his record suggests that since Curtin's mantle has fallen on him, he will wear it worthily.'

Chifley, too, had come up the ranks the hard way. A locomotive driver from Bathurst, he was elected in 1917 to the state general committee of the Locomotive Engine Drivers', Firemen's and Cleaners' Association.

When his union went on strike, Chifley was a model of restraint. His employers, however, held him to be the ringleader. First they punished him by refusing to reinstate him, then they re-employed him, demoting him to a fireman.

After several defeats, he entered the House of Representatives in 1929, but bitter faction fighting with Jack Lang saw him virtually destroyed. He faced the Great Depression without his seat in Parliament, expelled from his own union, and without a job.

Paradoxically it was his political opponents who rescued him. He was appointed to a Royal Commission on banking and four years later the Menzies Government made him wartime Director of Labour Regulation and Supply. However, Chifley resigned to contest the election that returned him to Parliament. Chifley became Curtin's Treasurer.

On 12 July 1945, Chifley entered the Federal Parliament for the first time as Prime Minister and was greeted by a chorus of cheers from members of all parties. His first job was to announce the surrender of the Japanese, and for this occasion he arranged the first national broadcast from the House of Representatives in Canberra.

Chifley's primary objective as Prime Minister was post-war economic and industrial development. His government set up shipping, aluminium, whaling and atomic energy industries. It started the Snowy Mountains Scheme and took over telecommunications. But it was Chifley's confirmed belief in nationalisation which led to his downfall; first with the airlines and then, more disastrously, with the banks. Menzies, who was then leader of the opposition, later recalled:

In my opinion he was the most authentic Labor leader in Australian political history. For him, the socialist objective was more than a slogan, it was a principle of action.

Chifley's first attempt to nationalise industry met with mixed success. He did not achieve a true monopoly, but Trans-Australia Airlines (later Australian Airlines—now part of Qantas) was a testament to his skill, and his initial sortie into the airline business did no harm to his standing at the next elections. Labor was returned to the helm with Chifley firmly in control.

During his second term as Prime Minister, however, Chifley made a decision which militant union leaders still regard with distaste. Strikes in the New South Wales coalfields were causing a critical shortage of supply and Chifley, believing a communist plan was at work, sent the army to work in the mines.

But Chifley's most serious tactical error was his attempt to nationalise the banks. He dissented from the findings of a Royal Commission into the banking system and introduced legislation that was passed through Parliament in 1945. It gave greater control to the Commonwealth Bank, but the Melbourne City Council mounted a challenge in the High Court, claiming that the legislation was discriminatory. The aborted bank nationalisation plans were a nail in the coffin of the old Labor Party, which was about to be cast out of office. Labor would not see power again for another 23 years. Ahead lay the agonies of the crippling party 'split' and the so-called 'years in the wilderness'.

The legacies of Labor in the 1940s are very much with us today. The visionary Snowy Mountains Scheme is one example. Another of Chifley's more symbolic acts in the last months of his Prime Ministership was to welcome the first Holden motor car off the assembly line. Chifley, a constant supporter of Laurence Hartnett, played a considerable part in the birth of the car that became an Australian institution.

Today Ben Chifley's humble cottage in Bathurst is a working-class shrine—a perfect time capsule of the 1940s down to the lino and Early Kooka in the kitchen. The sitting room and sideboard hold very modest memorabilia for a man who ran the nation. And out the back, of course, there's a galvo tank on a brick tank stand.

## ARTHUR CALWELL

On a cold winter's night in June 1966, Arthur Calwell was deep in conservative country campaigning against Australia's involvement in the Vietnam War. If Labor won the next election, he told the staunch upper-class residents of Mosman in Sydney, he'd bring the conscripts home. It was an orderly meeting, with just a few Liberal hecklers. When he was leaving, Mr Calwell, contrary to his usual fashion, left the car window wound up. The cold night helped to save his life.

A few seconds later, a young man walked up to the car, pointed a rifle at Mr Calwell's face and pulled the trigger. For the first few moments there was confusion. Calwell was rushed to hospital but it was revealed that the only damage done was to the massive chin so beloved by cartoonists. It was lacerated by glass fragments. Arthur Calwell left hospital the same day. But the frightening impact of this first attempted political assassination in Australia, coming less than three years after the death of John F. Kennedy, was felt across the country.

The morning after the shooting, a 20-year-old youth, Peter Kocan, appeared briefly in court. Kocan later pleaded guilty and was given a life sentence. He was released in 1977 after serving 10 years.

During the ensuing years since the shooting, Kocan immersed himself in academic study, obtaining a Bachelor of Arts degree with honours, majoring in English (creative writing). In January 1999 the University of Newcastle announced that he would be presented with a University Medal for academic excellence. It's been more than 30 years since he expected to die in a hail of bullets and acquire instant fame. In his own words:

> It was an act springing out of profound mental confusion. It was a process of probably three or four years during which time I was becoming more isolated and more alienated, more filled with this peculiar notion that this was a way to make oneself somebody. You know, the old hackneyed thing about identity crisis. I wanted to make myself feel real.
>
> Now for anyone who hasn't experienced the kind of psychological confusion that I experienced prior to the attack on Mr Calwell, that may sound a bit peculiar. But my problem really was that I didn't feel like a real person. I felt like some sort of shadow or ghost or disembodied wraith wandering the streets.
>
> And the significant thing about an act like that, the shooting, to me, was that at one stroke it would prove my realness. After all, you have to be real to pull a trigger, to set in motion the whole process of the media, and the headlines and so on.

While Kocan was in Morisset Psychiatric Hospital, Arthur Calwell kept in touch with the young man's mother to follow his progress. Just before he died, Calwell told Kocan he was planning to visit him at the hospital.

Left: Federal Labor opposition leader, Arthur Calwell, after he had been shot while in the back seat of a car in 1966. Glass fragments lacerated his chin. Bottom: The man who fired the shot, Peter Kocan, who served 10 years of a life sentence for the attempted political assassination of Calwell.

## HAROLD HOLT

The new Liberal Party leader, Harold Holt, won the 1966 election that saw the removal of Arthur Calwell from the opposition leader's chair to be replaced by Gough Whitlam. Holt 'ruled' until 17 December 1967—then he disappeared.

Holt was Menzies' faithful, hard-working lieutenant: a handsome, popular man with a vivacious wife, who immediately set about redecorating the conservative Prime Minister's Lodge in what was an avant-garde style for the 1960s.

Holt's hobby of skindiving was well known, and Australians looked on his enthusiasm for the sport with some humour. The thought of their Prime Minister slipping into a wetsuit had a faintly whimsical air. But why not? We all have our weekend relaxations.

Harold Holt loved his freedom and he was an experienced swimmer. At 59, he was fit and knew the waters around Portsea, on the Victorian coast, as well as the best divers. But surely it could only happen in Australia that the leader of a nation could walk on the beach with friends without security protection? In what other country could the head of government walk into dangerous surf and swim out to sea alone?

The alarm was raised at 12.40 p.m. on a summer Sunday, and within minutes a massive search operation was under way. The Prime Minister was missing, presumed drowned. Melbourne's police, Navy, Army and Air Force were thrown into the hunt. When the search was abandoned in the failing light that evening, it was obvious the exercise was futile.

Artist Clifton Pugh, an experienced skindiver, frequently swam with the Prime Minister. He described Holt's last day on Cheviot Beach:

I think he probably wanted to show off a little bit. I believe there was a young bloke and his young girl there and I think it was the story of the old bull and the young bull. You know, out he goes without his wetsuit. He'd had a few drinks and you get puffed very quickly. The young bloke had much more sense. He went a little way and came back. Apparently, right at that time, the tide changed and the water became an absolute millrace. And then, in that water is a lot of debris and kelp up to 30 feet long whipping about. He might have just got a bit exhausted. He could have been hit on the head by a bit of debris, or caught by a bit of kelp. It's all holes there and rock caverns. I think he probably just got pulled under.

Top: In what other country could a Prime Minister wander into the surf unwatched by security men and drown? Harold Holt had a passion for the sea and scuba diving but on 17 December 1967 he disappeared while swimming at Cheviot Beach, Portsea. Bottom: His wife Dame Zara Bate, 15 years afterwards, at the site of Holt's disappearance.

Holt's death upset the whole future of the Liberal Party, which had been so carefully planned by Menzies. The stately order of leadership was thrown into turmoil. There was a series of coups and counter-coups, four Liberal leaders and an election defeat before the Liberals could discover their new strong man. As the former British Prime Minister, Harold Wilson, once declared so accurately: 'A week in politics is a very long time.'

And if Wilson was right, how long does that make 100 years of politics— an eternity? In fact, Australia has seen around 30 Prime Ministers since Barton was first installed amid all that controversy in 1901.

They've ranged from Menzies, who was the only Prime Minister Australians knew for a generation, to Sir Earle Christmas Grafton Page, who was Prime Minister for a little over a fortnight, and Frank Forde, who was in power for eight days.

In 1904, we saw the world's first Labor Prime Minister, John Christian Watson, who actually came here via South America and New Zealand and who, despite playing a vital role in forging Labor's place in the Federal Parliament, was eventually a captive of capitalism. He became a director of various companies and Chairman of the National Roads and Motorists Association.

There was the rotund George Reid nicknamed 'yes/no' because of his ambivalent attitude to Federation and who was the only Australian ever to have sat in the Colonial, Commonwealth and Westminster Parliaments. Andrew Fisher, that man who gave Australia its rallying cry to defend England, 'to the last man and the last shilling', was Prime Minister three times. He was the first Labor Prime Minister to be actually voted into power and then lost it again by a single seat. He'd be the last Prime Minister to win a third term until Bob Hawke. There was Joseph Cook, who accompanied Billy Hughes to the Versailles Peace Conference. Cook said, 'I did a lot of the yarding he did a lot of the barking ... that's what little dogs are for.'

Billy Hughes, called everything from 'the Little Digger' to 'the Rat', was in Parliament for 58 years. And, of course, there was his arch enemy, Bruce, who was the first Australian to sit in the House of Lords; as well as Scullin, the brilliant orator of whom it was said, 'He simply chose the wrong time to be Prime Minister'; and his colleague, Joe Lyons, who led a splinter group away from Labor and who was described by Menzies as 'the best Parliamentarian I've ever known', yet somehow exuding the image of an amiable koala, warm, cuddly and benign.

After Lyons came the short-lived Page; Menzies for his first term; Artie Fadden, another stopgap Prime Minister in power only 40 days; Curtin; and then Francis Forde, who in 1935 lost the leadership to Curtin by only one vote, succeeded him when he died, but then spent only eight days in power before losing to Ben Chifley.

Then began the so-called 'Ming Dynasty', followed by the dramatic demise of Holt, and another stopgap period when the country was under the control of 'Black Jack' McEwen, king of the Country Party and king maker. He shocked but impressed the nation when he declared publicly that he would not serve under William McMahon and later withdrew his support from John Gorton. Despite these bloody encounters, McEwen retired from Parliament and spent a peaceful decade before his death in 1980.

Jolly John Gorton's political epitaph was inspired by a television send-up of his extraordinary and controversial reign—'This Day Tonight' decided that Frank Sinatra's version of 'I did it my way' should be his theme, and it stuck. Gorton, a former RAAF pilot whose face had been reconstructed after an aircraft crash, had a crooked, cheeky smile and a larrikin demeanour that kept him constantly in trouble.

Tall and athletic with an easy charm and a sense of humour, he'd risen to the elevated position of Leader of the Government in the Senate and descended to lead his party in the lower house when his other colleagues were apparently thought too grey and uncharismatic to be considered as leadership material. But Gorton, the loner, soon ran foul of the Liberal pack, most particularly with Malcolm Fraser, his Minister for Defence, who spoke in his resignation speech of Prime Minister Gorton's 'dangerous reluctance to consult Cabinet'.

He became the subject of scandalous rumour, particularly about his relationship with his young female secretary described by a colleague as, 'It's shapely, it wiggles, and it's name is Ainslie (Gotto).' In typical loose cannon style, he eventually voted himself out of office.

Meanwhile, Billy McMahon, after waiting in the wings as a not-too-blushing bridesmaid, finally got there just in time to send his party into political obscurity.

McMahon, a respected Treasurer but a somewhat comical, bird-like figure and a favourite butt of cartoonists, was the very antithesis of the next Liberal to become Prime Minister, John Malcolm Fraser. Fraser, tall, aloof and arrogant with a profile as haughty as that of an Easter Island statue, was nicknamed 'Freezer' by his school mates.

A descendant of a wealthy pastoral family, his private school education was followed by graduation from Oxford. Fraser came under the wing of Robert Menzies, who saw him as future leadership material. Such is history's capacity to reduce entire political careers to a few fragments, he's remembered for the fact that he was dubbed 'Kerr's Cur' by his arch enemy; the fact that he somehow lost his trousers in a Memphis Hotel; and that he had the temerity to tell Australians the truth with the line that will become his epitaph, 'Life wasn't meant to be easy.'

How Fraser and his rival Gough Whitlam will be remembered in the longer term is yet to be seen but as far as Whitlam's concerned, he was a magnificent Prime Minister. Never one not to blow his own alpenhorn, Gough has been accused in recent years of attending so many functions that he would 'go to the opening of an envelope'. Nevertheless, he's achieved something of an elder statesman status, and his old rival Malcolm Fraser certainly has—successfully striding the international stage while Gough spends much of his time launching books on the local scene.

Bob Hawke, at one stage Australia's most popular Prime Minister, the man who it seemed had single-handedly won the America's Cup, the Wimbledon tennis final, and broken the drought all in a matter of months has somehow managed to diminish in stature as time passes. This phenomenon no doubt has something to do with Hawke's combined penchant for self-aggran-disement, business and women other than his ex-wife Hazel, who in the meantime has become something of a national icon herself.

Official histories might be kinder to Hawke, recalling his Rhodes Scholarship, his persuasive leadership of the ACTU and his contribution to industrial relations reform with the establishment of the Accord; but to many, he's still 'the Silver Bodgie'.

Paul Keating, his successor, who could inspire his electorate with passionate and brilliant political statements on such causes as the Republic, the environment and land rights, could also instantly disenchant them with the French clock, Zegna-suit, piggery side of his political persona. His sudden and dramatic fall from grace and power seemed to send him into an almost monastic exile and it would be some time before he emerged again to give firmly argued Keatingesque advice on such subjects as media monopolies.

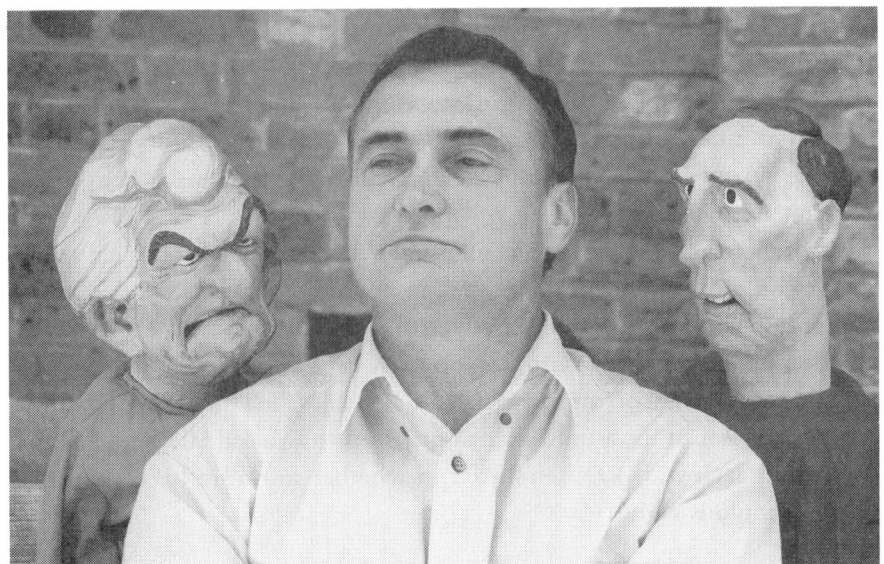

Top: A couple of 'Rubbery Figures' created by puppeteer Peter Nicholson. Hawke, dubbed 'the Silver Bodgie' by the press, had enough idiosyncrasies to keep the cartoonists going for years. His successor, Paul Keating, 'the Bankstown Bonaparte', was subtler and a little harder to satirise. Bottom: Liberal Party leader and Prime Minister John Howard at Liberal Headquarters, Charterbridge House, Sydney, in 1999.

Just like Fraser, Keating could well be remembered for two unfortunate aphorisms—'Banana Republic', and of course, 'the recession we had to have'— both comments about the economy under his own control. These typically cavalier Keating quotes had a sort of twentieth-century 'Let them eat cake' quality that incensed his electorate, who were doing it hard under huge interest rates.

Yet, if there was anyone who demonstrated better than even this illustrious band of brothers just how long a week in politics can be it was little Johnny Howard, spurned and elevated, rejected and raised, a political Lazarus who plodded and plotted his way to the top job with a deceptive set of skills that had the wise heads of the press gallery nodding their heads in acknowledgment. The man most unlikely had managed to succeed after all.

In an interview in 1999, I asked him whether or not in his view it had been a 'fabulous century':

Yes and no ... It's been an horrific century—the loss of life in war has been quite horrific yet it ends fabulously because we are starting to get the benefits of information technology—all the benefits in medical science that gene technology and gene research can produce. So it is simultaneously horrific yet fabulous.

And Australian society in general?

Yes, we are a far more open-minded, tolerant nation than we've ever given ourselves credit for. When I saw President Clinton here in 1996 we were talking about some of the similarities between Australia and America, and there are many but there are also dissimilarities, and I pointed out to him that Australia had had both Catholic and Protestant Prime Ministers long before America had elected its first Catholic President, and yet the religious distribution of the two nations as between Catholic and Protestant were roughly similar.

Now, I know we're not without blemish in these things and we suffered terribly from sectarianism and bigotry for a long time, but we're sometimes a little slow to recognise that in many of these fields we were a long way ahead of other people. I'm reminded of it only today. A very prominent Sydney businessman who is Jewish said to me: 'John, this is the most racially tolerant country in the world.' And this is a man who had many of his family members perish in the Holocaust. I think we sometimes forget that we have done things well in that area—much better than we give ourselves credit for. Look at how we've absorbed people from everywhere. Sure you've had some blips and you've had resistance and you've had people arguing at various stages that perhaps it's all happening too quickly and we've obviously done it badly in some ways, but by and large, we have done it very well indeed.

# Fads, fashion and feminism ...

## AUSTRALIAN FADS AND CRAZES

Possibly the earliest Aussie fad was 'Two-up', the game derived from the convict pastime of 'pitch and toss' and it has convicted a few more since then. Two-up (its other name 'the Swy' is a corruption of the German *zwei*, meaning two) has been played just out of grasp of the long arm of the law since the First Fleet arrived in 1788. The only times it's legally played is at licensed casinos and during the nation's most sacred day of commemoration, Anzac Day.

A very simple game with a rather complicated set of rules and lots of arcane terminology ('spinner', 'kip', etc.), it comprises two coins which are tossed into the air from a small wooden palette called a 'kip' to see whether they land 'heads' or 'tails'. Vast sums of money have been won and lost at the famous galvo (galvanised iron) two-up shed a few miles outside the robust gold mining town of Kalgoorlie, Western Australia. Winning punters are traditionally given a 30 minute head start to get back to town before their predatory mates, who might want to take their money, or at least want to be 'shouted' a drink at the pub.

In fact, in a country where the top-rating television program at the end of the century was the American sitcom 'Friends', the national dress was jeans and T-shirts, the national food was McDonald's or KFC, and the national drink was Coke, it's not always easy to find a distinctively Australian pastime. But now and then, in among a sea of weird imported activities that have ranged from the Fandango to phone box stuffing, there have been a few local innovations.

Left: Annette Kellerman, champion swimmer, actress and 'pin-up' girl of the early 1900s.

Indeed, some of them have been quite surprising. According to some pretty expert opinion, Australia, paradoxically, is the home of the sport of skiing. As a means of transport, of course, it had been known in Europe for at least 1500 years. It was brought to Australia by Norwegian miners during the gold rushes and as early as 1860 some of them came up with the idea of arranging a sports meeting on skis. If they'd formed an official ski club then they would have clinched first place without question, but as it turned out the Kiandra Ski Club is the second oldest in the world, formed shortly after the first one in Norway.

Our other big claim to fame in sport is motor cycle speedway racing, or dirt track racing, born when J.S. Hoskins organised the first races at the Maitland Agricultural Show in 1925. Other Australian sporting innovations were the aptly named position of 'silly mid-on' in cricket, a fielding position where a player can get his or her head knocked off pretty easily, the butterfly stroke in swimming, invented by Sydney St Leonards Cavill, a member of the renowned aquatic family, and the crouch seat for jockeys. Jockeys sat bolt upright until 1884 when Tot Flood and James Barden decided to streamline the whole business.

In the same year, the Australian sprinter, Bobby McDonald of Bourke, pioneered the crouch start for a sprint race. Actually, when McDonald first got down on the starting line, the starter ordered him to stand up in the proper manner but the runner, not the starter, stuck to his guns and made a little piece of history.

Our biggest claim to fame, of course, is the Australian Crawl introduced to us by the Solomon Islander Alick Wickham, also billed by promoters as 'Prince Wickyama', and developed by another member of the Cavill family, Dick. The new stroke was so effective that it played havoc with existing world records and for a while there was some argument that it should be banned.

While America had its drug stores and soda fountains, the milk bar was an exclusively Australian invention. The maiden 'strawberry malted' was poured at Australia's first milk bar, which opened in Martin Place, Sydney, in 1933. The same year, milk bars began opening in Melbourne and Brisbane, and it soon became the sport for milkmaids across the country to fill their tumblers by stretching the milk out at arm's length in front of them, in a sort of liquid, milky way. How and why this sort of long-distance decanting caught the public imagination is a mystery. But then, most fads are.

Sydney's first milk bar had an electric cow as decoration in the front window. Milkshakes were sold for fourpence each, extra if an egg was added. An American ice-cream soda cost sixpence and sundaes, dripping with chocolate syrup and topped with nuts and shiny green cherries, were ninepence, to be ordered only on special occasions.

Many fads pioneered by children are often also taken up by their parents. In the 1950s, Australian children and adults were crazy about bamboo hulahoops, another Australian invention. We whirled them around our necks, hips, arms and legs in backyards, at exercise classes, even at parties, and the nation was alive with the sound of slipping discs.

In 1958, when two Californian toy makers heard about Australia's hoop craze, they made their own version out of plastic. Within six months, with the help of the Wham-O Company, American children were spinning 30 million hoops across the United States, setting records of up to 3000 twists without stopping.

In the early 1930s, mini-golf was all the rage in towns and cities across our nation. At weekends we spent leisure hours with backs bent, putting a golf ball around a concrete obstacle course of fairytale medieval castles and miniature Sydney Harbour Bridges. In Sydney, one of the most popular courses was built in a temple overlooking picturesque Middle Harbour. This mock Grecian edifice was, in fact, all that remained of a previous fad. It was built during the 1930s by members of Sydney's Theosophist Society, purportedly to watch 'the Second Coming' of Christ, who, some were led to expect, would walk across the water through Sydney Heads and up the Harbour. These people were in fact victims of a persuasive Indian mystic, and while they were disappointed, the subsequent tenants of the temple were delighted with their spectacular venue for mini-golf.

The craze blossomed with 'links springing up like mushrooms', according to a newspaper report. There have been several revivals of the mini-golf craze over the years, but by the 1990s it had all but disappeared.

Another craze, huge in the 1950s but killed by television, was the drive-in theatre. Back then it was 'as modern as tomorrow'. Families often arrived while the sun was still up to get a good spot. Dad tried to get the front wheels perfectly on top of the bitumen mound, and then there was always that familiar crash as the loud-speaker was hooked onto the glass window. Somehow the knob always either stuck or came off. At interval, everyone

Top: So, Superman wasn't the first to wear his underpants on the outside. Bondi Surf Lifesaving Club's team march past at Manly Beach, 1909. They are wearing the 'proper' dress of the time—chests and thighs covered and 'vees' for added modesty. Bottom: Mini-golf was a craze of the 1930s, being played here at the old Theosophists' temple on Sydney's Middle Harbour—scene of an unfulfilled 'Second Coming'.

rushed out of the car and tried to be first to the hot dog counter. On the way back you couldn't find your car in the dark, and when you finally got there the main feature had invariably started. If it got boring, there was always the chance of some fun and games in the back seat; if not in your own, then in the car beside you. At worst, it rained and you had to sit peering through the windscreen wipers at Charlton Heston building the pyramids. How did television compete with all that?

Close behind drive-ins came another American family fad. In 1960, the first ten-pin bowling alley was opened at Hurstville, Sydney. Scores more followed, each decorated in the early 1960s American style, with snack bars and garish plastic furnishings. As with all true crazes, their fortunes have gone up and down like Alan Bond's bank balance, but the game itself has been assured a future as a big money television event.

America also gave us the pogo stick and the urge to break crazy records like phone box stuffing, a sport almost exclusively confined to university students.

And then there was that hardy perennial, the yoyo! Yoyos might seem as American as Coca Cola, but the United States can't claim to have invented this fad. Prehistoric man used yoyos as hunting weapons. King George IV of England played with one when it was called 'the bandalore'. And history tells us that aristocrats distracted themselves with yoyos on their way to the guillotine during the French Revolution.

Yoyos have been periodically and cleverly launched onto the Australian scene by the marketing gurus of companies like Coca Cola, and every time this simple device with no moving parts has always become a giant fad—selling more than a million just in the suburbs of Sydney.

## DANCING

For most of this century, dance crazes have been a favourite target for wowsers. In 1903, the Reverend Dr Torrey in Melbourne warned women in his congregation that if a girl knew what a man was thinking while he was dancing with her, she would never dance again. But that's exactly why she did dance again, and again. In 1914, the New South Wales Presbyterian Assembly denounced Sydney women for their shameful 'sleeveless' evening gowns and daring new dances. Waltzing was barely acceptable, and any other dance that brought young people close together was 'shocking'. But the ballrooms were as crowded as ever. It seemed there was no stopping the modern wave of sinful dancing. After the austerity of life during the First World War years, Australians were dancing the Foxtrot and Pride of Erin, often at musical evenings in homes where the lounge room carpet and chairs were pushed back to make a dance floor.

With the introduction of radio in 1923 came the hits of 'the Golden Twenties'. Australian flappers danced the American Charleston to the beat of 'jazz' music that reflected the hedonistic affluence of the times. A generation later we were copying the Americans again, this time dancing the Jitterbug in the merry-making days after the Second World War. The Jitterbug was the maddest dance of all. Not many people could do it well, and so just watching the experts became a craze. The Jitterbug's popularity produced teams of professionals who performed their acrobatic displays of dancing in front of huge crowds.

Aileen Joyce and Artie Smith won the New South Wales Jitterbug Championship at the Bondi Pavilion in 1945. They also danced the Lindy Hop and the Boogie Woogie, plus dozens more variations of their own invention. Aileen remembers:

> We used to dance to 'In the Mood', 'Twelfth Street Rag'—anything that was really jazzy. The music really got into us. When the music was on, you could see Artie just drift away. He just loved music. You know, once you've got the music you can just keep on going. It was very strenuous and entailed a lot of training. We used to train three days a week—like a racehorse. I think we were the only Jitterbuggers where the woman threw her partner.

And according to Artie Smith:

> We had precision. There was one routine where I used to put Aileen up on my shoulders and I'd throw her to the ground and she'd go into a complete split. We had a unique set of double throws. My footwork was pretty fast and my partner was double-jointed. She could twist herself any way.

Being dropped six feet onto the floor in the splits was not to the taste of every Australian matron, and soon we were looking for a modern step we

Top: In 1945, the Jitterbug reached such energetic heights it was left mostly to professionals such as Artie Smith and Aileen Joyce. Dignity was not a criterion. Bottom: Before the arrival of television, American-style drive-ins were popular during the 1950s. A few still operate around Australia but these days they're mostly for nostalgia buffs, some of whom courted there and some who were conceived there.

could all do. After a decade of rock 'n' roll, we discovered 'the Twist', a dance so simple that anybody could do it. For the first time since the Charleston, dancing partners actually let go of each other permanently and moved around the dance floor in separate motion. The Twist went up and down and round and round and just about any way you wanted to go. If you tired of your partner, you could twist off and dance with someone else. The Twist lasted only a few years, but in the meantime Australia was already inventing its own dance craze, 'the Stomp'.

To do the Stomp in regulation style, you needed a special uniform of rubber sneakers, jeans and extra-outsized jumper. It started on the Sydney beaches, and Sunday nights soon saw thousands of teenage 'surfies' flocking to the Avalon or Bronte stomp halls to stamp their feet to the music of young bands like the Bee Gees, who played the surf club circuit.

The dance spread west to Kings Cross in Sydney to a stomp hall called Surf City, which became something of a battleground for Sydney's rival teenage gangs, the stomping surfies and the 'rockers', who were mainly bike riders and their mates from the western suburbs. But apart from that, parents could stop worrying. The Stomp had no sex appeal whatsoever.

No-one is even sure where it started, but one little girl came to be identified with it more than anyone. Patricia Amphlett was just into her teens when she climbed onto the stage at her local surf club to sing 'Stomping at Maroubra'. Little Pattie went on to entertain Australian troops in Vietnam and has been a perennially successful singer on the Australian club circuit. As for Australia's one great contribution to the world of dance crazes, in her words:

Anybody could do it. It was less complicated than rock 'n' roll and even less complicated than the Twist. I mean, overweight people couldn't twist very well, but anybody could do the Stomp. It stayed for a little while, and it is Australian.

Interestingly, there haven't been that many dance crazes in the last few decades of the century. Formalised steps have tended to give way to individual expression. It's no longer considered socially odd for same-sex dancing, or even dancing by yourself—once the sign of a word that's gone almost totally out of fashion—'the wall-flower'.

The other somewhat paradoxical change is that in the seemingly more conservative and morally uptight years of the early part of the century dancers held onto each other and were even intertwined. In the more recent so-called permissive era where the discotheque is seen by some to be a den of debauchery, dancers rarely hold each other—indeed it's somewhat 'infra dig' for them to even make contact.

Of course, there are exceptions. There have been brief flirtations with the naughty Lambada and even lap dancing, but these are fads that have come and gone quicker than most. The short life of another craze, the Macarena, might have had something to do with the fact that its most high-profile exponent was the Federal Treasurer, Mr Peter Costello. The sight of Mr Costello disporting himself with 'Midday' chat show host, Kerri-Anne Kennerley, was amusing but not one to set the nation's feet tapping.

Nevertheless, it seems that some sort of dancing, like sex, is here to stay. It still does not always meet with the older generation's approval. But tripping the light fantastic is certainly not the picture of debauchery predicted by another Melbourne cleric, the Reverend Wallis of Fitzroy, who 60 years ago denounced meeting on the dance floor as, 'The nursery of divorce, the training ship of prostitution and a modern ulcer threatening public morality.'

## FASHION

When you went to town in the 1950s, you wore a hat and gloves. You wouldn't dream of going to town without a hat and gloves.

So said Australian fashion historian, Norma Martyn. Not until we dropped the old English customs, including the hat and gloves uniform, did Australians begin to develop a fashion style of their own.

In the early 1900s, 'a woman walked in beauty and in pain', as Norman Lindsay's wife, Rose, once said. She wore steel-ribbed corsets that cupped the breasts and layers of padding below a tiny waspish waist. Stiff necklines choked her lily-white neck. Men's fashion too made no attempt to suit Australia's hot, humid summers. Gentlemen went to the office dressed in three-piece tweed suits, more suited to the cold English climate.

Even if, very occasionally, they took their coats off, the waistcoat was never removed. Hats were also compulsory, and most men wore Australia's version of the English bowler, which we called 'the Boxer'.

Women wore large hats feathered with fancy plumes plucked from ostriches, which were bred on farms especially set up to supply the fashion. The sale or possession of ostrich feathers was banned in 1918.

The first breakthrough in modern fashion came soon after the turn of the century. Quite simply, the ankle was revealed. It was a most dramatic happening. In one sense, the revelation of the ankle was the point at which we started to enter the age of the 'permissive society'. But it was some time before tightly squeezed female bodies were released from their less visible constriction of voluminous underclothing. Women still wore layered skirts and steel corsets. One Sydney retail store even advertised that corsets could be returned for refund if they showed signs of rust.

In 1914, the first 'brassiere' was patented in America by a young heiress with the appropriate name of Caresse Crosby. There is much dispute among fashion historians as to whether this was, in fact, the first bra invented. Bust garments had been worn in Australia earlier this century at first only by 'stout' women. But by 1918 they were popular with all women and soon became a moral 'must' for all modest ladies.

As skirt lengths inched upward from the ankle towards the knee after the First World War, compulsory sleeves and high necklines also disappeared. The war years had brought a new, simple fashion. Tight waists and flared skirts gave way to soft, uninhibited styles that left a woman able to breathe and move freely.

By the 1920s, fashion-conscious women were aligning their clothing tastes with the prevailing mood of feminism. Skirts took a sudden leap to the knees and black wool and lisle stockings gave way to skin-tone sheer silk. 'Fast' young ladies openly smoked cigarettes in public and even made personal calls on the telephone without being formally introduced.

The flappers, with their new-found freedom, began wearing straight 'tubular' dresses that showed no bust, waist or hipline. Bobbed-cut hair, introduced as a practical measure for women doing war work during 1914–18, now became the fashion, and by the late 1920s, bobbed curls had given way to a more boyish cut, the Eton crop.

These boyish fashions eventually led to a return of femininity in the 1930s and women who could afford to copied French fashion photographs on their Singer sewing machines. Bodices were shaped around padded shoulders, and emphasised the bustline. Waists were tightened and skirts curved out to the hips and bottom, then back into narrow hems.

Rayon, made from wood pulp and first exhibited by a French scientist in 1889, was woven into cheaper stockings in the 1930s. The traditional white evening dress was replaced by a dramatic, brief black number called 'the cocktail dress'. Gloves were very vogue, worn up to 16 inches long at night, and elbow length by day.

With rayon came the age of synthetics—nylon, dacron, banlon—in fact, just anything that ended with 'on'. After the Second World War, baby doll shortie pyjamas introduced teenagers to a new American fad, the pyjama party. And, when older women went 'out' they dressed up in shiny Rita Hayworth numbers, or glamorous taffetas à la Monroe.

Yet soon all this formal elegance was gone, swept aside by the most potent fashion accessory of all—bare flesh. Most of the changes had been gradual, but the salons were set reeling by a sequence of sensational events that started to reveal more of the female form.

Swimsuits that had started off as woollen neck-to-knees were well established as being a 'two piece' by the 1940s, and in 1946, when the United States began testing the atom bomb at Bikini Atoll in the Pacific, the first 'bikini' was launched by a French designer, Louis Reard.

Bikinis gradually gained acceptance in the 1950s, especially on the Gold Coast of Queensland; although they took a little longer in Sydney where council beach inspectors were still ordering bikini 'birds' off Bondi Beach in the 1960s. Such was the state of the moral barometer that penalties were quite draconian and women were even taken to court and fined for wearing less than three inches (7.5 cm) of fabric at the hip. Ironically, the same council was the first to sanction topless bathing on a popular public beach in 1978.

But it was during Melbourne Cup week in 1965 that a battle between European models dramatically changed the course of Australian fashion. Representing 'pure wool' was French mannequin, Christine Borge. Appearing for 'synthetics' was Great Britain's Jean (the Shrimp) Shrimpton, at that time the highest-paid model in the world.

Borge had arrived in Melbourne in late October. As she stepped off the plane from Paris, she fell into an elegant faint straight into the waiting arms of the local Wool Board representative. The airport pictures made front page news. Later, Christine Borge told Melbourne columnist Keith Dunstan, 'I just can't think of anything the Shrimp can do to upstage me.'

Top: What the ladies were wearing to Flemington during the 1950s. Note the ^identical hemlines. Right: Eyebrows went even higher than English model Jean Shrimpton's raised hemline when she wore the first mini-skirt in Australia at Flemington during the 1965 Melbourne Cup week. To add insult to injury, the brazen hussy was not wearing any stockings!

Left: As far as young Australians were concerned, particularly the blokes, the bikini was the greatest invention in the history of the world. Bottom: In 1965, the Gold Coast Council came up with a terrific idea for tourism —bikini-clad maids who fed tourists' parking meters just as they were about to expire. They're still going strong.

But the Shrimp fought back in dramatic style. She arrived at the Flemington members' stand in a skirt that was four inches above her knees. Not only did she make every front page in the country, but she also had reporters flying out from London to cover the story.

To Melbourne's conservative social set, the Shrimp was a brazen hussy. Not only did she show almost a quarter of her thigh, but she wore no hat, no gloves and—horror of horrors—no stockings! To make matters worse, the cheeky little minx was wearing a man's watch. 'Where,' they asked, 'would it all end?' It's hard now to understand the uproar. But you have to remember that these were the first deliberately exposed human knees ever seen inside the members' enclosure at Flemington.

Fortunately, the next time Australia made world headlines with fashion we had learnt to admire, rather than gasp at, a shapely leg. This time, the scene was the White House in Washington and most Australians felt our First Lady had done us proud. As Sonia McMahon walked down the staircase of the White House, the skirt of her long white dress parted to reveal an arresting sun-tanned leg from ankle to thigh, with an illusory split in the fabric that went much higher. The photographers and press had a field day. That one daring evening gown kept any serious discussion between Prime Minister William McMahon and President Nixon, if there was any, off the front pages. President Nixon's problems with unsuccessful cover-ups were still to come, but for Lady McMahon it was a venture into foreign affairs that she will never forget:

> I never thought twice about wearing it. I actually was going to wear that dress to crown Miss Australia that year. But then President Nixon asked us to go over to the United States rather hurriedly so I took my white dress with me. Naturally if you have a new dress you think of wearing it to the White House.
>
> You know, it's not all that daring unless you get caught by photographers sideways walking up and down stairs.

Lady McMahon's famous dress is now a fashion icon and in the 1990s it was displayed at Sydney's Powerhouse Museum, still looking impressive and, strangely, even 30 years on, still looking like a dress that could set the White House on fire.

In many ways, the early 1970s were the end of an era for high fashion. The harsh modernism of Dior's 'sack' look had made a mockery of the word 'style'. At last Australians began to cast a critical eye over the strange plastic, metal and modular creations that kept arriving from overseas. We were ready to try a home-grown product. In the words of Carla Zampatti, one of the first contemporary Australian designers:

> Women used to say, 'I will buy my wardrobe in Paris or London or Italy or New York.' Today, the same people come to me and I outfit them for the trip.

Australian fashion, led by designers like Zampatti, Prue Acton and Trent Nathan, were soon helping to support more than 120 000 people working in the local fashion industry. At last, Australians had come to terms with the climate and our fashions had earned a place in international salons.

By the 1990s the rag trade was booming, spurred on ironically by the success of someone who specialised more in what she didn't wear than what she did—supermodel, Elle Macpherson. The extraordinary international love affair with Elle, nicknamed 'the Body', rubbed off very well on the antipodean fashion scene, and when a next-generation supermodel, Sarah O'Hare, not only charmed the world but beguiled the son of possibly the most influential Australian in history, Rupert Murdoch, Australian fashion was well and truly on the map.

Among the new breed of rising fashion stars is Collette Dinnigan, whose wispy, lacy, filigreed confections signify a total return to the feminine and took even tough old Paris by storm. In her words:

> I think Australia is quite unique and it has its own kind of sense of style and sense of design, whether it's in film or fashion or any creative side. I think it's being a lot more recognised now because Australia seems to be the flavour at the moment.
>
> Everyone wants to sort of head to Australia, whether it's for a holiday or to discover something new because, after all, the world is sort of becoming a smaller and smaller place.

## MISS AUSTRALIA

The search for a true Australian beauty queen has always been something of a national preoccupation. In 1909 the magazine *The Lone Hand* felt it should

Above left: Sonia McMahon made world headlines when she wore this split evening dress at President Nixon's White House in 1971.
Above right: Beryl Mills of Perth won the inaugural Miss Australia competition in 1926.
Right: Tania Verstak won the Miss Australia contest of 1961 and went on to become Miss International later that year. She was the best-known person in the nation.

defend our womanly honour and set off in search of an Australian entrant for the World's Beauty contest to be held in America later that year.

The judges narrowed the field down to a handful of aspiring queens by sifting through thousands of photographs. But it wasn't a foolproof system and the magazine reported with regret the exclusion of a young Queenslander of 'classic mould' when the unfortunate girl appeared in person for the judging:

> Accompanied by her sister, we met a tall girl of 18 summers. But, alack, not quite the girl imagination and photograph had pictured for us. It may be that five years hence, after exercise has developed what at present are promises, this young lady would be acclaimed the winner of a beauty contest.

In those days marriage was not considered a handicap and Mrs Otto Wunderlich and Mrs Della Carsons were starters. Daisy Clifton was a strong runner but eventually she was pipped at the post by Alice Buckridge, a 21-year-old drapery assistant who weighed in at a demure 10 stone 6 pounds (about 66 kilograms). The judges waxed lyrical about her 23-inch (58-centimetre) waist and her 'unblushing face full of the joy of life, and beautiful even in repose'. Miss Buckridge's photographs were forwarded to the *Chicago Tribune*, which by now seemed to have forgotten about the event. But the circulation of *The Lone Hand* climbed handsomely and the commercial potential of the beauty quest was established beyond doubt.

The official Miss Australia Quest, as we know it, began in 1926 when two Sydney newspapers, *The Guardian* and the legendary *Smith's Weekly*, set about the rather costly business of choosing the most gorgeous girl in the country. Badly damaged fragments from a film of the first Miss Australia Quest are the only visual records of the event. It seems the girls were thoroughly tested for Australian conditions, parading before judges in clinging woollen swimsuits. By modern standards they were, in fact, quite bold. Miss Australia contestants would eventually cease to pose in swimming costumes as the opinions of feminism prevailed.

With prizes of £1000 and two motor cars, the beauty quest caused tremendous excitement. And, when the big night finally came, it was the girl from the West, Miss Beryl Mills, who beat Monica Mack and Mascotte Rawlston to become the first official Miss Australia.

Beryl, a 19-year-old from Geraldton, Western Australia, was described as 'a splendid stamp of glorious Australian womanhood'. Hal Missingham, later Director of the New South Wales Art Gallery and a Miss Australia judge, recalled meeting Beryl when they lived in the same neighbourhood:

> She was a big bird, you know. All built right, a pleasant kind of look about her face. Open. She had a big mouth, big eyes. She really was something.

After her win, Beryl went to Hollywood for a screen test in the silent movies. When she returned she was soon taken up by the local advertising industry to spruik for Australian products.

After the death of her first husband, Beryl married again and went to live in America. She died in 1977 at the age of 70. In the late 1920s she was Australia's most famous girl, yet reports of her death made barely a couple of paragraphs in the papers.

There have been scores of Miss Australias since Beryl Mills and over the years, the Miss Australia Quest had many ups and downs. Outwardly it was a shiny pageant which raised tens of millions of dollars for charity. But for many years it was a tool for commercial interest. The image of Miss Australia was portrayed as being as sacred as motherhood and yet, in 1975, the Northern Territory withdrew from the Quest—its entrant was disqualified because she was in fact a mother.

By the 1990s, the advance of feminism and political correctness helped the whole concept of Miss Australia towards oblivion. When men rather cheekily demanded to become participants, reversing the whole notion of affirmative action, the Quest was clearly facing extinction and that's exactly what happened.

Few people can remember one year's winner from the next. Yet, even today, one beauty remains firmly in the memory of millions of Australians. Remarkably, she was not even born in the country she represented so successfully, not only as Miss Australia but as Miss International as well.

Tania Verstak was born in Shanghai. She was something of an ugly duckling as a child. She came to Australia at the age of seven with her White Russian parents who were refugees from the communist regime in China. The family settled at Manly and by the age of 16, Tania had begun to blossom as a beauty. She had brains as well as charm. She took an Arts degree at

Sydney University and spoke several languages. In all she won five beauty quests, from Miss Movie Ball and Miss Sydney University, to Miss New South Wales, Miss Australia and finally Miss International.

The daily press followed Tania's every move for three years. Hers was the best-known face in Australia. The story of the refugee child who grew up to conquer the world came to a fitting climax when she married Peter Young, a successful Australian businessman, and then retired from public life to have her baby girl. Tania was indeed a fairytale princess, one who did live happily ever after.

She went on to live in a quiet, wealthy part of Perth in a large house set among a spectacular garden. And this is how she described to me the changes in her life following those heady days when she was the nation's sweetheart:

> Tania Verstak has become Mrs Peter Young. I think she's been leading a very normal life. She has a daughter and a house that takes a lot of looking after. She plays sport, she takes part in a few social things and leads a normal life.
>
> It was very satisfying to have given 18 months of your life towards charity. Not many of us have a chance to do that. And I have a lasting memory of the effect my winning the Miss Australia Quest had on the new Australian community. I met girls of 13 or 14 who said they felt accepted because I had won the Miss Australia Quest, and that was a wonderful feeling.

## THE LADIES

Chevalier Jules Lefebvre's famous painting of a nude French woman, titled simply *Chloe*, is one of Australia's most admired paintings. But instead of hanging in a gallery, *Chloe* looks down on the patrons of a Melbourne pub. The painting has occupied pride of place in Young and Jackson's Hotel since it was bought for 400 guineas back in 1908.

Perhaps it says something about Australia's attitude to women that, for most of the following 70 years, only nude paintings like *Chloe* and the ever-present barmaid were allowed in our public bars. For much of this century, Australian womanhood, if it wanted to drink at all, was politely ushered into a special area quaintly called 'the Ladies Lounge'. It wasn't many years ago that all Australian women were expected to be much like *Chloe*, to know their place and be seen but not heard. A woman could be beautiful,

Top left: Annette Kellerman made a huge splash with her 1914 movie *Neptune's Daughter*, in which she appeared wearing only seaweed. Top right: Ms Kellerman was one of Australia's first truly liberated women. Bottom: Kellerman performed her lavish aquatic fantasies in specially-made giant tanks, one of which burst and almost killed her.

fashionable, witty—but she always understood her main role in life was to 'honour and obey'.

One young Australian woman who didn't take too much notice of convention was Annette Kellerman, the daughter of a Sydney music teacher. She became an international film star and the world's first screen 'pin-up' girl. As part of her recovery from a childhood illness, Annette was encouraged to take up swimming, and while still in her teens, she was winning state championship events. By 1903, her aquatic talents were spectacular enough to warrant a special show at the Melbourne Aquarium. As *Punch* reported: 'A lissom young lady gambolled fearlessly among the fishes and eels. She will become the rage of the town.'

In fact, when Annette added the rather bizarre trick of eating a banana under water, she was well on the way to becoming the rage of the world. In England, the Kellerman name shot into the headlines when she swam down the Thames, and before long she was commanding US$4000 per week for her lavish aquatic 'fantasies', which were performed on stage in giant tanks built especially for the purpose.

It wasn't long before Hollywood made Annette an offer to try her luck in the newly established world of celluloid fantasy, and she created a sensation with a brief 'nude' scene in the 1914 melodrama *Neptune's Daughter*. Annette's first entry to 'Tinsel Town' only fuelled her driving ambition. It was an overwhelming urge to succeed that her sister, Marcel, even at the ripe old age of 92 remembered well: 'I think it was that tenacity that she had. She never gave way on anything at all. Nobody counted. All she wanted to do was get to the top of the tree.' Annette did get to the top of the tree and her life story was immortalised by Esther Williams in the Hollywood extravaganza, *Million Dollar Mermaid*.

Annette married her manager and as she grew older, she seemed to live at an even more hectic pace. She no longer staged her water ballets in public, although at 60 years of age she could still perform amazing underwater feats for the cameras. She became famous for her views on exercise and diet, was elected to the United States Swimming Hall of Fame and passed on her skills to any youngster willing to learn.

When she retired to Surfers Paradise she was already a legend, and in 1975, in a fitting end to her life-long love affair with the water, her cremated remains were scattered in the seas of the Great Barrier Reef.

Annette Kellerman was one of Australia's first truly liberated women, but for many others, the struggle for freedom and equality would continue throughout the century. Australian women won the right to vote in 1902. But although they made up half the electorate, a woman was not voted into parliament for another 40 years. In the 1930s, at the height of the Depression, one in four women was battling against unemployment, hunger and poverty just to keep her family together. The new Prime Minister, Joe Lyons, was proving a skilful politician but, in public at least, he never seemed a very forceful personality. His popularity, it was often said, was partly due to his wife, Enid, 'the woman behind the throne'. At 83, Dame Enid told me:

> We were very close. We were one person really. Of course my role has often been exaggerated in this. People used to say I advised him on everything, which of course wasn't true. But all the big decisions—that affected the family, particularly—naturally he would discuss them. Especially with me having an interest in politics, as I always had. I know without my backing he probably wouldn't have done things. If I'd said I don't like it he probably would not have been able to do it.

Enid Lyons was a girl who always knew what she wanted, and usually got it. At 14 she decided to become a school teacher. Then she met Joe Lyons, at that time Tasmanian Minister for Education. She wanted to marry Joe, and she did so when she was just 17. He was exactly twice her age.

Enid Lyons wanted a large family. She had her first child at 19, and by the time the Lyons household moved into the Prime Minister's Lodge in Canberra, Enid had borne 12 children, of whom 11 survived.

While Joe Lyons settled into the leader's job, Enid became a national figure in her own right, often making three speeches in a single day. But to the media at least, she was still the classic, subservient woman. The newsreels delighted in depicting her as a hard-working devoted wife who ironed Joe's pants and did the mending. Dame Enid said:

> I see nothing derogatory in darning socks. I always used to say that some of my best ideas for speeches came when I was washing clothes. In those days it wasn't a washing machine, you know. You really slogged it out at the washing tub.

Joe Lyons died in April 1939. A few months later the world was plunged into war, and many Australians, particularly women, turned to Enid Lyons to raise their sinking morale. She knew enough about politics to recognise her own electoral potential and in 1943, just four years after her husband's death, she was elected to Federal Parliament—the first woman to take a seat in the House of Representatives and later the first female Cabinet Minister. She once told me:

> Women are of a different make-up from men. A man is a naturally aggressive person, and I think a woman has within her a certain desire to please. And, though I hesitate to say this because I'm sure I'll be torn to pieces by feminists, I believe they like to please men. A subservient role in certain aspects of their lives is normal.

Despite this now rather conservative utterance Dame Enid Lyons, in 1967, was dubbed 'the Germaine Greer of Tasmania' after she gave her official approval to 'much of women's lib'. It seemed a strange tag for a woman who, for 60 years, had reigned as the ideal of Australian motherhood. She told reporters: 'My great-grandson brought me a box of matches. I asked him why, and he said I would find them useful for burning my bra.'

The bra-burning bonfires lit by women's liberationists were blazing brightly in 1972 when a book written by expatriate Australian, Dr Germaine Greer, became almost the bible for the international women's movement. *The Female Eunuch* was acclaimed by critics as a work of notable scholarship. By the time she returned to Australia in 1972, after seven years working in universities abroad, Germaine Greer was the biggest celebrity in feminism.

Ms Greer was born in 1939 and came from a conservative, middle-class Melbourne family. Educated in convent schools, she went on to graduate in Arts from Melbourne University. She gained her MA with first-class honours at Sydney University, then moved on to Cambridge University for her PhD. When she came home to launch *The Female Eunuch* in Australia, 'respectable' women were shocked by this young Australian who encouraged abortion for women who didn't want to have babies.

But thousands turned out in the streets of Sydney to march behind and support Dr Greer. They were protesting at discrimination against women in the home, in the workforce and in public facilities like hotels, where

Right: Enid Lyons was the first woman to take a seat in the Australian Federal House of Representatives in 1943. Wife of Prime Minister Joe Lyons and mother of 11 children, she was also our first female Cabinet Minister.

Bottom: Prior to women's liberation, spearheaded by Germaine Greer during the 1970s, the only women allowed into public bars in Australia were barmaids and those hanging on the wall, for example, C.J. Lefebvre's *Chloe*, at Young and Jackson's Hotel, Melbourne.

women were still unwelcome in most public bars. Germaine Greer kept the memories:

> I can remember going into a pub in Gippsland, and I went into the public bar. The expression on the faces of the blokes drinking there was so appalled— their whole day was ruined. I mean, they were standing there quietly sousing. I stick my head around the door and they go. They weren't rude or anything. I just knew that if I stayed there I wouldn't do myself any good and I'd make myself uncomfortable, so I withdrew.
>
> The man I was with said, 'I didn't think you'd do that. I thought you'd be liberating the bar.' I said, 'You don't seem to get the point. I mean, why should I go somewhere where I'm unpopular? I'm not going to get anything out of it. It's obviously the place where they go to get away from the missus, and they're allowed to have it as far as I'm concerned. I'm not going to jostle for occupation of the men's lavatories.'

Many of the early liberation battles now appear to have been won. According to Dr Greer:

> People can no longer abuse women as thoughtlessly as they used to. But there's still no relish in women's company for men. I mean, they make an effort to kind of get you in a group that women are part of, but I think they'd rather have it the way it was.

For many years now, Dr Greer—or as she's still affectionately remembered from the halcyon days, 'Germs'—has been an expatriate where her writings, musings and spectacular brawls with other feminists and academics still cause headlines. Some regard her as a modern-day Joan of Arc, others as an irascible crackpot. Either way she's had a profound affect on the shaping of feminism, and her fearlessness certainly inspired other women of the world to take up the banner. Here in her motherland—or is it sisterland?—women now occupy, or have occupied, almost every position of power and influence in the community, except the positions of Prime Minister and metropolitan media proprietor. But, with the coming of the new millennium, it's clear those male bastions will soon crumble, too.

# Fear and tragedy ...

## ENVIRONMENTAL HAZARDS

Australia is a relatively safe place, especially when you consider how much of the planet it covers—from its equatorial north down towards the Antarctic. An earthquake was recorded in 1788, but in the past 200 years there have been only a few major tremors. Our volcanoes are extinct and cyclones relatively rare. Bushfires are our greatest natural killer of humans, followed by floods. Drought is the most destructive of the environment. We have few predatory creatures—at least in the animal kingdom—yet the dangerous creatures we live alongside are a great source of terror—snakes, spiders, and most of all, the shark. Our chances of being taken by a shark are around one in 20 million—nationally each year, on average, beestings kill 1.8 people, lightning 1.7, and sharks one person.

But fear is not related to statistics. For example, over the years more Australians have drowned in motor cars than in the Sydney to Hobart yacht race, but most Australians will go for a drive before climbing into a boat and heading to Tasmania on Boxing Day. And, ultimately, the most dangerous creatures on our landscape are us humans.

Foremost among our human predators has been 28-year-old Martin Bryant who, on 29 April 1996, killed 35 people in the historic town of Port Arthur, Tasmania. Bryant, who had a history of mental problems, was suspected of killing his father and a woman named Helen Harvey who left him $500 000 in her will. He drove to the Broad Arrow Cafe armed with semi-automatic rifles, killed 20 people in the café and then went searching for other victims, including children, who were mercilessly gunned down. Bryant was sentenced to life imprisonment and remains in gaol, despite

Left: Everything but the kitchen sink—the devastation of Cyclone Tracy, Christmas Eve 1974.

a couple of attempts at suicide. The Port Arthur massacre led the Australian Government to ban automatic and semi-automatic weapons, but fear and tragedy still stalk the Australian landscape.

## SHARKS

To most of us sharks are terrifying creatures, and Hollywood has proved that, even if you make one out of rubber and put a motor inside it, you can still scare the cossies off half the world.

Shark attacks have been recorded throughout our history, and it is a sobering thought that some of the most dangerous areas are in Sydney Harbour, just a few kilometres from the GPO.

In 1929, eight Australians were killed by sharks. At Bondi Beach, young Colin Stewart was mauled. 'He seemed to be pushing it away,' witnesses said. 'But it came back at him.' Colin died the following day. The same year, a girl was maimed by a shark at Collaroy Beach on Sydney's north side, and a youth was attacked at Maroubra to the south. Another man was killed while swimming in Sydney near the suburb of Balmain.

Sharks were causing so much concern in New South Wales that the government introduced a meshing system in 1937. There has not been a fatal shark attack at a meshed ocean beach since. But the problem in Sydney is that the busy harbour thoroughfares cannot be encumbered by nets. Swimmers bathing in the inviting bays and inlets are tempting, easy bait for sharks.

Australia's most notorious location of sharks has been Middle Harbour in Sydney, an idyllic stretch of placid water and picturesque beaches. Middle Harbour has seen six fatal shark attacks since 1942. The last and most horrific attack was in Sugarloaf Bay.

It was the Australia Day holiday in 1963; a hot, humid, overcast day—the sort that Sydneysiders call 'good shark weather', and yet also the sort they seem to spend in the water until late afternoon when the thunderstorms break. A young actress, Marcia Hathaway, was cooling off in just 75 centimetres of water. Her fiancé, Fred Knight, was swimming nearby when Marcia suddenly cried out, 'I've been bitten by an octopus.' But it was no octopus. By the time her fiancé and a friend had freed her from the jaws of the shark, her right leg had been torn off at the hip and the other mangled.

Marcia Hathaway died in the most tragic circumstances. The beach where

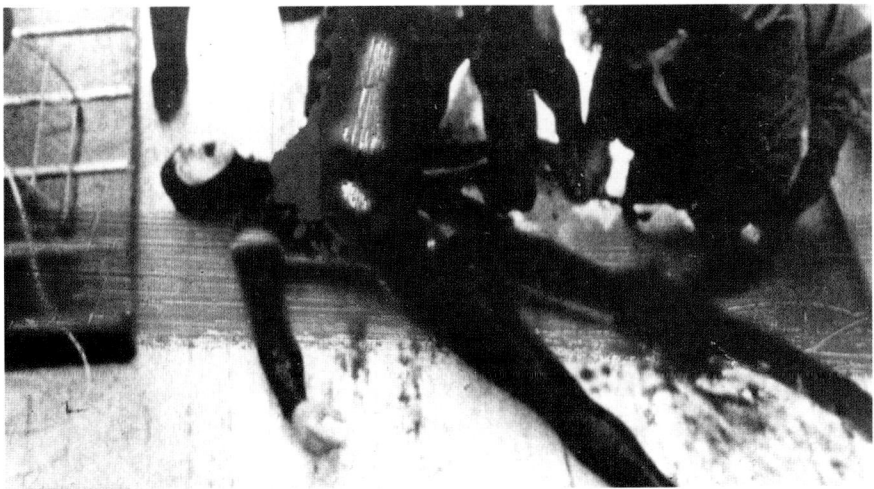

Top: There have been no fatal shark attacks on Sydney beaches since netting was introduced in the 1930s. However, there have been numerous attacks inside the Harbour. In 1963 actress Marcia Hathaway was mauled by a shark in 75 centimetres (30 inches) of water. The ambulance had trouble leaving the beach (top right), and the delay contributed to her death. Bottom: Henri Bource was attacked by a shark off the coast of Victoria in 1964. He was rescued by an incredibly brave young woman who dived into the blood-stained water.

she had been swimming was inaccessible by road. She was taken by boat to the nearest landing place while her fiancé dived back into the water and swam to the nearest house to call for help. An ambulance was waiting for the victim when she arrived, but as it started up the slippery slope, it began to lose traction and the clutch burnt out. A second ambulance had to be called. By the time it arrived and the girl was transferred, it was too late. Marcia Hathaway was dead on arrival at the hospital.

Many shark victims don't live to tell the tale but Henri Bource, a Melbourne scuba diver, who lost his left leg to a White Pointer shark off the coast of Victoria in 1964, was believed to be the only person whose attack was actually recorded on film. Henri used the film in a documentary to tell the story of his terrifying experience. In Bource's words:

> At the impact I knew immediately what had happened. I was dragged under the water and shook and shook—like a dog with a slipper. In a minute and a half it was all over.

Henri Bource owed his life to an incredibly courageous young diver, Jill Ratcliffe, who went to his assistance, diving into the turbulent, bloodstained water. With the help of others, she brought him back to the boat. He said:

> The leg came off and I had to get to the surface to get air. Everything after that just happened automatically. Everyone went into action. They got me on board the boat and they put a tourniquet on the stump and stopped the bleeding. It took an hour and a half to get me to hospital.
> If I hadn't lost the leg when I did, I would have drowned. There is no doubt about that. Although it was only a minute and a half under water, according to the lookout on board who put a time on it, that's a relatively long period of time without breath when you're under stress.

In 1997, I reunited Henri and Jill, now Jill Hinde, for the television show, 'Where Are They Now?' In Jill's words:

> Well, see, I was in charge of the whole dive so I sort of felt this incredible responsibility and then when I got to Henri, Henri said, 'Oh, God, help me!' And it was just this awful voice, and I still did not know what had happened,

and I started putting him into the side of the boat, and then two other divers jumped overboard and pulled him in right over the side of the boat. That's the first time I realised what had happened.

I asked her, did she feel heroic?

No. I felt very, very angry and all I wanted to do was get back in the water and go 'boom' with the shark, but powerheads were absolutely outlawed. But that's all I wanted to do. But, I mean, that's a ridiculous reaction—this is the person who was so brave. I mean, he was incredible. We had an hour and a half's journey back to Port Fairy and he'd lost half the amount of blood in his body, and he realised that if he lost consciousness he would die. Didn't you?

Henri replied, 'That's right. I really didn't have a leg to stand on.' Bource was soon back in his skindiving gear, more determined than ever to defy nature and make the sea his life as a contract diver and underwater photographer. He died in 1999 at the age of 63. At the same time we reunited Henri and Jill, we also brought together shark attack victim, Raymond Short, and his rescuer, Ray Joyce, whose story is just as gripping—literally. Ray had his arm down the shark's mouth during the rescue. Raymond said:

I was actually bitten on the left thigh first and then on the right thigh, and then she swallowed from the bottom. And the full realisation didn't hit until she came in and swallowed up to the knee and at that stage I was punching and thrashing around and I finally finished off by bending down and biting her back on the nose. I don't know if that was a good or a bad thing ...

Fortunately for Raymond, a number of lifesavers, including Ray Joyce, were at hand:

Well, when we got out to him he kept saying, 'It's still there. It's still there.' And, I mean, I didn't want that shark to be there ... 'No, it's not. You're all right, mate. I've got you.' And we couldn't figure out why he was so heavy and then the rest of the boys arrived ... And that was a relief to see them there, I mean, the more legs in the water, the better ... And the water receded the same time as his leg was coming up and my hand was sort of in the shark's mouth, and the head surfaced and there was the shark and all we saw was this big eye hanging onto his leg so I said, 'Well, grab its tail.' And I think Dallas—I didn't think anyone would—they grabbed the tail and pulled it in. We were all very fearful, but I think they were great mates to do it with.

## CRIME

Shark attacks have been much a part of our history since the first was recorded in 1788—no more so than in the bizarre story of 'the Shark Arm' murder. On the 18 April, 1935, a shark which had swallowed another shark was caught by fishermen and taken to the Coogee Aquarium. Before some horrified spectators it disgorged a tattooed human arm. What followed was a murky and convoluted tale involving some minor hoods in Sydney's underworld. The arm belonged to a small time crim named Jimmy Smith who apparently set out to blackmail a wealthy boat builder. Smith in turn was killed by a hitman and his arm cut off for proof that the job had been done. During the trial which followed, the boat builder himself was murdered. Keeping up? If it's any consolation the police couldn't either and the unsolved case remains an eternal mystery.

Australian history has had plenty of human killers and if ever there was a shark of the underworld it was 'Squizzy' Taylor. Taylor, who terrorised Melbourne in the 1920s, was one of those criminals who somehow managed to become part of our folklore. Another was a Sydney waiter named Antonio Agostini, husband of the mysterious 'pyjama girl'.

Perhaps the most infamous of all was a Hungarian migrant, Stephen Leslie Bradley, Australia's first kidnapper. Australia's most baffling crime is still the Bogle–Chandler case—brilliant scientist and his illicit lover found dead after a New Year's party but with no clues as to how or why they died. And by far, the most famous case which is officially not a crime at all—the death of Azaria Chamberlain, apparently taken by a dingo at Uluru in 1980.

## Squizzy Taylor

Joseph Leslie Theodore (Squizzy) Taylor was an evil little punk who showed that, if crime didn't exactly pay, it wasn't a bad way of making a name for yourself. Taylor was really a larrikin criminal, who dressed like

'Pretty Boy' Floyd, wrote doggerel like Bonnie and Clyde, and died like John Dillinger.

Taylor started his career as a pickpocket, graduating through standover tactics and blackmail to armed robbery. Unfortunately for many innocent people, most of the stories told about Squizzy Taylor were true. He was involved in at least six murders dating back to 1913, but was never convicted of any. They were mostly killings of unsuspecting law-abiding citizens.

In 1916, Taylor telephoned a Melbourne chauffeur service and ordered a car to call at an exclusive address. Taylor and an accomplice met the car outside, planning to use it for their getaway after robbing a bank messenger. When the driver refused to cooperate, he was shot dead. By the time Taylor appeared in court, the frightened witnesses somehow 'forgot' what they had seen and Squizzy had found himself an alibi.

On another occasion, Taylor sent two of his henchmen to the Melbourne suburb of Glenferrie. At 11.00 a.m. in the busy shopping centre, Thomas Berriman, manager of the Commercial Bank, was hurrying to the railway station past women with prams and small children. In a small bag he carried £1850 in notes, surplus cash he was returning to the bank's head office in the city. Taylor's men confronted him on the railway ramp. Berriman pulled out his security revolver, but the thieves were quicker and a bullet ripped into the bank man's chest. Men in the crowd chased the bandits, but they escaped with the money. Berriman died in hospital soon afterwards.

In the heady days after the First World War, Melbourne was the crime capital of Australia, and Squizzy Taylor was its undisputed boss. Around the notorious slum suburbs, rival gangs fought over two-up schools, racecourse rackets and cheap brothels. In the back alley area of Fitzroy, commonly called 'the Narrows', the bullets flew thick and fast.

The Police Department's only regret was that the criminals did not shoot straighter and wipe one another out. Squizzy, or 'the Turk' as he was known in the underworld, stood just 5 feet 2 inches (almost 158 centimetres) high, a diminutive spiv sporting flash clothes and flash girlfriends, including Mollie Jervis who was known as the 'decoy duck'. His loyal 'moll' was Ida Pender, a pretty teenage shoplifter.

But even in their moments of privacy, Taylor was not immune from police raids. Former CIB detective Harold Saker, who broke into Taylor's home in one of the many raids, told me:

I went to the back door and instead of knocking I just put the jemmy in. I dashed up the front and Squizzy Taylor was in bed with Ida Pender. I just put up my guns and told them to jump out of bed. Squizzy said, 'She can't get out, she's got nothing on.' And I said, 'Well, she won't bloody frighten me, so she can come out.' She was a good sort, too.

The raids on Taylor's various homes never gained the police much more than good publicity. But in 1921, they caught him red-handed during a warehouse robbery. Taylor skipped the £3000 bail and went into hiding. He evaded the police for a year, arrogantly teasing them with newspaper correspondence like this:

Dear sir, I can't understand what the fuss is about. [Your story] says I was seen in St Kilda. That's a lot of rot. I haven't been there for months. Last month I went to see *Johnny Get Your Gun* at the Theatre Royal and had supper at the Sawdust Factory and then went home on the Toorak line. As soon as I have finished my business, I will pop up to the CIB where I'll be welcome because I know I can't keep running around much longer.

There is no doubt that the idea of a criminal skipping bail and writing to the newspapers to tell them about the shows he had seen appealed to the larrikin instinct in many Australians and, if it wasn't for Taylor's viciousness, it could have been amusing. He eventually telephoned the detectives to announce his surrender and they sent a car around to pick him up. By now Taylor's every move was front page news. Out on bail again, he was shot and wounded by a rival gangster the night before his trial was due to begin. But this time he turned up, on crutches, to hear the jury find him not guilty yet again.

Taylor was now at the peak of his career. He was perhaps the first real folk hero of Australian crime since Ned Kelly, and with more murder and armed robbery charges hanging over his head, Squizzy could not be suppressed. Warned off the race tracks, he continued to show up until one day at Caulfield the stewards threw him out into the street. That night, Squizzy was back to settle the score. He took matches and fuel and burnt the members' stand to the ground. It was an effective demonstration of Taylor's power.

Undeterred by police harassment, he continued his career. He was as hated and feared by criminals as he was by the public.

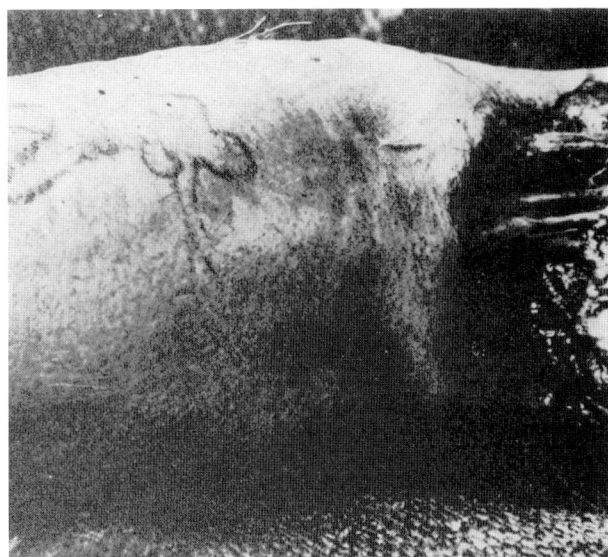

Top left: 'The Shark arm' murder—exhibit A. Top right: Ida Pender, the loyal 'moll' of cold-blooded killer Squizzy Taylor, Australia's most notorious criminal in the early part of this century. Bottom: Taylor's cheeky interaction with the police while on the run made him perhaps the first folk hero of crime since Ned Kelly. Here he is with off-sider Bush Thompson (left).

He was a police informer, 'sneaking' on his underworld colleagues, and there were prisoners in Pentridge Prison who had sworn to poison his food if he was put behind bars.

The fitting finale to the Taylor legend came when he died from bullet wounds received during a gunfight while defending the 'honour' of a prostitute. In October 1927, it was reported that Taylor, with his gun drawn, had burst into the home of an up-and-coming young standover man, 'Snowy' Cutmore. Cutmore was asleep when Taylor burst into his bedroom, but in a second he had woken and pulled a gun from under his pillow. The two gangsters shot each other dead.

Some historians, however, have found this climax just a little too pat. There are theories that Cutmore and Taylor were set up by rival criminals, and even that the police were somehow involved. Certainly, if they weren't, many would have liked to have been.

Whatever the answer to the mystery, it was hardly a day of national mourning when Joseph Leslie (Squizzy) Taylor—'the Turk'—met his spectacular demise.

## The 'pyjama girl' case

During the Second World War, Antonio Agostini was an Italian waiter at Sydney's plush Romano's restaurant. One of his regular customers was Police Commissioner Bill MacKay.

The New South Wales Police Force had been trying for 10 years to solve what had become known as the 'pyjama girl' case. In 1944, the Police Commissioner and the waiter found themselves sitting face to face across a desk in the Commissioner's office. Suddenly one of the world's strangest murder mysteries unfolded.

It all began in 1934 on the Howlong Road, a few miles outside the New South Wales border town of Albury. A young farmer, Tom Griffiths, was leading a prize bull along the side of the road when he stumbled across the body of a young woman in a culvert.

Her face was mutilated and her body badly burnt. A bag had been drawn over her head and shoulders. She was loosely clad in yellow crêpe Chinese pyjamas. When Tom rushed home to telephone the police, neighbours asked him whether he had seen a ghost. He replied that he thought maybe he had.

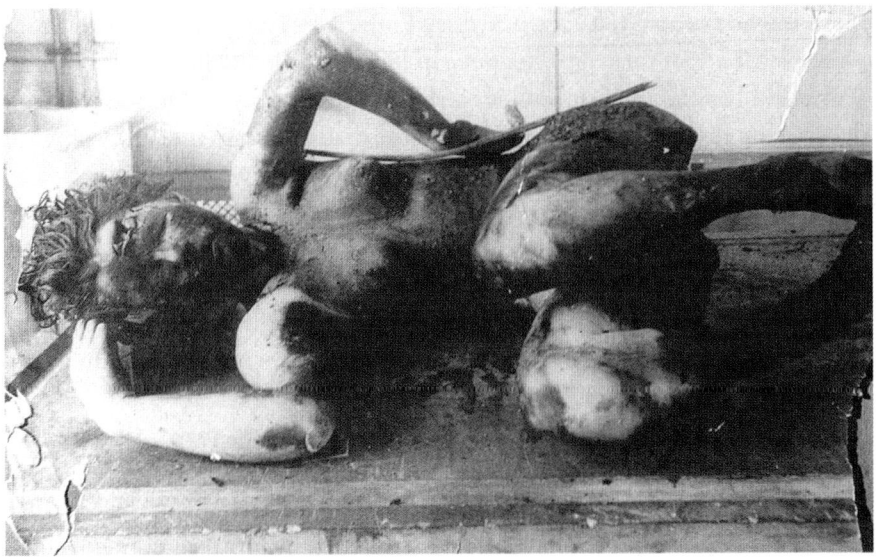

Top left: Antonio Agostini was a lucky killer—saved by undetected clues. When the 'pyjama girl's' body was found in 1934, the initial dental examination did not match that of his wife, Linda Agostini (top right). Ten years later, a subsequent dental examination proved otherwise. Bottom: The partly burnt body, found loosely clad in pyjamas in a culvert near Albury.

Establishing the woman's identity seemed routine enough. Missing persons' files were checked, and this description was issued by the police:

... between 20 and 30 years of age, 5 feet 2 inches to 5 feet 3 inches, slim to medium build, blue-grey eyes, light-brown hair.

One of the women who seemed to fit that description on the missing persons' list was Linda Agostini, a young English woman who had settled in Melbourne, and her husband, Antonio, became a suspect. But when police investigated Mrs Agostini's dental chart it appeared slightly different from that of the 'pyjama girl', as the murder victim would become known—not only in Australia but around the world. A dentist had made a subtle mistake during the initial post-mortem, and his error would cost police 10 years of laborious and mostly unnecessary work.

Initially the body was kept on ice, but when a newspaper reporter in Albury pointed out that it was developing green spots, it was decided to move the body to a mortuary at Sydney University. There the pyjama girl was placed in a bath of formalin. No-one could have realised what a weird exhibit she would become or just how long she would lie in state. During the next decade, hundreds of people peered at the bath, noting the girl's physical peculiarities: her large hands, peroxided hair and ears with almost no lobes. They went away horrified. However, no-one could identify her. At one stage police made checks on every young woman who had not voted in the federal elections. Inquiries were made in almost every country of the world.

Determined to solve the murder, Police Commissioner Bill MacKay decided to put a fresh team of detectives on the case every few months in the hope that someone would come up with new evidence.

In 1944, a team of three dentists was asked to make yet another examination of the pyjama girl. This time the dentists noticed a tiny gap in an upper bicuspid not previously recorded. After all that time in the formalin bath, a porcelain filling had fallen out. It had been overlooked in the original dental reports. Then the dentists found another porcelain filling. The dental comparisons were made again. This time the pyjama girl's modified dental chart matched that of Linda Agostini in every detail.

With the mystery solved at last, police were ready to arrest Agostini. Commissioner MacKay spoke to Antonio at Romano's and suggested the waiter 'drop into headquarters for a chat'. He did, and within a few minutes had confessed to the murder. It was now the best part of a decade since he was first taken by police to see the body of his wife in the formalin bath, and had expressed no signs of recognition.

Time was much kinder to Agostini than it had been to his wife. After the drawn out search to establish the pyjama girl's identity, the inquest and trial were almost an anti-climax. The inquest was complicated enormously by the claims of a certain Dr Benbow who, with the mother of another missing girl, Anna Philhomena Morgan, almost persuaded the authorities that they had been mistaken and that the cadaver was in fact Anna Morgan's and not that of Linda Agostini. At the trial, with the evidence now confused and blurred, Agostini was convicted only of the manslaughter of his wife. In 1948, after serving less than four years of his sentence in Pentridge Prison, he was deported to Italy where he re-married. He died in 1969.

The pyjama girl was the most famous corpse in our history. By the time the case was over, she had been reconstructed, put on public display, and even made up with lipstick and rouge in the hope that someone might identify her. Today, she is all but forgotten. Her body lies in plot 8341 at Preston Cemetery in Melbourne. The government spent hundreds of thousands of dollars trying to find out who she was; yet, when she was finally laid to rest, there was not enough money in the coffers to put a headstone on her grave.

## The Thorne kidnapping

Stephen Leslie Bradley picked up a newspaper one day in 1960 and read that Bazil and Freda Thorne had won first prize in the £100 000 Opera House lottery. The Thornes, who had a daughter, Belinda, aged three, and an eight-year-old son, Graeme, lived in a modest Bondi flat. They were ecstatic about their windfall. But the joy in the Thorne household lasted exactly one week. On 7 July, Freda Thorne answered the telephone and a voice said, 'I have your son.' It was the beginning of a nightmare.

The Thornes had been determined that the lottery win would not affect Graeme's school life. Every morning he left home at the same time and walked down the street to the corner shop where he bought himself a packet of chips. He ate them while he waited for the mother of one of his school friends to pick him up and drive him to Scots College.

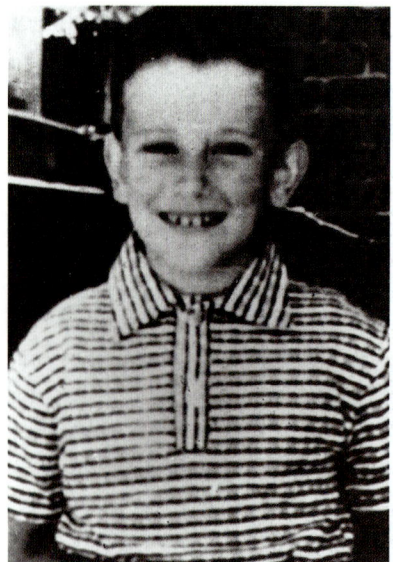

Top left: Eight-year-old Graeme Thorne disappeared from Bondi on 7 July 1960, kidnapped and murdered during an extortion attempt by Stephen Leslie Bradley (top right), a parent himself. Bottom: Memorabilia from the case, including the Bradley family's stuffed Pekingese dog, the fur of which helped police to positively establish Bradley's guilt.

On the morning of 7 July, he stood outside the shop as usual. An older boy who knew him told police he had seen Graeme from a car as he went past. It was the last time he was seen alive.

Graeme's mother was convinced her son's disappearance had something to do with the lottery win. But, when Sergeant Laurence O'Shea of Bondi police was sent to the Thorne's flat to take down a detailed description of the missing boy, he knew nothing about the large amount of money the family had won. By sad coincidence, while the policeman was in the flat, the phone rang again. O'Shea took the receiver from Mrs Thorne and a man spoke in a foreign accent: 'I want £25 000. If you don't pay the money, I'll feed him to the sharks.' O'Shea responded with the question: 'Where would I get that sort of money?' Immediately suspicious, the caller hung up. It would be the only contact the kidnapper would make with the boy's parents. A reward of £15 000 was immediately offered for information leading to Graeme's return. His heartbroken father spoke on the newsreels, appealing to the kidnapper to return his son:

All I can say to this person—if he's a father, and has children of his own—well, for God's sake, send him back to us in one piece.

The search quickly moved to Frenchs Forest where the missing boy's school case was found a few days after he disappeared. With it were Graeme's school cap marked with his name, a maths book and an apple from his packed lunch. Five weeks after he disappeared, Graeme Thorne's body was found in a patch of scrub in the northern suburb of Seaforth. The body, wrapped in a travelling rug, was jammed into a rock crevice. A post-mortem showed Graeme Thorne had suffered a fractured skull. A silk scarf was knotted around his neck.

Police were convinced that forensic examination of the plant clippings that had stuck to the rug would help them to find Graeme Thorne's murderer. They consulted a botanist who specialised in Australian grasses; a quiet woman scientist who worked in a laboratory in a corner of Sydney's Royal Botanic Gardens. Finally, she gave them the much-needed lead. Dr Joyce Vickery found two peculiar plants on the blanket. She told me:

We knew the two plants were garden plants, but they were not present at the site where Graeme Thorne's body was found. Therefore, they must have become attached to the rug somewhere else. In the course of identification, one of my colleagues went out into the Botanic Gardens and brought in a twig of each. When Detective Sergeant Alan Clarke came to get our report, I showed him these. He looked at them with intense interest and asked if he could keep them.

Those two innocuous cuttings helped to seal Bradley's fate. One was an uncommon plant and, as Dr Vickery explained to the police, it would be unusual to find the two shrubs growing together. Another detective working on the case suggested that the pink powder found on the boy's clothing might be mortar, like that used in housing foundations some years earlier. This was also confirmed. So began weeks of laborious searching. As Sydney crime reporter Bill Archibald later described in his book, *The Bradley Case*:

> Detective Sergeant Clarke had been able to tell the searchers ... they should look for a building with high foundations. They should look also for the shrubs. The type of building had been deduced from observation that most places in which pink mortar had been used were built at ground level and had well-kept gardens around them. Grains of mortar were not likely to lie undisturbed in these places. The most probable place for the boy's body to have lain so that it would collect the mortar was under a house or in a garage.

It was a Clontarf postman working his rounds just a few miles from Seaforth who finally found the house the police were seeking. The house was empty, but the police soon established the name of the previous tenant. It was Stephen Leslie Bradley, who had already fled Australia aboard the passenger ship *Himalaya* with his wife, Magda, and their three children. Mrs Magda Bradley told police they were taking their youngest child, Robert, five years old, to England where he was to have specialist treatment for deafness. Bradley was arrested aboard the *Himalaya* at Colombo in Ceylon (now Sri Lanka) and extradited to Australia to face a charge of murder.

Bradley's trial was conducted amid public demonstrations of outrage and hatred. When the jury handed down its inevitable verdict, nine months of accumulated anger was unleashed. People in the court screamed abuse. One woman called out, 'Feed him to the sharks.' Bradley was sentenced to life imprisonment. In October 1968, Stephen Leslie Bradley suffered a heart attack and died after playing a game of tennis with the prison governor.

Today, Bradley is long forgotten but his pet dog is preserved for posterity for public viewing in Sydney. The dog, which resides at the Justice and Police Museum, was an exhibit at the trial—hairs of the Pekingese breed were used to confirm that the picnic rug found wrapped around Graeme's body was, in fact, Bradley's. During the course of the trial, the dog was accidentally run over and killed. It was duly stuffed and mounted and is a forlorn reminder of a truly horrible 'first' in the story of Australian crime.

## The Bogle–Chandler case

During the early 1960s, Chubby Checker was teaching us how to twist, but the hip generation was experimenting with 'free love' and drugs, and acid was about to leave the laboratory. It was also the era of nuclear testing when 'the Cuban Crisis'—a stand off between the United States' President John F. Kennedy and Russian President Nikita Kruschev—took the Cold War to a boiling point. In fact, it was the closest the world had ever been to a third world war. It was the scenario that all seemed a million miles from the quiet suburbs of Sydney's north shore. But, on 31 December 1962, the spectres of sex, psychedelia and espionage were unwelcome guests at a party at a respectable address in Chatswood.

Among the guests were Dr Gilbert Bogle and Mrs Margaret Chandler. What happened to them remains one of the most baffling mysteries in the history of Australian crime. Dr Bogle was a brilliant radio physicist who was about to take leave from the CSIRO to work on a secret project in the United States involving masers, the forerunner to lasers. He also had an appetite for sex with other men's wives. Margaret Chandler was married to Geoffrey Chandler and they reportedly had an 'understanding' about extramarital affairs. As an entry ticket to the Chatswood party, each guest was required to bring something creative and Dr Bogle arrived with a very bizarre surrealistic drawing, which is still retained by the State Coroner of New South Wales. 'Gib', as he was known to colleagues and friends, had drawn a beautiful woman with blue eyes but with two mouths, a severed hand and foot and a rainbow—all rather unusual, indeed—so left of field that people speculated whether or not Dr Bogle had been dabbling with drugs.

Bogle arrived on his own but left the party an hour before dawn with Mrs Chandler, when they drove to the banks of the Lane Cove River.

A few hours later they would be dead, found by two boys looking for golf balls. Even the way the bodies lay was peculiar. They were some distance apart and there was evidence that both had been physically ill. The bodies were also partly covered with beer cartons and, according to those two witnesses who discovered the bodies when I spoke to them 30 years later:

> *First witness*: His clothes weren't actually on him, they were draped over him, pulled apart by the seams ...
> *Second witness*: She was in a partial stage of undress ...
> *First witness*: Oh, I'd say definitely there was a third party because of the way that he was covered up and then the way that she was covered up ... underneath the beer cartons ... his pants were split, pulled apart by the seams and actually laid on the body.
> *Second witness*: Yeah. Laid down his leg ...
> *First witness*: So he could never have done that himself. Someone would have to do it, you know, because it was too precise and exact.

The boys called the police and stayed to watch the proceedings. They say they couldn't help noticing that there seemed to be a somewhat rough and ready examination of the site—so much so that even 30 years later they felt their evidence which could have been vital had been dismissed:

> When we were in court we started to talk about the police around the scene of the crime disturbing any clues there might have been and we were hushed up in the court by the judge at that time.

But there were no clues as to what killed the couple. Were they murdered, or was it death by misadventure? The police could never work it out, nor could the coroner. But Margaret's husband, Geoffrey Chandler, sees a more sinister scenario—a weird one but, given that the scientists were working on secret technology during the Cold War, also possible. From a 1997 interview:

> *Chandler*: I know that the whole thing was very thoroughly covered up—that the inquest was orchestrated. Special Branch was involved and instructions

The bodies of Dr Gilbert Bogle and Mrs Margaret Chandler were discovered on the banks of the Lane Cove River on New Year's Day 1963. Earlier they had left together from a New Year's Eve party, which required a 'creative' entry ticket. This surrealistic painting by Gil Bogle is still held by the Coroner. Its subject matter lends support to the theory that his death was caused by an LSD overdose, a theory doubted by Mrs Chandler's husband, Geoffrey, who suspected a federal conspiracy.

came from the Prime Minister's Department ... Menzies ... I know that the two
people who did it left on an aeroplane about half-past nine that morning ...
*Luck:* Who were 'they'?
*Chandler:* 'They' are the ones that killed Margaret and Gib.
*Luck:* Hired hands? Assassins?
*Chandler:* Hired hands.
*Luck:* Government agents?
*Chandler:* Yes.

Given that at the time masers (microwave sound amplifiers) were a secret
military technology, conspiracy theories could easily be given some
credence, and over the years the rumour mills have worked overtime with
this most intriguing mystery.

However, in the late 1990s came a sudden new development. Dr Godfrey
Oettle, former Director of Forensic Medicine at the Sydney Morgue, had
been among the experts initially involved in the investigation of the deaths
and he came to the following conclusion:

Because the findings of the post-mortem excluded injury and had the characteristics
of natural causes—that is, acute heart failure in young people who had no reason
to have acute heart failure—it was felt that this was probably the result of a drug
overdose, and the question was, what drug overdose that might have been?

My belief after seeing the drawings was that it was probably LSD because
that was an hallucinogen that was being used at the time, given by Sandoz,
who were the manufacturers, to selected psychiatrists for an evaluation.

Oettle believes that 'home brew' LSD was soon being manufactured locally:
'Any good high school lab could do it.' So as early as 1962 one of the
country's leading experts had the solution.

So why has the mystery continued, in fact, deepened during the past three
decades? Dr Oettle:

The problem was that there was little in the way of published material
because at the time the only recorded death as a result of LSD was that of an
elephant—which sounds really bizarre—but there was no evidence of a
human animal dying from it and so for them to have died while taking it when

it was being used in psychiatric centres around the world therapeutically meant that they had to have had a major overdose.

In 1993, Dr Oettle was speaking with colleagues at an international forensic meeting and conversation once again came round to the Bogle–Chandler case. It's a little known fact, but as with the pyjama girl, the hearts of the two victims had been retained and they were initially put into formalin. A colleague of Oettle's examined them once again and 'found large amounts, as I understand it, of LSD in the tissues'.

Geoffrey Chandler, once a prime suspect in this suspicious case, told me that the loss of his wife was 'shattering' and that he thinks the two were killed with some sort of nerve gas. Whatever, he says, the whole affair destroyed his life—his children suffered and his career was terminated because of the notoriety. As for his opinion of the LSD theory, well, that's succinct enough: 'Bullshit.'

And there's another macabre twist to the tale. Ruth Nash, who hosted the fatal 1962 party, died on New Year's day in 1974. Her husband Ken shot himself dead two years later on New Year's day.

## The Chamberlain case

Whether you call it Uluru or Ayers Rock, it's perhaps no accident that this mysterious, symbolic place was where Australia's most fascinating killing took place. It's a place where heaven meets the earth, where people meet nature, where Aboriginal people have lived for 50 000 years and where white people have been arriving for holidays for around 50 or so.

For the traditional owners, the Anangu, it is a sacred site—and it's also a place for Seventh Day Adventists to pitch a tent. It's a place watched over by *Tjukurpa* or Aboriginal law—and a place where there's a cop every few hundred kilometres. But on 17 August 1980, it was white fellers' law and a white feller's mystery that drew the eyes of the nation, and eventually the world, to Australia's 'Dead Heart'—a tale that began with a cry in the wilderness and wouldn't let up until it had divided the nation:

And I just yelled—there wasn't time to go and tell people. I just yelled out, 'Has anyone got a torch? A dingo's got my baby. A dingo's got my baby.'

Whatever your opinion, it was impossible to ignore the sight of a young attractive woman on every television set in the nation sobbing as she told a story of the disappearance of her baby Azaria Chamberlain.

The story was so bizarre that many people found it hard to believe—nine-week-old Azaria plucked from the Chamberlains' tent as they holidayed at Ayers Rock. It is pointless now going into all the minutiae: $23 million spent on legal proceedings, three Coronial Inquests, two Appeals, a Royal Commission, a Court of Criminal Appeal Hearing, tens of thousands of pages of evidence, numerous witnesses, some of them now dead ... But what's more telling are those haunting echoes that never seem to leave us:

> I knew the dog had something ... I thought it was one of my husband's shoes because it was going like this as it was getting out of the door of the tent. (Lindy shakes her head.)

And there was her husband, Michael—blonde, youthful, handsome—a metaphorical echo himself, always by Lindy's side:

> ... and I rushed into the tent, and we looked around quickly and we couldn't see anything. I felt—my hat!—a dingo, and I rushed out into the blackness and I felt as hopeless as I ever felt in my life ...

Rumours flew that these were strange people. Unusual, perhaps, but not so strange. Just New Zealand-born Seventh Day Adventists—those who avoid alcohol, tobacco and drugs, dress modestly and use expletives like 'my hat!'— those who gave us Weetbix for breakfast, the Sanitarium Hospital and Bob Ellis. There was even talk of dark Satanic forces at play, and at first Lindy patiently responded to the press, which at times became feral itself:

> A lot of people think the name Azaria ... this is another one of the old rumours, that it meant 'bearer of sin', and was known specially for this reason ... The name Azaria is an old Hebrew name and it means 'blessed of God' and we felt we truly were blessed when we got our little daughter.

There were those, too, who leapt to the defence of the dingo. But there seemed to be no question of how clever they are—locals even told of one that could take meat out of a caravan fridge. And, of course, there were a thousand other ponderables and conspiratorial theories ... Why would you take a nine-week-old baby to Ayers Rock in the first place?

Were the parents covering up for another of their children? Despite an intensive search around the rock, Azaria's body would never be recovered. Most of her clothing was found a week after she disappeared, five kilometres from the camp site, and all that was missing was a white matinee jacket, which Lindy swore Azaria was wearing on the night she disappeared.

The case generated tremendous public interest from the outset. So much so that in the first inquest, Coroner Denis Barritt invited the media to the broadcast of his Biblical finding live on television:

> I doth find that Azaria Chantel Loren Chamberlain, a child then of nine weeks of age, and formerly of Mount Isa, Queensland, met her death when attacked by a wild dingo.

The Chamberlains were exonerated from any involvement, but the public's imagination had been fired. The Chamberlains were devoutly religious: Michael was a church minister, and they were uncannily calm in their public grieving. There would be few more tears from Lindy, who showed her resentment at the position she found herself in when facing packs of the media and the public. In fact, the Chamberlains legal saga, rather than being over, had only just begun.

When the eminent United Kingdom pathologist, James Cameron, viewed Azaria's clothes, he concluded her throat had been cut, and not by a dingo. The police widened their investigation, there was a second inquest, and the Chamberlains were charged—the now pregnant Lindy with murder, and Michael with being an accessory after the fact.

On 13 September 1982, Lindy and Michael Chamberlain arrived at Darwin's Supreme Court building for a sensational trial that would last 33 days. On each of those days, the pregnant Lindy Chamberlain would ascend the stairs with her husband and lawyer, Stuart Tipple, before a media pack that had soon become just as interested in maternity dresses as the murder case. After each appearance, the questions, like the answers, were the same. How was Lindy looking? Was that a new outfit? And most importantly, did she look any closer to giving birth? The trial itself became a battleground of forensic experts blinding one another and us with science.

The Chamberlains' yellow Torana became a key exhibit, with the Crown alleging that Lindy cut baby Azaria's throat in the front seat.

The prosecution case rested heavily on so-called foetal blood samples scraped off the footwell and the rear carpet. This evidence was later discredited, but not before a jury found Lindy guilty as charged, and sentenced her to life imprisonment.

Yet the drama was still far from over. Nineteen days after being found guilty, Lindy gave birth to another baby girl, Kahlia Shonell Likari. By now, the Chamberlain case had polarised the nation—everyone had an opinion, but more than ever the dingo was seen as the culprit. The 'Free Lindy' movement gathered pace, despite two Appeals being rejected by the highest courts in the land.

Then, suddenly, a breakthrough. Remember the missing white matinee jacket? Five and a half years after the tragedy it was found during a search for the body of a tourist who'd fallen from the Rock. The very existence of the jacket had been brutally challenged during the trial. The press eagerly questioned Michael:

*Michael*: I'm stunned and amazed, but very grateful.
*Reporter*: Grateful. Why?
*Michael*: Because I think that just goes to show once again that my wife was telling the truth.

The case against Lindy was falling apart rapidly, and the authorities knew it. Television news services in Australia and around the world carried the same story: 'Lindy Chamberlain walks from jail—free at last.'

But even with her release, the media wouldn't let her go. It had become the crime story of the decade—and Lindy Chamberlain was a household name. 'How different is the Lindy Chamberlain of today?' asked one interviewer. 'I think I'm harder,' Lindy replied.

Her life sentence might have been remitted, but the new-look Lindy wanted justice. In 1987, after a Royal Commission, she was officially pardoned. 'Well it's great to be pardoned for something that never happened,' she said with a hint of bitterness. And that's how it still stands, with the large matter of compensation still not satisfactorily resolved.

It's a sobering story about how scientists, police officers and journalists can be manipulated to reflect prejudice and ignorance. It's a story about the inability of our judicial system to admit mistakes. But ultimately, it's about a family's loss. The case has spawned nine books, three documentaries and a movie, *A Cry in the Dark (Evil Angels)*, with Meryl Streep and Sam Neill as Lindy and Michael Chamberlain.

And the real Michael and Lindy? The years of misery told in their 1991 divorce. They came together briefly in 1995, 15 years after the tragedy, when a third inquest was held into the disappearance of baby Azaria. The result— an open finding. Over the years, the tragic couple has gradually faded from view. Lindy is living now in the United States and Michael has ironically been working as a photo journalist.

## DISASTERS

Australia has suffered relatively few natural disasters, and perhaps because of this the nation has been deeply traumatised when a major tragedy has occurred. The city that has suffered most is Darwin, which has been through three major cyclones in living memory and was almost bombed out of existence during the Second World War.

For the most part, however, the nation has been shocked by 'man-made' disasters; in particular, an extraordinary series of bridge collapses, and a bizarre chain of tragic circumstances that involved ships of Her Majesty's Royal Australian Navy.

### The *Melbourne–Voyager* collision

HMAS *Melbourne* must be the only ship in history unlucky enough to have sunk two destroyers in peacetime and none in war.

In 1964, Australians were becoming increasingly conscious of the country's defences. We'd had a taste of confrontation with Indonesia and were getting involved in Vietnam. Our Army, Navy and Air Force were being strengthened, and military manoeuvres and joint exercises with the allies were popular subjects for newspapers and television.

It was against this background of 'war games' that in February 1964 the Australian Navy was training off the coast of New South Wales. The aircraft

Top: Anxious relatives wait for news of their loved ones after the freak collision between aircraft carrier HMAS *Melbourne* and destroyer HMAS *Voyager* near Jervis Bay on 10 February 1964, which killed 82 sailors. Bottom: The *Melbourne*'s captain, John Robertson, was eventually cleared of blame and received $30 000 as 'an act of grace'.

carrier *Melbourne* and the destroyer *Voyager* were cruising together at night about 30 kilometres south-east of Jervis Bay.

On receipt of *Melbourne*'s signal to take up a 'plane-guard' position, *Voyager* moved from behind so that it was about 1800 metres to the right and ahead of the carrier. It turned further to starboard and headed away from *Melbourne*, which was steaming straight ahead. Then the situation changed drastically.

A few minutes before 10.00 p.m., Captain John Robertson was on the bridge of *Melbourne* when he noticed *Voyager* had swung back to port. He assumed it was 'fishtailing' or zigzagging to reduce speed while *Melbourne* overtook it. When the two ships were about 1800 metres apart again, Captain Robertson moved across to the compass platform just as the navigator looked up to see *Voyager* crossing towards them. Instantly alarmed, the navigator ordered, 'Stop both engines. Half astern both engines.'

A second later, Captain Robertson issued the order, 'Full astern both engines.' Afterwards, Captain Robertson said:

It all happened so quickly. One minute all was well, and one minute all was not well. There was a collision. It was too late to do anything then. I guess you just wait for the crash. I don't know how quickly one thinks in those situations. The whole thing from start to finish was over in just over one minute. I think it struck me in a flash of lightning that this was probably the end of my Naval career.

By the time the situation was realised, *Voyager* was sinking fast. It plunged to the bottom in two sections with 82 seamen dead, either crushed or drowned. *Melbourne* rescued 197 crew members.

Among the bodies of the dead was *Voyager*'s captain, Duncan Stevens. *Melbourne*, with its bows gaping like the jaws of a wounded shark, arrived back in Sydney the following morning. The scene, as the injured and the bodies of the dead were unloaded, was reminiscent of war.

In March 1964, a Royal Commission was set up to hear the complex evidence surrounding our worst Naval disaster. After 55 days, it was found that *Voyager* was largely to blame. But *Melbourne*'s officers were criticised for not warning *Voyager* of the impending danger.

By now, Robertson's days as captain of an aircraft carrier were over. Under his command, another ship, HMAS *Vendetta*, had earlier been involved in a collision with a dry dock. Captain Robertson was transferred to a shore position soon after the Royal Commission ended. He resigned and forfeited a large pension.

Meanwhile, Lieutenant Commander Peter Cabban, an officer aboard *Voyager* at the time of the collision, alleged in certain documents that Captain Stevens had 'a reputation for drunkenness'.

Intriguingly, the documents containing the evidence were in the hands of Liberal politicians, who faced the choice of remaining quiet or embarrassing their own government.

In his very first speech in Parliament, the new Liberal Member for Warringah, Sydney barrister Edward St John, questioned the government about the evidence, and at one stage even the Prime Minister interjected. St John told me in retrospect:

I felt sorry for Robertson. I think he had been made a scapegoat. I was appalled really that the government ministers and public servants should cover up the truth the way they did. They had obtained statements from Naval officers on board *Voyager* which clearly corroborated what Cabban said, and they were still maintaining in Parliament that there was no corroboration of Cabban; in fact, they had it in their hands.

By 1968, the attacks by Edward St John and other politicians forced a second Royal Commission into the *Voyager–Melbourne* collision. The official finding this time was that Stevens was not a drunkard, but the whole responsibility for the accident was placed on *Voyager*.

Captain Robertson was cleared of any blame and received a payment of £30 000 as an 'act of grace'. He became a businessman, ran a charter yacht service in New Guinea for some years, and owned a hotel in Sydney's Surry Hills district before his death in the 1980s. He told me:

A big organisation tends to be very impersonal when it comes to an individual being. If you face the facts of life, however good a captain you are, if you're the captain of a ship and it has a collision, whether you're right or wrong, then there's going to be a reluctance to employ you again at sea. It's happened to other captains who've been involved in collisions—it's one of those facts of life, you know!

Ahead of the *Voyager* survivors lay a battle for compensation that would last for decades; indeed, a battle that would outlast many of them.

But within two years, something else incredible happened. In 1969 HMAS *Melbourne* was involved in an almost identical collision with the United States destroyer *Frank E. Evans*. Both ships were taking part in a joint exercise in the South China Sea. This time, 74 American sailors were killed and, once again, it was found that *Melbourne* was not responsible.

But *Melbourne's* problems were still not over. In 1974, the passenger liner *Australis* bumped the aircraft carrier while it was moored at Garden Island Naval dockyard in Sydney Harbour, causing minor damage. The following year, four crewmen were rescued from the sea off the New South Wales coast when their anti-submarine aircraft overshot *Melbourne's* landing deck. In 1976, a Japanese freighter, *Blue Andromeda*, sideswiped *Melbourne* when it was moored at Garden Island. In early 1979, eight crewmen were injured aboard *Melbourne*, again while it was moored at Garden Island. A nylon tie-line snapped, whipping into the sailors. Seven crewmen were admitted to hospital. Then in May, *Melbourne* was the scene of yet another drama, when two costly airforce aircraft, both on the same day, overshot their landings and were sunk. The crews were rescued by the carrier. Another aircraft was lost overboard in late 1979.

It is said that *Melbourne,* long since scrapped, was the 'the unluckiest boat in the Navy', something Navy public relations people like to deny. All ships have accidents, and running an aircraft carrier is something like driving a block of flats. But, with two major disasters on its log, there is little doubt that this is how the best-known ship in the Australian Navy will be remembered.


## Three bridge tragedies

The West Gate Bridge collapse on 15 October 1970 was Australia's worst ever industrial accident. Thirty-five of the 46 men who were working on the site were killed on, or under, the 2000 tonne concrete span when it broke loose and plunged about 45 metres to the ground.

Many more workmen were seriously injured. Among the lucky ones were Paddy Hanaphy and Eddy Halsall, who were coming down in the lift at the moment of impact:

*Paddy*: Well, it was like someone shooting bullets—bolts going everywhere—and I turned around and I had a look and I could see it bending, buckling, and then all of a sudden it came down. Eddie walked underneath and as we walked a few inches, Eddie got blown with the impact ...

*Eddie*: The downdraft of the bridge blew me away like a paper bag you know—30 metres—it blew me out onto the main road ... Lucky there was no traffic, you know, otherwise I would have been run over.

Another worker, Bob Setka, had an even more incredible escape—he actually rode the collapsing bridge span right down to the ground and was rescued by Tom Watson.

I asked Bob what it was like riding a 2000 tonne concrete surfboard: 'I was thinking about my family.' Tom had the horrifying experience of seeing two of his close mates killed:

When we got over there he had one of the actual bolts that were holding the bridge together ... he had a bolt right through his skull and it killed him instantly.

Another friend, engineer Ian Miller, was hanging from a support high up on the bridge but his mates were powerless to help him:

He must have been hanging there for about five minutes when we got there and me and another person started to climb up the lift well because there was no other way to get to him. We got about a third up the lift well and he just couldn't hold any longer and he just screamed and let go and he just hit the bottom. We just couldn't get to him in time.

West Gate was a tragedy that affected more than just the people on the bridge. It touched lives all over the city of Melbourne. One of those was only a kid with a camera who happened to be there on that day, now Naval Lieutenant Commander, Udo Rockman:

I was taking a photo of a seagull on a pylon in the middle of the river, and as I was focusing, I heard a loud crash. I turned around and saw a plume of dust going into the air. I just re-focused and took another photo, and that was the one that was on the front page of *The Sun*.

Top left: The collapse of Melbourne's West Gate Bridge while under construction on 15 October 1970 was Australia's worst industrial accident, killing 35 workers. Top right: Beleslaw Pelc about to steer another boat under the Tasman Bridge, which collapsed on top of the *Lake Illawarra*, the ship he was captaining when it collided with one of the pylons on the morning of 5 January 1975. Bottom: Aftermath of the Granville Bridge disaster on 18 January 1977, in which 83 people perished.

However, even as a little boy, Udo had some recriminations about his first encounter with the media:

> While I was being interviewed the reporter asked me to smile for a photo, to have my photo on the front page of *The Sun*, and even as a 10-year-old I thought this isn't right I shouldn't be smiling here—this is a tragedy and I was smiling and I regret that ever since it happened.

In the bitter aftermath that followed, two contracting companies were dismissed, and work on the bridge was delayed for two years. By the time it was finished, the price had soared to $200 million.

And the workers are still bitter about what happened in the wake of the tragedy. Tom Watson said:

> Earlier that year there was a bridge in Milford Haven in Wales that collapsed and killed four people, and it was a smaller-type feature of the West Gate Bridge; it was a box girder bridge. Nobody from the company came and told us about it. So one morning we just refused to go to work. We said, we're not going to go to work any more until somebody gives us some guarantees. The Chief Engineer ... he told us that if he thought it was unsafe, then he wouldn't be on the bridge, too. When the bridge collapsed, he was the first one killed.

And that wasn't the end of it:

> I don't know anybody who worked on the bridge who got injured on the bridge got any counselling whatsoever ... I went to the local hotel, I rang my family to say I was still alive. Nobody had been in touch with my family whatsoever to say we were alive or dead. We worked Thursday, Friday, we got the last body out on Saturday and on Monday we all got terminated ... everybody.

Since the tragedy of West Gate, two other Australian cities have witnessed shocking bridge disasters. On the morning of 5 January 1975, commuters travelling to work in Hobart were greeted by an amazing scene. Two cars were perched on the brink of the new Tasman Bridge, which had just been scissored open in a weird accident. During the night, the bridge's long, sweeping span, like a sleeping dinosaur, had been neatly split in two when it was struck by the ship, *Lake Illawarra*. A fisherman, who saw it from his boat, described the incident:

> The two sections of the roadway collapsed and the debris of the roadway just collapsed onto the ship. It started going down front first almost immediately. I saw a car, and it careered straight off the end in a swallow dive.

At least four cars plunged into 27 metres of water, drowning their trapped occupants. In all, 12 people died. The subsequent inquiry revealed that *Lake Illawarra* had been off course and had sailed between the wrong pair of pylons under the bridge. For the tiny island state of Tasmania, the destruction of the bridge was an economic disaster—40 000 people were cut off from their places of work and, during the period of public shock and outrage, the Prime Minister, Gough Whitlam, said angrily that, 'It is beyond my imagination how any competent person could steer a ship into the pylons of a bridge.' His premature comments caused an uproar and he apologised. Captain Beleslaw Pelc was suspended for six months by a court for 'careless navigation'. Theoretically he could have gone back to sea and he was given a shore job with his old employer, ANL, but he said life on shore didn't suit him and he retired a captain without a ship. At his Sydney home, he wiled away the day painting voluptuous nudes and seascapes. Almost a decade later he told us:

> There is a term in English, 'human error', but it was more than human error and less than negligence ... I agreed when the court was held in Hobart, but judging of the distance of, say, six years, I could have conducted my defence differently.

But the big question was whether or not he could ever bring himself to take the helm again and confront those ghosts that still haunted him? In a much smaller boat than the 10 000 tonne *Lake Illawarra*, we took him once again under that multi-span that he'd seen hurtling down onto the bow of his ship in 1975. As he steered under the bridge, he described what happened on that fateful night:

> When the ship was three lengths from the bridge, I realised that she wouldn't answer the helm. I put the helm hard over, hard to port, but the ship still kept

going hard to starboard. So I gave the engines a double ring and stop on full astern—it means that if something is wrong that they should use as much engine power as possible, even risking wrecking the engines. I was under the impression that the ship is going to stop before reaching pylons; but she didn't, she still kept going and I hit the pylon on the starboard side and that pylon collapsed.

Did he have any regrets? 'I am really sorry that some people lost their lives but that's about all.' Would he have done anything different if he'd had his time over again? 'I am under the impression that it would have been better if I went a bit slower.'

Australia's bridges seemed to be 'jinxed' throughout the 1970s. Just two years after the Tasmanian incident, the nation was shocked by the most gruesome bridge disaster in our history. On 18 January 1977, Granville's Bold Street Bridge was carrying early morning peak-hour traffic across Sydney's western railway line. As the 6.09 a.m. train from Mount Victoria in the Blue Mountains was about to pass underneath the bridge, the engine ran off the lines, striking the bridge supports. The 170-tonne concrete span collapsed on the packed passenger carriages below. The final horrific toll of Granville was 83 people dead. Another 213 passengers were injured, many psychologically and physically crippled for life. At the scene of the accident, where crushed carriages lay flattened under slabs of concrete, one of the many rescuers said:

We were nine hours cutting those girders out. Of course, we got a few surprises—like people speaking to us that later died. One old fellow said, 'Don't worry any more about me. I'm done for. You rescue the young people.' Eventually he died. Imagine that.

There were many heart-rending moments at Granville, but perhaps the most inspiring story of all is of Debbie Woodgate who, by a tragic stroke of bad luck, only caught the train that day because her car had broken down. She became the most severely injured person to survive the bizarre disaster, crushed in her seat into a space 30 centimetres high. But, she went on to build a new life with a miraculous denouement. She was just 19, full of energy and the joy of life, with plans to become a policewoman. In the next instant, she thought a plane had fallen on top of the train, and at the end of the day, doctors thought she would not live let alone walk again:

I was crushed from the neck down, all of my body ... hearing people screaming, crying. I heard one, I think he was an elderly man, saying the 'Lord's Prayer'. He was to my right ... I just wanted the aeroplane to get off to go to work. I was thinking, 'My boss will kill me.'

Almost exactly 20 years after the accident, I reunited Debbie with the man who rescued her, Police Rescue team member, Gary Raymond:

I couldn't believe that there would be anybody alive underneath ... A slab had come down and the people were crushed down to within about 14 inches of the deck of the carriage ... And she was entrapped in every part of her body, but the crucial part was that her head was pushed downwards and backwards and she was having an airway obstruction ... And I thought she was going rather purple. I thought to myself, I've got to move her head and neck. And I felt, well, if I do, I could actually ... I suppose, putting it bluntly, I could have killed her.

So, very gently and carefully, Gary began moving Debbie's head to the side. She suddenly gasped for breath and she started breathing normally. Then her rescuer began to ask her questions about how she was feeling towards the toes and the feet. This exchange during the reunion gives some indication of the extraordinary rapport between two human beings as life is ticking away:

Gary: It was not a pretty picture ...
Debbie: Did I answer you?
Gary: You did.
Debbie: Did I? What did I say? What did I say?
Gary: You started saying, 'How's everybody else?' And I said, 'They're OK.' And you said, 'And you crawled in all the way for me?' And I said, 'Yes ... and it's a good way to meet somebody, isn't it?'

At one stage the rescuers had to clear the site as the situation became too dangerous. Gary remembered of that time:

It's the worst thing I've ever had to do. At one stage the message came through the bridge was shifting and at the same time we had a leaking LP gas cylinder that was on the train and we had liquid petroleum gas creeping through there as well. So at first, to get Debbie out, I couldn't use mechanical equipment. I had to use my hands and I had to take the gloves off because I needed the tips of my fingers to feel very closely to you.

But I had to leave and they ordered me to leave and I remember coming back and I remember saying to you, 'Told you I'd be back.' And you said, 'I've got a pain in my tummy.' And I said, 'Well, that's probably because you're compressed for some time.' And you said, 'Do you reckon I'll ever have a baby?' And I just said, 'I know that God performs miracles and I reckon you're gonna have a baby.'

Gary got a medal for rescuing Debbie and others and, amazingly, 20 years later, Debbie had her baby.

In that intervening time she'd been at death's door, had lost a leg and had scores of painful operations, but she had also met Steve Woodgate, who became her husband. Steve proposed to Debbie on April Fool's Day ('Just in case she said "no".')

The two fostered and then adopted a daughter and then, by an uncanny coincidence, on the day they signed the adoption papers Debbie found out that she was pregnant. To cap it off, the baby was born on, you guessed it, April Fool's Day.

The coroner found six causes for the catastrophe, including the poor condition of the track, and wear on the leading wheels of the engine. The New South Wales Public Transport Commission accepted liability and expressed its deep regret. But the promise to upgrade the system must have meant little to the hundreds of people whose lives were shattered when Locomotive 4620 went off the rails on that terrible Tuesday.

## Cyclone Tracy

Darwin today is 'the town that Tracy built', a rising landscape of specially engineered, strong cyclone-proofed houses.

On Christmas Eve 1974, Darwin residents waited for the cyclone they knew was coming. They had survived these storms every summer. This one would come and go like all the rest. It took Cyclone Tracy just a few hours to prove them wrong and flatten the entire city.

The eye of the cyclone arrived at 3.00 a.m. on Christmas morning. By then, people were literally praying for their lives. The official toll was 65 people dead, 140 badly injured, and thousands left homeless.

Broken glass and sheets of jagged metal flew through the air as roofs were lifted off houses and walls smashed to the ground. Parents shielded their children as whole families lay cut and bleeding in the hot, furious rainstorm of that awful Christmas night.

The noise of the cyclone was as terrifying as the wind and rain. It was, according to a person who witnessed the cyclone, 'The sound of a million sheets of corrugated iron being scraped across the ground at 200 miles an hour.' Mr Ron Bell was one of Darwin's residents whose family still suffered from the shock of Cyclone Tracy years later:

> The noise—I think the noise is what caused my boy to have sleepless nights. A couple of years afterwards, he wouldn't sleep at all without the light on. But the daughter, she was different. She had a wild outburst of crying, nearly all day. Then it was gone and over with—finished.

When the Bell family rebuilt their Darwin home, they spent another $4000 to have a steel and concrete cyclone shelter built within easy reach in their front yard. Another Darwin man described how, two minutes after the cyclone struck, his house—the floor, roof and walls—all disappeared:

> We spent four hours huddled in the yard where the house was. We had no protection. My wife was killed by flying debris.

And a little boy, who later received hospital treatment for his injuries, told how his badly injured father sought help:

> All I can remember is my Dad saying, 'Keep down, keep down.' When it got a bit lighter we went over to our car where my brother was and my Dad was nearly fainting from loss of blood. He started to beep the horn and our neighbours came and helped us.

One of the most telling images that Australians down south saw of the disaster was ABC television journalist, Mike Hayes, sitting red-eyed and

Top: Heartbreak—a man
returns to the ruins of his
home and street after
Cyclone Tracy had
demolished Darwin on
Christmas Eve 1974.
Right: Hardly a scar—at least
on the surface... Darwin in
1974 and 1998.

forlorn in the ruins as he delivered a memorable piece to camera.

A quarter of a century later, I took him back to the same place that he'd left soon after:

> I was asked to do a piece to camera and I was just squatting down here in the wreckage of the suburb of Stuart Park which had been completely annihilated. No houses were standing, no gardens, no trees and I remember saying something like: 'I'm just wondering about the new Darwin ... It might be safer, it might be newer, but Darwin was always a place of character. It wasn't a very pretty place, but it was a place of people with a unique lifestyle. I just hope the new Darwin has a character. This is Mike Hayes of ABC News in the wreckage that was once a bloody good place to live.'
>
> And that was about it, and it was lucky it was it, because as I've stood up the camera ran out of film and it was the last frame of the film in the whole Northern Territory and I just didn't have another piece in me to repeat it anyway.

That use of the word 'bloody' caused a great deal of heartburn among ABC executives in Sydney but Hayes' piece was, in fact, the perfect evocation of the mood of the town. Mike went south to try his luck on the land and went on to become an Aussie icon on ABC Radio as 'The Prickle Farmer': 'I just had to stop feeling sorry for myself and get on with my life.' This is how he described Boxing Day, Darwin, 1974:

> One of the most amazing things out here was driving through all these suburbs where you were quite convinced everyone had been killed, and there were little kids coming out literally from under the wreckage like little mice or cockroaches, grasping stuff that Santa had left them—half a teddy bear with its ear missing or shredded, sodden books, bikes with wheels missing and smashed whatever—and saying, 'Oh, mister, look what I got for Christmas.'

Among those little 'cockroaches' with their Christmas toys were brothers Stephan and Arnold Walters, who in 1997 were veteran Darwin residents. Remembering the night, they said:

> *Stephan*: I woke up about 12 o'clock and I got my Christmas bear and then I went back to my bedroom and I was about nine years old and I woke up,

got out of the house, and it was like a Hiroshima had hit.

*Arnold*: I woke up about 12 o'clock with water soaking into my bed and trying to mop it up and then the winds came. I thought I was going to die that night. I still can remember it.

I was in my bedroom there and the wind was that strong it pushed the louvres open and the water was coming in and it got the whole room wet. There was about so much water on the floor so we decided to move the table out of the lounge and put it in the hallway and we all held onto one leg and we just prayed, and I prayed myself to sleep.

But the boys survived:

*Stephan*: Oh, I went away for a little while but always intended coming home and making my life here.

*Arnold*: I call Darwin home and we all love this place. The whole family is still here and we've still got the original house.

Darwin today bears remarkably few scars of that night that shocked the nation. As with all events of national trauma, there was some recrimination about how the authorities handled the chaos that followed and there would be inquiries and post-mortems now filed for posterity.

But within six months of the cyclone, most of the population was preparing to go back home, and Darwin residents held their first 'Back to Darwin' celebration to thank the millions of Australians who had donated clothing, food and more than $15 million to the city.

Perhaps the final word should go to one of Darwin's colourful identities, one who still props up the bar at the Hotel Darwin, Cowboy Bill. In 1974, television crews found him sitting among the ruins relatively unscathed, saying:

A man's livin' good, he's livin' real good ... He's got a curry ... He's got a cold beer and a smoke ... But right now, today, I'm gonna get good and darned drunk.

When I interviewed him 25 years later, he still had a beer and a smoke—but no curry—and I asked him what Cyclone Tracy meant to the town. 'Cyclone Tracy,' said Cowboy Bill, 'blew away a way of life.'

## The *Greycliffe* and the *Rodney*

Sydney Harbour is one of the busiest waterways in the world and the traffic at peak hour can be just about as hair-raising as a drive through the city. On the whole, our most famous body of seawater has a remarkable safety record, but in the days before radar and radio control, the harbour saw two major disasters in the decade. The first involved the ferry *Greycliffe*.

On 3 November 1927, Sydney was stunned by the news that the ferry *Greycliffe* which, because of its departure time of 4.15 p.m. carried dozens of schoolchildren, had been run down by the steamer *Tahiti*. The 7000 tonne ship sliced through the smaller craft like butter, and the people on board had no time to panic. One passenger, John Pfeiffer, remembered:

> I was upstairs on the *Greycliffe* doing my homework on the starboard side when the deckhand we all knew as 'Curly' came running up the stairs and said there was going to be a crash. I looked upwards and saw the green bows of a boat crashing into the side of the *Greycliffe*. So I don't know what made me do it, I acted on impulse, just ran outside on to the port side, took off my shoes and I dived overboard. I don't know what made me take off my shoes but I just took them off.
>
> The next thing I can remember was the *Tahiti* passing very quickly and I was looking up at a lot of faces staring down at me when I was sucked under by the ship as she passed. And I can remember being quite frightened of being injured—cut up by the propellers.

John Pfeiffer escaped with barely a scratch but many were mutilated by the propellers, and in all, 40 died. Many of them were children, and the Taronga Zoo wharf resembled a pit head after a mine explosion as relatives waited anxiously for news.

When the *Tahiti* left Australia on the very night of the accident there were complaints about its 'indecent haste'. In Sydney its pilot, Captain Carlson, faced a long ordeal in the inquiries which followed. He was dismissed and had to wait until the *Tahiti* returned from America seven months later before hearing the official conclusions about the accident. Eventually, after a long and bitter argument between the owners of the ferry and the steamship company, the judge apportioned three-fifths blame to *Greycliffe* and two-fifths to *Tahiti*.

Top: Artist's impression of the collision between the steamer *Tahiti* and the ferry *Greycliffe* on Sydney Harbour, 3 November 1927. Many school children were among the 40 who died when the wooden ferry was chopped to matchwood. Bottom: The roof of the small ferry, the *Rodney*, proved too popular for well-wishers farewelling the American USS *Louisville* from Sydney Harbour in 1938. When the ferry capsized, US sailors suddenly found themselves trying to rescue girlfriends they had met only a few days before.

But, fate had its own penalty for the steamer. Three years later, workers on the new Harbour Bridge watched as it steamed under them for the last time. In mid Pacific, a propeller shaft broke and tore away, leaving a gaping hole in the side of the ship. The crew tried to bail it dry, but it was a futile battle. The passengers and crew were picked up by a Norwegian freighter, and a few hours later, *Tahiti* sank.

Ten years later, the memories of the *Tahiti* and *Greycliffe* had faded. There was plenty of excitement on Sydney Harbour. The fleet was in, and it was time to farewell the American warship *Louisville*. People in little boats crowded to get a glimpse of it, and on the small ferry *Rodney*, there was standing room only. But suddenly, as people crowded to one side to wave to the American sailors, the *Rodney* gave a sickening lurch and rolled over.

For Sydneysiders it seemed like history repeating itself. Only this time, most trapped in the stricken craft were women, some of whom had made boyfriends among the crew and were getting a last glimpse of their new beaux. Sailors from the *Louisville* jumped over the side and rescued those who managed to get clear of the ferry. Members of a police band on another boat also dived into the water and rescued others, but a number of people were trapped inside the ferry and those on the outside literally heard their death throes. Nineteen drowned. Two survivors remembered:

The panic was dreadful ... We heard the noise, that was most harrowing, of them trying to scratch to get out from the bottom of the boat. You could hear this thumping with their hands on the upturned hull.

The aftermath was just as sad as that which had followed the *Greycliffe* incident. There was a long inquiry and savage accusations about the number of people who had been allowed on the top deck. The boat was salvaged and quickly renamed *Regis*, and later, *Regalia*. She still plies the harbour trade— few realise the little craft spent some of its life as a coffin.

# Stage and screen ... AND

## THE ENTERTAINMENT OF A NATION

The twentieth century differs from all others in that it is the first to have been recorded throughout with moving pictures, and while we enjoy quite a distinguished history in the theatre, it is in the cinema that Australia can actually claim to have led the way.

In radio and television, however, as with the rest of the world, we have spent most of our time aping the Americans and the British. The most popular television program in Australia in the penultimate year of the twentieth century has been the American sitcom, 'Friends'. Yet Australia can take some heart from the knowledge that at least nowadays that's the exception rather than the rule.

During the first 15 years of television, it was very rare to find any homemade product in the top 10 Australian programs and, even at the beginning of the 1970s, the line up went like this: 'Number 96'; 'Six Million Dollar Man'; 'Planet of the Apes'; movies/specials; 'Police Woman'; 'Doctor at Sea'; 'Little House on the Prairie'; 'Father Dear Father'; and 'Bewitched'—in other words, only one local program in the top of the charts.

Five years later, however, the gradual dawning that we were capable of making something worth watching all by ourselves was starting to gain momentum. The top 10 programs in the last year of the 1970s were: 'This Is Your Life'; 'This Fabulous Century'; 'Restless Years'; 'Prisoner'; 'Willesee at Seven'; movies; news and weather; 'The World Around Us'; and 'The Muppet Show'—nearly all Australian.

Left: Kylie sets off for fame from the set of 'Neighbours'.

Among the pioneering radio and television programs that were an expression of our own ethos were such humble offerings as the incredibly long-lived 'Blue Hills', to the trail-blazing, larrikin and often slapstick satirical offerings of 'The Mavis Bramston Show'. As for the art of making ourselves known to the rest of the world, that's a much harder task, invariably achieved only by those who made the long and lucky journey from down under to Hollywood and beyond ... Annette Kellerman, Louise Lovely, Snowy Baker, Errol Flynn, Rod Taylor, Peter Finch, Olivia Newton-John, Mel Gibson, Jack Thompson, Judy Davis, Bryan Brown, Nicole Kidman, Geoffrey Rush—a distinguished but short list of big if not megastars.

## ON STAGE

In the closing decades of this century, Australian theatre has enjoyed something of a nationalistic boom. Spearheaded by the witty and at times eviscerating works of David Williamson, plays written, acted and produced by Australians have done well at the local box office and made a significant impact overseas.

We've also exported a distinguished array of Thespians as diverse as Dame Judith Anderson, Leo McKern, Keith Michell and Cate Blanchett, to strut their stuff at the smarter end of the market on the British stage. But for most of this century, the flow has been all the other way. Australians waited breathlessly for each new shipload of culture to arrive from Europe.

In 1948, England sent us the legendary Old Vic Theatre Company headed by two of the truly 'big guns' of the international stage: Laurence Olivier and his wife Vivien Leigh. They were feted wherever they went—the newsreel cameras even followed them on a visit to Taronga Zoo in Sydney. Olivier exploited this media attention, repeatedly urging Australia to set up its own national theatre. Yet it took another six years and a visit by Queen Elizabeth before the Elizabethan Theatre Trust came into being. Its first play, *The Sleeping Prince*, opened on 27 July 1955 at the Trust's Elizabethan Theatre in Newtown, Sydney. It starred Dame Sybil Thorndike, Meriel Forbes and her husband Sir Ralph Richardson. The critics were quick to point out that Australia's National Theatre had begun with an English play, an English cast and an English director.

The former Governor of the Reserve Bank, the late Dr H.C. 'Nugget' Coombs, a co-founder of the Trust, once put it to me in these words:

Australian creative effort in drama was thought to be a pretty ambitious idea. Some of us believed that it would come, but I don't think you can get creative effort in as organised an art form as the theatre until you have a vigorous institution of theatre. Frankly, I am astonished, when I look back on it, at how quickly Australia has produced genuine creative artists of real quality in the theatre.

*The Summer of the Seventeenth Doll* was our first successful post-war Australian play. Sumner Locke-Elliot's *Rusty Bugles*, produced in 1948, had made a spectacular impact, but mostly because it was banned for a short period by an over-zealous New South Wales Chief Secretary's Department. From its premiere in 1955, 'the Doll' burst upon Australian audiences with an almost embarrassing impact. Packed theatres around the country felt the shock of recognition, seeing the language and emotions of their own lives portrayed on stage. Author Ray Lawler about the mood of the time:

> There was a growing awareness of Australia as an identity. Certainly after the war, one could feel it in many fields, and I think theatre was one of them. It was a lucky play. There was sufficient awareness of Australian identity to make people go and see it, and it just happened to strike a note at the time. I've never felt it was more than that.

Big name Australian playwrights this century are few and far between, yet it could be argued that David Williamson is a name that might be known to anyone in the street—not a bad claim to fame for such a rare trade as a playwright. This could be partly due to the eclectic nature of the observational genre of this former lecturer in thermo-dynamics from Melbourne.

Williamson began writing for university reviews in the late 1960s under the nickname of 'Lofty' Williamson, and apparently his stuff clicked with the audiences. In 1970, his first fully professional play hit the boards and not surprisingly it took the big stick to the sort of antics going on around the university campus. This from *The Coming of Stork* ...

> *Teacher:* I see we have a comedian in our midst. Are you aware young man that we have a lady of the cloth present who may find your humour somewhat offensive?

Right: Press and public here and overseas responded enthusiastically to Ray Lawler's *The Summer of the Seventeenth Doll*, a very Australian play about sugarcane cutters and their seasonal girlfriends.
Bottom: Cast of the movie version of 'The Doll' included Angela Lansbury, Ernest Borgnine and John Mills.

Australia's first national theatre, The Elizabethan Theatre Trust, was launched with an English play and an all-English cast in Newtown in 1955, but at least it was officially ours. Later, to everyone's delight, The Elizabethan Theatre played *The Summer of the Seventeenth Doll*, a totally fair-dinkum affair.

*Stork*: There's nothing offensive about a jockstrap. It's what's in it that you've got to worry about.

I've made a number of films with Williamson over the years and while he's seen by some as awkwardly shy, he sees himself as quite the opposite:

I don't like the garret existence. I like to get out in amongst people because that's ultimately where you draw your material from.

I think playwrights are probably more voluble and outgoing than say, poets or novelists, and they always have been in history. I mean, Bernard Shaw dominated the whole of English intellectual life. He had opinions on every subject under the sun, so playwrights have traditionally been loud-mouths.

A large number of Williamson's plays, including *The Coming of Stork*, *The Removalists*, *Don's Party*, *The Club*, *Travelling North* and *Emerald City*, have been made into feature films, and Williamson himself has written screenplays for a number of Australian films, including the critically acclaimed *Gallipoli* (1980), *The Year of Living Dangerously* (1981), and *Phar Lap* (1982).

The truth is, however, that the Australian theatrical industry today still relies heavily on British and American writing, and we continue to import overseas celebrities. But there has been a growing acceptance of local and even indigenous plays, and the large numbers of small theatre companies in the capital cities are evidence of a continuing interest in 'live' drama.

Works by Alex Buzo, Jim McNeil, Tony Morphett, Ron Blair, Jack Hibberd, Dorothy Hewett, Kevin Gilbert and Steve Spears have all attracted enthusiastic reviews and audiences, and the international success of Barry Humphries' shows—a unique form of theatre in themselves—has done much to encourage original work throughout the Australian theatrical world.

## THE BIG SCREEN

Australia can claim two firsts in world cinematic history. *Soldiers of the Cross*, a religious epic made in 1900, was 3000 feet long, cost £600 to make and is believed to be the world's first full-length dramatic presentation including film. Unfortunately, the film itself has been lost, although glass slides and photographs still survive to give an impression of the lavish sets and costumes.

*The Story of the Kelly Gang* made in 1906, was 4000 feet long and took six months to make. It is claimed to be the world's first full–length feature film and the discovery of three scenes from the film more than 70 years after it was made would seem to support this claim.

*Soldiers of the Cross* was a grand presentation of film, slides and music put together by the Salvation Army's Limelight Division, probably the earliest regular film production unit in history.

The religious epic turned out to be an enormous box office success. On a rainy night in 1900, 4000 people braved the elements to attend the premiere. Newspapers such as *The Age* hailed the novelty with unrestrained enthusiasm:

> To have some of the most tragic episodes of Christian history carried out in all savage but soul-stirring realism is an accomplishment essentially of today. It is a thrilling, novel and instructive lecture.

In the following years, Australians became fascinated with the new marvel of cinematography. They flocked to theatres that sprang up in the cities showing film of Australian scenery and people. Commercial feature films were a logical development and it's not surprising that for its first attempt Australia should choose the popular legend of Ned Kelly.

*The Story of the Kelly Gang* was produced on weekends by two theatrical entrepreneurs, John and Charles Tait. A dairy farm at Heidelberg on the outskirts of Melbourne was transformed into the village of Glenrowan. The film was shown with voices and sound effects supplied by stand-ins behind the screen. The acting was outrageously overdone by modern standards, and the scene that showed Kate Kelly's set-to with the policeman could go down in history as the first blending of sex and violence on screen. Actually, Kate Kelly was a bloke in drag. The other good thing about making Kelly movies was you didn't need any stars—stick a bucket over a head and anyone would do. Consequently, we would remake the movie six times, way up until 1970, when Rolling Stones singer Mick Jagger played the outlaw in the film directed by Tony Richardson. Alas, not even a bucket over his head could make Mick a convincing Ned.

While still photographs taken from the 1906 film have been preserved, the original print was lost years ago. But in 1979, a section was discovered under a bed in an empty house. It was sent to me during the making of the original

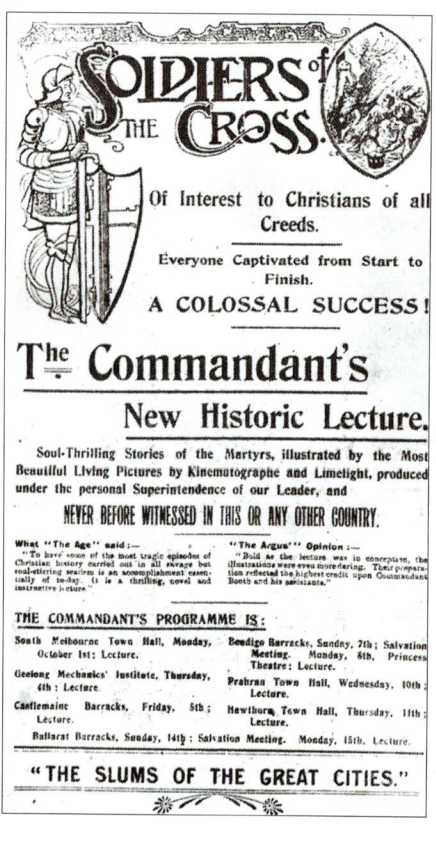

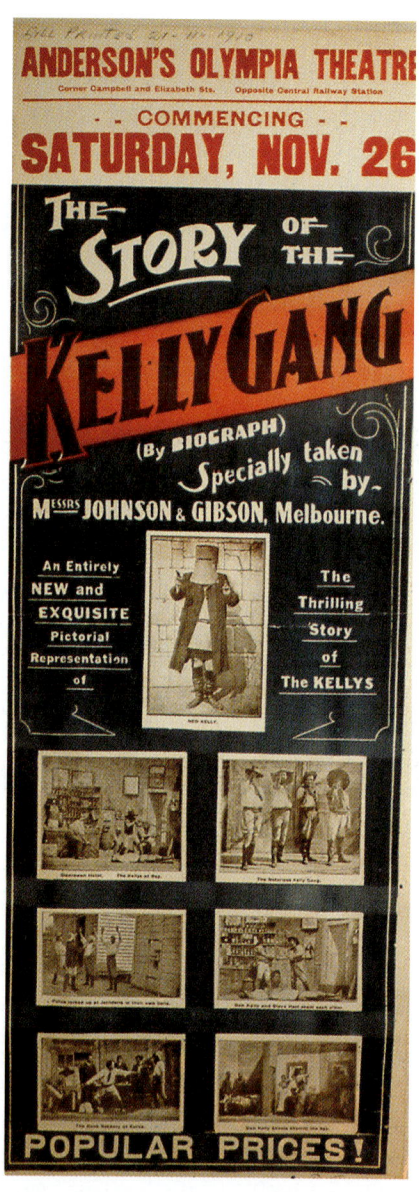

The Salvation Army's epic *Soldiers of the Cross*, was premiered to 4000 people in
Melbourne in 1900. A thrilling combination of film, magic lantern slides and theatrical
address, it has been described as probably the world's first colossal multi-media presentation. While no film, only glass plates from *Soldiers of the Cross* survive, three film

scenes from another local production by two Melbourne chemists, John and Charles Tait, *The Story of the Kelly Gang*, made in 1906, have been recovered. Experts claim it is the first full-length feature film in the world. It was far from silent—stand-ins added voices and sound effects from behind the screen.

'This Fabulous Century' television series by a Melbourne collector, Mr Ken Robb, and has since been authenticated at the National Film and Sound Archive, now called ScreenSound Australia.

The film cost the Taits just £1000 to make, but grossed a colossal £25 000 at the box office. So, Australia began churning out bushranger pictures, including the first *Robbery Under Arms*. Bushranger pictures became to the Australian film industry what Westerns represented to Hollywood, and were made just as fast.

But the important question is: did Australia produce a work of lasting merit during the silent film era? The nation's leading authority on film, Ray Edmondson, Deputy Director of ScreenSound Australia, says:

> The obvious answer to that is *The Sentimental Bloke*; although it's possible that other films made before that which don't survive now would have had similar significance. Certainly The Bloke is our first claim to a true international classic. It had enormous impact in England and it was released in America. It's a very fine piece of film from anybody's point of view and, as a piece of silent film art, it typifies the best characteristics of the medium.

C.J. Dennis, author of *The Sentimental Bloke*'s verses, said of the film (made in 1919), 'It could not have been pictured better.' The classic verse-tale of working-class romance in the slums of Sydney was ideally suited to the silent screen, and the written title cards which helped the story along retained the charming flavour of the slang language employed in the original book.

To add to the authentic feel of the film, all the exterior scenes were shot on actual locations around the dock areas of Sydney. There was even a scene filmed on the Manly ferry.

Its director, Raymond Longford, was the leading filmmaker of his day. Longford's story is, in many ways, as sentimental as that of 'the Bloke' himself. He should have been acclaimed as a genius and, in any other film-producing country, he might have been. Despite the popularity of *The Sentimental Bloke*, and its sequel, *Ginger Mick*, Longford never raised the money he needed for later films.

Behind the scenes of Longford's film romances was a real romance, far more poignant than the fantasy. Longford had been an actor before becoming a director. He directed the biggest star of the day, Lottie Lyell, in some of her films, but she, too, had more of an interest in movies than merely acting in them. Longford and Lyell became lovers and formed a creative partnership as well. It was the magic of that partnership which gave such an aura to their creation, *The Sentimental Bloke*.

In the film, Lottie played the Bloke's girl, Doreen, who worked in a pickle factory. In reality she would become scriptwriter, designer, editor and associate director. Unfortunately, however, she was suffering from tuberculosis. They made more films together under increasingly difficult circumstances, personally and financially. For a start, Longford could not divorce his Catholic wife. The two also ran foul of the powerful international forces which controlled the local film industry—a group called 'the Combine'.

Little Lottie was as frail as her appearance suggests and she died, a melancholy figure, at only 34. Longford battled on to make Australian films but, after he gave telling evidence at a Royal Commission into the film industry in the 1920s, he was a marked man. The ultimate irony and humiliation for Longford was that he was eventually forced to go cap in hand to the Combine for work. He persuaded the syndicate to produce the epic Australian story *For the Term of His Natural Life* but he was then passed over in favour of the American director, Norman Dawn.

Longford's career waned and he was reduced to playing bit parts in other people's movies, but he was still optimistic. 'I would like to see the industry go ahead in leaps and bounds,' he said near the end of his life. 'Particularly the good Australian stories; stories indigenous to Australia and full of sentiment. After all's said and done, aren't we all sentimentalists at heart? As for myself? Well, I'm the Sentimental Bloke.'

Longford spent his last days as a tally clerk on the wharves at Woolloomooloo. And the ending of the Longford/Lyell romance is worthy of Mills and Boon. Raymond Longford and Lottie now lie together in the same grave. His family granted his extraordinary request that he be buried with his lover, whom he outlived by 30 years.

*The Sentimental Bloke* would be made again as a talking film in the 1930s but with none of the skill or charm that flickers through the original. The advent of 'the Talkies' brought a boom in the cinema trade, but there was no guarantee that any of the films to be shown would be locally made. Even before the 1930s began, the sad truth was that the Australian film industry, so promising in the early 1900s, had already fallen into foreign hands.

Top: The ballad verses of C.J. Dennis' *The Sentimental Bloke* were brought to life in the film directed by Raymond Longford in 1919. His charming masterpiece is regarded by film buffs as Australia's one true classic of the silent era. It starred actors Arthur Tauchert and Lottie Lyell (left), later Longford's lover. Right: Ken Hall, pioneer Australian director, whose many films such as *The Squatter's Daughter* and *Smithy*, about Charles Kingsford Smith, were produced by the Cinesound company, which Hall himself later ran in Australia.

But, while the Americans were making the big money, a few local directors still struggled to get home-grown films on to the screen. *The Squatter's Daughter*, one of 19 features made for the Cinesound company by Ken Hall was as Australian as two-up. Yet it still reflected the style and bally-hoo of a Hollywood production. As Ken Hall told me:

> I was greatly influenced by American films, and I don't see anything wrong with that because they, after all, were the best in the world. If you could follow their example and have anything like their success, then you'd be doing something worthwhile for Australia.

And Ken was guided by that philosophy throughout his long and successful career that saw him go on to run the Cinesound newsreel empire and even Channel Nine in its infancy. He was unashamedly commercial in his outlook and considered his finest film was *Smithy*, the story of Kingsford Smith and the Southern Cross, starring American actor Ron Randell as Smithy. Yet, if he had no qualms about American cultural imperialism, he also gave the industry a good dose of common sense, making features with only a fraction of the Hollywood budgets. He developed a pool of filmmaking skills which survived to see in the new boom that has occurred in Australian filmmaking. He also had plenty of anecdotes about the bad old days of film and the Hollywood Hayes Code whereby the censors wielded the scissors like machetes.

Hall's films, such as a remake of *The Silence of Dean Maitland*, a highly melodramatic saga about a seductive village belle and the trouble she gets herself into with a young parson, raised the censor's ire:

> We had a love scene in that, a very strong one where he kissed the girl, but you could only allow a kiss to run for something like, oh, a half a minute, about 30 seconds or less than that. If it lasted longer than that, well, it would have been cut.
>
> If a man was in a room with a girl, or husband and wife when they were in the bedroom, he had to keep one foot on the floor while he was sitting on her bed. He had to. If he raised one ... any two feet off the floor, that was it.

One foot on the floor—same rules as snooker, and it now seems laughable—but the battles between censor and creator in the film business have raged for all of this century. There was, in fact, only one section of Saturday night at the flicks that was always Australian: the newsreel. Almost from the day the Talkies started, two companies, Cinesound and Movietone, competed furiously with each other to produce the best newsreel review of the week's events.

Over the years, the newsreels developed tremendous expertise in filming everything from cyclones to singing dogs. But they suffered badly from the advent of television. In 1970, the two companies were forced to amalgamate and by 1975 they had ceased production altogether. Sadly, the men who had helped to sustain the traditions of Australian filmmaking through 40 lean years went out of business just when the local industry was on the brink of another boom.

After 100 years of filmmaking, all we can say with certainty about our early film industry is that its home-grown products were all, to say the least, Australian. *Forty Thousand Horsemen*, an epic made on the eve of the Second World War was enormously successful for director, Charles Chauvel. But Chauvel, in his other films, often sacrificed box office profits by using only parochial subjects. Chauvel's film *Jedda* was no exception. The first full-colour feature film made in this country, *Jedda* explored a theme that would have been struggling for mass appeal even in countries with more sophisticated film audiences. Based on the book with the painfully corny title of *Eve in Ebony*, the film is about the conflict of emotions of a black girl raised in a white society—a girl who, according to the film, feels 'the call of the wild', the desperate urge to 'go walkabout'.

Ngarla Kunoth was just 16, a shy child with a mission education, when she was found by the Chauvels after exhaustive screen tests. And the true story behind the fantasy of the film proved to be far more traumatic and moving than anything the screenwriters could have dreamt up. Ngarla, now Mrs Rosalie Kunoth-Monks, told me:

> Well, looking back on it to me it was all—the part in that film—was trauma to me. Simply because I couldn't understand being away. It was the first time I'd been away from my surroundings. It was the first time I'd been away from having some of my relatives around me, and of course my communication wasn't, you know, as good as it is now. I can communicate with you but in those days, and especially going through my teens at the same time, it was a nightmarish thing.

The film would change her life completely. The Chauvels had taken her under their wing in Sydney and the real life scenario was somewhat more fascinating and subtle than the one they'd managed to capture on celluloid. Elsa Chauvel:

> She was like a little normal 16-year-old girl. I was anxious that she didn't go back to the Territory. I knew that she'd ... after a home with us in Sydney, her own lovely little bedroom, her own pretty frocks. I was very worried and I was very keen to have her remain in Sydney and study. And she was so fond of children that I thought she would be an excellent kindergarten teacher.

Eventually Ngarla Kunoth did go back to her people. But she found it hard to return. There were new problems and expectations, and finally she sought solace in religion. She entered a convent in Melbourne where she spent the next 10 years. During this time she learned that her co-star, Robert Tudawali, had failed to cope with his success. Alone and derelict, he died in a fire in Darwin.

After a decade, Sister Rosalie felt the urge to be free again. She left the convent, married a white brewery clerk and became a social worker looking after numerous Aboriginal foster children. Now a proud mother herself, she spends much of her life back at Utopia, 300 kilometres east of Alice Springs and she's also a social worker at the Alice Springs base hospital.

After the Second World War, there was a complete slump in the local film industry. Any other country the size of Australia might have given up years before, but against enormous competition from Hollywood, we've persisted with our dream of having a film industry.

The struggle to make successful Australian films based on Australian subjects is best symbolised by *The Summer of the Seventeenth Doll*. It was our finest drama, yet it starred English and American actors: Ernest Borgnine, John Mills, Angela Lansbury and Anne Baxter.

The re-birth of the local film industry got off to a spectacular false start with the film of John O'Grady's comedy *They're a Weird Mob*. Despite its success, the film failed to set off the long-awaited boom. It was now clear that the industry would need support from Canberra.

Melbourne producer, Phillip Adams, was one of a group of Australians herded together to advise the government on film funding. Adams said:

Top: *Forty Thousand Horsemen*, an Australian film epic made in the sand dunes of Cronulla Beach, Sydney, was an enormous success for director–producer Charles Chauvel (centre). It starred two Australian acting heroes, 'Chips' Rafferty (left behind Chauvel) and Peter Finch (far left). Bottom: Elsa Chauvel, Charles' wife and co-everything. They 'discovered' Errol Flynn from a Sydney newspaper photograph. Errol landed his first role as Fletcher Christian in the Chauvels' *In the Wake of the Bounty* (1933).

When Harold Holt was about to appoint us, he drowned. Gorton then got the list and asked who Holt wanted to appoint, then crossed them all off. I was left over, and this is the way you have greatness thrust upon you. Barry Jones and I, with the help of some others, really worked Gorton over. We wrote him speeches and stuff and next thing we had a blank cheque. In pretty rapid succession, we set up the Experimental Film Fund, the AFDC, which is now the Australian Film Commission, and later, the Film School. To my astonishment, all our fantasies came true overnight.

Gorton is regarded as a sort of father figure of the modern film industry. Controversially, when he was replaced by Billy McMahon as Prime Minister, Gorton actually crossed the floor in support of legislation for the film school.

Initially, the so-called '10BA' tax incentive scheme, led to rampant exploitation by many of the sharks of the industry. But then came a period of commercial and creative settling that has produced a steady stream of moderately successful films with a few spectacular highlights.

In fact, the Australian film industry now considers itself to be among the world's leading filmmaking nations—not in terms of bulk, for countries like India and Turkey each produce far more films than even Hollywood—but in terms of product which can be taken seriously here and around the world. During the 1960s, only 17 pictures were made, but with government support, the 1970s saw the production of 153 films.

Australia's first dedicated film and television school began in 1973 and was officially opened in 1975. Gough Whitlam's Labor Government picked up the baton and ran just as hard. During the 20 years that followed the demise of the short-lived Whitlam Government, other politicians took up the cause and between mid-1970 and mid-1993, 524 feature films and 251 telemovies were made. That's more features than were produced in the preceding 70 years. The Film School has produced some major success stories—among its graduates are Jane Campion (*The Piano*) and P.J. Hogan (*Muriel's Wedding*).

Without question Australia's most successful feature film has been *Crocodile Dundee*, a rumbustious, ratbag flick about a larger-than-life Indiana Jones-style of character named Mick Dundee, created by the former Sydney Harbour Bridge rigger turned comedian, Paul Hogan. Hogan's commercial nous is legendary. However, while the sequel to *Crocodile Dundee* was also a hit he's failed to produce any similar successes. But then again he hardly needs to, having married his beautiful star and gone off to live happily in a Randolph Hearst-style pleasure palace at Byron Bay whence he commutes to Tinsel Town.

Even more successful, cumulatively, have been the 'Mad Max' movies, an allegory of the American western and an orgy of ultra-violence which helped to launch Mel Gibson's international career and crossed cultural boundaries even into Japan where it needed no sub-titles.

Just how good we are really as filmmakers is infinitely arguable. Many critics feel that Peter Weir's *Picnic at Hanging Rock* was part of the Australian film industry's 'coming of age' and, certainly coupled with Fred Schepisi's *The Devil's Playground*, made around the same time, it was a watershed period. To save bickering, however, it might be better to simply list some of the major films of the 1970s, 1980s, and 1990s:

*The Chant of Jimmie Blacksmith* (1978)
*Mad Max* (1979)
*My Brilliant Career* (1979)
*Breaker Morant* (1980)
*Gallipoli* (1981)
*Mad Max II* (1981, a.k.a *The Road Warrior*)
*The Man from Snowy River* (1982)
*Crocodile Dundee* (1986)
*Evil Angels* (1988, a.k.a. *A Cry in the Dark*)
*Strictly Ballroom* (1992)
*The Piano* (1993)
*The Adventures of Priscilla: Queen of the Desert* (1994)
*Muriel's Wedding* (1994)
*Babe* (1995)
*Shine* (1996)
*The Castle* (1997)

Since our first Academy Award presented to Cinesound for a compilation of Damien Parer's footage from New Guinea in 1943, *Kokoda Front Line*, Australia has won dozens of Oscars—'the Biggies' being Peter Finch's post-humous Best Actor Award (*Network*, 1976) and Geoffrey Rush's Best Actor Award (*Shine*, 1996).

Other significant Oscars have gone to Dean Semmler for Best Cinematographer (*Dances With Wolves*, 1990), John Seale, Best Achievement in Cinematography (*The English Patient*, 1996), and Jane Campion, Best Original Screenplay (*The Piano*, 1993).

Among the standout nominations have been Peter Weir for Best Director for *Witness* (1985), *Dead Poets' Society* (1989) and *The Truman Show* (1998), along with a nomination for Best Screenplay for *Greencard* (1990). Bruce Beresford was nominated for Best Director for *Tender Mercies* (1983). He was hard done by not to get a nomination for *Driving Miss Daisy*.

Judy Davis received a nomination for Best Actress in *A Passage to India* and Best Actress in a Supporting Role in *Husbands and Wives*, 1992. *The Piano* was nominated for eight Academy Awards in 1993, *Babe* was nominated for seven Academy Awards in 1995 and *Shine* was nominated for seven Academy Awards in 1996.

## REG 'SNOWY' BAKER

Reg 'Snowy' Baker was Australia's first great screen hero, a fine example of Australian manhood. In the silent movie era when actions spoke louder than words, handsome Snowy was a dead 'cert' to be a star.

Even before he faced his first hand-cranked movie camera, Snowy had become a legend in Australia. He excelled in no less than 29 sports. He was Australia's top diver and New South Wales swimming champion. He represented Australia playing rugby union, and he went to the Olympics as a boxer. He was Australian middleweight champion and also held the New South Wales heavyweight title. He breezed into the Olympic final with just four punches. Then he lost the gold medal on a points decision, perhaps, Snowy claimed later, because the referee was the winner's father.

Snowy was also a boxing promoter and owned the Sydney Stadium. It was on a trip to California to find boxing champions to fight local talent like the famous Les Darcy that he became enchanted with the film industry.

A shrewd and, by reputation, extremely hard businessman, he realised the enormous potential of the new industry, and set up a film company to exploit his own talents. The theme of his movies was always much the same. Snowy was a kind of Ocker Superman—faster than a speeding horse and dray, able to leap verandahs at a single bound. He despatched villains all over the place.

He managed to do all his own stunts, despite a back injury that kept him out of service during the First World War. In 1919, when Australian cinema audiences were already in the millions, Snowy Baker was the biggest matinee idol of the day. Snowy then decided to have the inevitable crack at Hollywood, but the Americans weren't too sure about accepting him as a star. After making five mediocre films, Snowy decided to use his horse riding talents to run a successful polo ranch called the Riviera Club. If you believe the legends, he taught Valentino to ride, Douglas Fairbanks to crack a stockwhip and Harold Lloyd to crack jokes. Whatever the truth, Reg 'Snowy' Baker, sound of mind and sound of body, with his faithful horse 'Boomerang', became a permanent part of the Hollywood scene.

## ERROL FLYNN

The doctors said Errol Flynn died of a combination of tuberculosis, malaria, gonorrhoea and kidney disease. Hardly sound mind, sound body.

Flynn took over where Snowy Baker left off. He really was larger than life. He faced danger on and off the screen, but his greatest danger was himself. As he said in his autobiography: 'My biggest problem is reconciling my gross habits with my net income.'

The son of a university professor in Hobart, Flynn was a knockabout adventurer who was literally 'discovered' from a newspaper cutting. He had been skipper of a commercial schooner that was wrecked on the coast of New Guinea. The shipwreck wasn't a big story in the newspapers down in Sydney, and the pictures were small and blurred. But the report was read by Charles Chauvel, and the pictures were enough to convince Chauvel and his wife that they had found the star for their new film *In the Wake of the Bounty*.

Flynn knew nothing about acting, but for £10 a week he was happy to play the legendary mutineer, Fletcher Christian. It was far from a distinguished debut. His acting was wooden to say the least, but as Elsa Chauvel told me, all he really had to do was stand on the set and the women swooned. One of his more memorable lines in the film was, 'Where will it all end?' And the answer, before too long, was Hollywood. Emboldened by his early success in Australia, Flynn tried making a career in repertory theatre in England. But the British required their leading men to not only be handsome, but to know something about acting as well. So he headed across the Atlantic to America.

His first role in a Hollywood feature was as a corpse lying under a kitchen table in a B-grade gangster movie. But even as a 'stiff', the Flynn face and body were so appealing they demanded attention. The wife of the film's producer suggested that the unknown Australian might be star material, and before long Errol Flynn had been given his first leading role. *Captain Blood* (1935) was a run-away hit, and he followed with a string of similar swash-buckling epics, including *The Charge of the Light Brigade*, and appeared as a dashing hero in *The Adventures of Robin Hood*. Flynn soon became a celebrity in Tinsel Town. He was a favourite with the tennis set, as well as being a member of the exclusive Hollywood Cricket Club. It was a time when to be an English gentleman was terribly chic in America, and Flynn and David Niven were two of the most sought after sex symbols in Hollywood, with their classic good looks and debonair manner.

But Flynn never took himself seriously. He treated Hollywood and his own legend as a joke. However, behind his crisp and smiling facade, hard living was taking its toll. His house was called 'Cirrhosis by the Sea'. He was rejected for war service because of ill health and in 1942 he was involved in a celebrated morals case that led to the famous phrase 'in like Flynn', and made him a scapegoat for the gossips. Despite critical acclaim for some of his later movies such as *The Sun Also Rises* and *The Roots of Heaven*, Flynn became little more than an ageing ladies' man. The swash was beginning to buckle, and for the last two years of his life the dissipated actor lived with a teenage girl and played in pathetic films such as *Cuban Rebel Girls*.

It was 30 years since Flynn had been discovered through a shipwreck, and coincidentally he was on his way to sell a yacht, when he collapsed as a result of his virulent cocktail of diseases. The handsome young adventurer from Australia was finally scuttled by his own crew: an uncooperative heart, rebellious lungs and mutinous kidneys. He died at the age of 50, and the doctors expressed amazement he had managed to live that long.

## CHIPS RAFFERTY

For 30 years, Chips Rafferty was the screen embodiment of everything the Australian male liked to think of himself—a bronzed, dinkum, all-round, true-blue ocker mate. He was as dry as the drought and as big as Queensland.

In fact, 'Chips' was born John Goffage in 1909 in the far-west New South Wales mining town of Broken Hill. Determined to get into the film business somehow, Chips hung around the Cinesound studios and cutting rooms until he was noticed by Charles Chauvel, the feature film director who at the time was casting his First World War epic *Forty Thousand Horsemen*. To Chauvel, the Rafferty face, voice and stature seemed perfect for a part as one of the gallant Australian light horsemen in Palestine. From that film until his last role in 1974, Chips Rafferty was a household word. Throughout the 1940s and 1950s, hardly a film was made in Australia without Chips taking the part of some homespun, good-natured bush character. He was in the British productions *The Overlanders*, *Bitter Springs* and *Bush Christmas*, as well as in the two *Smiley* features and a variety of lesser movies.

His career seemed to be taking an international turn when he was cast in the Hollywood epic *Mutiny on the Bounty*, which starred Marlon Brando in the role that Errol Flynn had tried 30 years before. But Chips had a fierce pride in his Australian origins, and he particularly wanted this country to develop a film industry of its own. On his return from Hollywood, Rafferty's faith in the potential of the local industry was unshaken. To an interviewer:

> Give the Australian technicians a go! Give the actors a go! Give the musicians a go! Give the Australian industry the money today and we can take the world, boy. This is what I've been screaming about for 15 years. Backed by top writers, the material they're getting on the screen at the present time, they must win!

Sadly, just at the time the local industry was beginning to get on its feet, Chips was running out of steam. For 20 years he'd been a good actor without decent films to star in. He did manage to record a finely crafted performance in his last film, *Wake in Fright*, but a few months later in 1974 he collapsed and died while taking a walk near his home at Elizabeth Bay, Sydney.

## PETER FINCH

The first Australian actor to win an Oscar for Best Actor, Peter Finch, was in many ways the antithesis of the Rafferty image of an Australian. He was a sophisticate—a highly gifted and versatile actor who could play any part, from the gawkish country simpleton he portrayed in *Dad and Dave Come to Town*,

Top: Australian actor Peter Finch (centre) faces Bert Bailey in *Dad and Dave Come to Town* (1937), a film produced by Cinesound based on Steele Rudd's *On Our Selection* book series. Bottom: Peter Finch as the demented newsreader in *Network* (1976), the role which won him an Oscar, even though he was not alive to receive it.

his first screen role, to the demented New York television newsreader he created for *Network* nearly 40 years later. His professional life was a series of triumphs and lavish praise, while his private life was usually chaos.

Born in England, Peter Finch came to Australia as a child and always considered himself an 'Aussie'. He fought as a gunner in the Australian Army during the Second World War, but soon landed in the AIF Entertainment Unit helping to produce a variety of stage presentations. When the war ended, Finch was in demand as a radio actor but, after some encouragement from the great English actor Laurence Olivier during his visit here in 1948, the young Finch was ready to test his ambitions overseas. Allan Ashbolt, an old Army comrade who also worked in the theatre with Finch during the late 1940s recalled his remarkable powers as a dramatic actor:

> … there was that marvellous meditative stillness he had about him—those large luminous, expressive eyes and that brooding, pervasive intensity, the tightly reined emotional explosions. He was a beautifully disciplined actor.

Finch quickly established himself as one of the most accomplished screen actors in Europe and America. His list of credits is impressive: *A Town Like Alice*, *No Love for Johnnie*, and *Sunday Bloody Sunday* are three contemporary dramas which confirmed his stature. He attracted critical acclaim in *Far From the Madding Crowd* and *England Made Me*, but it was his last major role in the frenetic black comedy *Network* that eventually earned him his long-overdue Academy Award. With an almost Shakespearian touch of tragedy, Peter Finch died just a few months before he would have received the Oscar in 1977. It was accepted—to a standing ovation—by his widow Elethea.

## GEOFFREY RUSH

The only other Academy Award for Best Actor in Australia's movie history this century went to another knockabout bloke playing a tortured soul, Geoffrey Rush, as the emotionally disturbed concert pianist, David Helfgott, in the movie *Shine*.

Born in Toowoomba in 1951, Rush's background is primarily in theatre— his first hit stage role was as Snoopy in *You're a Good Man, Charlie Brown* with the Queensland Theatre Company. On the night that he won the English

Geoffrey Rush, the only other Australian to win a 'Best Actor' Academy Award this century, for his role as the disturbed concert pianist David Helfgott in *Shine*. Rush also received a Golden Globe, the English equivalent to the Oscars, and many thought some awards should have gone to young Ben Mendelsohn who played the adolescent Helfgott. Geoffrey in turn was rushed off his feet with offers including starring roles in two of the biggest hits of 1998, *Shakespeare in Love* and *Elizabeth*.

equivalent of the Oscar, the Golden Globes—the first leg of the grand slam, if you like—I asked him how it felt after so long in theatre to be considered 'an overnight success'? He replied, 'I still have the wonderful experiences of the 25 years I've spent working in Australian theatre, very much with me.'

The somewhat dishevelled actor's history, including sharing a flat with NIDA graduate, Mel Gibson, in their 'bones-of-your-arse days', helped to give Rush a healthy perspective on the heady lunacy of Oscar week that was soon to descend upon him. Everyone, including the doyen of American chat shows, Jay Leno, wanted to know about the artists-in-the-garret days:

> *Rush*: We had a bag of carrots in the kitchen and a blender. We'd wake up in the morning, we'd have a carrot juice, we'd go off to rehearsal and I think we might have smoked a little bit of Woody Harrelson's jacket ...
> *Leno*: Really?
> *Rush*: Well, we put it on but we didn't actually model it ...

Rush is the Aussie actor of the 1990s as Finch was of the 1970s. Rush too had played the gormless Dave in Australia's most recent *Dad 'n' Dave Movie* with Joan Sutherland and Leo McKern—but no amiable ocker is this one—rather, a sophisticated player who knows the arcane nuance of Hollywood today. I followed him to Los Angeles for the big Oscar week and he told me that he and Mel were shamelessly building up the folklore:

> I met up with Mel last night at a party and I said, 'This story I've been telling about the time we shared the flat together for three or four months in Australia has now become sort of folkloric.' And he said, 'Oh, yes, I'm embroidering it, I'm pushing it further and I keep adding bits to it as the press keep asking me questions ...'

Among those questions were inevitably those about the famous scene in which Helfgott meets his future wife, Gillian. She arrives at his backyard to be greeted by the spectacle of the eccentric genius jumping up and down on a trampoline wearing only an open overcoat. Rush to Leno on the filming of that scene: 'It's fairly liberating because, after a while, when you've been standing around with nothing on and the wedding tackle is there, totally revealed ...'

'Wedding tackle?' splutters Leno as the audience breaks into hysterical laughter.

So maybe the grand old tradition of Aussie larrikinism prevails after all, even with the new breed. How did it feel, I asked Geoffrey, to have introduced the phrase 'wedding tackle' to the American lexicon?

Well, I have to pay a due literary footnote to H.G. and Roy, who I'm a great fan of. That sort of popped into my mind and again, I thought, in those chat show contexts, I thought a little bit of genuine Australian linguistic flavour might go down well.

And so it did. Rush was subsequently also nominated for Best Supporting Actor for his role in *Shakespeare in Love*, a film in which he played Rose Theatre owner Philip Henslowe, who relies on young William Shakespeare to write a 'crowd tickler' that will rescue the theatre from debt.

Australians can take some pride in the fact that our two winners of the ultimate Academy Award have been extremely talented actors—Finch and Rush. But that does not necessarily make them our biggest stars. Mel Gibson, born in America and ultimately a Hollywood star with a formative Aussie period sandwiched in between, still attracts more publicity; and Nicole Kidman, with a solid body of work in Australia but always battling to shed the sobriquet Mrs Tom Cruise, is a star in her own right. Whether or not she enters the ultimate Hall of Fame of those who are already famous remains to be seen.

## RADIO

In early 1919, a young Englishman called Ernest Fisk set up an office at York Street, Sydney. Fisk was a friend of Marconi—the man who invented the radio—and he'd come to Australia as the representative of the Marconi Wireless Company.

On the night of 13 August, he was a few blocks down the road from his offices, addressing the conservative membership of the Royal Society of New South Wales. At a pre-arranged time, Fisk finished his talk and switched on a receiving apparatus that had been set up in front of the members. Back at the York Street office, an assistant broadcast by radio a recording of the national anthem, which the members listened to with amazement. Australia had entered the world of radio.

The earliest wireless sets were big enough to be classified as furniture. They were a status symbol, and manufacturers put as much work into designing the box and horn as they did into building the electronics inside.

The public was still so suspicious of the new marvel that advertisers had to assure everyone that it was not necessary to open the windows to receive radio broadcasts. Come to think of it, I still don't know why you don't need to open the windows. Anyway, radio broadcasting soon brought its own social revolution to Australia, and by the mid 1930s, the Postmaster General's Department had sold one million licences.

Wireless was bringing news, music and laughter to a far-flung population, and before long Australians were trying to live up to the BBC's motto that 'nation shall speak unto nation'. The 1933 'Empire' broadcast caused as much excitement in its day as a satellite hook-up. Among the official broadcasters on the great day were Sir Charles Lloyd Jones, and the young man who started it all, Ernest Fisk.

Fisk was now a man of substance, and head of his own radio company, Amalgamated Wireless (Australasia) Ltd, AWA. As business thrived, the company built ambitious new offices that soon became a landmark in Sydney. Today the building still stands among the skyscrapers, and the intricate AWA tower, a replica of the Eiffel tower, is a quaint reminder of the days when the wireless was as modern as tomorrow.

Radio still had a long way to go in the 1930s. What people most wanted to hear was the cricket. Don Bradman was demolishing the British bowlers at Leeds and Lord's, but live broadcasts from England would have been far too complicated and expensive. A young ABC announcer named Charlie Moses used his ingenuity to devise a coverage that almost had the nation's cricket fans fooled. The announcer went on to become Sir Charles Moses, ABC General Manager from 1935 to 1965. He once described to me just how they did those early broadcasts:

> It was an attempt to give our listeners the impression that they were listening to a cricket match actually being broadcast from the ground, although before the broadcast we announced that it would be a simulated description done in the studio. Although, many people didn't believe it. I'd arranged to get the scorer

Top: Radio was introduced commercially to Australians by Ernest Fisk, Marconi Wireless Company representative, in 1919. Before television, the family radio was the centre of home entertainment. Below: Gwen Meredith, writer of the epic radio serial, 'Blue Hills'. Grown men were known to climb out of the sheep dip to tune in to the gentle saga of mundane rural life, which ran for 30 years.

from the Sydney Cricket Ground and we had a small scoreboard and we put the scores on the scoreboard so that we could look at the board and check. The sound effects were done by Dion Wheeler and he was very good indeed. He knew the game and he never fluffed by getting loud applause for something that was a very stodgy stroke. One of the difficult things in this simulation was to get the sound of the ball on the bat. I tapped a pencil on a piece of wood and it made the exact sound of a full-blooded drive.

So, with announcers improvising around cryptic telegrams, and the various sounds of a match in progress being concocted in the studio, the nation's cricket lovers were lulled into the belief that they were listening to the actual match 'live' from England.

But, as Sir Charles remembers, the days of 'synthetic' or 'simulated' cricket were not without their occasional dangers, such as when a telegram was delayed and the announcers had to *ad lib*:

> … and it was on those occasions that Larwood had to have a look at his boot, or he would have to go to the pavilion and change his boot if necessary, and on one occasion, a dog ran onto the field … that sort of thing. Although I never actually said 'I can see …', one of my colleagues did once say, 'I can see rain coming down in sheets.' I thought that was going a little far.

By the 1940s, radio was at its peak of popularity. It was the golden age of the valve wireless. Competition between the stations was fierce, and for the first time announcers were becoming celebrities. A young woman named Gwen Meredith began writing a simple serial for the ABC titled 'Blue Hills', which eventually became an institution.

'Blue Hills', an inoffensive saga of country life, has been called the most successful radio serial in the world. It ran for a staggering 5795 episodes. Even grown men were known to clamber out of the sheep dip at lunchtime to find out how Dr Gordon and Granny Bishop were getting on. For 30 years, Gwen Meredith improvised her mundane country adventures straight into an office dictation machine. How did she feel when it finally ended, I asked her:

> A little bereft … and the general tenor of the letters was, 'Well, if you're bereft, what about us?' One letter was from North Queensland, and this woman said

that when she heard it announced on the air that the serial was going off, she went around in a state of shock all day. When the shock wore off, she said perhaps I was doing her a favour because as I was getting old and tired I might have died, and then she would never have known what happened.

'Blue Hills' was an institution in radio, but it was never what the commercial stations called a 'commercial success'. The big money was in advertising sponsorship. Sponsors demanded shows with plenty of action, drama and suspense. With television still decades away, the radio producers tried to create all the glamour and prestige of the theatre. The broadcasts were played on stage before packed audiences who supplied the necessary applause in return for the free entertainment. Even the sound effects men were required to dress in dinner suit and bow tie as they dashed about the stage frantically keeping up with the action, creating the sounds of door knocks, telephones, car crashes and gun shots.

Radio drama died with the advent of the new medium of television in the 1950s. 'The wireless', in turn, had to reinvent itself, including that name, 'The Wireless'. Within 10 years of the advent of 'the Gogglebox', radio had turned pretty well exclusively to talk—news, gossip, and a new phenomenon, listener participation—what would be known in the 1990s as 'inter-activity'.

The pioneer of talk-back radio, or 'open-line' as it was called when it was first borrowed from America in the 1960s, was the former disc jockey named John Laws, who would become a *cause célèbre* 30 years later in a furore over what radio announcers should be paid, or paid not, to say.

One of the early criticisms of talk-back was that it quickly became abusive. The ignorance of some of the on-air personalities who suddenly found themselves having to talk extemporaneously on a variety of subjects was exceeded only by the ignorance of some of the callers who rang in. So, at times, the new genre began to sound more like theatre of cruelty than good old-fashioned information and entertainment.

Shortly after he launched that first 'Open Line' program, I asked John Laws in an interview, given that radio kings couldn't see their subjects, how did they know they weren't hitting little old ladies with walking sticks? 'I can usually tell when they've got a limp in their voice,' Laws responded, which I guess is the sort of repartee that has kept him in business for most of the latter half of the century.

Laws and his fellow morning announcer in Sydney, former Australian Wallabies coach, Alan Jones and Neil Mitchell in Melbourne, claim huge cumulative audiences—although still only a fraction of an actual television audience—and wield some influence in the corridors of power among politicians anxious to appease their constituents. Undoubtedly one of the wittiest and most talented of the modern breed of radio talk-back announcers is Mike Carlton (son of the famous sprinter, Jimmy Carlton, who was at one stage the fastest man in the world but who, on the eve of the 1932 Los Angeles Olympics, entered the priesthood for 10 years before returning to normal civilian life to marry and raise a family).

By the end of the century, radio had become a different creature with other eccentric talents like Andrew Denton, Richard Stubbs, Martin and Molloy, Wendy Harmer and crew, and Doug Mulray, all pushing the comic boundaries, with the latter pioneering a new milieu linking live radio with the Internet. Until then the only real innovation in the medium had been the introduction of FM radio, a technical advance perfected in the 1920s but deliberately stifled during commercial warfare in the United States. As for the shape of the future, it seems that radio is a sort of exploding universe, still growing but more fragmented with scores of stations now narrowcasting to smaller individual groups in the cities and around the country.

## TELEVISION

The medium that eclipsed radio in popularity is now itself obsessed with its relative popularity with the viewing audience. The infamous 'Ratings', the statistical measure which tells television executives how many people were watching a particular program at a particular time down to the minute—but not how good it is—have come to rule the airwaves much as the ballot box rules politics. Every day a computer spits out the figures that show which television station is attracting the most viewers, and for many people within the industry, these can be life or death results.

But television wasn't always such a cut-throat business. As early as 1934, Dr Val McDowell of Brisbane assembled a bizarre jumble of apparatus and with it somehow managed to transmit a television picture the grand distance of 10 feet. His workshop wall sported a sign which read, 'Television. Keep clear!'

Australian electronics buffs had been fiddling with television since the 1920s, but it wasn't until the world radio convention of 1938, and the visit of

James Logie Baird to Australia, that we began to realise that 'radio with pictures' might soon be a reality.

Twelve years after Baird produced his first flickering television images, thousands of Londoners were watching a regular television service twice a day. As it turned out, Baird's system was not the process adopted for television transmission, although his middle name, Logie, lives on as the title of our television industry's top awards.

By the early 1950s, when British and American audiences were already watching television at home, Australia was still staging experimental broadcasts in places like Sydney's Hotel Australia. Sir Ernest Fisk, poised to swing his vast AWA empire behind the production of television sets and equipment, extolled the advantages of television above radio:

> Television is a new kind of radio broadcasting. You will have a set in your home with which you will see plays, variety shows, pageantries, sports and a great variety of things as they occur in your own receiving set.

By the mid 1950s, the race to be first was hotting up. At Sydney's Channel Nine, Sir Frank Packer was so determined to win, he didn't even wait for his studios to be finished.

The first Australian television programs were produced as outside broadcasts from a tiny church hall in Surry Hills in Sydney. The dazzling variety line-up included 'The Johnny O'Connor Show', 'Accent on Strings', 'What's My Line?' and a show, 'Campfire Favourites', starring a yodeller named Ifield.

When the big day came on 16 September 1956, Bruce Gyngell had the dubious and uncomfortable honour of uttering the first words, 'Ladies and gentlemen, good evening and welcome to television.' He told me he practised saying the phrase with a variety of emphases but ultimately there weren't that many ways to utter it and he decided to play it pretty straight. Gyngell, who later became the first Chairman of the Australian Broadcasting Tribunal, the first head of the Independent Multicultural Broadcasting Corporation (later SBS, the Special Broadcasting Service), and still later back as a faithful lieutenant to the Packer family, remembered the seminal moment like this:

> On the opening night I was sitting in a chair in a very small little room; in fact, people commented as to why this announcer, who was unknown, appeared

like this. It was because of the confinement of the space and the only way the camera man could get the panning handle of his camera in. The chair wouldn't move any further so I sat the entire night with my left shoulder dropped and my right shoulder up saying, 'Ladies and gentlemen, good evening and welcome to television.'

Once it became established, Australian television spent most of its time transmitting English and American programs, but we did manage to produce shows of our own. 'Consider Your Verdict', a courtroom melodrama, and 'Homicide', the legendary cops-and-robbers saga, were early successes, as was Graham Kennedy, one of the few radio personalities to make a triumphant new career on television. His 'In Melbourne Tonight' show became one of the longest-running programs in the history of Australian television, along with other stalwarts such as the ABC's current affairs program 'Four Corners', and Channel Nine's 'Hey Hey It's Saturday'.

'The Mavis Bramston Show', Australia's first satirical show, kept the nation laughing through the mid 1960s, and the cast of Barry Creyton, Noeline Brown, Ron Frazer, Carol Raye and Gordon Chater all became stars.

In the 1970s, 'Number 96', a sinful soap-opera made perhaps the biggest impact of any drama series. Producer Bill Harmon has attempted to explain its amazing success:

Well, number one, it was the first of its kind. Secondly, it goes back to radio. People like to follow characters all the way through. They like to know their innermost thoughts, they like to feel they're part of the family. I think also comedy was a very big part of the success of the show. They could laugh at each other and they could laugh at the characters.

But, like every other television show except the news, the drama of 'Number 96' eventually came to an end, killed off by the dreaded ratings.

At the end of the century, as television itself approached its 50th birthday, the medium that had been relatively stable for decades faced considerable change and volatility. Nothing much had threatened its owners and pro-prietors except themselves. Cannibalistic commercial warfare is still the order of the day but for the first time there were new technological threats in the air waves.

Top: KEEP CLEAR!—Dr Val McDowell of Brisbane is about to fire a television signal the grand distance of 10 feet in 1934. Alas, his system like many others proved unworkable and Australia had to wait until 16 September 1956 for the first real television signals to be transmitted to about 3500 sets in Sydney. Below: 'The Mavis Bramston Show', a super satirical success, kept the nation laughing through the mid-1960s.

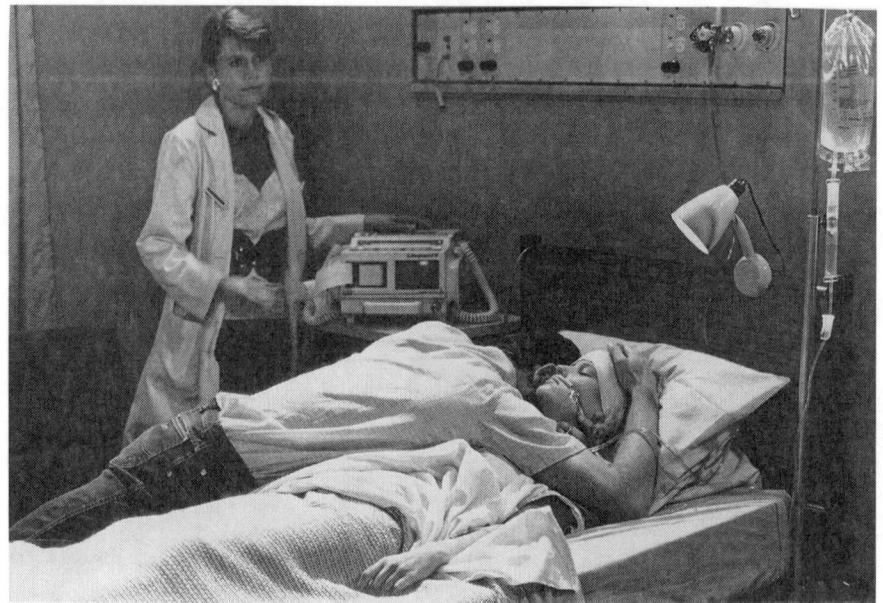

Top: Soapie sentiment—Daph (Elaine Smith) carks it on 'Neighbours' as Des (Paul Keane) mourns. The highly exportable and long-running soap opera (this scene is from episode 690) launched the international careers of Kylie and Jason. Below: Lisa McCune, star of the popular 'Blue Heelers' television show, the day after winning her third gold Logie in April 1999.

Firstly, so-called 'free-to-air' television, which somehow painlessly extracts about three billion dollars in revenue from someone or other, found itself facing a new rival—cable television—whereby subscribers pay to have many channels thereby having, theoretically, more choice of what they want to see. In the initial flurry to establish territory in the marketplace, various operators lost almost a billion dollars, but the long-term stakes are apparently worth the pain. In the bad old days, the solution for cable television's commercial rivals would have been simply to buy it, but anti-monopolistic legislation, while not exactly watertight, has so far prevented all of Australia's media falling into a single pair of hands.

The other new threat to traditional television has been the Internet. Initially dismissed as an introverted pastime for nerds, the Net has increasingly become a source not only of information, home shopping and pornography but a possible interface for a dynamic global entertainment system. Each of Australia's major television networks, already required by law to begin the era of digital broadcasting, has been making aggressive thrusts, as far as they are able, into Internet and Pay TV opportunities.

Change has been rapid in the television industry, yet the stations that have offered the most stability and the least changed are the ones that have been most successful. Evergreen programs such as '60 Minutes', 'Sale of the Century' and 'A Current Affair' have been cemented into their time slots, even when the performances have looked like failing, and have became institutionalised goldmines for their owner, Kerry Packer.

Perhaps the most fascinating thing about television is how, after even half a century, we haven't seemed to tire of it, despite all the predictions. While television viewing has declined a little, even on a quiet night 70 per cent of Australians are still watching 'the idiot box', and the average Australian watches more than three hours of television a day.

Television's been accused of being a deeply shallow medium—indeed, it is 'a medium because it's never well done'—but in the long run it's only as good as we are, a mirror to the society we live in and perhaps, to bend that old aphorism about politicians, 'we get the television we deserve'. Media commentator Phillip Adams' famous line has often been repeated but still holds true, nevertheless: 'We haven't had 30 years of television; we've had one year of television 30 times.' Now as television approaches its half century, he could well change it to: 'We've had 50 years of television, but once is enough.'

# The sunburnt country ...

## BEYOND THE URBAN BOUNDARIES

I love a sunburnt country,
A land of sweeping plains,
Of ragged mountain ranges,
Of droughts and flooding rains,
I love her far horizons,
I love her jewel-sea,
Her beauty and her terror,
The wide brown land for me!

When Dorothea Mackellar wrote her famous verse 'My Country' at the beginning of the century, Australia was already becoming one of the most urban countries on Earth. Far from being a nation of bushies, less than 10 per cent of the population of around 19 million people live on the land. Indeed, more than 90 per cent of the population live less than 50 kilometres from the sea.

Dorothea Mackellar's country is a land relatively few modern Australians have seen, the wide brown land of mirages and kangaroos, back of Bourke, back of beyond—'the Never Never'. Today, most of us are more likely to have tried roti than damper. We're certainly more familiar with swimming pools than billabongs.

Yet the Australian ethos is still influenced by that magical, mystical and often forbidding place, 'the bush'. The power of the land is still amply illustrated by the fact that our Liberal Prime Minister can only work—indeed, is only Prime Minister—because of the fact that the Libs are in coalition with

Left: Drought—otherwise known as 'the seventh state', is a fact of life in outback Australia.

Right: Isobel Marion Dorothea Mackellar, whose evocative, anthemic Australian poem 'My Country' was first published in *Spectator*, a London magazine, in 1908. Bottom: Pages from the original manuscript of the poem, at first called 'Core of my Heart'.

the National Party, formally the Country Party and still not sure why it changed its name. Even in the late 1990s, when John Howard was absent, his place would be taken by an amiable bloke in a big Akubra called Tim Fischer. Another former leader of the party, which in those days had a bob each way and called itself the National Country Party, was Doug Anthony, whose own family property is among the rich, pastoral valleys on the New South Wales coast near Murwillumbah. Like most men on the land, the then Deputy Prime Minister saw his property as more than just a farm and he told me:

My father came back from the First World War and was given a small soldier settler's block, 14 acres, to grow bananas. So he went and cleared the country and grew bananas. He was ravaged by bunchy-top and went broke. He tried growing sugarcane and went broke. He became an auctioneer and then went back to growing bananas. That was the beginning and we've always had a battle.

Yet the biggest struggle on the land is not against overdrafts, but against sheer uncertainty. Even with scientific farming, mechanised war against disease, superphosphate bounties and guaranteed minimum prices, life is often still a bitter fight against the elements. One year's record crop is often followed by the next year's failure. What the Lord giveth, he can also take away, even unto last year's Mercedes.

The ravages of the Australian way of life are legendary, a colourful part of our folklore, perhaps best summed up in the ironic words of the famous poem 'Said Hanrahan' by P.J. Hartigan ('John O'Brien'). Hanrahan is a bush pessimist who is first found lamenting the onset of the drought:

'If we don't get three inches, man,
Or four to break this drought,
We'll all be rooned,' said Hanrahan,
'Before the year is out.'

Then of course it rains and now he bemoans the arrival of too much water:

And every creek a banker ran,
And dams filled overtop;

'We'll all be rooned,' said Hanrahan,
'If this rain doesn't stop.'

And, lo, after the rain, the grass grows as high as the fences and Hanrahan gazes around the sky:

'There'll be bushfires for sure, me man,
There will, without a doubt.
We'll all be rooned,' said Hanrahan,
'Before the year is out.'

## FLOODS

The Hunter River, flowing lazily past the New South Wales town of Maitland, is part of a tranquil scene, typical of much of rural Australia. But, when you live on the land, nature can be a harsh mistress. In 1955, after weeks of heavy rain, the northern New South Wales rivers, including the Hunter, rose and broke their banks. In the floods which followed, 22 people were killed and 10 000 homes ruined. The flooding of Maitland, the worst-affected town, was fast and furious. In low-lying areas, houses were completely submerged beneath the muddy, swirling water. Thousands fled their homes, and those who refused to go had to be removed by force. The Mayor of Maitland appealed to surf clubs on the coast, and lifesavers rowing their surf boats helped to rescue more than 600 people.

At the height of the flood, hundreds of people watched as a railway signal box swayed and rocked under the force of the waters. Inside, two men struggled for their lives while a helicopter circled overhead. Within minutes, the signal box collapsed, hurling the men into the torrent. As they grabbed at a line lowered from the helicopter, the crowds cheered what seemed like an amazing rescue. The helicopter climbed to 30 metres and veered towards a nearby railway bridge, where the pilot hoped to lower the two men to safety. But, as the helicopter turned to avoid power lines, the men's holds slipped. One man hit the water and disappeared, the other landed across high-tension wires and was incinerated in an explosion of blue flame. Then the dangling rope tangled in the power lines and the helicopter spiralled out of control into the water. The crew of two was incredibly lucky. They survived the crash

"First the drought killed some of the sheep, then the flood drowned some more, and now the grass has grown so high, I can't find what's left of 'em!"

Top: In the Maitland floods of 1955, 22 people died and 10 000 homes were ruined. For the locals this shot must have some bleak, ironic humour, because if ever there were another place subject to flooding over the years, it was Brisbane. Below: Cartoonist Emil Mercier with a variation on the theme of 'We'll all be rooned, said Hanrahan.'

and, wearing lifejackets, were plucked from the floodwaters about three kilometres downstream by an Army 'duck'.

So savage was the flowing flood that at one stage, 20 houses in one street were picked up by the rushing waters and smashed against a bridge. Seven people clung to the roof of one of the houses, but only three of them survived. By the time the rain finally stopped, more than 10 inches had fallen in just four days. The damage was estimated at £20 million. And, as the floodwaters slowly subsided, Maitland was still cut off from the rest of the nation by water. Food and medical supplies, blankets and clothing were dropped into the town by parachute. It was weeks before the town could return to its normal life. Since 1955, Maitland's levy banks have been strengthened and its flood warning system improved.

Of course, Maitland is not the only district to suffer from flooding in Australia. But there was something particularly dramatic about this disaster which captured the attention of the newsreels in their last gasp before the advent of television. In fact, such was the coverage given to the event that it in turn inspired one of Australia's most successful films, *Newsfront*, which built a thrilling story around the intriguing and ultimately tragic behind-the-scenes adventures of the newsreel teams involved.

Some of Australia's worst flooding occurred in 1909 in the north-west of New South Wales and then in the following five years widespread record floods were recorded through South Australia, Western Australia and Tasmania. Parts of Tasmania were flooded again in 1929 and 14 lives were lost near Derby.

In the 1960s, Tasmania experienced its worst floods ever but none would be as spectacular as the torrent that submerged much of the city of Brisbane in the last week of January 1974. A freak flood, brought on by the torrential rains of Cyclone Wanda, overran about one-third of the entire metropolitan area of the Queensland capital, Australia's third-largest city. Forty suburbs were under water, some to the amazing depth of more than 10 metres. Fifteen people died, scores were injured and many thousands had to be evacuated from their homes. The city centre was swamped and an oil tanker broke its moorings in the Brisbane River and narrowly missed a block of flats before slamming into a wharf.

In more recent times, there have been heart-breaking floods in New South Wales and Queensland; but such is the contrary nature of the Australian climate that one of our most spectacular floods in the last two decades has been in the desert near Kalgoorlie, Western Australia, where the Indian Pacific train was embarrassingly marooned.

For many people, particularly the thousands who found that their insurance policies meant naught in the face of 'an act of God', the floods have spelt ruin. And the problem with the elements in this exasperating country is that they can so easily switch from one extreme to another.

## DROUGHT

'I am the master, the dread king drought, and the great west land is mine,' said Ogilvie's poem of half a century ago, and it has always been the same. Some part of Australia is always in the grip of 'the Dry' and that's why they call the drought 'the seventh state'. It's a grim, cruel fact of Australian life and it breeds its own brand of sardonic humour. It's a time when graziers tend to call clouds 'empties coming back from the coast', a time of the so-called 'darling showers'—three thunderclaps, two drops of rain and one dust storm.

It is impossible not to be profoundly emotionally affected when travelling into a drought-stricken area, and the desolation, death and despair have made their mark on Australia's writers. In the face of drought, the doggerel that characterises so much Australian poetry, including that of Lawson and Paterson, is somehow elevated to a different plane. And even Australia's unknown bards have been moved to a rare eloquence:

Eerily wails the drover,
When the drought wind sweeps the sky,
And men say, 'Hear the Plover,'
As he moves the ghost mob by.
And they never speak of rain,
When the blazing sun is setting,
Like a disc of shining brass,
And they wouldn't steal a copper,
But they all steal grass.

The name of the writer of this old ballad is lost to time. But many of Australia's well-known writers have been inspired by the spectacle of drought, and their words, considering the circumstances of their inspiration, have an almost indecent beauty. Mary Durack linked beauty with the tragedy of drought in this passage from *Kings in Grass Castles*:

> Every morning clouds piled up to the north to melt in the midday heat and evening skies were agate bright fading to amethyst. Cracks widened on the parched plains and hot winds filled them with the brittle remnants of precious grass.

Geoffrey Dutton described the land with no rain as 'drought country ... when the light strikes nothing but ruin as response', and time and time again observations about the drought pierce the general greyness of Australian literature with a special clarity. From Judith Wright's poem 'Drought Year':

> I heard the dingoes cry
> In the whipstick scrub on the Thirty-mile Dry.
> I saw the wagtail take his fill perching in the seething skull.
> I saw the eel wither where he curled in the last blood-drop of a spent world.

## BUSHFIRE!

They conjure up a litany of tragedies for almost every day of the week ... Black Tuesday, Ash Wednesday, Black Friday, Black Sunday. Bushfires have taken more lives than any other natural disaster in Australia.

On 6 February 1851, Victoria experienced a bushfire, smoke from which could be seen in Hobart—hundreds of kilometres away. Fires raged right across the state from Barwon Heads to Mount Gambier in South Australia. By 11 o'clock, the temperature in Melbourne was 47° Celsius in the shade. Ten people are known to have died in the fires which were called 'Black Thursday', a name which has applied to several similar disasters since the 1850s.

But Victoria's worst single bushfire occurred on a Friday the 13th—the 'Black Friday' of 13 January 1939. The blaze, which had been burning for several days, reached its peak when the whole town of Noojee was destroyed. The fire covered almost two million hectares. More than 100 homes were lost and 71 people died. In that same month, a week-long

Bushfire is Australia's greatest natural killer and Tasmania has had more than its share of disastrous blazes. Smoke from some of them has been seen on the mainland. Top: Hobart's *Mercury* newspaper printed this picture of ironically named Forest Road, after the 1967 fires, and the Melbourne *Sun* (left) describes the disaster which came within two kilometres of Hobart's city centre. Sixty-two people perished, hundreds of cars and houses were destroyed and thousands of animals died.

bushfire burned over a huge area of southern and eastern New South Wales and six people were killed.

In 1957, five people died in three weeks of bushfires in the Blue Mountains near Sydney. Damage was estimated at more than two million pounds and in two townships, Leura and Wentworth Falls, fire destroyed 158 houses and other buildings.

In 1962, Victoria suffered the worst fires since those on the eve of the Second World War. Nine died in the fire that raged east of Melbourne and came within 20 kilometres of the city centre. Six-hundred homes were gutted and eight died. Seven years later, fires in Victoria claimed 23 lives. This total included 18 people, some of them fire fighters, who died at Lara, near Geelong.

During 1983, South Australia withered under the onslaught of the 'Ash Wednesday' fires which killed 71 people in that state as well as Victoria on two terrible days in February. In South Australia, the Adelaide Hills and the south-east corner of the state were ablaze and damage was estimated at $400 million. Much of the property has been rebuilt and restored and the land regenerated, but the psychological scars have not healed, even today.

The capacity of the Australian landscape to heal itself rapidly, with many native shrubs having quick-growing, short lifespans for this reason, has in turn made suburbs on the outskirts of Sydney particularly vulnerable in recent years. Another cruel feature of bushfires is their ability to strike at random. Reporting on the fires at Menai in 1998, I spoke to residents in Barnes Crescent where every second house had been destroyed by tongues of flame that had whooshed up the valley and amazingly had somehow left the houses in between unscathed. I also spoke to a woman and a boy, each clutching a piece of amorphous metal in their hands. One piece had once been a lawn-mower and the other the hubcap of a motor car.

Of course, all states of Australia have endured terrible bushfires, but perhaps none has suffered quite like the tiny island of Tasmania. Hobart, Australia's second-oldest city has been recording fires since it was founded in 1803. In 1915, bushfires burned in the Huon River area for more than two weeks and in 1920, the north-west suffered the severest fire since 'Black Friday'—31 December 1897. The following year, fires occurred in the north-east. By this time the fire brigade's foot-powered and horse-powered vehicles had been totally replaced by motorised fire engines, but even they were of little avail.

Huge fires again paralysed the state in the 1930s and 1940s, but one of the most disastrous bushfire days in Australia's history occurred on 7 February 1967. In the terrifying Tasmanian bushfires of 1967, nine houses were destroyed in Forest Road, Hobart, just a mile from the city centre.

Bushfires consumed much of the south-east of Tasmania and came to within two kilometres of the centre of Hobart itself. Sixty-two people were killed. High temperatures, high-velocity winds and dry terrain made the fire fighters' jobs impossible and incredibly hazardous for them personally. Hundreds were hurt and losses included 1400 buildings and 1500 cars. Among the animals killed were 1400 cattle, 50 000 sheep, 25 000 poultry and 900 pigs. Losses were estimated at $40 million.

Among the hundreds of buildings gutted in the bushfires of 1967 was Hobart's landmark Cascade Brewery built in 1823. The top three storeys were added in the 1920s. The Cascade Brewery is now restored to its former glory. The name preserves an earlier form of the name of the district in which it is situated. Perhaps they should change it to 'the Phoenix Brewery'.

## THE RABBIT

In the middle of the nineteenth century, Mr Thomas Austin, a gentleman farmer of Barwon Park near Geelong, was feeling homesick. He missed his native England and he missed his favourite sport—hunting. In 1859, Mr Austin decided to import live game and later that year the first animals arrived in Victoria on the clipper ship *Lightning*. The animals Mr Austin had chosen were *Oryctolagus cuniculus*, the common European rabbit. Mr Austin had made a terrible mistake.

Domesticated pet rabbits had come to Australia with the First Fleet, but their breeding was controlled. Mr Austin's rabbits soon reproduced to the point where by 1870 they had become a popular delicacy for Melbourne society. There were now so many, they were regularly offered for sale in the *Geelong Advertiser*. The Barwon Park rabbits were bred near the main house and became so famous that when the Duke of Edinburgh visited Australia in the 1880s, he made a special trip to Geelong to enjoy the hunt, shooting 450 rabbits in a single day. By this time, the rabbits were breeding and spreading at an unbelievable rate, and from Barwon Park came what scientists now call the greatest animal invasion of any continent in history.

Feeling homesick and missing his favourite sport of hunting, Mr Thomas Austin, the owner of Barwon Park near Geelong (top), imported rabbits from England in 1856. By the turn of the century, however, those rabbits had reproduced so quickly that they

had reached national plague proportions. It wasn't until the South American myxomatosis virus (which painfully affects rabbits' eyes before killing them) escaped from a test site near Corowa in South Australia in 1950 that their numbers began to diminish.

Ironically, while rabbits were overrunning Australia, South American countries were facing the opposite problem. Rabbits raised for meat and fur were dying from a mysterious disease called myxomatosis. Early this century, a Brazilian scientist named Dr H. de B. Aragao approached the Australian Government and suggested that myxomatosis could be the answer to our problems. The government, on the advice of Australian scientists, ignored the Brazilian's solution to our ever-increasing rabbit problem. According to Professor F.J. Fenner, author of the book *Myxomatosis*:

> They poured cold water on it. They responded by saying that the rabbit was a very important animal for the carcass and fur trade. They didn't want to interfere with the trade by destroying rabbits totally. They realised that they did have to contain them but they didn't want to destroy them.

Australian scientists would soon regret their decision not to introduce myxomatosis to Australia. Within a few years, rabbits were completely out of control. The pests became so prevalent that, in the west of New South Wales, land which had supported 15 million sheep in the 1890s could carry less than half that 40 years later. For half a century, Australians on the land fought a futile battle against the rabbit. Trapping, shooting, poisoning and even clubbing the rabbits to death was futile.

In the 1930s, a new scientist entered the myxomatosis saga. She was Dr Jean McNamara, a Melbourne paediatrician, who had been overseas studying poliomyelitis when she met a group of scientists working on myxomatosis. Dr McNamara was convinced the disease and its effect on rabbits had not been adequately tested. Myxomatosis is a particularly horrible virus, which spreads only under certain conditions. A rabbit infected in the eye with ugly sores will take more than a week to die. The disease is transmitted to other rabbits by flies or mosquitoes. Convinced of its effectiveness, Dr (later Dame Jean) McNamara hammered away at the authorities for years. As Professor Fenner says:

> She wrote some very pointed articles in the Melbourne newspapers and insisted that myxomatosis must be given another trial. This was started in May 1950 and carried out right through the winter, which, with hindsight, is when mosquitoes aren't about.

But they didn't think of that at the time. The scientists had pretty well written it off as a failure. But then, just before Christmas 1950, reports came from 10 miles away from Corowa, the nearest trial site, that there were rabbits with a horrible disease wandering over Corowa Common. It was obviously myxomatosis.

The myxomatosis, which had escaped from that testing site in the Murray Valley in 1950, soon changed the entire face of rural Australia. With government support, a large-scale campaign was established which ensured the rapid, and deadly, spread of the myxomatosis virus throughout the Australian rabbit population. Half a century after a Brazilian doctor had first told us about myxomatosis, we finally had the rabbit plague under control.

When first introduced, myxomatosis killed 99 per cent of rabbits, but it's that 1 per cent left that's always the problem and the kill rate today is often less than 50 per cent. In recent years, the rabbit calicivirus, first reported in China in 1984 and soon after in Europe and Mexico, became a new *cause célèbre*. Amid claim and counter claim and general political hysteria, the CSIRO eventually began a three-year laboratory project. However, desperate farmers were urging that the disease be introduced immediately into the wider environment. Since leaving the confines of its test site at Wardang Island, South Australia, calicivirus has met with only mixed success.


## PRICKLY PEAR

The common prickly pear, *Opuntia inermis*, an innocuous-looking cactus, was first introduced to Australia as a pot plant in 1839, and grown for its decorative value at Scone in the central west of New South Wales.

By 1916, the prickly pear was estimated to be increasing at the rate of a million acres a year, threatening to destroy all the pastures and arable land of Queensland and northern New South Wales. In 1920, vast areas of eastern Australia were totally infested with the fast-growing plant. It was so dense that farmers found it difficult to find their way across their own paddocks. The more prickly pear was cut back, the more it grew. Eventually the pest covered 50 million acres of Australia. How the nation came to be saved from the scourge is one of the most fascinating stories of modern science coming to the rescue.

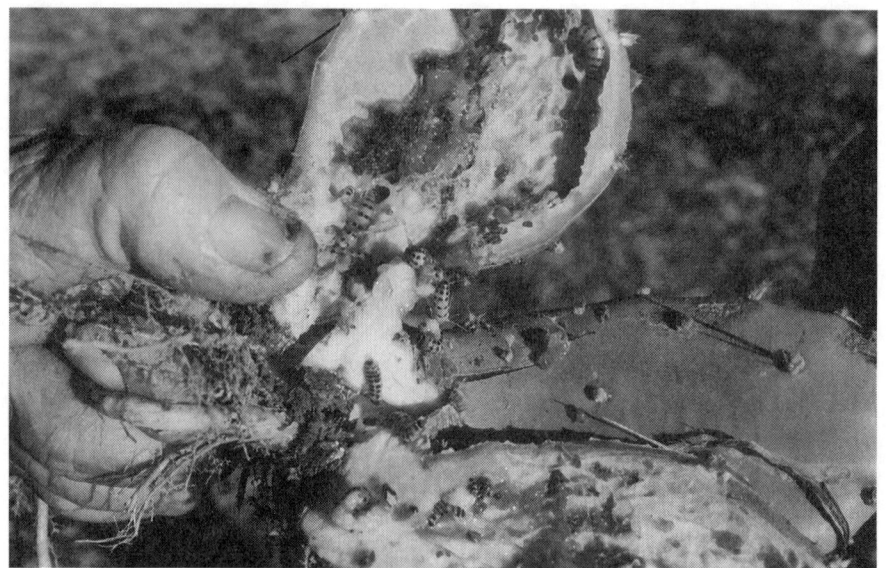

Another introduced species which multiplied to plague proportions was *Opuntia inermis*, otherwise known as the prickly pear. It arrived as a harmless pot plant in 1839, but eventually it covered 50 million acres of arable land in eastern Australia. Top: In 1925, its biological enemy, the moth *Cactoblastis cactorum*, again from South America, was set to work on the plant. Bottom: Grateful to the moth, the township of Boonarga erected a memorial hall.

The same site before *Cactoblastis* and after *Cactoblastis*, scenes that pictorially reflect the moth's onomatopoeic name.

The reason the prickly pear spread so quickly was that, when the early settlers brought it to Australia, they neglected to bring its natural enemies as well. By 1920, the situation was so desperate that the newly established Prickly Pear Board sent a team of experts to America in search of insects which, if introduced to Australia, might attack and destroy the pest.

There were, however, grave dangers in introducing another pest to an already disturbed ecology. Science, playing God and tampering with the balance of nature, had found itself in trouble before. So for many years the scientists worked patiently in the Americas, raising dozens of different insect species, making sure that they were free from parasites which would stop them multiplying.

Finally, in 1924, the scientists were ready to bring the insects on the long and difficult journey to Australia. Eventually, after more painstaking experiments, they narrowed down the field of candidates to one tiny creature, which now faced the extraordinary task of destroying millions of tons of encroaching vegetation.

*Cactoblastis cactorum*, introduced from the Argentine in 1925, proved to be as powerful as its name. Cactoblastis is a moth that lays its eggs on the prickly pear's spines. When the young caterpillars hatch, they immediately enter the pear and tunnel inside until fully grown. Then they spin cocoons and change to the chrysalis stage from which the moths emerge. The results are spectacular. After the grubs eat out the hearts of the pear, bacteria and fungus rot take over and destroy the plant completely.

In the mid 1920s, cactoblastis eggs were supplied to farmers in tiny quills that were stabbed into the flesh of the prickly pear. Many farmers, sceptical of the work of the scientists, threw the quills away, and then came to regret it. Their neighbours, who'd spread the cactoblastis eggs, soon watched with amazement as their 10-year scourge was quickly demolished. As the ground came back into view, the timber was burnt and crops planted again. Thousands of farms in Queensland and New South Wales were reborn.

In the small farming district of Boonarga near Chinchilla in Central Queensland, the locals were so grateful for the way their farms had been saved that they named the modest civic hall the Boonarga Cactoblastis Memorial Hall in honour of the tiny insect. It might not be the most attractive name for a public building but the people of Boonarga wouldn't have it any other way.

# CANE TOADS

*Bufo marinus*—reddish-brown to olive-brown, warty skin, a large, bony ridge over each eye and enlarged poisonous glands on each shoulder which can ooze white venom ... Why, couldn't you fall in love with one?

No. Even for 'frogaphiles', the cane toad is an ugly specimen. The species was introduced into Australia from Central and South America in 1935 to combat the sugarcane pest, known by some as 'the Brayback' or 'the grey-backed' beetle. It proved to be of limited use in the fight against the beetle but, being a highly adaptable amphibian and able to live in brackish water, it is now thriving, sometimes in pest proportions, in sunny Queensland. It has spread to the Northern Territory where there are fears it will establish itself in Kakadu National Park, and the creatures have been seen as far south as Sydney, but there are no signs of any breeding population so far.

They are primarily insect feeders but will eat pretty well anything except the beetle that they were bought out here to get rid of. Their diet includes everything from ping pong balls to mice.

The cane toad venom can kill an animal within 15 minutes of contact. Although they are not as dangerous to humans, it is advisable to wash your hands after handling because, if the venom comes into contact with your eyes, it can cause extreme pain and temporary blindness. Needless to say, the cane toad, its eggs and tadpoles should never be eaten. Only the Keelback snake can detoxify the venom and water rats, ibis and crows can eat the non-poisonous internal organs.

Over time, it appears that some native animals have learned not to eat the cane toad, but it is a sober lesson in what can happen when an exotic species is introduced to a new environment.

There are, believe it or not, people who actually love them. In fact, many Queenslanders early this century kept them as pets, but the authorities these days are trying to discourage that pastime. Mind you, they do have some intriguing, if not polite, habits. For example, they have spectacular sexual proclivities. Male toads will try to mate with anything, including goldfish and dead females. The mating position of toads is known as amplexus. The female lays 40 000 eggs but, of course, only a couple need to survive, which explains how the 102 original toads released at Gordonvale in 1935 now cover just about a quarter of Australia.

For some Queenslanders the preferred method of eradication is to use a golf club; however, according to the experts, the most humane way to kill them is to throw them in a freezer where they simply go into permanent hibernation.

## THE FLY

When Chairman Mao Zedung was in power in China half a century ago, one of his edicts was that the nation must get rid of its flies. Every citizen was directed to kill at least a fly a day and, after some years, China's fly problem reportedly diminished. That sort of pest control might work when you have more than a billion people to swat flies, but here in Australia we attack the problem with characteristic twentieth-century biological overkill. We spend tens of millions of dollars a year on pest sprays—when you're on a good thing, nuke it.

The 'Louies' we see in television commercials are actually raised in science laboratories, such as that at the Department of Entomology at the University of New South Wales. But, while the scientists supply the victims for fly spray ads, they don't necessarily approve of the battle strategy. Dr Eric Shipp, one of the country's leading experts on bush and house flies once told me:

> I don't think big companies are really aiming to try and get rid of flies and I don't think people are expecting the companies to do this. The only way to really get rid of flies is to look at their ecology and the whole background of their biology and breeding. Chemicals are not the answer to that at all.
>
> I believe someone once calculated the number of flies that would result if you started with a single pair and there was nothing to eat them, and plenty of food for them. At the end of 12 months, they would be 10 to the 18th. That is, 10 million, million, million—and that's not just flies—that's tons-weight of flies. That's enough to cover the Earth to a depth of 12 feet.

Flies are incredibly significant in the fields of medical and veterinary ento-mology and their history and relationship with the Australian environment is extremely complex. Few Australians who've been overseas have escaped the undignified ritual of being sprayed in an aircraft by inspectors who never seem to crack a smile in what seems like a comic spectacle. Their job, though, is of critical importance. Fruitfly can wipe out the economic livelihoods of whole communities.

Much of the interaction of flies goes unnoticed; for example, one plant-infesting fly seemingly accidentally introduced to Australia from South America attacks the seeds of the Bathurst burr and another species attacks the Noogoora burr. Another introduced in 1952 assists in the control of Crofton weed. Yet another was introduced in 1914 to control Lantana.

The fly most of us are familiar with is *Musca domestica*, the common house fly, which early this century was blamed for spreading infantile diarrhoea, dysentery, typhoid, cholera, yaws and anthrax.

During the first half of this century, control was pretty primitive—the buzzing of flies caught on curly strips of sticky fly paper was familiar music in most Australian homes. In the latter half we've become more accustomed to the sight and sounds of flies and mossies being zapped by ultraviolet fly zappers—'One flash and they're ash.'

The bloke who was quick to realise that the pot of gold was right under his nose was John Hagemann who, around 1880, began importing a Pyrethrum powder from Germany and marketed it under the brand name Mortein. He appointed Samuel Taylor as wholesale distributors and in 1942 they took over ownership. Their slogan, 'When you're on a good thing, stick to it', is still used.

But whatever the realities of our war against the fly, a succession of anonymous blowies have left their own distinctive mark on Australian life. The characteristic wave of the hand across the face to dislodge a persistent fly from crawling up a nostril, crawling inside one's mouth or hanging about in the corners of the eyes has become known as 'the great Australian salute', and there's plenty of photographic evidence that flies have been present at many of the nation's most solemn historical moments. There were flies at Gallipoli, and the famous flies of Canberra made the first of their many appearances on film when Prime Minister Joe Lyons introduced his Cabinet for the newsreel cameras in 1932.

And—horror of horrors—flies even turned out to plague Her Majesty Elizabeth Regina II when she toured outback areas during the royal visit of Australia in 1954.

When you can't even say there are no flies on the Queen, what hope is there for the rest of us?

## HORSES, DOGS, SHEEP AND GALAHS

The ceaseless battle against plague and pestilence and the elements has bred a familiar stereotype—the laconic man on the land who is fazed by very little, except perhaps some bludger who misses his shout in the pub.

It would appear from Australian history that, rather than complain about his lot, the dinkum country man has spent a good deal of his time sitting around thinking of more colourful ways to describe the adversities that beset him. Not the least of problems facing a 'bushie' has been crook tucker. Australia has never been noted for its cuisine and yet, even when faced with abysmal food, somehow the bushman has managed to keep his sense of humour. What, for example, does he do when confronted with one of the world's gastronomic horrors; namely, a galah? Certainly he didn't complain but rather he invented this famous recipe as quoted in Bill Wannan's marvellous book *Australian Folklore*:

> Select three average-sized stones and place the plucked and gutted cockatoo or galah on top of them in a pot of water over a good fire. Boil hard for 10 hours and then simmer for another five or six (the longer the better). Tip out the water, give the cockatoo to the dog and eat the stones.

Another version goes:

> First catch your cockatoo. Pluck and gut it, and place it in the pot of hot water with two stones. Boil steadily. When the stones are soft the cockatoo is ready to serve.

Birds have always played a prominent part in the annals of the Australian bush—perhaps because they have been the only other creatures in the landscape that actually talked. Bill Wannan sources this story to one of the readers of his famous column 'Come In Spinner', which became an institution in the magazine *Australasian Post*:

> I reckon the best-known talking bird in Australia was Mudie's crow, a familiar figure at Alec Mudie's Federal Hotel, Bemboka, New South Wales, for many years.

The bird developed a habit of drinking tailings from the beer mugs, and there were times when it would stagger around. On one occasion, a chalk line was drawn along the bar and the crow was told to walk along it.

After making several attempts the bird turned to the publican and said, 'Put me to bed, Alec, I'm as drunk as an owl.'

The Australian bird with the most famous name is 'the Drongo', found in the north-east, although the use of the word to describe someone as slow or 'not the full quid' comes from Drongo the racehorse of the 1920s, which had a remarkably unsuccessful career. The horse was the butt of several jokes created by *The Melbourne Herald* cartoonist Sam Wells and thereafter became the national symbol of 'the no hoper'.

It is perhaps not surprising in a country so preoccupied with the problems of distance that animals, particularly horses, have featured so strongly in our folktales. From 'the colt from Old Regret' to Carbine, our horses have been raised to an exalted position few human beings have achieved. The faster they were, the bigger the legend.

An Australian dog, on the other hand, was required to be not so fast, but smart—quick on his paws, in other words. Here's a chestnut:

A kelpie dog was being discussed in a country pub in Queensland.

'That there dog of mine's a bloody marvel,' said the proud bushman. 'He does just about everything. He brings in the cows, goes out after rabbits, gets the mail from the post office, yards the sheep ... Yes, he does just about everything.'

'Well,' said the stranger, 'if he's such a flaming marvel, why don't you call him in and let me buy him a beer?'

'Now, fair go,' said the bushman, 'that's one thing I won't allow. It wouldn't be right, seeing as how he's got to drive me home.'

Paradoxically, though, the king of all Australian animals is one which most of the human population thinks is basically stupid. The sheep is a much-maligned creature and yet Australia is so proud of its premiere industry that you could be forgiven for thinking that we invented wool.

The simple fact is that Australia has quite literally ridden on the sheep's back for most of its modern history. Even by 1871, as Anthony Trollope wryly

Top: For much of our history 'Australia rides on the sheep's back' has been an apt slogan. But the wool itself rode on the 'backs' of camels and oxen on those epic journeys from station to mill. Bottom: The shearing shed—a cacophony of sound and a kaleidoscope of images, a tin temple at the heart of a nation where there are more sheep than people.

observed, there were 24 sheep for every man, woman and child in the colony. At the height of our sheep numbers in the 1940s, it took half a million sheep dogs to round them up; even by 1860 there were 20 million sheep in Australia, and by the turn of the century, around a 100 million.

Sheep came to Australia with the First Fleet but the animal that really put Australia on the economic map was the Merino. We didn't create the breed but we did have a lot to do with its evolution. Its fascinating history can be traced back to Macarthur who, while he was in exile in England, bought half a dozen Spanish Merinos from the stud flock of George III.

Macarthur, who planned to develop a wool industry in New South Wales, was warned that if he tried to ship his Merinos to the colony they would be confiscated and he would be severely penalised. But he disregarded their warnings. He had influential friends and he obtained a special Treasury warrant to transport the animals in spite of the efforts of his old enemy, Sir Joseph Banks.

The fears of his rivals were well founded because within two years Macarthur was back in London flogging his fleece for a small fortune, 10 shillings a pound.

Macarthur's sheep became the backbone of an industry that determined the destiny of this country. It was a history colourful and dramatic; a story of hardship and incredible wealth—from the 'pound a pound' days of the Korean War when American wool spinners' stocks were depleted to those tragic times when sheep have been worth less than the bullets used to kill them.

The drought of the 1890s reduced Australia's sheep flock by half. It caused a major depression and at the same time it reinforced one of the earliest major industrial forces in Australia—the shearers. Between 1860 and 1890 there had already been more than 3000 cases of strike action by shearers and the problems at the beginning of the twentieth century made them even more militant.

Shearers were striking about automation even in the early 1900s when the introduction of machine shears was considered to be a technological outrage.

All in all, the shearers lived in an intensely union-orientated atmosphere with its own fascinating rituals. Even the cook was elected by secret ballot and, according to the federal politician, Clyde Cameron, a former shearing organiser whose father was a foundation member of the shearers' union, it was a decision taken with gravity and some humour. The usual thing was, 'Who called the cook a bastard?' And the chorus would come back, 'Who called the bastard a cook?' It was generally reckoned that, if the most paralytic person who staggered out of the hotel was the cook, the shearers would have had a fairly good menu. The reason might be that, as they became more famous and competent, the good cooks were better able to afford to get drunk, while the bad cooks had to try to make up for their cooking by their sober habits.

Today, despite intense competition from synthetics, wool is still the fabric of our society. Interestingly, much of the synthetic revolution has been spearheaded by the Japanese who are very much part of the Australian wool tradition. Many Japanese have been involved in the local wool scene longer than some Australian companies, and the remarkably long and complicated relationship between the two countries has survived even war and its bitter aftermath. Mr Kanematsu, founder of the famous company, was in the wool business when Ned Kelly was a boy. His company established its Australian office in the 1890s and there has been a constant interchange of business and cultures up to the present day. The only real interruption was during the Second World War when Kanematsu's Japanese staff was sent home for a few years. Discriminatory trade regulations were enforced until 1957, when it was business as usual. In the words of Hiroshi Tachibana, a former wool manager of Kanematsu–Gosho:

We think that the Australian people are very open and very friendly and more or less optimistic. That's what we think. Typical thing is that you can say, 'She'll be all right, mate.'

And as far as enterprising Australians are concerned, she will be right. Perhaps nothing represents the inexorable nature of the wool industry more than the continuing business relationship between nations through thick and thin. Eventually not even a few million lives stand between a healthy trading situation. Wool itself is an industry that has survived tremendous ups and downs during more than two centuries of Australian life. No doubt it will suffer many more vicissitudes. It is, after all, a billion-dollar industry based on such shaky foundations as an imported, ill-equipped animal set loose in an environment noted for its wretched excesses.

Constant research and development by organisations like the CSIRO, which created revolutionary spinning processes such as Sirospun and other technological advances which may see sheep of the future shorn chemically, have helped to keep the wool business alive in the face of withering competition. Meanwhile, innovative knitters such as John Macarthur of Sydney, who bears the apt name of his forebears in the industry, have spread the word at the grass roots level with ventures such as his cheekily named shop, Purl Harbour. Others like John J. Hilton and his brother Emil established a fashion group that exported 300 000 garments a year to places like Japan, Hong Kong, Bangkok, Singapore, Manila and Canada. The John J. Hilton Group proved that wool was as suitable for an elegant evening dress as it was for a footy jumper. Holeproof, with the slogan, 'The socks that will help put Australia back on its feet', export to Russia, Holland, Denmark, Taiwan and Singapore.

In the meantime, the man on the land can only watch all the developments with his fingers crossed. As long as there is drought and flood and fire, and a fluctuating market, working the land is always going to be a risky way to make a quid. Yet most country people wouldn't dream of changing their environment, even if they could. In the words of Dorothea Mackellar:

Core of my heart, my country!
Her pitiless blue sky,
When sick at heart, around us,
We see the cattle die—
But then the grey clouds gather,
And we can bless again,
The drumming of an army,
The steady soaking rain
Though the earth holds many splendours,
Wherever I may die,
I know to what brown country,
My homing thoughts will fly.

# Landmarks in time ...

## THE SPIRIT OF ADVENTURE AND ENTERPRISE

Perhaps because the country itself is so bloody big, Australians have always been obsessed by size. If it's not 'the biggest in the world', then it's 'the biggest in the Southern Hemisphere'. If it's not the biggest in the Southern Hemisphere, then it's hardly worth bothering about. We seem to have this 'edifice complex' whereby we build on a grand scale as if to prove there really is someone down here on the bottom of the world. Certainly, this mixture of assertiveness and inferiority is reflected in our institutions and monuments and nearly all of our man-made landmarks in time have been accompanied with some controversy and not a little folly.

## CANBERRA

The story of Australia's national capital is a mixture of vision and farce, of shameless junketing and destructive bickering. But, while the building of Canberra reflects government bungling on a grand scale, it also represents the realisation of a noble ideal.

Canberra is also the story of American architect Walter Burley Griffin who, like Denmark's Jørn Utzon with his Sydney Opera House 40 years later, was so troubled by government interference that he handed over his project to see it finished by others.

In 1902, W.M. (Billy) Hughes, then the new federal member for West Sydney, led a group of Parliamentarians in search of a suitable site for our national government. Choosing New South Wales, the oldest state, they

Left: Tread carefully, for you tread on my icon.

journeyed from town to city, feted and feasted by eager country folk who were hoping their district might be chosen as the lucky spot. Through Bega, Bombala, Tumut, out to Orange and down to Albury, they stopped to tour rainforests and take a dip in cool springs. This jolly junketing at taxpayers' expense became so blatant that the Sydney magazine *Table Talk* finally thought it was time to satirise their fruitless explorations with verse:

Each hill and dale, each stream and lake,
Seems all the more alluring,
When sandwiches and bottled ale,
Alleviate our touring.

Then the general public joined in the fun, suggesting bizarre names for the nation's capital: Australopis, Kookaburra, Woolgold, Cooeeton.

When, at last, a site was chosen beside the Molonglo River, months of speculation ended. It was declared 'Canberra' after its common local name. But debate still persists today on the origin of that name. Some say it means 'place of winds'; others that it is derived from the Aboriginal 'Canberra' as the locals called Robert Campbell, owner of the original Yarralumla homestead. Or perhaps it comes from the Aboriginal word Kanburra, meaning a young kookaburra.

Whatever its origin, Canberra was officially named on 12 March 1913, just a few months before Walter Burley Griffin arrived to take up the position of Federal Capital Director of Design and Construction. When he won the highly coveted competition to design Australia's national capital, Griffin, 36 years old, was a 'modern' architect from Chicago, designing American cities for the future, cities for motor cars and electricity and aircraft. But, even before he arrived, Commonwealth public servants were criticising the design as 'too ambitious'. Griffin had planned for Canberra's development over the next 100 years, but the bureaucrats refused to accept that Canberra would ever be larger than a country town. In fact, at the end of the century its population had just exceeded 300 000.

The government men often ignored Griffin's detailed instructions, even approving the construction of new buildings without his knowledge. The architect opposed the expense of putting up temporary buildings, claiming it would cost less to start work on the permanent designs.

Top: The Federal Minister for Home Affairs, King O'Malley, knocks in the first peg for the construction of Canberra on 20 February 1913. Bottom: Dame Nellie Melba sang at the opening of the Canberra's Parliament House on 9 May 1927. Local wags wasted no time in lampooning the decision to build the capital on grazing land near a sheep property called 'Canberra'. Thirty years later when this shot was taken, the first Parliament House was still not immune from a flock of jumbucks. Spot the Pollie!

The public servants saw the affable, idealistic young American as an 'artist', the sort of person not to be trusted by 'sensible' administrators. In 1916, a Royal Commission into the National Capital criticised the bureaucrats for withholding information from Griffin, but the findings made little difference. By 1919, Griffin's contract had ended, and he left Canberra, with at least its distinctive triangular layout already formed. But he was never to be involved again in the city's development. Griffin worked in private practice designing buildings such as Melbourne University's Newman College and the Capitol Theatre, as well as a good part of the unusual suburbs of Castlecrag in Sydney and Eaglemont in Melbourne. Towards the end of his stay in Australia he made a living out of designing council incinerators, and those which still stand reflect his unique modern design concepts. Walter Burley Griffin, whose works in Australia ranged from our capital city to restaurants and water towers in country towns, eventually went to India on a commission to design a city. He died there from peritonitis in 1937.

Ten years before, on 9 May 1927, Canberra had celebrated the opening of its Parliament House with the architect of the city noticeably absent from the invitation list. It was a grand occasion. The opening of the first proper venue for our national Parliament also marked the true establishment of Canberra as our national capital. As the politicians and public servants began their move up from Melbourne, what had recently been little more than a country town found itself a potentially great city. The opening ceremony was performed by the Duke of York (later George VI). Dame Nellie Melba sang the national anthem to the enthralled spectators who had travelled by motor car, buggy and excursion train to watch the spectacle unfold among the sheep pastures. With only two cafés in town, thoughtful organisers arranged caterers for the crowds they confidently expected to reach the grand figure of 100 000. Consequently they ordered 30 000 pies and sausage rolls, and on its opening day Canberra witnessed its first major example of overspending. A mere 6000 people did their darnedest and ate 10 000 pies, and the government had to pay up for the rest. After everybody had gone home, the embarrassed officials buried 20 000 leftover Sargents pies in a mass grave on Capitol Hill behind Parliament House.

Canberra has been the butt of public service jokes ever since, but despite the funds that have been poured into the place, it is a city which now inspires most Australians with some sense of national identity. After 50 years the original 'temporary' and familiar art deco-style wedding-cake Parliament House, which had been erected on the edge of Lake Burley Griffin while flocks of sheep roamed around it, was superseded by the bold new glorified flagpole of a building that now houses our Parliament on Capitol Hill.

Canberra still has its critics as being 'a bit soulless'—something which the Duke of Edinburgh said about the place to the dismay of its residents—but it is a crisp, clean metropolis with its sights set firmly on the future, and almost everyone agrees, resident or non-resident, that it's 'a good place to raise the kids'.

## SYDNEY HARBOUR BRIDGE

We're building a bridge in Sydney.
Over the harbour, too.
We'll all cross in safety
And busy trains pass through.
A wonderful thing of beauty,
Arching the skies of blue,
The best brains started it, brave men wrought it,
Bridge of Our Dreams Come True.

The unlikely lyrics of this old gramophone recording were sung by the popular Len Maurice, backed by Gil Dech and his Syncopators. But, quaint as that song might seem now, back in 1930 it was sentimental enough to stir the souls of Sydneysiders day by day as they watched the two half-arches of the Sydney Harbour Bridge inch closer together. It was truly 'the bridge of our dreams'.

As early as 1815, convict architect Francis Greenway was designing bridges to span Sydney Harbour. The New South Wales Railways drew up plans in the 1870s and a few years later, the state government actually negotiated to build a bridge for £850 000, but again, nothing happened.

By 1900, Sydney was a thriving metropolis but virtually cut off from the north by water. The only way to move people and vehicles across Sydney Harbour was by ferry. In 1912, Dr J.C. Bradfield, a government engineer, was commissioned to build a bridge. His early plans were delayed during the steel shortages caused by the First World War and it was 1924 before an

Top: Sydney Harbour Bridge, the famous 'coat hanger', under construction. Bottom left: During August 1930, the two halves of the bridge's arch were ready to be joined; however, the temperature had to be just right. Bottom right: Jim Barbour, a riveter, one of the few men who worked on the bridge's construction from start to finish. Sixteen of his fellow workers were killed. The bridge opened on 19 March 1932.

English design for the bridge was selected and a British company was contracted to build it.

Against criticism of the high cost (the successful tender was for £4 217 721/11/10), the New South Wales Premier, J.T. (Jack) Lang insisted the bridge be wide enough for Sydney traffic as he foresaw it 50 years later.

The plan itself was simple. Two half-arches would be built, one from Dawes Point in the city, the other from Milson's Point on the northern shore. The arches, on hinges, were cantilevered out over the water, each one held in place by giant tension cables looped through tunnels dug from subterranean granite. When the half arches were completed, the hundreds of cables were gradually slackened until the two halves closed and were bolted together.

At a time when much of the traffic was still horse drawn, it was a stupendous engineering achievement. The span weighs 65 000 tonnes. More than 1000 men were employed building the bridge under the watchful eye of Lawrence Ennis, director of construction for the British contractors. Jim Barbour of Sydney, who worked on the bridge from 1924, to 1932, remembered Ennis well:

> I was screwing a bolt with the washer on and I dropped the nut. Mr Ennis was at the back of me and he saw me drop it. 'Don't forget to pick that up and put it on,' he said. 'That cost sixpence, that nut.'

For some men it was like any other job. The old hands became as agile as mountain goats as they strolled down the slippery steel slopes, over 90 metres above the water. But for many workers, it was bitterly tough. It was 1930 and some men, who had been forced to lie about their skills to get a job in the Depression, worked in a state of utter terror. Jim Barbour was there when the first of the 16 who died, fell:

> I remember I was standing there with one hand on the wire rope, and I had to prise my fingers off it with my other hand. I was quite safe where I was. But it was the shock—it was just seeing him go down. I knew he'd be killed.

Each time a man died, representatives were sent to his funeral and money was collected, half a day's pay from each worker, for the widow.

Late in 1930, the two half-arches had been lowered to the point where they were only inches apart. Completion of the span now depended on the weather, and 24 thermometers were placed along the surface to warn of even slight variations in temperature. In hot weather, the bridge might have expanded suddenly and jeopardised the complex and delicate operation. It was a cool, cloudy August day in 1930 when the arch was successfully joined. The contractors claimed the bridge as 'a triumph for British engineering', but really it was very much an Australian achievement, and the bridge was indeed at that time one of the modern wonders of the world.

Huge girders were hung from the giant arch to support the roadway that was being built like a cradle underneath. After another 18 months, the last of six million rivets was driven home and the steel structure was complete.

To show off the new marvel, imaginative public relations staff ran 92 steam engines onto the bridge in a rather extravagant test of its strength. No-one seemed too worried that if the test had failed half of the New South Wales Railways might have wound up on the bottom of the harbour. But as far as the public was concerned it did prove that our £10 million—double the original quote—had been well spent.

The opening ceremony was planned for 19 March 1932, and thousands crowded the foreshores for a long-distance glimpse of the celebrities on the bridge. The Premier Mr Lang made the major official speech concluding with the words: '... in a few moments I shall complete the opening ceremony by severing the ribbon stretched across the highway.' They were some of the most famous last words in our history. Just before the Premier stepped forward to perform the ceremony, Captain Francis de Groot rode up on a horse and sliced through the ribbon with his sword, shouting: 'I declare this bridge open in the name of the decent and respectable citizens of New South Wales.'

In his slightly tatty uniform and mounted on a decidedly skinny horse, de Groot seemed like a latter-day Don Quixote. He was dragged to the ground by the New South Wales Police commissioner, Bill MacKay, and carted off to the reception house.

Officials hastily restored the ribbon and the Premier was again handed the ceremonial pair of scissors. As the slashed ribbon was cut for the second time, tens of thousands of people around the harbour cheered and shouted as hundreds of ships, tugs and small craft hooted. Aircraft flew in formation across the city and over the bridge.

Captain de Groot, the villain of the day, was a member of the extreme right-wing political group, the New Guard. They were violently opposed to

Lang's socialistic policies aimed at combating the Depression. The following Monday, de Groot appeared in court and was fined five pounds for offensive behaviour after the judge refused to declare him insane. Afterwards, he described his one moment of glory for the newsreel cameras:

> The job was easy. Wearing my uniform, which I wore in France, I merely joined the Governor-General's escort of 'mounteds' as they came out of Government House. I saluted the Governor most punctiliously as I passed, proceeded to the place where the ribbon was stretched, and before our Premier could get a chance to open it, slashed it through with a sword that I also wore in France.

Whatever the fun and political games of opening day, there's no doubt that the grand old pile of nuts and bolts that spans Sydney Harbour is today part of Australian folklore. It has an interesting story or fact for almost every one of its six million rivets. Much of what you hear about the famous paint job is true—it is a never-ending job that costs millions of dollars each year. The bridge used to have its own special paint and the colour was created on the site but that is now tendered out to commercial companies, and what most people don't realise is that the bridge has to be painted on the inside as well as out. The bridge has a hinge at the top as well as each side and gets about 10 centimetres higher in hot weather.

Detonators were allocated to strategic parts of the bridge to blow it up if the Japanese invaded during the Second World War and it's true that someone climbs the bridge daily to raise and lower the flag, although recently that task has been made much easier with the addition of a glass lift and new cranes to replace the old creeper cranes that used to take a week to reach the top.

Despite nearly 50 years of toll collection, and despite the fact that these days more than 150 000 cars cross the bridge daily, it took until the late 1980s for the bridge to be paid for. Sadly, while the bridge has been the symbol of triumphant optimism for most Australians, others saw it simply as a place to end it all. In fact, in the year the bridge opened during the Depression, more than 60 people leapt to their deaths, prompting authorities to install an overhanging protective fence. More than 100 determined souls have still managed to suicide from the bridge in the ensuing decades.

## THE HOLDEN

To most Australians, the Holden is 'Australia's own car'. It means plentiful spare parts and quick service. In the 1950s, it used to be said you could 'buy a fan belt in any milk bar in the country'.

But the Holden is far from a home-grown product, and the story of how an American car became an Australian institution is one of the great marketing sagas in our history. Indeed, even the famous television advertisements, 'We love football, meat pies, kangaroos and Holden cars' was a pinch from the United States.

In 1946, the first three prototype Holdens arrived on a boat from Detroit, in America. Alongside locally built prototypes they were road tested at Fishermen's Bend in Victoria and in the nearby countryside. Mr Laurence (later Sir Laurence) Hartnett, managing director of General Motors-Holden's between 1934 and 1947, once told me:

> The deal, as I saw it, was that we would be responsible for the styling, and the mechanical work would be done in Detroit. But Detroit seemed to take the whole thing under their wing. And they produced the prototype.

But if the first Holden was designed and built by Americans, at least the name was Australian. In the 1850s, James Alexander Holden and his friend, Henry Frost, established a highly successful saddlery and coach building business in Adelaide. When the horseless carriage arrived, the Holden Company turned its hand to motor bodies.

In the early 1920s, General Motors came to Australia. It made good sense for the local and overseas companies to work together. By the end of the decade, they were making everything from flivvers to hearses.

When the Depression struck, the two companies merged and continued to produce the General Motors range of Oldsmobiles, Pontiacs, Chevrolets and a variety of other vehicles in Australia. But the business merger did not work out so well, and soon the company began to run at a loss. In 1934, a young engineer, Laurence Hartnett, was sent out from England to untangle the mess. With Hartnett at the wheel, the losses turned into profit and the company expanded its operations, building a new plant at Fishermen's Bend. Hartnett's long-cherished dream was to produce an Australian car for

Left: Sir Laurence Hartnett, the father of the first Holden, stands somewhat forlornly beside his own car, the Hartnett, built after he left GMH in 1948. He disagreed with GMH about what sort of car was suitable for Australia. Bottom: Prime Minister Ben Chifley sees a private dream come true when the first 'Australian' Holden came off the production line on 29 November 1948. The Labor leader's idea was for a low-cost 'people's car', but with American involvement that's hardly what it was.

Australian conditions, and he was greatly encouraged by the wartime Prime Minister John Curtin and his successor Ben Chifley. He went to America to persuade his American superiors to help fulfil the dream. But the boss of General Motors, H.P. Sloane, considered the Australian Government of the day to be 'dangerously socialist'. Hartnett countered with the argument that it was, in fact, the military and not private enterprise which had built America's proudest achievement, the Panama Canal, and he got the begrudging go ahead. He was allowed to take an existing prototype, which he considered was the ideal basis for an Australian car, from a backlot in Detroit.

But from then on the Americans dictated what type of vehicle 'Australia's own car' would be. Despite Hartnett's vision of a cheap car for the local market—a car with straight-pressed body sides and 'no fancy chrome grille'—the Americans were insistent. They were the biggest business in the world and they drove some very hard bargains with the Australians. They would be taking their share of the profit, but they would not be tying up their capital. For that, Hartnett had to take loans from the Commonwealth Government and the Bank of Adelaide.

Eventually, when it seemed inevitable to Hartnett that 'the Holden' was going to be simply a scaled down version of other General Motors cars, he gave up his struggles and resigned on the eve of the release of the first car. The honour of greeting the first one off the assembly line on 29 November 1948 went to his friend and mentor Ben Chifley.

Those original Holdens were the 48/215 (now commonly and mistakenly called the FX) and they sold for £733/10/–. GMH built just 163 cars in that first year. By 1951 they were producing 100 a day, and Australians bought them as fast as they reached the showrooms. The basic design hardly changed for the best part of a decade. In 1953 they made a small alteration to the grille and called it the FJ. Today the FJs are nearly 50 years old but there are still quite a few on the roads.

With the hindsight of history, perhaps the Americans had a better idea of what Australians really wanted in a motor car. By 1960, one million Holdens had been built and the second million took only another six years. Later, Toranas, Commodores and Geminis could claim engineering pedigrees stretching from Germany to Japan, but they all sported the Holden name and the familiar tag, 'Australia's own car'.

Holden afficionados salivate at just the initials: FJ, FE, FC, FB, EK, EJ, EH, HD, HR, HT, HG, HQ, HJ, HX, HZ, Commodore VB, VC, VH, VK, VN, VP, VR, and VT. By the late 1990s, the Commodore could do zero to 100 kilometres per hour in just over nine seconds and would cost around $30 000.

The real sequel to the story is the fate of little Larry Hartnett, 'the father of the Holden'. He still had dreams of building a cheap 'people's car'. After resigning from GMH he produced a small, French-designed car called the Hartnett. But government contractors failed to supply essential parts, and while Hartnett won a massive damages case in the courts, the delays killed the project. Only 350 were ever built, one of them lovingly kept under a tarpaulin in a shed on Sir Laurence's spectacular estate at Mount Eliza. The registration expired in 1950.

## QANTAS

Qantas is the second-oldest international airline in the world (after KLM) and its bald-tyred beginnings can be traced back a long way, to a stony paddock and a galvanised iron shed in the town of Longreach in central Queensland. These days the closest Qantas goes to Longreach is about eight kilometres straight up, but in 1920 this was the scenario: after you'd collected your tickets at the old wooden-verandah building in Duck Street, you made your way out to the hangar at the aerodrome. There was only one plane to choose from, an Avro 504K. It did 65 miles an hour (about 105 kilometres an hour) and it wasn't cheap. A joy flight cost three guineas and charter flights cost two shillings a mile. The facilities weren't exactly luxurious but right from the start there was a healthy demand in the remote centre of Queensland. Qantas was soon ferrying mail and the odd grazier between Cloncurry to the north and Charleville to the south.

The story of the birth of Qantas is as intriguing as the name itself—the letters stand for Queensland and Northern Territory Aerial Services Ltd and it was begun by two men who, in 1919, had the task of surveying by motor car the proposed route for the £10 000 competition for the first flight between England and Australia. While Ross and Keith Smith took the glory for that flight, two other young pilots named Hudson Fysh and P.J. McGinness founded Qantas with the backing of a group of graziers. Hudson Fysh (later Sir Hudson) once recalled:

Top left: Queensland grazier Alexander Kennedy, who invested in the foundation of Qantas when it was better known by its full name, the Queensland and Northern Territory Aerial Services Ltd, holds ticket No. 1, from 22 November 1922. Top right: A Qantas Kangaroo Route advertisement from the1930s. Bottom: The first booking office in Duck Street, Longreach, which was leased from local auctioneers.

Our first trip into Queensland nearly ended in disaster. We ran into some very rough weather, and the clouds closed right in on me and I got lost in them and I'm afraid I came out of them in the first turn of what could have been a fatal spin. However, I righted the plane and managed to land on the side of a hill near what turned out to be Redhead Coalmine. We taxied up this hillside and to a miner's cottage and the miner's wife rushed out and offered us a cup of tea.

On another occasion, Fysh landed in a paddock to be greeted by the owner of the property thus: 'G'day God, my name's Smith.' Soon young bush pilots were buzzing around the outback delivering people and mail. They were harum-scarum days, when you chocked the wheels with a mallee log, didn't worry too much about smoking on the tarmac, and took off and landed in a cloud of dust.

The first Qantas passengers flew open cockpit but it wasn't long before 'the Propeller Set' were getting a bit fussier. In 1924, Qantas bought its first cabin aeroplane and a brochure told the passengers, 'Flying cap and goggles are quite unnecessary, sit at ease in your machine because your movements will not affect its balance whatsoever.' It sounded pretty good but for those who were still a bit queasy about flying there were some really comforting words: 'The fact that many invalids have used our facilities, including people with weak hearts,' it said, 'demonstrates the ease of air travel.' Not that everyone enjoyed the luxury. While the passengers travelled inside, the pilot stayed out on top in the wind and the weather.

Over the years, Qantas would fly a host of different aircraft including the pretty little DH86s which made Singapore seem like a long way indeed. They were grounded after a series of crashes but the airline repainted older aircraft and pressed on with its ambitious plans.

And then came the golden years of the Empire Flying Boats, run in partnership with a British company. They were extremely popular; Sydney to Southampton took nine and a half days but it was luxurious travel. The 15 passengers were provided with reclining seats, a smoking cabin and a promenade deck.

In 1947, the first of the huge but graceful Lockheed Constellations arrived in Sydney for service on the now famous Kangaroo route between Australia and the United Kingdom.

The next decade saw a period of rapid expansion. At the beginning of the 1970s, the airline which had been started in the scrub by two men barely out of their teens was half a century old and proudly taking delivery of its first Jumbo Jet.

Qantas, which many Australians remember as our international airline, has in recent years become a domestic carrier as well and is now the tenth-biggest airline in the world. It operates more than 4000 flights a week and carries 17 million passengers a year to nearly 100 destinations in Australia and around the world.

The winged kangaroo symbol familiar to older Australians was adapted from the Australian one penny coin and first appeared in the late 1940s to coincide with Qantas' introduction of the Lockheed L749 Constellations. These aircraft first began operating on the United Kingdom service in December 1947 and were the first to operate right through to London with Qantas crews. The flying kangaroo was later placed in a circle but in the 1980s the logo was changed, the kangaroo lost its wings and was refined to a more stylised presentation.

## VICTA AND HILLS

Mr Merv Richardson, an engineer and compulsive tinkerer, was almost 60 when he emerged from the garage of his suburban house in 1952 with the contraption that would soon revolutionise the Australian weekend. What he had produced from some billycart wheels, old piping and even a peach tin, is now almost an archaeological relic. In the 1970s I recall mucking around with it in the front yard of the Victa factory—now it's such a holy object it can only be handled by company curators in white gloves and, believe it or not, cannot be placed on real grass but is ceremoniously set down upon a piece of astro-turf for television crews to take pictures. Not all that surprising perhaps, because since it was created, more than six million Victas have been sold, and they now come off the assembly line at the rate of up to 1000 a day in peak time and are sold in 57 countries.

It's all a far cry from the days when Merv Richardson sold the mowers direct from the garage, but after he'd placed a tiny advertisement in the local paper, demand outstripped supply so quickly that he knew he'd stumbled on a bonanza. Within a year Richardson was building a small factory and even the carpenter on the roof couldn't help noticing how much the Victa business

Left: Victa lawnmower *numero uno*—it's now practically an archeological relic. The first of more than six million Victas, is now handled only by curators wearing gloves and cannot be set down upon real grass. The prototype was created by Merv Richardson in a backyard shed in Concord, Sydney, in 1952. Bottom: In some Australian suburbs there are more Hills Hoists than trees. Mr and Mrs Lance Hill of Adelaide began another post-war phenomenon, when they began making rotary clothes hoists on the back verandah of their suburban home.

was booming. The carpenter, Mr Ken Blight, went on to become sales promotion manager for Victa Limited:

> Well, you see, they needed the space so badly that by the time we got a roof and some walls up, they were moving in to start the manufacturing of the lawnmower. There were about six fellows working there then and it fascinated me so much that I just couldn't keep my interest on the factory, as a matter of fact. To be honest, I hated every minute of the factory roof; when it rained I was delighted to get down and go inside and help them building lawn-mowers. They really excited me.

In fact, they seemed to excite most of the adult population of Australia, helped along by slogans such as 'Turn Grass Into Lawn' and advertising that even gives the big horsepower mowers some of the mystique of sports cars. Victa is now a part of Sunbeam, a company with its own fascinating history. Founded in the United States in the 1890s to manufacture horse clipping machinery, it began manufacturing in Australia in the 1930s and in 1947 manufactured its first electrical appliance which itself became an institution—the Sunbeam Mixmaster. This was followed by the Shavemaster Electric Shaver in 1951. During the 1960s and 1970s, the company concentrated on expanding its production of domestic appliances as well as sheep-shearing equipment.

Merv Richardson spent a frustrating and unsuccessful period of his life trying to develop a local aircraft manufacturing industry, but the mowers remained the firm foundation of the empire. Statistically, the chances are that almost every backyard in Australia has at some time had a going over from a Victa.

The other great Australian backyard success story is the rotary clothes hoist. In some Australian suburbs there are more Hills Hoists than trees.

The story began when Mr and Mrs Lance Hill of Adelaide planted two orange trees in the backyard of their home to commemorate the birth of their daughter. While Lance was at the war, the trees grew and grew until there was little space left to hang clothes across the yard.

So the dutiful husband built his wife a rotary clothes hoist, and soon afterwards he was travelling to town in a tram when he overheard a conversation. Lance Hill told me that just a few words changed his life:

There were two ladies sitting opposite me in the tram and I couldn't help but hear their conversation and one said, 'I'm going into town to buy a rotary clothes hoist because my line's just broken and all my washing is down in the mud.' And number two replied, 'Well, you can't get them. They are not available.' Number one said, 'They are available somewhere, because my neighbour's just got one.' So, with that in mind, I stewed it over and I got out of the tram next stop and caught the following tram back home and said to Mum, 'We're going to make clotheslines.'

Just as Merv Richardson had done, they gathered up material to make half a dozen units and put a small ad in the paper. The calls started at 6.00 a.m. and continued all day and all the next day. People arrived at the Hills' house and left cash for the first hoist available. Lance Hill:

We had a long verandah on the house, which had been converted into a kitchen, and at the end of that was a little old cash box and people would say 'Here's £5 or £7' or what have you. Sunday night my voice had gone and the cash box was overflowing on to the floor, and we were most ecstatic. We just didn't know that things could be like this. We'd never seen so much money.

Materials were extremely scarce but the demand was so great that Lance Hill was soon going to the most extraordinary places to get his precious tubing. A lot of material for the early hoists came from the submarine boom that had been stretched across Sydney Heads during the war. Early deliveries were made by the Hills and their relatives pushing a handcart. By the 1970s, Hills Industries was a multi-national company exporting to many countries, and responsible for planting three million hoists in the backyards of this country alone. Any Aussie kids who haven't swung from a Hills Hoist and nearly broken something, either on themselves or on the hoist, are probably rare.

## THE SYDNEY OPERA HOUSE

If ever there were a symbol of modern Australia it is the Sydney Opera House. Overseas it is as familiar an image as the kangaroo, the boomerang and the Sydney Harbour Bridge. The Opera House has become an indelible part of the Australian consciousness in a comparatively short time, and no doubt this is due partly to the architect's importance, the form of the building and its unique setting; but it also has much to do with the fact that the building came into being after 20 years of trials and tribulations. It was a difficult birth. As early as 1948, Eugene Goossens had advocated an opera house for Sydney and his idea was taken up by an unlikely crusader, the Labor Premier J.J. (Joe) Cahill, who on the down side also gave us one of the great blights on the Sydney landscape, the Cahill Expressway. Opera is essentially not a sport of the working class, and although there were few votes in it for Joe Cahill, he pushed ahead with zeal.

In 1956, his £10 000 international design competition attracted 234 entries from 36 countries. The four-man panel of judges chose a bold sketch of graceful sails by a 37-year-old Danish architect Jørn Utzon. Utzon, a devotee of such architectural giants as Frank Lloyd Wright and Le Corbusier, started work on the Opera House in 1957. At that time the cost was quoted at about seven and a half million pounds.

The trouble was that nothing quite like Utzon's building had ever been built. Utzon did not really know how his magnificent sails could be con-structed and soon, like Griffin before him, he ran into tremendous difficulties with the bureaucrats and politicians over time, cost and management.

To everyone's horror it soon became clear that the shells as drawn could not even support their own weight. Years later he told me: 'We were half-finished with the base and I was sitting there with a big problem.' (Laughter.) I asked him whether, when he made his original drawings, did he really have any idea how to make those shells?

> Yes, I thought we could make them as thin concrete shells ... but we couldn't get enough height and so we tried with engineers for two years, two and a half years, to make up the shells and other things. And the engineers one day came in and said, 'We give up. Go somewhere else.'

Eventually the problem of the sails was solved but only after the engineers spent six years, 350 000 man hours and 18 000 computer hours to work out a solution. The new shape of the shells was finally resolved by producing them all from a single sphere. They were more upright but some thought that was for the better.

As Utzon and the contractors grappled with incredibly complex engineering, the costs began to mount. Soon we had a monumental architectural problem on the scale of the pyramids, except of course the Pharaohs did not have the benefit of a pyramid lottery. The £100 000 Opera House Lottery made the extraction of money relatively painless.

The problems seemed interminable and, at times, insoluble. The battles between Utzon and the authorities were complicated still further by different demands from the eventual tenants of the building, including the ABC. Half way through the project it was decided to change the whole nature of the building. At one stage, three million dollars' worth of stage machinery had to be scrapped when the ABC demanded the main hall for its symphony concerts and this pushed opera into the smaller second hall. Joan Sutherland, La Stupenda herself, joined the fray saying, 'The concert hall is better. If only the ABC hadn't taken it for themselves.'

The wars would continue for more than a decade. The opposition in the State Parliament found the Opera House a wonderful weapon with which to bludgeon the government. When the Liberals came to power in 1965, Utzon had to deal with a new and tough Minister for Public Works, Mr Davis Hughes. Hughes pinned most of the blame for the troubles on the hapless architect. In 1999, and now in his 90s, Sir Davis Hughes told me:

When we got to the stage of wanting the thing finished, he wasn't able to give us anything. The point I want to make is he had no plans for anything beyond the shells.

Utzon would deny this—but there's no doubt that he was struggling to find the solutions to the myriad of problems that had never before been encountered in this, the most unusual building in the world. Eventually, though, it all came down to a question—as it always does—of 'bums on seats'.

Utzon's concept, complicated by the demands of the various parties and crippled by the problems of how to place stage machinery, could only accommodate 1700 bums in the main hall, and the government, having insisted on a role reversal of the two major halls, was demanding a thousand more.

Ironically, Utzon's original plan before all the changes that were asked of him provided for 2800 seats in the main hall. For a year the architect

Top: Bennelong the Aborigine lived there first, then there was a fort, later a tram shed and finally an opera house. Bottom: The towering shells of the Sydney Opera House roof presented staggering problems for the designers, engineers and builders. It took six years, 350 000 work hours and 18 000 computer hours to solve it. And, while construction began in 1957, the Opera House was not opened until the Queen's visit in 1973.

Top: Just like Walter Burley Griffin, who designed Canberra, and Laurence Hartnett, father of Australia's Holden, Jørn Utzon as the designer of the Sydney Opera House was stymied by external power plays. He left Australia in 1966 and, at the turn of the century, had still not returned. Right. Sir Davis Hughes, the Minister for Public Works, who moved to demote Utzon in 1965.

defended his right to design the interior, but when Mr Davis Hughes moved to downgrade Utzon's role on the project, the architect suddenly resigned.

'What was your reaction when you received an envelope containing Utzon's resignation?' I asked Sir Davis.

'One of relief … great relief,' he replied.

'More than that?' I persisted. 'Did you jump in the air … click your heels?'

'No, I didn't … but I could have.'

More than 1000 architects and artists marched through the streets of Sydney in protest. They formed the 'Utzon In Charge' group, opposed by the 'Utzon Go Home' faction. Michelangelo's letters describing the problems he faced building St Peter's in Rome were reprinted and distributed by the Sydney University Architects Club. A Sydney sculptor even went on a three-day hunger strike in protest over the government's treatment of Utzon. Reluctant to continue as the centre of controversy any longer, Jørn Utzon left Australia in April 1966 with his wife and family, under assumed names to avoid publicity. In 1972, I spent a year pursuing him for an interview, which he finally gave me on a remote island off the north coast of Sweden. It would be his only interview on the subject for 25 years:

> I left with great, great regret. I fought for the perfect idea. The years I worked with my team were marvellous, but very hard, and we gave up only because I couldn't see the alternatives Mr Hughes wanted. I thought our work would be ruined and as it actually has proved now, it is ruined. You cannot make a piece of art and let somebody else finish it. I think if the architects who took over had been slightly more 'good colleagues', it could have been settled easily. But they were very eager to grab the case. Normally in this, if you take something over from another architect, you're not supposed to do that before the first architect is completely satisfied with his fees and everything else.

Utzon has never returned to Australia. The job of finishing the Opera House was passed to a conglomerate firm of Sydney architects, Hall, Todd and Little-more. All of them have now passed on but before he died Peter Hall told me:

> I suppose I was fairly young and reckless. I thought it was a fascinating idea. The job wasn't represented as what it turned out to be. The drawings that were left did not describe the kind of building the community thought it was getting.

I thought it would be necessary for us to complete drawings and build what Utzon had designed for the interior. But he hadn't designed very much. We did all the working drawings and made the final decisions on colour. There was a great deal more designing to do than I'd bargained for. I think people imagined that because I came into the job, it stopped Utzon finishing it. In fact, he'd left the country. I spoke to him and I gave the Utzon faction full information as to where the negotiations were between the minister and me. If he'd wanted to reopen negotiations at the eleventh hour, it was definitely open to him.

When the Opera House was finally completed just in time for the Queen to open it in 1973, Utzon did not attend. The cost had risen to more than $100 million, and Australians flocked to Bennelong Point in the thousands to see what their lottery money had bought. There was criticism that the outside and the inside of the building didn't match, which was to be expected since it had been created by different minds. But, on the whole, Sydneysiders love their Opera House. It has numerous flaws, but it compensates by being a most magnificent piece of sculpture. Like the pyramids, it is not so much a functional object but a decorative symbol—the jewel of Sydney Harbour.

The building has had thousands of knockers. One Sydney wit said, 'It would have been cheaper if they built it overseas and sailed it across.' And another dubbed it 'the New South Whale'. But others, like Sir Tyrone Guthrie, have said, 'Although Australians might consider the Sydney Opera House the stock joke, the rest of the world is not giggling. It will lift Sydney out of its crimson imitation of British suburbia.'

Jørn Utzon went on to design buildings 40 times more costly than the Sydney Opera House such as the Kuwaiti Parliament. An architect of huge international repute, in 1978 he was awarded the Queen's Gold Medal for Architecture for his design of the Sydney Opera House. His recommendation came from the British Institute of Architects and it was said of Utzon at the award ceremony that he was 'the greatest architect of the twentieth century'. In 1972 I asked him in light of everything that had happened to him in Australia would he design another building here and I was rather taken aback with his reply: 'Certainly,' he said. 'Yes, with great pleasure.' But he would have to wait until he was in his 80s before feelers were sent out from Australia to see whether or not he'd be interested in being a consultant on refurbishing the interior of the building that remains his unfinished symphony.

# Acknowledgements

Thanks to the Edwards family, and my thanks go also to the close family who breathed new life into 'This Fabulous Century' two decades after it first became such a fabulous success on Channel 7. Indeed, it won a Logie and this will sound a little like those award speeches—the fact is, big television series require a dedicated band of souls, among them cameramen David Knight, Scott Barnett and David Rose along with sound recordists Rob Beck, Wayne McKelvie, Andy Laidlaw and Rick Creaser who shot the new series and Nick Glover of Towcutter who edited it; Mark Tanner who post-produced the sound, field producers Andrew Farrell, Clare Bonham and Rob Wallace, production manager Allison Haigh, production co-ordinator Antoinette Siskovic and publicist Jason Volbeda. My sincere thanks to my partners Southern Star, in particular Errol Sullivan and business manager Maureen Barron, and to the Seven Network's executive producer of the project Brad Lyons, network head of production Janeen Faithfull and Chris O'Mara, Network Director of Programming and Production.

Most critical to a project such as this have been the researchers Carolyn Martin and Claire Middleton and my wife, Penny, who transcribed the original series and book and also did some of the research. New Holland's publisher, Averill Chase, senior editor Pauline Kirton and editor Karen Enkelaar have done a wonderful job producing this book.

But above all my thanks go to the brilliant young man who shaped and sculptured and built the new 'This Fabulous Century' series, my co-producer David Galloway. Thank you.

Most of the illustrations in this book come from the photo libraries of John Fairfax and Sons and Peter Luck Productions (Australia).

The author would also like to thank the following:
The Australian Broadcasting Commission, *The Age*, Art Gallery of NSW, Elizabeth Bource, the late Elsa Chauvel, Filmworld, General Motors Holden, *Herald & Weekly Times*, Vane Lindsay, the Mawson Institute, University of Adelaide, Denis Mercier, the Mitchell Library, Museum of Victoria, the NSW Government Printer, NSW Rugby League, the National Library, Old Parliament House Canberra, Bruce Petty, the Seven Network, ScreenSound Australia (formerly The National Film and Sound Archive), Les Tanner, Channel 10, News Ltd, Norman Lindsay copyright holder Janet Glad c/o Curtis Brown Aust Pty Ltd, Qantas, Queensland Museum, the Australian War Memorial.

# Index... EX

Published in Australia 1999 by
New Holland Publishers (Australia) Pty Ltd
Sydney • Auckland • London • Cape Town

14 Aquatic Drive Frenchs Forest NSW 2086 Australia
218 Lake Road Northcote Auckland New Zealand
24 Nutford Place London W1H 6DQ United Kingdom
80 McKenzie Street Cape Town 8001 South Africa

First published in 1980 by Lansdowne Press

National Library of Australia Cataloguing-in-Publication Data:

Luck Peter, 1944–
This Fabulous Century
Includes index
ISBN 1 86436 598 6
1. Australia – History – 20th century. I. Title
994.04

Publisher: Averill Chase
Senior Editor: Pauline Kirton
Project Editor: Do Write, New South Wales
Permissions Editor: Kirsti Wright
Designer: Nanette Backhouse

Reproduction: DNL and PICA
Printer: Griffin Press